Cyber Conflict

Cyber Conflict

Competing National Perspectives

Edited by
Daniel Ventre

First published 2012 in Great Britain and the United States by ISTE Ltd and John Wiley & Sons, Inc.

ISTE Ltd
27-37 St George's Road
London SW19 4EU
UK

www.iste.co.uk

John Wiley & Sons, Inc.
111 River Street
Hoboken, NJ 07030
USA

www.wiley.com

© ISTE Ltd 2012

Library of Congress Cataloging-in-Publication Data

Conflicts in cyberspace / edited by Daniel Ventre.
 p. cm.
Includes bibliographical references and index.
 ISBN 978-1-84821-350-0
 1. Cyberterrorism--Prevention. 2. Cyberspace--Security measures. 3. Computer networks--Security measures. 4. Information warfare. 5. National security. I. Ventre, Daniel.
 HV6773.15.C97C66 2012
 363.325'6004678--dc23

                                                                          2012008022

British Library Cataloguing-in-Publication Data
A CIP record for this book is available from the British Library
ISBN: 978-1-84821-350-0

Printed and bound in Great Britain by CPI Group (UK) Ltd., Croydon, Surrey CR0 4YY

Table of Contents

Introduction

The year 2007 was marked by the cyber-attacks against Estonia, and the well-publicized waves of cyber-attacks against various State institutions across the world, often attributed to China and Russia. Following this, 2010 was marked by the Stuxnet worm attack on industrial infrastructures. Since then, a number of nations, led by the United States (US), have entered a new era in terms of their policies and strategies for security and national defense, integrating the cybernetic dimension. This can be seen in the publication of White Papers, national cyber-security strategies, military doctrines, the reorganization of players in cyber-security and the creation of cyber-defense units, both civilian and military (national cyber-security agencies, cyber-commands, etc.).

For nearly two decades prior to this turning point, theories and concepts, mainly American in origin, fueled debates about the informatization of armies, revolution in military affairs and the new techno-centric way of waging war. The first Gulf War was presented as the first war in this era of digital information. Since then, the thoughts and strategies developed by the US Department of Defense have been observed, analyzed, copied and adapted by various nations. Russia and above all China have made their presence felt as new major actors in cyber-conflict.

Following years of musings, costly programs and successive plans to improve cyber-security, the US came to a bitter realization: the security policies pursued up to that point had failed, not yielding the results expected (cyber-attacks were never ceasing to increase in number and were upsetting the stable functioning of the global economy). They no longer seemed capable of avoiding the worst, which is yet to come, in the form of attacks against vital, critical infrastructures that are essential to the nation.

Today, all States connected to cyberspace are concerned by the same questions, stakes, problems, challenges and difficulties. However, not all of them can pursue the same ambitions as the US or China – to develop both defensive and offensive capabilities, with equivalent means.

Yet when cyberspace is shared by all and international cooperation appears to be one of the options for dealing with common stakes in terms of security and defense, a place must be offered to the diversity of analyses.

In the West, most of the publications that dominate the field of cyber-security, cyber-defense, cyber-warfare or information warfare, are written in English – and they are mainly American in origin. We need only look at online library databases for proof of this.

Production is not monopolized by the US – merely dominated by it – and little room is left for international works that could offer other perspectives on these questions, which are increasingly a part of issues of security and defense the world over.

The structure of this book

The nine chapters of this book offer an analysis of the strategies and policies developed in Canada, Cuba, France, Greece, Italy, Japan, Singapore, Slovenia and South Africa (the chapters are presented in alphabetical order) in terms of cyber-security and cyber-defense. They offer a key to the way in which these States interpret the concepts of cyber-warfare, information warfare, cyber-conflict, cyber-attacks and cyber-threats. The chapters are drawn from multiple questions that integrate into the field of studies in international relations:

– Most states underline their dependence in terms of cyberspace (the dependence of society built on technology; dependence on the rest of the world by way of that space; mutual interdependence of their systems). How do States deal with the negative effects of that dependence, or get around it?

– What level of autonomy do States have in their strategic choices? To what degree are policies influenced, oriented, guided and determined by the international, geopolitical and economic environment, international alliances and the technical constraints peculiar to cyberspace?

– How efficient are cyber-security and cyber-defense policies? How can that efficiency be defined, measured, evaluated?

– Do these strategies succeed in dealing with all of the issues? Are strategies needed that break away from the traditional approach to problems of security and defense, or should they treat cyberspace like other conventional dimensions?

– What options are foreseeable in terms of security and defense? Should we focus on dealing with threats at the source; limiting the effects of attacks; reducing the scope of attacks; adopt a strictly defensive stance; or adopt an offensive stance? What impact does a nation's posture in terms of cyber-security and cyber-defense have on the international community (both allies and enemies alike)?

– Do cyber-defense policies take account of the stakes involved in international relations? For instance, is the security dilemma one of the factors restricting options in terms of cyber-defensive strategies?

– Is there a single mode of thinking in terms of cyber-security and defense the world over? Are all States driven to pursue the same objectives, deal with the same challenges, and apply the same solutions to problems that seem to arise in a similar way the world over? Is there a place for 'national' approaches?

– What are the factors that could favor a genuine absence of strategic diversity: the weight of the influence of the hegemonic American strategy? The constraints imposed by technologies, and consequently by the owners of those technologies?

– Does cyberspace tend to unify approaches, and impose immovable solutions? Can there truly be national approaches to cyber-security/cyber-defense?

– Can we identify significant differences or original aspects between the various approaches to cyber-security/cyber-defense?

– How do States manage to get around the constraints to impose their own vision of the treatment that can be afforded to cyberspace and its use?

– Not all States integrate the cybernetic dimension into their security/defense policies at the same rate: how can these differences be explained? Which variables lead States to integrate the cybernetic dimension, and which result in them rejecting or delaying it?

– What happens when concepts/theories that are American in origin, and applicable to an American-centered cyberspace (because of its infrastructure), meet States, modes of government, cultures, etc., which are different?

– Are there notable differences in the definitions of cyber-security, cyber-defense, cyber-warfare and information warfare? How do these concepts fit into the trajectories of the defense policies and strategies of the States examined herein? Has the relatively recent introduction of these questions into policies of national defense and security significantly altered these policies? Can we speak of a revolution in terms of security and defense policies, or of prolongation and continuity? Is cyberspace a central or peripheral factor in policies relating to security and defense?

– Do these States desire more international standardization and dependence in terms of international and supranational instances, to guarantee their cyber-defense, or, on the contrary, do they favor national initiatives? What place does the expression of sovereignty have?

These are only some of the questions to which we attempt to provide a certain degree of a response in this book.

Canada

The development of a cyber-security policy in Canada has clearly accelerated between 2001 and 2011. Throughout this period, the Canadian federal government's major concern in terms of national security related to the protection of the essential infrastructures. These infrastructures, particularly the computer networks of the different governments in Canada, are mutually interdependent to an increasing degree, but are also dependent on the country's other essential infrastructures. Hence, during the decade in question, we observe a raised awareness of the vulnerabilities this interdependence implies. Thus, computer security has become the main issue in trans-border security. The different versions of Canada's cyber-security policy are aimed at reducing the scope of and the effects of potential cyber-attacks and responding to them efficiently.

In 2010, the Canadian federal government published the *National Strategy and Action Plan for Critical Infrastructure*, and later the same year, *Canada's Cyber Security Strategy*. These two documents implement a plan to combat cyber-threats and protect Canada's cyber-systems.

Cuba

In Cuba, the political regime views cyberspace as a threat to its stability, believing that by way of the Internet, the country could fall victim to foreign influence, its subversive ideas and attempts at destabilization. Thus, cyberspace is not allowed to exist unless it defends the principles of the revolution. For this reason, a germ of cyberspace exists in this country, but is subjected to control, surveillance and strict regulation, the objective being to control the flow of information by controlling this tool.

Cuba has one of the world's lowest ratios of Internet users to head of population. The regime blames the US for this situation. Despite this, it is careful to control Internet access, to create national content, and to isolate its Internet users from the rest of the world.

France

In the chapter on France, we go back to the 19th Century to discover the origins of musings on the creation of a telecommunications space, the ancestor of today's cyberspace (still largely founded on the telephonic infrastructures of the last century), when visionaries imagined the outlines of what would become the Internet, and information technology (IT). This foray into the past lends itself to a reflection on the evolution of the concepts and their introduction into the areas of policies and strategies for national security and defense.

The chapter looks at the way in which France defines cyberspace, cyber-security, cyber-defense, the threat, information warfare, and information operations. What is France's view of the world, and of its challenges and threats? What are its responses to these threats, and how does it structure its security and defense in order to deal with these challenges?

Greece

Greece's geopolitical importance is such that the country's approach to information operations and cyber-warfare has a bearing in several international contexts, including maritime transportation, banking, energy, telecommunications, the Balkans, the Middle East, NATO and the European Union.

Although Greek conceptions of information operations and cyber-warfare are still emerging, it is safe to say that they will continue to be decisively shaped by the country's particular historical experiences and strategic concerns, particularly in relation to its geopolitical arch-rival, Turkey. The asymmetrical promise embedded in the concept of information warfare appeals to Greek defense planners, who seek ways of maintaining Greece's internal military equilibrium, combating the growing demographic gap between Greece and Turkey, and reinvigorating Greece's geopolitical dynamic without directly antagonizing the Turkish military.

These broader strategic parameters have been revised through the prism of several formative experiences in information operations, including – but not limited to – the Öcalan affair, the Vodafone wiretapping of 2004–2005, and the Ergenekon conspiracy. While damaging on a number of fronts in exposing substantial holes in Greece's defensive info-dominance, these experiences have also proved constructive in highlighting – even to non-experts – the urgent need to reinterpret Greece's traditional geopolitical concerns and strategic interests through the all-encompassing lens of the information society. These experiences have therefore helped make the country's decision-makers progressively more aware of the country's vulnerability to information operations.

Italy

After a brief introduction on information and cyber warfare, Chapter 5, "Moving toward an Italian Cyber Defense and Security Strategy", analyzes the current Italian geo-political situation from a perspective comparing it with other countries, and the legal framework upon which Italy is constructing its cyber-security and cyber-defense strategy.

The active involvement of Italy in peacekeeping operations abroad, its role within NATO and its high dependence on information and communication technology systems and networks, make it particularly vulnerable to information and cyber-warfare. While Italy has successfully built up agencies and policies to tackle cybercrime and protect intellectual property rights, it is still at an early stage in developing its information and cyber-warfare strategy, as demonstrated by the fact that studies and conferences on the subject have only recently been delivered, the outcomes of which are presented.

This chapter then introduces the debate about the creation of a cyber-defense command and the other solutions put forward. It concludes by examining the necessity for a Cyber Security National Strategic Plan entailing an integrated and coordinated approach among key stakeholders. This should be achieved through the establishment of a one-stop coordination center for national cyber-security and defense.

Japan

The Constitution of 1947 forbade Japan from resorting to war to solve its international problems. Since then, Japan's defense policy has always been restricted by the conditions imposed by the Constitution and subjected to the conditions of the alliance with the US. However, in the past few decades, the international environment has changed: the emerging figure of China is exerting pressure in the Asia-Pacific region – economically, politically and militarily; North Korea, by way of its military saber-rattling, represents a significant threat to peace in the region, and in the world at large.

Japan has gradually regained its autonomy in terms of defense and now plays a role in maintaining regional and international peace. In 2009, the Democratic Party of Japan's rise to power marked an important turning point in the definition of political choices in terms of defense. A new strategy has been put forward, which for the first time includes cyberspace and the use of it in the field of defense policy and military doctrine. Does the introduction of the cyberspace dimension into strategy and doctrine constitute a major step in Japan's evolution? Does the strategy of cyber-defense alter the trajectory of Japan's defense policies? Possible answers to these questions are discussed.

Singapore

The Singaporean government officially treats information warfare in two ways.

First, acting upon the threat label of "cyber-warfare" – which encapsulates attacks by sources employing the World Wide Web and attacks by insiders with access to intranets – the government has created the Singapore Infocomm Technology Security Authority. This watchdog and strategic controlling outfit, housed in the Ministry of Home Affairs, is trying to engage private sector firms and individuals to collaborate with the government in establishing a joint Cyber Defender Program to defend against threats to the island state's highly globalized economic links with the world. This takes place against the background of a steep increase in the number of hacking and viral attacks against private sector corporations in the past three years. Whether this will be a foolproof territorial defense remains to be seen.

Second, the Singapore Armed Forces (SAF) largely subscribe to the American-originated understanding of information warfare as a realm of military operations aimed at disrupting the enemy's decision-making capabilities while enhancing its own. However, the implementation of military informational measures is often subsumed to the rhetoric of general high-tech improvements. This sort of logic is typical of the militaries of developing countries aspiring to modernize by acquiring missiles and aircraft with offensive and defensive capabilities. This chapter will argue, however, that the Singaporean defense planners have creatively treated information warfare in three dimensions of capability expansion:

– redoubling their forces;

– generating asymmetrical advantages in operational transparency; and

– continually revitalizing existing conventional arms capabilities.

In short, the Singaporean military approach is not revolutionary but evolutionary in nature.

In summary, the approaches to both civilian cyber-warfare and military information warfare render the case of Singapore unique on the grounds of its division of focus, but the question of effectiveness, as for most nation-states, remains unanswered in this new realm of national defense.

Slovenia

The Republic of Slovenia is a small and relatively marginal country with its own language. The Slovenian information and communication technology infrastructure ranks amongst the most highly developed countries in the world. Slovenia is one of the 27 European Union Member States (EU-27) and a member of NATO, so it must act in the field of information and communication technology security in such a way as to meet its obligations to both organizations.

Beyond a commitment to fulfill its EU-27 and NATO obligations, unfortunately the Republic of Slovenia does not possess a clear strategy defining the objectives it needs to pursue to achieve sufficient information and communication security policies, and much less clear directions on how it will achieve these objectives. From most of the strategic documents adopted we can conclude that the problem of information and communication technology security in Slovenia is underestimated.

Besides the high cost, which is extremely difficult to justify, the main barrier to investment in information and communication technology security is the relatively high sense of security, which can be seen throughout Slovenian society. In almost all strategic documents, cyber-threats are only mentioned, mostly in the domain of cyber-crime. Defense against these threats is limited to general responses and intentions to design new strategies and new government bodies. At the present time, Slovenia is not adequately prepared for cyber-attacks, especially for advanced cyber-attacks on critical information and communication infrastructure.

South Africa

South Africa has the most developed communications infrastructure in Africa, and it is exhibiting rapid growth. This developed infrastructure necessitates the development of a national cyber-defense plan to protect it from potential attackers, which has been identified as an area of national strategic importance. The chapter on South Africa outlines and compares the national models and structure of information warfare with those of other nations, and the potential limitations of information warfare on the African continent.

South Africa is in the process of developing relevant legislation and policies for cyber-security, and the national stance and agencies involved in cyber-defense are described. The cyber-environment of Africa exhibits widespread vulnerabilities and the potential for exploitation in a cyber-warfare scenario. The cyber-environment on the continent is discussed, along with existing reports of cyber-conflict, and the authors' estimations of the threats and potential for future conflict in the cyber-domain are presented.

About the authors

The chapter on Canada is written by Hugo Loiseau and Lina Lemay.

Hugo Loiseau has held the post of professor at the School of Applied Politics at the University of Sherbrooke, Quebec, Canada, since 2004. He holds a bachelor's degree in history from that university. He also has a Masters in political science from Laval University, Quebec, Canada, where he obtained his doctorate in political sciences in 2006. He teaches and conducts research in the field of research methodology in political and social sciences, in the domain of military sociology and in studies on cyberspace. In addition, he is a specialist in the political systems of Latin America. He co-authored *Carte mentale et Science Politique, Regards et Perspectives Critiques sur l'Emploi d'un Outil Prometteur* (The Cognitive Map and Political Science – Views and Critical Perspectives on the Use of a Promising Tool) with Sandra Breux and Min Reuchamps [BRE 10].

Lina Lemay is a professional in emergency measures and sustainable development at the Centre de Santé et de Services Sociaux – Institut Universitaire de Gériatrie (Center for Health and Social Services – University Institute of Geriatrics) in Sherbrooke, Quebec, Canada, having held this post since 2011. She is the holder of a Masters in applied politics from the University of Sherbrooke, Quebec, Canada, obtained in 2010. During her masters, she received research grants from the Social Sciences and Humanities Research Council and the Fonds de Recherche sur la Société et la Culture (Social and Cultural Research Fund), as well as being a research assistant from 2008 to 2010. Her research interests relate to public policies, management of risks and threats and civil security. During her studies and in parallel to her current job, she continues to pursue her research and has presented lectures, including one at the Congrès Annuel de la Société Québécoise de Science Politique (Annual congress on political sciences in Quebec society) in May 2011 in Montreal, entitled: *"La sécurité civile: une politique publique comme une autre? Réflexion à partir du Québec"* (Civil Security: a public policy like any other? Reflections from Quebec), that was produced with Dany Deschênes and Vicky Chainey.

The chapter on Greece is written by **Joseph Fitsanakis**, who coordinates the Security and Intelligence Studies program at King College in Tennessee, USA, where he teaches classes on intelligence, espionage, terrorism, security, covert action and geopolitics, among other subjects. He has written extensively in the areas of communications surveillance [FIT 98] and communications interception [FIT 03]; the US National Security Agency [FIT 06]; information warfare [FIT 09]; and the impact of social networking on intelligence gathering [FIT 11]. Dr Fitsanakis is senior editor of *intelNews.org*, and a frequent commentator on intelligence and security. His work has been referenced in international media outlets including *The Washington Post*, ABC Radio, RT Television, *The Boston Herald*, *The Guardian*,

Político,   Al Jazeera,   *The Diplomat,*   *Le Monde Diplomatique,*   *Libération,*
The Huffington Post, El País, Wired and *Studies in Intelligence* (the journal of the
Central Intelligence Agency [CIA]). Dr Fitsanakis is a member of the Association of
Former Intelligence Officers, the International Association for Intelligence
Education, and the International Advisory Board of the Mediterranean Council for
Intelligence Studies, among other professional bodies. His research interests lie in
the areas of international espionage, domestic security and surveillance, and the
history of intelligence with particular reference to the CIA and the National Security
Agency.

The chapter on Italy is written by **Stefania Ducci**, who is senior analyst at the
Research Institute for European and American Studies, Deputy Chair of the
Mediterranean Council for Intelligence Studies, Director of Cyber Intelligence and
Cyber Security Studies at the European Intelligence Academy, and freelance Open
Source Intelligence (OSINT) Analyst. She holds a Doctorate in Law (University of
Bologna, Italy) and an MA in Criminology and Security Studies (University of
Turin, Italy); both her Doctoral and MA degrees were earned *Summa Cum Laude.*
From September 2003 to December 2008, Dr Ducci held the position of Research
Fellow at the United Nations Interregional Crime and Justice Research Institute, as
well as the post of Program Manager on projects regarding organized crime,
particularly cybercrime, human trafficking and smuggling. She currently lectures at
postgraduate level on the subjects of peacekeeping intelligence and security studies,
at the University of Roma Tre (Rome, Italy) and International University of Social
Sciences (Popular University UNINTESS, Mantua, Italy). In addition, Dr Ducci
regularly publishes articles, scholarly papers and books, as well as contributing to
the development of training manuals on national and international security issues
[DUC 08, DUC 11a, DUC 11b]. She regularly participates as a speaker and lecturer
at academic institutions, international conferences and seminars.

The chapter on Singapore is written by **Alan Chong**, who is Associate Professor
at the S. Rajaratnam School of International Studies in Singapore. He has published
widely on the notion of soft power and the role of ideas in constructing the
international relations of Singapore and Asia. His publications have appeared in *The
Pacific Review, International Relations of the Asia-Pacific, Asian Survey, East Asia*
(an international quarterly), the *Journal of International Relations and Development,*
the *Review of International Studies,* the *Cambridge Review of International Affairs*
and in *Politics, Religion and Ideology.* His recent book was *Foreign Policy in
Global Information Space: Actualizing Soft Power* [CHO 07]. He is currently
working on several projects exploring the notion of "Asian international theory". His
interest in soft power has also led to inquiry into the sociological and philosophical
foundations of international communication. Taking off from his interest in the
transformative impact of IT on politics, he is presently exploring the role of
information warfare as a matter of national strategy, and is currently completing a

book manuscript titled *The International Politics of Communication: Representing Community in a Globalizing World.* He has frequently been interviewed by the Asian media and has consulted in think-tank networks in the region.

The chapter on Slovenia is written by Igor Bernik, Iztok Podbregar, Gorazd Praprotnik and Bojan Tičar.

Igor Bernik, PhD, is Assistant Professor of Information Sciences and the Head of Information Security Department at the Faculty of Criminal Justice and Security, University of Maribor, Slovenia. His research fields are information systems, information security and the growing requirement for information security awareness. He has recently been involved in the international project: eSEC – Competency Based e-portal of Security and Safety Engineering. He is a member of the editorial board of the *Organizacija – Journal of Management, Informatics and Human Resources* and *European Journal of Security and Safety*. He is co-author of articles on cybercrime, information warfare, cyber terrorism and risk assessment in information systems and has published a book about cybercrime and information warfare.

Iztok Podbregar is a Full Professor and a Senior Research Scientist in the field of leadership and management of security organizations, lecturing and researching in several faculties at the University of Maribor. He is Head of the Security Sciences Department at the Faculty of Criminal Justice and Security, Professor of Crisis and Strategic Management at the Faculty of Organizational Sciences and Head of the Military Logistics Department at the Faculty of Logistics. He was appointed to the rank of Full Professor at the University of Maribor in 2011. He holds a PhD in organizational sciences (human resources management) from the University of Maribor (Faculty of Organizational Sciences), which was awarded in 2000. Prior to that, he was an National Security Advisor to the President of the Republic of Slovenia, Director of the Slovenian Intelligence and Security Agency (SOVA), National Counter-terrorism Coordinator, Minister-Counselor in the Prime Minister's Office and State Secretary at the Ministry of Defence. In 1999 he held a lecture on the developed model including smaller countries in peace operations at the US Army War College, in Germany, Denmark and Bulgaria, at the UN headquarters (in New York) and at NATO (in Brussels). Prior to that, he held the positions of Deputy Chief and later Chief of the Slovenian Armed Forces General Staff. He was also a member of the Slovenian delegation appointed to initiate dialog on the Republic of Slovenia's accession to the NATO Alliance, International Inspector for Weapons Supervision within the Organization for Security and Co-operation in Europe (OSCE), and Chief of the Air Force Section in the Republic Territorial Defence Staff. He holds the personal Slovene military rank of Lieutenant Colonel General.

Gorazd Praprotnik is a Lecturer at the College of Information Technology, where he teaches Computer Networks and Communications. He is also a professional programmer. He has held a MSc in electrical engineering sciences from the Faculty of Electrical Engineering (University of Ljubljana) since 2002. He is a PhD candidate at the Faculty of Criminal Justice and Security (University of Maribor) and a PhD candidate at the Faculty of Electrical Engineering (University of Ljubljana). He has also completed military Reserve Officer training and holds the military rank of Lieutenant.

Bojan Tičar holds a PhD in public and financial law from the Faculty of Law, Ljubljana, Slovenia. In 2005, he joined the University of Maribor, Faculty of Criminal Justice and Security and the University of Primorska, Faculty of Management, where he is an Associate Professor for Administrative Law and Legal Regulation of Management in the Public Sector. At present, he is Vice Dean of the Faculty of Criminal Justice and Security of the University of Maribor.

The chapter on South Africa is written by Brett van Niekerk and Manoj Maharaj.

Brett van Niekerk completed his BSc in electronic engineering in 2002 at the University of Natal, and graduated with an MSc in electronic engineering (his dissertation was on next-generation communications) in 2006 from the University of KwaZulu-Natal. He worked at ThoroughTec Simulation on mining and military projects, and managed the electronic design department. He is currently completing his PhD research in information systems and technology at the University of KwaZulu-Natal, analyzing potential vulnerabilities in 3G communication infrastructures from information warfare and electronic warfare perspectives. He has published journal articles on information warfare, most recently on the Arab Spring events [VAN 11a] and proposing a consolidated information warfare model [VAN 11b]. He has also spoken at conferences and as a guest lecturer on information warfare.

Manoj Maharaj, PhD, is currently Associate Professor at the University of KwaZulu-Natal, where he teaches information systems, specializing in information systems strategy and information security. He has supervised numerous postgraduate students from throughout Africa at MA, MBA, DBA and PhD levels. He has consulted widely in the IT industry and has presented workshops on topics including IT Auditing, IT strategy, information security, risk management and others. He has published extensively, and his most recent publications on information warfare include analysis of the Arab Spring [VAN 11a] and the proposal for a consolidated information warfare model [VAN 11b].

The chapters on France, Cuba and Japan are written by Daniel Ventre, who is the editor of this book.

Daniel Ventre, CNRS (Centre National de la Recherche Scientifique – National Center for Scientific Research) conducts research at the Centre de Recherche sur le Droit et les Institutions Pénales (Center for Research on Law and Penal Institutions) laboratory of the CNRS, the University of Versailles and the French Ministry of Justice. He is Secretary General of Groupe Européen de Recherches sur les Normativités (the European Research Group on Norms). His work in political sciences/international relations deals with cyber-conflict, cyber-security and cyber-defense. He has published numerous articles as well as several books (monographs and edited collections) about information warfare and cyber-warfare – particularly [VEN 07, VEN 09, VEN 10, VEN 11a, VEN 11b, VEN 11c, VEN 11d]. Since 2010, he has been in charge of the Cyberconflict and Cybercrime series published by ISTE-Wiley (London), and also published in French by Hermès-Lavoisier. He is a part-time lecturer at Telecom ParisTech and is regularly called upon to dispense courses in France and abroad, to talk at international conferences and to the media.

Bibliography

[BRE 10] BREUX S., REUCHAMPS M. and LOISEAU H., "Apports et potentialités de l'utilisation de la carte mentale en science politique", *Transeo Review*, vol 2-3, 2010.

[CHO 07] CHONG A., *Foreign Policy in Global Information Space: Actualizing Soft Power*, Palgrave, 2007.

[DUC 08] DUCCI S., CHIESA R., CIAPPI S., *Profiling Hackers. The Science of Criminal Profiling as Applied to the World of Hacking*, Taylor & Francis, 2008.

[DUC 11a] DUCCI S., "Leggi, direttive e standard in material di protezione delle infrastrutture critiche", *MCIS*, August 2011, available at: www.mcisitalia.net.

[DUC 11b] DUCCI S., *Strategic Cyber Exploitation of Social Media and Networks. The Islamic Terrorists Underground Community*, August 2011, http://ideasthatshape.com/?p=494.

[FIT 98] FITSANAKIS J., *Subversive Technology: From Video-Revolt to Digital Democracy*, Kalendis Publishers, Athens, 1998 [in Greek].

[FIT 03] FITSANAKIS J., "State-sponsored communications interception: facilitating illegality, information", *Communication and Society*, vol. 6, no. 3, pp. 403-428, 2003.

[FIT 06] FITSANAKIS J., "National Security Agency: The historiography of concealment", in de LEEUW, K., and BERGSTRA, J. (eds.), *The History of Information Security Handbook*, Elsevier BV, Amsterdam, pp. 523-564, 2006.

[FIT 09] FITSANAKIS J., ALLEN I., Cell Wars: The Changing Landscape of Communications Intelligence, Research Paper No. 131, Research Institute for European and American Studies, May 2009.

[FIT 11] FITSANAKIS J., BOLDEN M.S., "Social networking as a paradigm shift in tactical intelligence collection", *Intelligence Studies Yearbook*, vol. 1, no. 1, pp. 28-40, 2011.

[VAN 11a] VAN NIEKERK B., PILLAY K., MAHARAJ M.S., "Analysing the role of ICTs in the Tunisian and Egyptian unrest from an information warfare perspective", *International Journal of Communications*, vol. 5, pp. 1406-1416, 2012. Available at: http://ijoc.org/ojs/index.php/ijoc/article/view/1168/614.

[VAN 11b] VAN NIEKERK B., MAHARAJ MS., "The information warfare lifecycle model", *South African Journal of Information Management*, vol. 13, no. 1, 9p., 2011, available at: http://www.sajim.co.za/index.php/SAJIM/article/view/476.

[VEN 07] VENTRE D., *La Guerre de l'Information*, Hermès Lavoisier, Paris, 2007.

[VEN 09] VENTRE D., *Information Warfare*, ISTE Ltd, London and John Wiley and Sons, New York, 2009.

[VEN 10] VENTRE D. (ed.), *Cyberguerre et Guerre de l'Information: Stratégies, Règles, Enjeux*, Hermès Lavoisier, Paris, 2010.

[VEN 11a] VENTRE D. (ed.), *Cyberwar and Information Warfare*, ISTE Ltd, London, and John Wiley and Sons, New York, 2011.

[VEN 11b] VENTRE D., *Cyberespace et Acteurs du Cyberconflit*, Hermès-Lavoisier, Paris, 2011.

[VEN 11c] VENTRE D., *Cyberattaque et Cyberdéfense*, Hermès-Lavoisier, Paris, 2011.

[VEN 11d] VENTRE D., OCQUETEAU F., *Contrôles et Surveillances dans le Cyberespace*, Problèmes Politiques et Sociaux, La Documentation Française, no. 988, 2011.

Chapter 1

Canada's Cyber Security Policy: a Tortuous Path Toward a Cyber Security Strategy

1.1. Introduction

In this day and age, no developed nation is immune to computer attacks. The attack on many Canadian federal government servers in January 2011[1] was indicative of the state of affairs in this matter. Canada had been developing a greater awareness of the significance of this type of threat since 2001, a turning point that led to the introduction of more drastic security measures, particularly with regard to electronic security. In 2009, the Office of the Auditor General of Canada then warned the Canadian federal government that: "Threats to computer-based infrastructure, or cyber threats, are increasing and Canada is certainly not immune to them."[2] The incidents related to the viruses I Love You in 2000 and MYDOOM in

---

Chapter written by Hugo LOISEAU and Lina LEMAY.

1 *Cyberattaque contre le gouvernement Canadien, La Défense nationale aussi ciblée*, February 17, 2011, [Online]: http://www.radio-canada.ca/nouvelles/National/2011/02/17/001 -cyberattaque-federal-reactions.shtml, accessed January 29, 2012.
2 OFFICE OF THE AUDITOR GENERAL OF CANADA, Report of the Auditor General, December 2009. available at: www.oag-bvg.gc.ca/internet/English/osh_20091202_e_33489.html, accessed January 29, 2012. The Office of the Auditor General of Canada is the equivalent of the *Cour des comptes* in France and of the Government Accounting Office in the USA.

2004, as well as the Slammer and Blaster worms in 2003[3], illustrate the reach and impact of risks emanating from cyberspace and the problems these may cause for Canada's national security.[4] Moreover, these "events [...] demonstrate cyber-related vulnerabilities resulting from the interdependence among critical infrastructure sectors."[5]

In this context, a major concern of the Canadian federal government in matters of national security pertains to the protection of the critical infrastructure (CI),[6] which is defined as "processes, systems, facilities, technologies, networks, assets and services essential to the health, safety, security or economic well-being of Canadians and the effective functioning of government."[7] In Canada, CI includes 10 sectors, with each being a complex system in and of itself. Nevertheless, these sectors are interrelated and therefore interdependent. As has been shown, the interdependence of systems, and thus of the CI in this case, leads to an interdependence of risks, which increases the vulnerability of contemporary societies. Canadian society is not exempt from this challenge.

Faced with this reality, "cyber security [is] at the forefront of the transborder challenge to Canada's critical infrastructure (CI)."[8] This calls for the public management of the associated risks as well as the need to improve Canadian national cyber security. The protection of CI is inextricably linked to cyber security. According to the Canadian federal government, cyber security is related to cyber attacks in that:

> "Cyber attacks include the unintentional or unauthorized access, use, manipulation, interruption or destruction (via electronic means) of electronic information and/or the electronic and physical

---

3 CANADIAN SECURITY INTELLIGENCE SERVICE, *Examples of Electronic Attacks*, www.csis-scrs.gc.ca/prrts/nfrmtn/xmpls-eng.asp, accessed January 29, 2012.

4 P. VAN LOAN, *Standing Committee on Public Safety and National Security,* 40th Parliament, 2nd Session, Evidence of the Minister of Public Safety, April 2, 2009, www.parl.gc.ca/HousePublications/Publication.aspx?DocId=3801940&Language=E&Mode=1&Parl=40&Ses=2, accessed January 29, 2012.

5 CANADIAN SECURITY INTELLIGENCE SERVICE, *Examples of Electronic Attacks*, www.csis-scrs.gc.ca/prrts/nfrmtn/xmpls-eng.asp.

6 In fact, "Cyber-attacks are a growing concern that have the potential to impact on a wide range of critical infrastructure that is connected through computer networks." Privy Council Office, *Securing an Open Society: Canada's National Security*, April 2004, pp. 11. www.pco-bcp.gc.ca/index.asp?lang=eng&page=information&sub=publications&doc=natsec-secnat/natsec-secnat_e.htm, accessed January 29, 2012.

7 PUBLIC SAFETY CANADA, *National Strategy for Critical Infrastructure*, www.publicsafety.gc.ca/prg/ns/ci/index-eng.aspx, accessed January 29, 2012.

8 PUBLIC SAFETY AND EMERGENCY PREPAREDNESS CANADA, *Government of Canada Position Paper on a National Strategy for Critical Infrastructure Protection*, pp. 3, www.acpa-ports.net/advocacy/pdfs/nscip_e.pdf, accessed January 29, 2012.

infrastructure used to process, communicate and/or store that information. The severity of the cyber attack determines the appropriate level of response and/or mitigation measures: i.e., cyber security".[9]

Canada's national cyber security strategy thus consists of minimizing the impacts of possible cyber attacks and of conducting effective response actions to incidences. For example, in 2010 Canadian cyber security measures emphasized mitigation (reduction of the impact of possible attacks) and intervention (a wide range of actions to be performed in the case of an attack). The Emergency Management Act, which regulates cyber security, however, also contains provisions on prevention, namely through risk management and preparedness – two dimensions that seem removed from Canada's national priorities in that domain in terms of implementation. Moreover, in the case of offences, the Canadian government battles against cyber crime, which it defines as "a criminal offence involving a computer as the object of the crime, or the tool used to commit a material component of the offence."[10] Two categories of cyber crime are targeted: one where the computer is a source of perpetration; and one where the computer is the object of the crime.

To reduce the reach of the risks emanating from cyberspace, the Canadian federal government commits to protect the CI, increase cyber security, and fight against cyber crime, with the view of ensuring the security of the cyberspace within its territory, and so its institutions and population. For this, progress has been made with regard to emergency management, which includes the protection of CI and cyber security. At the legislative level, the Emergency Management Act was adopted in 2007, and at the administrative level developments were instigated to improve coordination, decision-making and cooperation within emergency management. Specifically, with regard to the protection of CI and cyber security, diverse centres were created for monitoring the risks and responding to incidents. In addition, two strategies were developed and one intervention plan was implemented.[11] As for cyber crime, legislative and administrative amendments have

---

9 PUBLIC SAFETY CANADA, *Canada's Cyber Security Strategy. For a stronger and more prosperous Canada,* pp. 3, www.publicsafety.gc.ca/prg/ns/cbr/_fl/ccss-scc-eng.pdf, accessed January 29, 2012.

10 STATISTICS CANADA, *Cyber-Crime: Issues, Data Sources, and Feasibility of Collecting Police-reported Statistics,* 2002, pp. 5, http://dsp-psd.pwgsc.gc.ca/Collection/Statcan/85-558-X/85-558-XIE2002001.pdf, accessed January 29, 2012.

11 The newly created organizations were the Government Operations Centre, the Integrated Threat Assessment Centre and the Canadian Cyber Incident Response Centre. In 2010, two strategies were adopted: the "National Critical Infrastructure Protection Strategy" and "Canada's Cyber Security Strategy. For a Stronger and More Prosperous Canada." In December 2009, the Federal Emergency Response Plan was adopted, which has enabled intervention in the case of national emergencies.

been made, mainly with the view to improving the investigative powers and the implementation of tools that promote awareness-raising and denunciation.

Although effective and pertinent, the measures to advance Canada's CI protection, cyber security and fight against cyber crime are too insignificant in scope and the speed of their implementation is certainly too slow, especially considering that the emergence of cyber space goes back to the early 1980s. The lack of speed had been assessed by the Auditor General of Canada in December 2009, mainly with regard to the implementation of emergency management measures.[12]

This finding raises questions as to the capacity of the Canadian federal authorities to identify and respond to current and emerging risks in cyberspace. In other words, is Canada equipped to respond to the threats posed by cyberspace? And, in that context, how does the Canadian federal government ensure the security of cyber space and what strategy has it developed since the emergence of the phenomenon? Finally, has Canada developed a cyber security policy that corresponds to the realities of 2012?

Of importance here is to analyze the role of the Canadian State in its capacity to ensure the security of its population and its institutions against the risks posed by the development of cyberspace. In this chapter, we will determine how the Canadian federal government ensures the security of cyberspace at the national scale and, more specifically, examine the strategy it has developed and promoted since the emergence of the phenomenon.

The chapter begins by presenting the emergence and the constraints of the national security policy in Canada, as well as the initial developments in terms of cyber security. It then proceeds to explain the acceleration of the development of cyber security policies after 9/11 and their relation to the fight against terrorism. Thereafter, the chapter analyzes the slow progression of the diverse initiatives and policies toward a strategy for the protection of CI. In conclusion, the chapter describes Canada's current cyber security strategy.

1.2. Canada in North America: sovereign but subordinate?

The development of cyber security in Canada is largely concurrent with the development of information and communication technologies (ICTs), and in particular with the emergence of computer and Internet networks in the early 1990s. Overall, the effort of the Canadian federal government to ensure national security

---

12 OFFICE OF THE AUDITOR GENERAL OF CANADA, *Report of the Auditor General of Canada*, December 2009.

through the protection of telecommunications goes back to the end of World War II, and was again spurred with the onset of the Cold War.

The development of cyber security in Canada is also closely tied to its position on security and defense within the North American space. For this, the chapter will provide a brief historical overview illustrating the close link between technological developments and the Canadian military doctrine. This link determines the evolution of Canada's defense and national security policies, and in the later development of the country's national cyber security. The significance of this link is explained by the fact that the development of Canada's national cyber security is largely determined by the level of importance the Canadian federal government has accorded to national and international security, within the context and the priorities established over time. This reality was thus crucial in the development of Canada's national cyber security in terms of the directions that the Canadian federal government has pursued since the emergence of cyber space.

Canada's national security and defence policies have always been largely determined by its relations with its immediate neighbor, the United States. To this day, Canada's geographic location has been a main factor in the development of these policies. Moreover, US–Canadian relations have generally qualified as exceptional, although they have also been marked by tension, in particular as to the expansionist, if not continentalist, project of the US. Historically, the US expansionist drive has been contained by the influence of the United Kingdom. Formerly the motherland of the *dominion* and recognized as an imposing economic and military power, the UK greatly contributed to the maintenance of Canada's sovereignty. Thus, the fact that Canada retains privileged relations with both of these two economic and military powers explains in part why, since its creation in 1867, it has experienced sustained peace, if not a certain isolationism.

However, the occurrence of the Second World War changed the course of events and marked the onset of the US–Canadian cooperation for the defense of North America. This cooperation proved to be a determining factor in the development of Canadian defense and national security, and in the reach of the American influence in these areas. We are reminded that in 1938, US President Roosevelt and Canadian Prime Minister Mackenzie King signed the Kingston Dispensation, which stipulated that the security of the neighboring state should be considered a matter of national security.[13] The treaty contributed to the defense and national security of Canada in that the US committed to cooperate with Canada to ensure continental security as such in the case that Canadian capacities were to become overextended. However,

---

13 The Kingston Dispensation was signed on August 18, 1938. K. R. NOSSAL, S. ROUSSEL and S. PAQUIN. *Politique Internationale et de Défense au Canada et au Québec,* Les Presses de l'Université de Montréal, 2007, p. 61 and 71.

Canada as a country nevertheless remained sovereign in these domains. The treaty obliges Canada to improve its investments in defense and national security and to consider threats directed at the US as being its own. Canadian defense and national security policies were thus to reflect these priorities. In 1940, this cooperation was further strengthened with the creation of the Canada–US Permanent Joint Board on Defence (PJBD) and then, in 1941, with the Hyde Park Declaration on the production of war material.[14]

The Cold War then ushered in a new strategic era for Canada with regard to both defense and national security. In terms of defense, this period was characterized by the strengthening of Canada–US cooperation, in particular with the 1946 establishment of the protection of the Arctic as a priority, and then, in 1949, with the signing of the North Atlantic Treaty, which culminated in the creation of the North Atlantic Treaty Organization (NATO) in 1951. In 1957, the newly founded North American Aerospace Defense Command (NORAD) solidified, if not embodied, the Canada–US cooperation on defense.

With the onset of the Cold War, and parallel to this the acme of Canada–US cooperation on defense, the need to ensure national security through the protection of telecommunications then emerged as a further priority for the Canadian federal government. It was in this historical context that Canadian cyber security evolved.

The ghost of the Cold War led to developments in the security of telecommunications, because "[t]he Government of Canada believes that intelligence is the foundation of our nation's ability to effectively provide for the security of Canada and Canadians."[15] Then in 1946, by order-in-council, the federal government created the Communications Branch of the National Research Council (CBNRC), giving it the mandate to ensure the security of telecommunications and, more generally, national and international security in the context of the Cold War. To optimize its field of action, the CBNRC collaborated with diverse international partners, among them the US, UK, Australia, and New Zealand.[16] In 1975, the CBNRC became the Communications Security Establishment Canada (CSEC). Since then, it has reported to the Department of National Defence (DND) and is governed by the National Defence Act. Moreover, "CSEC functions entirely within all Canadian laws, including the Canadian Charter of Rights and Freedoms, the

14 K. R. NOSSAL, S. ROUSSEL and S. PAQUIN, *Politique Internationale et de Défense au Canada et au Québec*, pp. 61-63.
15 COMMUNICATIONS SECURITY ESTABLISHMENT CANADA, *National Security*, www.cse-cst.gc.ca/home-accueil/nat-sec/index-eng.html, accessed January 29, 2012. Government of Canada, *Communications Security Establishment Canada*, www.cse-cst.gc.ca/index-eng.html, accessed January 29, 2012.
16 This may well be the beginning of cooperation in cyber security, as these same partners collaborated in 2010.

Criminal Code, the Canadian Human Rights Act and the Privacy Act."[17] Following technological developments and emerging priorities concerning national security, the mandate of the CSEC was due for modification.

Further, the considerable development of ICT and the arrival of personal computers in the early 1980s transformed Western societies at all levels: social, political, economic, legal and institutional. That context generated a new notion of the development of societies, while also giving rise to new risks. Especially in the context of the still-ongoing Cold War, the accelerated development of ICT led to a greater recognition among governments of the need to protect citizens and institutions against the risks posed by ICT.

To this end, the Canadian federal government adopted the Canadian Security Intelligence Service Act in 1984.[18] This act gave rise to the Canadian Security Intelligence Service (CSIS), which has the mandate "to investigate threats, analyze information and produce intelligence. It then reports to, and advises, the Government of Canada to protect the country and its citizens."[19] To realize its mandate, "Parliament has given CSIS extraordinary powers to intrude on the privacy of individuals. SIRC (Security Intelligence Review Committee) ensures that these powers are used legally and appropriately, in order to protect Canadians' rights and freedoms."[20] CSIS activities consist of the collection, analysis, and sharing of information with diverse partners and the public as well as security screening and research in collaboration with diverse experts.[21] Lastly, to be discussed later, CSIS had a determining role in the development of Canada's national cyber security, in particular on the basis of the development of ICT and the emergence of new risks.

---

17 COMMUNICATIONS SECURITY ESTABLISHMENT CANADA, *CSEC: An Overview*, www.cse-cst.gc.ca/home-accueil/about-apropos/overview-survol-eng.html, accessed January 29, 2012. DEPARTMENT OF JUSTICE, Canadian Charter of Rights and Freedoms, http://laws.justice.gc.ca/eng/Charter/; Criminal Code, laws-lois.justice.gc.ca/eng/acts/C-46/; Canadian Human Rights Act, http://laws-lois.justice.gc.ca/eng/acts/H-6/; Privacy Act, http://lois-laws.justice.gc.ca/eng/acts/P-21/index.html; sites consulted January 29, 2012.
18 DEPARTMENT OF JUSTICE, Canadian Security Intelligence Service Act, http://lois.justice.gc.ca/PDF/Loi/C/C-23.pdf, accessed January 29, 2012.
19 CANADIAN SECURITY INTELLIGENCE SERVICE, *Role of CSIS*, www.csis-scrs.gc.ca/bts/rlfcss-eng.asp, accessed January 29, 2012; Canadian Security Intelligence Service, *History of CSIS*, www.csis-scrs.gc.ca/hstrrtfcts/hstr/brfcssndx-eng.asp, accessed January 29, 2012.
20 The Security Intelligence Review Committee (SIRC) monitors operations of the CSIS. SIRC has been an independent organization since 1984 and reports to the Parliament of Canada. Security Intelligence Review Committee, *About SIRC*, www.sirc-csars.gc.ca/abtprp/index-eng.html, accessed January 29, 2012.
21 CANADIAN SECURITY INTELLIGENCE SERVICE, Role of CSIS, www.csis-scrs.gc.ca/bts/rlfcss-eng.asp.

The early 1990s were marked by the end of the Cold War and the breathtaking speed of ICT developments, which raised new issues with regard to national and international security. This called for a change in the mandate of some federal organizations, among them the CSEC, which was then expected to advise "the federal government on the security aspects of government automated information systems."[22] From then on, CSEC also functioned as Canada's national cryptologic organization, which means that it analyzes and approves "cryptographic algorithms for the protection of all sensitive information processed by GC (Government of Canada) information technology systems."[23]

Parallel to these developments concerning ICT security, the end of the Cold War had repercussions on Canada–US cooperation in defense, one being the reduced strategic importance of NORAD, which constituted a decrease in Canada's power with regard to defense. Nevertheless, NORAD still exists and remains pertinent, particularly with regards to the antimissile defense project and the threat of terrorist attacks. Moreover, a multilateral cooperation in defense was implemented during the Gulf War in 1991, which was considered to be the first war characterized by the extensive use of information warfare.

The Gulf War was influenced by developments in ICT that posed new stakes with regard to defense and national and international security. The Gulf War was also a determining event in the development of cyber security. During the "Desert Storm" operation, information operations (IOs) were executed by the Canadian authorities to compromise the capacities of the adversary.[24] IOs are defined as "physical and computer-based operations used by military forces to compromise the access to and viability of information received by the decision-makers of an enemy, while at the same time protecting their own information and information systems."[25] At that time, the concept of IOs referred to a new military doctrine on information warfare. We are reminded that, traditionally, the responsibilities of national defense concern the [translation] "management of the country's armed forces, the development of defense policies, the building of alliances, the maintenance of self-defense capacities, and intervention beyond the national territory [and] the maintenance of the technological superiority required for conquering potential

---

22 CANADIAN SECURITY INTELLIGENCE SERVICE, *Backgrounder No. 11 – Information Operations*, www.csis-scrs.gc.ca/nwsrm/bckgrndrs/bckgrndr11-eng.asp, accessed January 29, 2012.

23 COMMUNICATIONS SECURITY ESTABLISHMENT CANADA, *Cryptographic Services*, www.cse-cst.gc.ca/its-sti/services/crypto-services-crypto/index-eng.html, accessed January 29, 2012.

24 IOs are synonymous with "computer network operations" (CNO). J. CARR, *Inside the Cyber Warfare. Mapping the Cyber Underworld*, O'Reilly, 2010, p. VI.

25 CANADIAN SECURITY INTELLIGENCE SERVICE, Backgrounder No. 11 – Information Operations, www.csis-scrs.gc.ca/nwsrm/bckgrndr11-eng.asp.

enemies on the battle field."[26] The notion of IOs is thus embedded in this framework.

From this perspective, a new area of security and defense evolved that views cyber space as [translation] "a 'place' that must be protected, a territory where the risks to the national security must be managed."[27] In this way, IOs became a new military tactic for responding to an emerging need.

However, this raises the question of whether the IOs perpetrated during the Gulf War can be associated with the concept of a [translation] "revolution in military affairs" (RMA) that has its origins in that armed conflict.[28] The RMA is defined as [translation] "a drastic change in the weapons systems and in the way of using them"[29]. It led to the integration of information technologies. In this way, the RMA introduced a new way of planning defense strategies, and even of conceptualizing war.

Since the Gulf War, IOs have thus been regarded as a new technological means for staging attacks. For the US armed forces in particular, IOs have integrated certain military strategies. This recourse to information warfare, through the use of IOs represented a distinct transformation in Canadian military strategy. Nevertheless, the use of IOs by the Canadian national defense does not constitute an RMA *per se*, as it has not modified Canadian military doctrine. In fact, to this day, [translation] "the integration of technologies that have the capacity to change the structure and characteristics of the armed forces takes place very gradually. At this stage, 'evolution with a revolutionary potential' is a more appropriate way of putting it.[30]"

This finding appears to apply to Canada, even though according to Gagnon DND has been expressing its interest in developing the RMA since about 1994. In fact, Canada's defense policy, the Defence White Paper,[31] was silent as to the RMA.

26 A. MacLeod, E. Dufault, F. G. Dufour and D. Morin. *Relations Internationales. Théories et Concepts*, Outremont, 3rd edition, Athéna Editions, pp. 64-65.
27 B. Gagnon, *Informatique et Cyberterrorisme*, pp. 135. In: S. Leman-Langolis and J.-P. Brodeur, *Terrorisme et Antiterrorisme au Canada,* Les Presses de l'Université de Montréal.
28 B. Gagnon. *La Révolution dans les Affaires Militaires au Canada: une Erreur Stratégique?* Masters thesis, University of Quebec, Montreal, 2004. J.-P. Racicot, "La lutte antiterroriste et les guerres de quatrième génération" in C.-P. David, et al. *Repenser la Sécurité. Nouvelles Menaces; Nouvelles Politiques*, Fides, 2002, pp. 111-133. (
29 B. Gagnon, *La Révolution dans les Affaires Militaires* […], p. IV.
30 J.-P. Racicot, "*La lutte antiterroriste et les guerres de quatrième génération*", […], pp. 131.
31 In 1994, the Canadian federal government presented its Defence White Paper. The position paper discusses the use, management and planning of the Canadian armed forces, the

It was not until 1999 that a first mention of the RMA was made, namely in *Shaping the Future of the Canadian Forces: A Strategy for 2020*, the document that launched the official national defense strategy with regard to the RMA.[32] However, the fact remains that in 2004 delays were observed and that the resources allocated to this effect were limited.[33] Yet, this reality did not keep Canada from confirming its intention of developing the RMA. According to Gagnon, the Canadian reason for integrating the RMA is to [translation] "minimize the effects of the military imbalance with its neighbor to the south."[34] Moreover, [translation] "by setting up its own RMA, DND is reducing Canada's subordination to the United States."[35] This finding clearly illustrates the subordination of Canada in the US–Canadian cooperation with regard to defense.

Thus, the recourse to IOs by the Canadian national defense during the Gulf War should be differentiated from the actual development of the RMA in Canada. Nevertheless, the use of IOs by Canadian Forces during that war provides evidence for the fact that concrete modifications had been made to the Canadian military combat strategy, in addition to demonstrating a case in which Canada engaged in information warfare.

Although IOs lived up to expectations of them in terms of effectiveness during the Gulf War, however, they ultimately turned out to be partially counterproductive, to the point of becoming a threat to national security for many nations that had been their instigators. With the expansion of the Internet and its use at a global scale, IOs could be realized by all types of aggressors. From then on, IOs were increasingly directed against the CI of Canada and became a real threat, to the point that the authorities considered them tools of aggression of the same order as the proliferation of weapons of mass destruction or massive corruption.[36] In IOs perpetrated by aggressors, the threat can take on diverse forms, among them non-authorized intrusions,[37] system operations, material attacks and even cyber-war.[38] As is to be expected, the pace of the evolution of these threats is as rapid as the evolution of the

---

vision of a safe world, and Canadian values and interests, which it tackles at three levels: 1. the protection of the nation; 2. the US–Canadian collaboration; and 3. the maintenance of global security. See also: GAGNON, B. *La Révolution dans les Affaires Militaires* […], pp. 65, 68 and 69.

32 B. GAGNON, *La Révolution dans les Affaires Militaires au Canada* […], pp. 76.

33 B. GAGNON, *La Révolution dans les Affaires Militaires au Canada* […], pp. 2.

34 B. GAGNON, *La Révolution dans les Affaires Militaires au Canada* […], pp. 92.

35 B. GAGNON, *La Révolution dans les Affaires Militaires au Canada* […], pp. 94.

36 Public Safety Canada, *Backgrounder No. 11 – Information Operations*.

37 Among these are viruses, worms, Trojan horses, etc. Public Safety Canada, *Backgrounder No. 11 – Information Operations*.

38 The term "cyberwar" appears in official documents of the Government of Canada. Public Safety Canada, *Backgrounder No. 11 – Information Operations*.

technologies they are based on. Thus, vulnerability increases to the extent that the complexity of networks continually evolves. In such a context, "One of the greatest challenges in countering the threat in the realm of IO is that borders have become meaningless to anyone operating in a virtual environment."[39] This finding reaffirms the existence of the challenge that the security of cyberspace represents for national and international security. IO-related risks have thus been determining factors for cyber security, particularly in Canada.

"As a result, governments will have to set procedures in place to allow security initiatives to evolve to deal with new threats as they arise."[40] Due to this need for continued adaptation, the concept of IOs has evolved over time and has eventually come to mean "the need for a state to maintain national security by protecting its critical information (CI) infrastructure."[41] This transformation of the concept of IOs demonstrates the close link between defense, national security, and CI protection. It constitutes the beginnings of Canadian cyber security. Thus, given the importance of CI protection for the Canadian federal government in terms of national security, it has become a priority to take stock of the state of cyber security development.

Thereby, starting in 1997, CSIS initiated the Information Operations program, which has the objective of ensuring national security through the protection of information-based CIs against intrusions and attacks.[42] This constitutes an expansion of the concept formerly held by the federal government on cyber security in that, in addition to ensuring the security of ICT, it also includes the protection of the CI.

This idea was again brought forth in 1999 by the Senate Special Committee on Security and Intelligence. In its report, the Committee stipulated that the need to protect the CI has arisen due to "the growth of, and our increased reliance on, the critical infrastructure, combined with its complexity, has made it a potential target for physical or cyber-based terrorism."[43] In this context, the Senate Special Committee proposed recommendations, among them the need to develop policies to prevent and evaluate this type of threat, to fend off attacks, or to strike back if required. Moreover, the Committee recommended allocating additional resources and evaluating the existing limits of the CI in view of improving them. Lastly, the report recommends the evaluation of the National Counter Terrorism Plan and its updating as well as the establishment of partnerships between all parties

---

39 CANADIAN SECURITY INTELLIGENCE SERVICE, *Backgrounder No. 11 – Information Operations.*
40 CANADIAN SECURITY INTELLIGENCE SERVICE, *Backgrounder No. 11 – Information Operations.*
41 CANADIAN SECURITY INTELLIGENCE SERVICE, *Backgrounder No. 11 — Information Operations.*
42 That program is mandated by the CSIS Act. Public Safety Canada, *Backgrounder No. 11 – Information Operations.*
43 CANADIAN SECURITY INTELLIGENCE SERVICE, *Backgrounder No. 11 – Information Operations.*

concerned.[44] This last aspect illustrates that there is a growing interest in adopting an integrated approach to national security.

Following these recommendations, the Canadian federal government created the Office of Critical Infrastructure and Emergency Preparedness. This organization "work[s] closely with the provinces and municipalities, private industry and other countries to protect Canada's electronic infrastructure against possible cyber-based attacks and natural disasters."[45] Thereafter, the government implemented the Liaison/Awareness Program, which is the responsibility of CSIS. This program aims to:

> "develop an ongoing dialogue with both public and private organizations concerning the threat posed to Canadian interests from cyber-based attacks. The purpose of the program is to enable CSIS to collect and analyse information that will assist it in its investigation of these threats which could have implications for Canada's national security".[46]

The program thus restates the need to develop an integrated approach to national security. It also innovates, by affirming that such an approach has become imperative for fending off cyber attacks, which constitutes a significant progress with regard to Canadian cyber security.

A further milestone in the development of Canadian national cyber security was the 1998 creation of the Canadian Computer Emergency Response Team (CanCert). CanCert "is a trusted centre for the collection, analysis and dissemination of information related to networked computer threats, vulnerabilities, incidents and incident response for Canadian governments, businesses and academic organizations."[47] We point out, however, that CanCert activities are almost exclusively executed by Electronic Warfare Associates-Canada (EWA-Canada). Nevertheless, the creation of this center demonstrates the interest in and commitment of the Canadian federal government to the management of the risks related to cyberspace as well as the existence of effective collaborations between the public and private sectors on cyber security. It is known that [translation] "the management of emergency computer systems by for-profit organizations entailed

---

44 CANADIAN SECURITY INTELLIGENCE SERVICE, *Backgrounder No. 11 – Information Operations*.
45 CANADIAN SECURITY INTELLIGENCE SERVICE, *Backgrounder No. 11 – Information Operations*.
46 This program also serves to protect against economic espionage. Public Safety Canada, *Sharing Information with the Public*, www.csis-scrs.gc.ca/bts/shrngpblc-eng.asp, accessed January 29, 2012. Public Safety Canada, *Backgrounder No. 11 – Information Operations*.
47 ELECTRONIC WARFARE ASSOCIATES (EWA), *CanCERT Overview*, www.ewa-canada.com/cancert/index.php, accessed January 29, 2012.

the risk of making the networks less secure."[48] In fact, computer security does not constitute a priority for private businesses, because [translation] "their time and money investments are above all focused on profit and client satisfaction."[49] It can even be the case that [translation] "flaws of the computer network turn out to be a benefit."[50] Thus, although CanCert has contributed to Canada's cyber security, it has also raised questions as to the presence of the private sector in the sphere of national cyber security, especially as the private sector is often the main holder of the national CI.[51]

In other words, is Canada now reliant on private interests for the protection of its CI and cyber security, despite having maintained sovereignty with regard to defense and national security? The subsequent events of 9/11 changed the direction that had been pursued until then in this domain and incited the Canadian federal government to take concrete steps to ensure its national cyber security.

1.3. Counter-terrorism for the improvement of national security

The terrorist attacks of 9/11 were determining with regard to the defense, national security and the development of Canadian national cyber security.

For one, these events modified the perception of the risks. From 9/11 onwards, the sociopolitical risk related to terrorism was real and threatened national and international security. From then on, terrorism changed the notion of national security among the Canadian political authorities, as well as the approach to managing that risk. This, in turn, raised a significant debate within the Canadian federal government as to the existing framework concerning national security. The main topics in question pertained to the inability to anticipate these attacks or detect the risk or any information prior to execution, to the reliability on the exchange, information and communication networks, and to the capacity to respond to such events. In other words, 9/11 revealed the existence of gaps within the Canadian national security system.

This context called for a revision of the direction in which national security was headed, which took place gradually and culminated in the development of an integrated approach.[52] The task was to improve the collaboration between the parties

---

48 B. GAGNON, *Informatique et Cyberterrorisme*, pp. 132.
49 B. GAGNON, *Informatique et Cyberterrorisme*, pp. 130.
50 B. GAGNON, *Informatique et Cyberterrorisme*, pp. 130.
51 In the US, 85% of the CIs belong to private interests. B. GAGNON, *Informatique et Cyberterrorisme*, pp. 130.
52 CANADIAN SECURITY INTELLIGENCE SERVICE, *Integrated Threat Assessment Centre*, www.itac.gc.ca/index-eng.asp, accessed January 29, 2012.

involved in national security and with international partners, in particular through the sharing of information and the coordination of actions. To improve efficiency, the integrated approach to national security applies a type of risk management that takes into consideration the knowledge of the risks, their evaluation and the management of the consequences, depending on the case.[53] Thus, this approach focuses mainly on prevention, preparation and intervention. This integrated approach to national security was made official in 2004 with the adoption of the first Canadian national security policy.

Gradual progress in that direction started to take place after 9/11. Among such progress is the development of statements, policies and legislative and administrative amendments with regard to national security. More concretely [translation]:

> "The Canadian government had to, in the months following the attacks of New York and Washington, adopt a certain number of laws to counteract terrorism, increase the budgets of the various security and defence organizations, and enter into many agreements with the United States, in particular on the safety of the borders, thereby implicitly creating what is now referred to as the North-American security perimeter."[54]

In the following, we will present the milestones toward national security that were determined in the development of the Canadian national cyber security.

Starting with Fall 2001, legislative amendments were made with regard to national security. First, on November 22, the federal government adopted Bill C-42 of the Public Safety Act.[55] This act aims to improve emergency preparedness in the context of terrorist risk. However, amendments to the initial bill led the government to adoption a new bill, Bill C-44.

---

53 PRIVY COUNCIL OFFICE, *Securing an Open Society: Canada's National Security*, April 2004, p. 16, www.pco-bcp.gc.ca/index.asp?lang=eng&page=information&sub=publications &doc=natsec-secnat/natsec-secnat_e.htm, accessed January 29, 2012.
54 K. R. NOSSAL, S. ROUSSEL and S. PAQUIN. *Politique Internationale et de Défense au Canada et au Québec,* Les Presses de l'Université de Montréal, 2007, pp. 69.
55 H. HASSAN-YARI, "Perspectives de changement pour la défense et les forces armées du Canada" in C.-P. DAVID and C. RAOUL-DANDURAND. *Repenser la Sécurité: Nouvelles Menaces, Nouvelles Politiques*, Montreal, Fidès, 2002, p. 239.

This bill affected many acts, in particular [translation] "the Aeronautics Act, the Canadian Air Transport Security Authority Act, the Criminal Code, the Quarantaine Act."[56] Bill C-44 received royal sanction on December 18, 2001.

On that same day, the federal government adopted Bill C-36 on the Anti-terrorism Act (ATA).[57] This act "creates offences that criminalize activities, such as participation in a terrorist group, that takes place before a terrorist event can occur."[58] The law thereby regulates and promotes the integrated approach at two levels. First, it introduces the level of prevention to risk management. Second, it promotes collaboration between the participants from the federal departments and organizations, namely through information sharing.[59]

Moreover, the ATA led to the amendment of other acts, in particular the National Defence Act,[60] the Criminal Code,[61] the Canada Evidence Act, the Proceeds of Crime (Money Laundering) and Terrorist Financing Act, the Canadian Human Rights Act, the Access to Information Act and the Personal Information

---

56 H. HASSAN-YARI, "Perspectives de changement pour la défense [...]", pp. 240.

57 DEPARTMENT OF JUSTICE, *The Anti-terrorism Act. Context and Rationale*, http://canada.justice.gc.ca/antiter/contextandrational-contexteetraisondetre-eng.asp, accessed January 29, 2012.

58 DEPARTMENT OF JUSTICE, *The Anti-terrorism Act. Context and Rationale*, http://canada.justice.gc.ca/antiter/contextandrational-contexteetraisondetre-eng.asp, accessed January 29, 2012.

59 The participants from the federal departments and organizations are "intelligence, foreign policy, border and customs, immigration, critical infrastructure, and law enforcement and prosecution communities." DEPARTMENT OF JUSTICE, *The Anti-Terrorism Act. Context and Rationale*.

60 DEPARTMENT OF JUSTICE, *The Anti-terrorism Act. The ATA in Perspective*, www.justice.gc.ca/antiter/actloi/perspective-perspectives-eng.asp, accessed January 29, 2012.

61 "Prior to September 11, 2001, the *Criminal Code* had been amended as required to implement UN counter-terrorism instruments adopted since 1970. Law enforcement relied on the normal processes of investigation, prosecution, and conviction under the *Criminal Code* to address terrorism. After September 11, 2001, the Government determined that it was necessary to include specific terrorist offences in the *Criminal Code*, in large part to confront the issue that once a terrorist event takes place, it is too late." Moreover, the *Criminal Code* was subject to amendments that had an impact on cyber security, well before the adoption of the ATA. Among these, in 1985, were the non-authorized use of a computer (section 342.1), mischief in relation to data (section 430.1.1), possession of device to obtain telecommunication facility or service (section 327), and theft of telecommunication service (section 326). In 1997, an amendment introduced diverse modifications to the *Criminal Code*, in particular as to the possession of devices to obtain computer service (section 342.2). STATISTICS CANADA, *Cyber-Crime: Issues, Data Sources, and Feasibility of Collecting Police-Reported Statistics*, p. 7, http://dsp-psd.pwgsc.gc.ca/Collection/Statcan/85-558-X/85-558-XIE2002001.pdf, accessed January 29, 2012. DEPARTMENT OF JUSTICE, *The Anti-terrorism Act. Context and Rationale*.

Protection and Electronic Documents Act.[62] Even though these amendments have raised many questions as to the effective reach of the ATA, the government reassures us that "[t]he ATA was designed to create a balance between the need to protect the security of Canadians and the protection of their rights and freedoms. Provisions of the ATA are clearly defined in order to target terrorists and terrorist groups."[63] Moreover, the Act "did not change other pieces of legislation designed in part to address terrorist threats, such as the Immigration and Refugee Protection Act, the Security Offences Act or the Canadian Security Intelligence Service Act."[64] Nevertheless, the ATA has improved national security in the face of the risk posed by terrorism, which is crucial for the development of Canadian national cyber security.

The ATA has a specified reach with regard to national cyber security. In fact, "[t]he Government of Canada, in response to growing cyber dependencies and global threats, has recognized the urgent and critical need to address rapidly developing IT security threats and vulnerabilities. The Information Technology Security Program provides the Government of Canada with timely, credible, unbiased insight and the technical leadership required to guide critical IT security decisions [information technologies]."[65] Given this context, and following the legislative amendments, the next step is to implement administrative amendments.

Due to the ATA and the amendments it has brought about for the National Defence Act, the CSEC assumed a new mandate: it is to develop an integrated approach by optimizing collaboration with national partners to guarantee the protection of the critical information infrastructure.[66] More concretely, the aim is to

---

62 DEPARTMENT OF JUSTICE, *The Anti-terrorism Act. The ATA in Perspective*, www.justice.gc.ca/antiter/actloi/perspective-perspectives-eng.asp, accessed January 29, 2012.
63 DEPARTMENT OF JUSTICE, *The Anti-terrorism Act. Context and Rationale*.
64 DEPARTMENT OF JUSTICE, *The Anti-terrorism Act. The ATA in Perspective*, www.justice.gc.ca/antiter/actloi/perspective-perspectives-eng.asp, accessed January 29, 2012.
65 COMMUNICATIONS SECURITY ESTABLISHMENT CANADA, *Information Technology Security Program*, www.cse-cst.gc.ca/home-accueil/about-apropos/its-program-sti-eng.html, accessed January 29, 2012.
66 Specifically, the Act "officially recognized CSEC's three-part mandate: A) To acquire and use information from the global information infrastructure for the purpose of providing foreign intelligence, in accordance with Government of Canada intelligence priorities; B) To provide advice, guidance and services to help ensure the protection of electronic information and of information infrastructures of importance to the Government of Canada; C) To provide technical and operational assistance to federal law enforcement and security agencies in the performance of their lawful duties." Moreover, the CSEC retains its initial mandate of advising the Canadian government in matters of information technologies. Communications Security Establishment Canada, *Information Technology Security Program*. Communications Security Establishment Canada, *What we do*. Department of Justice, *The ATA in Perspective*.

improve efficiency in the analysis of threats and vulnerabilities.[67] "The Anti-Terrorism Act also strengthened CSEC's capacity to engage in the war on terrorism by providing needed authorities to fulfill its mandate."[68] This intention resulted in the allocation of additional resources for improving its actions.[69] Moreover, the CSEC developed, and then implemented, the Information Technology Security Program, mandated to "ensure the reliability and the safety of the cyber-networks and of the critical infrastructure of the clients of the government of Canada."[70] The program adopts a preventive approach by improving knowledge of the risks and by sensitizing collaborators to cyberprotection. Nevertheless, the intervention remains targeted in that it seeks "to make cyber security a business enabler." [71]

Moreover, even though the ATA "did not change [...] the *Canadian* Security Intelligence Service *Act*"[72] or the mandate of the CSIS, the budget of the organization nevertheless increased due to the fact that CSIS is now responding to an increased range of threats.[73] More specifically, CSIS contributes to CI protection by protecting "the physical and information technology facilities, the networks and assets [...], which, if disrupted or destroyed, could seriously affect the health, safety, security and economic well-being of Canadians."[74] Moreover, CSIS monitors the threats related to information security, among them cyber attacks, which it currently defines as "the use of information systems or computer technology either

---

67 COMMUNICATIONS SECURITY ESTABLISHMENT CANADA, *The Antiterrorism Act and CSEC's Evolution*, www.cse-cst.gc.ca/home-accueil/nat-sec/ata-lat-eng.html, accessed January 29, 2012.
68 COMMUNICATIONS SECURITY ESTABLISHMENT CANADA, *What we do*.
69 The attacks of September 11 have led to a 25% increase of the CSEC budget. Moreover, CSEC performs analyses of the vulnerabilities, by "working to predict and prevent cyber attacks, developing and approving cryptographic systems, supporting research and development, and providing IT security advice and services in support of national interests." Privy Council Office, *Securing an Open Society* [...]; Communications Security Establishment Canada, *CSEC: An Overview*, www.cse-cst.gc.ca/home-accueil/about-apropos/overview-survol-eng.html, accessed January 29, 2012.
70 COMMUNICATIONS SECURITY ESTABLISHMENT CANADA, *Information Technology Security Program*.
71 COMMUNICATIONS SECURITY ESTABLISHMENT CANADA, *Information Technology Security Program*.
72 DEPARTMENT OF JUSTICE, *The Anti-terrorism Act. Context and Rationale*.
73 The terrorist attacks of 2001 have led to a 30% increase in the CSIS budget. Since then, CSIS has monitored diverse threats, among them "terrorism, the proliferation of weapons of mass destruction, espionage, foreign interference and cyber-tampering affecting critical infrastructure". CANADIAN SECURITY INTELLIGENCE SERVICE, *Role of CSIS*, www.csis-scrs.gc.ca/bts/rlfcss-eng.asp, accessed January 29, 2012; PRIVY COUNCIL OFFICE, *Securing an Open Society* [...].
74 PUBLIC SAFETY CANADA, *Information Security Threats*, www.csis-scrs.gc.ca/prrts/nfrmtn/index-eng.asp, accessed January 29, 2012.

as a weapon or a target."[75] Diverse motives are at the origin of cyber attacks, among them malicious attacks and political motivation.[76] The aggressors include people, information organizations,[77] terrorists, and criminal and extremist organizations. Moreover, the CSIS is interested in two types of cyber attacks: the denial of services and the operation of networks, both of which aim to generate instability. Nevertheless, the "CSIS confines its investigation to computer intrusions conducted with a 'political motivation'[78]" because these risks can have impacts on the critical sectors of Canada, in particular the CI. In this regard, CSIS collaborates with many federal departments and organizations,[79] among them the Royal Canadian Mounted Police (RCMP), which demonstrates the effective development of an integrated approach to national cyber security.

The RCMP is the federal police service and was established by the Royal Canadian Mounted Police Act.[80] Since the adoption of the ATA, which amended the Criminal Code, the RCMP has been granted increased authority, mainly in view of preventing and combating technological crime.[81] Since this time, the fight against cyber crime has been pursued by enhancing Canadian cyber security. While CI protection remains an imperative of national security, the emergence of a new trend is taking place at the same time to advance the fight against cyber crime. To this effect, we underline that "Canada was one of the first countries to enact criminal laws in the area of computer crime (Convention on Cyber-Crime: 2001)."[82]

---

75 PUBLIC SAFETY CANADA, *Information Security Threats*.

76 Please note that "[t]here is an increasing potential for politically motivated DoS [denial of services] or network exploitation activities." PUBLIC SAFETY CANADA, *Information Security Threats*.

77 This concerns espionage from certain governments. PUBLIC SAFETY CANADA, *Information Security Threats*.

78 "CSIS focuses its investigations on threats or incidents where the integrity, confidentiality or availability of critical information infrastructure is affected. Three conditions must be present in order for CSIS to initiate an 'information operations' investigation. The incident must: be a computer-based attack; appear to be orchestrated by a foreign government, terrorist group, or politically motivated extremists; and be done for the purpose of espionage, sabotage, foreign influence, or politically motivated violence (terrorism)." PUBLIC SAFETY CANADA, *Working Against Information Security Threats*, www.csis-scrs.gc.ca/prrts/nfrmtn/wrkng-eng.asp, accessed January 29, 2012.

79 Among these are Office of Critical Infrastructure Protection and Emergency Preparedness, the Department of National Defence, through the Communications Security Establishment Canada (CSEC), and the RCMP.

80 DEPARTMENT OF JUSTICE CANADA, *Royal Canadian Mounted Police Act*, http://lois-laws.justice.gc.ca/eng/acts/R-10/index.html, accessed January 29, 2012.

81 Technological crime is defined as "the use of computers or other high-tech equipment in the commission of a criminal act." ROYAL CANADIAN MOUNTED POLICE, *Technological Crime*, www.rcmp-grc.gc.ca/tops-opst/tc-ct/index-eng.htm, accessed January 29, 2012.

82 STATISTICS CANADA, *Cyber-Crime: Issues, Data Sources, and Feasibility of Collecting Police-Reported Statistics*, 2002, pp. 7,

Moreover, on June 10, 2002, the government adopted Bill C-15A on the protection of children against sexual exploitation.[83]

To further combat technological crime, the RCMP developed a Technological Crime Program that allows us to realize diverse types of inquiries concerning "cyber-threats and/or criminal activity on computer networks, which could have the potential to threaten one of Canada's critical infrastructures."[84] In parallel, the organization developed an Integrated Technological Crime Unit that has the mission to investigate "pure computer crimes, to provide forensic expertise in computer-assisted crime investigations, and to investigate significant cyber crime incidents."[85] Moreover, information and denunciation centers were created in connection with cyber crime, among them the National Child Exploitation Coordination Centre – Child Exploitation Tracking System[86] and RECOL (reporting economic crime on-line).[87] The sum of these legislative and administrative amendments illustrates the emergence and then the improvement of the fight against cyber crime in Canada, which optimizes national cyber security.

Nevertheless, at this time, a lot remains to be done according to the Auditor General. The report of April 2002 stipulates that "the operational and technical standards for IT security are still out-of-date, and plans and a timetable to update

---

http://dsp-psd.pwgsc.gc.ca/Collection/Statcan/85-558-X/85-558-XIE2002001.pdf, accessed January 29, 2012.

83 The objective of the Act is to prevent the proliferation of child pornography. STATISTICS CANADA, *Cyber-Crime: Issues, Data Sources, and Feasibility of Collecting Police-Reported Statistics*, pp. 7.

84 ROYAL CANADIAN MOUNTED POLICE, *Technological Crime*.

85 ROYAL CANADIAN MOUNTED POLICE, *Integrated Technological Crime Unit*, www.rcmp-grc.gc.ca/on/prog-serv/itcu-gict-eng.htm, accessed January 29, 2012.

86 This centre is aligned with Canada's "National Strategy to Protect Children from Sexual Exploitation on the Internet". It has the mandate to "reduce the vulnerability of children to Internet-facilitated sexual exploitation by identifying victimized children; investigating and assisting in the prosecution of sexual offenders; and, strengthening the capacity of municipal, territorial, provincial, federal, and international police agencies through training and investigative support." ROYAL CANADIAN MOUNTED POLICE, *National Child Exploitation Coordination Centre*, www.rcmp-grc.gc.ca/ncecc-cncee/index-accueil-eng.htm, accessed January 29, 2012.

87 RECOL is a part of the National White Collar Crime Centre of Canada and allows for the online reporting of acts of white collar crimes, among them those related to cyber crime. National White Collar Crime Centre of Canada, *Reporting Economic Crime On-Line*, www.rcmp-grc.gc.ca/scams-fraudes/recol-eng.htm, accessed January 29, 2012.

them have not been completed."[88] This finding demonstrates that the development of Canadian cyber security remains at the preliminary stage.

This context incited the Office of Critical Infrastructure Protection and Emergency Preparedness to present its National Critical Infrastructure Assurance Program in November 2002. The program aimed to stimulate dialog between the diverse participants concerned and the experts, as well as to promote information sharing, partnership building, and ultimately, the development of a national strategy for the protection of the CI, including those related to information.[89] The program is crucial for designing and then implementing the integrated approach to national cyber security. However, although a declared goal, the development of an integrated approach nevertheless appears to rank second among the government priorities with regard to national security, which is focused more on the improvement of coordination.

For example, starting in 2003, organizational changes were instigated to optimize the coordination of national security. The federal government began with "the integration of the Office of Critical Infrastructure Protection and Emergency Preparedness into the Department of Public Safety and Emergency Preparedness [...]."[90] Then, in the same year, the department became Public Safety Canada (PSC). Created with the goal to "ensure coordination across all federal departments and agencies responsible for national security and the safety of Canadians,"[91] PSC states that "from natural disasters to crime and terrorism, our mandate is to keep Canadians safe."[92] To reach this objective, PSC integrates diverse organizations and maintains five fields of responsibilities: national security, emergency management, law enforcement, correctional services, and crime prevention.[93] Cyber security reports to the sectors of national security and emergency management, mainly

---

88 OFFICE OF THE AUDITOR GENERAL OF CANADA, *Report of the Auditor General of Canada*, April 2002, http://oag-bvg.gc.ca/internet/English/parl_oag_200204_03_e_12376.html, accessed January 29, 2012.

89 PUBLIC SAFETY AND EMERGENCY PREPAREDNESS CANADA, *Government of Canada Position Paper on a National Strategy for Critical Infrastructure Protection*, pp. 5-6.

90 "[...] which merged into a single area the Government's strategic response capabilities for both non-terrorist emergencies and terrorist emergencies, and buttressed the ability of the Government to effectively connect with provincial and territorial emergency preparedness networks." Privy Council Office, *Securing an Open Society* [...], pp. 20; PUBLIC SAFETY CANADA, *Backgrounder No. 11 – Information Operations*.

91 PUBLIC SAFETY CANADA, *About us*, www.publicsafety.gc.ca/abt/index-eng.aspx, accessed January 29, 2012.

92 PUBLIC SAFETY CANADA, *About us*.

93 PUBLIC SAFETY CANADA, *Donnez un Sens à Votre Avenir*, publication of the Government of Canada, pp. 2-3.

through its participation in CI protection and the fight against cyber crime.[94] Within PSC, CSIS and the RCMP are the main organizations in charge of national cyber security.

The creation of PSC therefore demonstrates the formal commitment of the federal government to improve national security, in particular by optimizing the coordination of its actions. Moreover, the implementation of such coordination within one and the same department can be expected to promote the development of an integrated approach to national security and therefore to cyber security.

Nevertheless, even though this realization contributes to national security, it is insufficient. In March 2004, "the government did not have a management framework that would guide investment, management, and development decisions and allow it to direct complementary actions in separate agencies or to make choices between conflicting priorities."[95] This finding questions the actual willingness or capacity of the federal government to ensure national security through a framework of formal integrated management. Despite this finding, however, the federal government reaffirmed its commitment to reaching this objective by adopting its first Canadian national security policy "Securing an Open Society", in April 2004.[96]

With this policy, the Canadian federal government officially recognized the security problem posed by cyberspace and affirmed that cyber security is a determining aspect of national and international security. The policy put cyber security on the agenda of federal politics, thereby greatly advancing its development.

Securing an Open Society allows the federal government to reiterate that its "core responsibility [...] is to provide for the security of Canadians".[97] Moreover, it recognizes that "national security is closely linked to both personal and international security".[98] This is explained by the fact that the presence and emergence of new risks give rise to issues concerning both national and international security. Among these are threats posed by terrorism, infectious diseases, natural disasters, and cyber

---

94 The management of emergencies is regulated by the Emergency Preparedness Act. DEPARTMENT OF JUSTICE, *Emergency Preparedness Act*, http://laws-lois.justice.gc.ca/eng/acts/E-4.6/, accessed January 29, 2012.

95 The federal government has invested more than additional C\$7 billion over five years to ensure the public safety and to counter terrorism. OFFICE OF THE AUDITOR GENERAL OF CANADA, Report of the Auditor General of Canada, March 2004, http://oag-bvg.gc.ca/internet/English/parl_oag_200403_03_e_14895.html, accessed January 29, 2012.

96 PRIVY COUNCIL OFFICE, *Securing an Open Society* [...].

97 PRIVY COUNCIL OFFICE, *Securing an Open Society* [...], pp. 1.

98 PRIVY COUNCIL OFFICE, *Securing an Open Society* [...], pp. 3.

attacks on the CI.[99] In this context, "strengthening our security is also about managing and reducing risks".[100] The policy promotes prevention and intervention in particular.[101]

The general objective of the policy is "to address the security interests of Canadians".[102] It is categorized into three parts: "1. protecting Canada and Canadians at home and abroad; 2. ensuring Canada is not a base for threats to our allies; and 3. contributing to international security."[103] To reach these objectives, the federal government commits to developing an integrated approach to national security at the governmental scale.[104] This approach is based on the collaboration and contribution of diverse partners, as well as coordination in the case of emergency.[105]

The policy is "a long-term strategic framework" and will be funded with a budget in the order of C$690 million.[106] This amount will be invested in six principal strategic sectors: information, emergency planning and management, public health, transportation safety, border security, and international security.[107] Of this initial amount, C$105 million is allocated to the second sector, namely emergency planning and management, which cyber security falls under.[108] The improvement of this sector is based on establishing the priorities starting from the gaps identified and developing a national emergency management system via an integrated approach. The main gaps in the emergency management sector concern

---

99 PRIVY COUNCIL OFFICE, *Securing an Open Society* [...], p. 8. Government of Canada, *Securing an Open Society: Progress Report on the Implementation of Canada's National Security Policy*, April 2005, pp. IX, www.pco-bcp.gc.ca/docs/information/publications/secure/secure-eng.pdf, accessed January 29, 2012.

100 PRIVY COUNCIL OFFICE, *Securing an Open Society* [...], pp. 11.

101 The prevention consists of the evaluation of the threats and of interventions in the management of threat-related effects. Privy Council Office, *Securing an Open Society* [...], pp. 12.

102 PRIVY COUNCIL OFFICE, *Securing an Open Society* [...], pp.12.

103 PRIVY COUNCIL OFFICE, *Securing an Open Society* [...], pp.vii.

104 In a report, the Auditor General states that the lack of integration was a major weakness of national security. With this policy, the government wishes to respond to this critique by developing the integrated approach. PRIVY COUNCIL OFFICE, *Securing an Open Society* [...], pp. 12.

105 The partners involved in national security policy are the provinces, territories, communities, the private sector, and allies as well as individual Canadians. PRIVY COUNCIL OFFICE, *Securing an Open Society* [...], p. iv, 9.

106 This amount is added to the C$8 billion already invested in the effort to reduce the gaps previously observed. These investments have allowed the realization of organizational changes. PRIVY COUNCIL OFFICE, *Securing an Open Society* [...], preface.

107 PRIVY COUNCIL OFFICE, *Securing an Open Society* [...], pp. 4-6.

108 PRIVY COUNCIL OFFICE, *Securing an Open Society* [...], pp. 22.

the "capacity to manage emergencies in the areas of overall strategic co-ordination, critical infrastructure protection and cyber-security".[109] To absorb these gaps, the policy targets three areas:

– developing a CI protection strategy;

– strengthening the cyber security of federal government systems; and

– forming a public–private working group on a national strategy of cyber security.[110]

This raised the need to modernize the Emergency Preparedness Act, in particular by improving "mitigation programs, critical infrastructure protection, cyber-security, information-sharing between federal departments, agreements with international and private sector partners, and protection of sensitive private sector information."[111]

Moreover, in emergency planning and management, "the federal government will often play only a supporting role in the emergency management to provinces and territories, communities, and the private sector."[112] Nevertheless, that role does not limit the contribution that the federal government can and should make to the integrated approach, as it has demonstrated with this policy. According to this role, the government should "provide the leadership, resources and structures necessary to build a fully integrated and effective security system."[113] More specifically, the government develops orientations, statements of principles, as well as policies and acts concerning national security, and thereby cyber security.

Finally, by guiding the development of an integrated approach, Securing an Open Society constitutes an innovation with regard to national security and cyber security. This position translates into the gradual implementation of administrative amendments concerning national cyber security.

First, the CSEC has experienced a growth in its budget and activities related to prevention, all the while improving its collaboration with multiple partners, which advances the integrated approach promoted by the policy.[114] Then, in October 2004,

---

109 PRIVY COUNCIL OFFICE, *Securing an Open Society* […], pp. 20 and 22.
110 PRIVY COUNCIL OFFICE, *Securing an Open Society* […], pp. 22.
111 PRIVY COUNCIL OFFICE, *Securing an Open Society* […], pp. 25.
112 PRIVY COUNCIL OFFICE, *Securing an Open Society* […], pp. 22.
113 PRIVY COUNCIL OFFICE, *Securing an Open Society* […], pp. 9.
114 An increase in the budget allocated to the emergency planning and management sector allowed CSEC to improve its capacities for data collection, analysis, and evaluation, to increase its antiterrorist activities, and to improve collaborations and interdepartmental communications. Among the achievements was the cryptography modernization project as well as the creation, in January 2005, of a forum on cyberprotection, in collaboration with diverse participants such as government representatives, computer security professionals, and

the Integrated Threat Assessment Centre (ITAC) was created.[115] This center reports to CSIS and has the mandate to "produce comprehensive threat assessments, which are distributed within the intelligence community."[116] In this way, ITAC exercises a role linked to prevention, by evaluating the threats, and to intervention, by coordinating actions, depending on the situation. The creation of ITAC reflects the dual commitment of the Canadian federal government to promote an integrated approach to national security and to improve the management of risks through prevention. This commitment is important to cyber security.

Then, still in the field of emergency planning and management, the federal government developed a Federal Emergency Response Plan (FERP) in 2004, which constitutes "a framework that outlines a decision-making process to be used to coordinate emergency response activities."[117] FERP was born out of the need to improve the coordination of actions, in particular in the case of cyber threats or attacks. Thus, even though the national security policy recognizes the need to optimize prevention, this plan responds to the immediate priority in emergency management: intervention.

Nevertheless, the development of the integrated approach to national security remains a priority of the federal government and the statement of the national CI protection strategy confirms its commitment in that sense.

---

representatives from the private sector. The emergency planning and management sector has a budget of C\$56 million over five years. Moreover, the 2005 budget for national safety granted additional financial resources of C\$1 billion over five years. If including this amount, the overall investment has amounted to C\$9.6 billion since September 11, 2001. PRIVY COUNCIL OFFICE, *Securing an Open Society* […], pp. 5, 19 and 24. COMMUNICATIONS SECURITY ESTABLISHMENT CANADA, *The Anti-terrorism Act and CSEC's Evolution*, www.cse-cst.gc.ca/home-accueil/nat-sec/ata-lat-eng.html, accessed January 29, 2012.

115 ITAC is a new component of the national safety policy. PRIVY COUNCIL OFFICE, *Securing an Open Society* […], pp. 13 and 15. The centre has been in operation since October 15, 2004 and reports to the CSIS. It has a five-year budget of C\$30 million. CANADIAN SECURITY INTELLIGENCE SERVICE, *Integrated Threat Assessment Centre*.

116 This community consists mainly of PSC, the CSIS, Canada Border Services Agency, Communications Security Establishment Canada, the DND, Foreign Affairs and International Trade Canada, the Privy Council Office, Transport Canada, Correctional Service Canada, the Financial Transactions Reports Analysis Centre of Canada, the RCMP, the Ontario Provincial Police, and *Sûreté du Québec*. If need be, other partners can be invited, such as the Agriculture and Agrofood, Health, Environment, and Natural Resources departments of Canada. CANADIAN SECURITY INTELLIGENCE SERVICE, *Integrated Threat Assessment Centre*.

117 However, at the end of 2009, the plan was still under development. OFFICE OF THE AUDITOR GENERAL OF CANADA, Report of the Auditor General of Canada, December 2009.

1.4. The long path to a national CI protection strategy and national cyber security strategy

First announced in 2002 and then formalized in the national security policy, the federal government released a position paper on the development of a National Critical Infrastructure Strategy on November 10, 2004.[118] The overall objective is to reduce the vulnerability of the national critical infrastructure.[119] More specifically, the task is to promote a national dialog with the diverse stakeholders in that field, given that "over 85 percent of Canada's infrastructure is owned and operated by the private sector and the provinces and territories."[120] In its mission statement, the paper declared that the strategy – to be part of the integrated approach – was to be completed by the fall of 2005.[121] This demonstrates the commitment of the government to "predicting and preventing cyber attacks."[122] CI protection thus depends significantly on the capacity to manage cyberspace-related risks that comprise national cyber security.

The position paper lists nine principal elements that the future strategy should have. They are:

– the guiding principles;[123]

---

118 PUBLIC SAFETY AND EMERGENCY PREPAREDNESS CANADA, Government of Canada Position Paper on a National Strategy for Critical Infrastructure Protection, www.acpa-ports.net/advocacy/pdfs/nscip_e.pdf, accessed January 29, 2012. The development of such a strategy was one of the innovative aspects of the national security policy of 2004. PRIVY COUNCIL OFFICE. *Securing an Open Society* […], pp. 23 and 35.

119 In 2004, the national critical infrastructures are defined as the "physical and information technology facilities, networks, services and assets, which if disrupted or destroyed would have a serious impact on the health, safety, security or economic well-being of Canadians or the effective functioning of governments in Canada." The national critical infrastructures have been divided into the following 10 sectors: energy and utilities; ICT; finance; healthcare; food; water; transportation; safety; government; and manufacturing. PUBLIC SAFETY AND EMERGENCY PREPAREDNESS CANADA, Government of Canada Position Paper […],pp. 5.

120 PUBLIC SAFETY AND EMERGENCY PREPAREDNESS CANADA, *Government of Canada Position Paper* […], pp. 5.

121 By the end of 2009, PSC was still in the process of developing "an implementation plan for its proposed national critical infrastructure strategy and has taken the first step in drafting the strategy. […] However, progress has been slow and it has not yet determined what infrastructure is critical at the federal level or how to protect it." OFFICE OF THE AUDITOR GENERAL OF CANADA, 2009 Fall Report of the Auditor General, December 2009.

122 Public Safety and Emergency Preparedness Canada, *Government of Canada Position Paper* […], pp. 3

123 The guiding principles are: awareness, integration, participation, accountability, and an all-hazards approach. PUBLIC SAFETY AND EMERGENCY PREPAREDNESS CANADA, Government of Canada Position Paper […], pp. 6.

– the orientations for establishing a framework of integrated risk management;

– the importance of information sharing;[124]

– the development of an inventory of CI assets;

– the analysis and evaluation of threats and the communication required;[125]

– raising awareness of the interdependencies of CIs;

– governance;[126]

– research and development; and

– international cooperation.

In order to achieve this, the federal government restates the three areas targeted by the national security policy.[127] Then, in terms of actions, the government in the context of trust and governance intends to:

– establish an overview of the current measures with regard to CI;

– establish the priorities and present them, announce the principles and objectives; and

– establish the roles and responsibilities of each of the participants.

Lastly, with this paper, the federal government committed to the development of an integrated and new national CI protection strategy, which can be expected to benefit national cyber security. This commitment will result in concrete realizations at the administrative level.

In February 2005, the federal government launched the Canadian Cyber Incident Response Centre (CCIRC). The center ensures "the protection of national critical infrastructure against cyber incidents"[128] and is integrated in the Government Operations Centre (GOC).[129] To realize its mandate, CCIRC performs diverse

---

124 Given the diversity of participants involved in the CI, the federal government is taking on the mandate of coordinating information sharing. PUBLIC SAFETY AND EMERGENCY PREPAREDNESS CANADA, *Government of Canada Position Paper* […], pp. 8.

125 ITAC has a determining role with regard to this. PUBLIC SAFETY AND EMERGENCY PREPAREDNESS CANADA, *Government of Canada Position Paper* […], pp. 10.

126 This applies to coordination at the national scale. PUBLIC SAFETY AND EMERGENCY PREPAREDNESS CANADA, *Government of Canada Position Paper* […], pp. 11.

127 We are reminded of the creation of a working group, the development of a national cyber security strategy, and the revision of the Emergency Preparedness Act.

128 PUBLIC SAFETY CANADA, *About CCIRC*, www.publicsafety.gc.ca/prg/em/ccirc/abo-eng.aspx, accessed January 29, 2012.

129 GOC retains an operational role by ensuring coordination at the national level of interventions in the case of disasters or incidents related to the national security. PUBLIC

activities and offers services related to the prevention and detection of cyber attacks coming from within or outside the country.[130] In this regard, CCIRC collaborates with diverse partners within Canada[131] and internationally, and in the private sector. The creation of CCIRC and GOC are tangible results of the Canadian national security policies, which contribute to improving the integrated national security system as well as the cyber security.

Nevertheless, despite these realizations, the Auditor General emphasized in 2005 that the funds allocated to emergency management remain under-utilized and that the formerly announced legislative and administrative frameworks are still under development.[132]

Indeed, it took until 2007 for the Emergency Management Act to become adopted.[133] Since then, the Act has been regulating the integrated approach to emergency management and national cyber security. The Act improves coordination and collaboration by establishing "clear roles and responsibilities for all federal ministers across the full spectrum of emergency management. This includes prevention/mitigation, preparedness, response and recovery, and critical infrastructure protection".[134] Moreover, the Act assigns Public Safety Canada the leadership role concerning the management of national emergencies.[135] The Act also

SAFETY CANADA, *Government Operations Centre*, www.publicsafety.gc.ca/prg/em/goc/index -eng.aspx, accessed January 29, 2012. GOVERNMENT OF CANADA. *Securing an Open Society* […], pp. XI, 4 and 19.

130 CCIRC monitors cyber-related threats, manages information (collect, analyze, and disseminate), ensures the national coordination of responses to cyber incidents, fosters information sharing, and builds partnerships. In addition, it issues security publications and provides encryption services, diverse products and recommendations. It also has a Cyber Duty Officer as a point of contact. PUBLIC SAFETY CANADA, *About CCIRC*; PUBLIC SAFETY CANADA, *Analytical releases 2011*, www.publicsafety.gc.ca/prg/em/ccirc/anre-eng.aspx, accessed January 29, 2012. Privy Council Office, *Securing an Open Society* […], pp. 23.

131 CCIRC collaborates with many federal departments, among them the RCMP, CSIS, CSEC, DND, the Treasury Board of Canada Secretariat, Foreign Affairs and International Trade Canada (DFAIT) and Health Canada. It also collaborates with "provincial and territorial governments and owners of major critical infrastructure." PUBLIC SAFETY CANADA, *About CCIRC*.

132 OFFICE OF THE AUDITOR GENERAL OF CANADA, Report of the Auditor General, April 2005, http://oag-bvg.gc.ca/internet/English/parl_oag_200504_02_e_14933.html, accessed January 29, 2012. PRIVY COUNCIL OFFICE, *Securing an Open Society* […], pp. X.

133 This Act replaces the Emergency Preparedness Act and results from the announcement made by the federal government, in the national security policy of 2004, to modernize the Emergency Preparedness Act. DEPARTMENT OF JUSTICE, Emergency Management Act, http://laws.justice.gc.ca/PDF/Loi/E/E-4.56.pdf, accessed January 29, 2012.

134 PUBLIC SAFETY CANADA, Emergency Management Act.

135 OFFICE OF THE AUDITOR GENERAL OF CANADA, Report of the Auditor General of Canada, December 2009.

constitutes a determining tool for structuring the effective implementation of the integrated approach to national security, particularly with regard to emergency management and cyber security.

Then, in April 2009, the Standing Committee on Public Safety and National Security announced the development of a national cyber security strategy.[136] Although pertinent, this declaration proposed nothing concrete and was limited to repeating the intentions of the national security policy as well as the position paper on CI protection, both dating back to 2004.

Moreover, the slowness of the effective developments in emergency management was again underscored by the Auditor General in November 2009. In fact, one of the main challenges of the federal government consists of developing policies in ways that can be effectively and efficiently implemented.[137] In addition, PSC is working to improve the coordination of emergency measures, a task that led to the founding of PSC in 2003. Specifically, the gaps identified by PSC concern policy implementation and the responsibility of advisory departments to develop a common, and thereby integrated, approach. In this regard, the Auditor General pointed to the contradiction between the obligation to develop a common approach to emergency management (as stipulated by the Act of 2007) on one hand, and the development of standards unique to each organization according to its respective mandate on the other. This contradiction in part explains why the integrated approach is still under development in the field of emergency management.

This reality impedes the development of tangible measures for improving CI protection and national cyber security. Nevertheless, following the recommendations of the Auditor General on emergency management, the PSC committed to provide "tools and guidance for sectors to determine their processes, systems, facilities, technologies, networks, assets, and services,"[138] in addition to advising the governmental actors involved in the evaluation of CI-related risks. Moreover, PSC committed to developing "policies and programs to prepare plans for their protection."[139] Although remarkable, this commitment illustrates that in that

---

136 STANDING COMMITTEE ON PUBLIC SAFETY AND NATIONAL SECURITY, *Evidence*, April 2, 2009, www.parl.gc.ca/HousePublications/Publication.aspx?DocId=3801940&Mode=1&Parl =40&Ses=2&Language=E, accessed January 29, 2012.
137 For this, the risk analysis, resources, and impacts of the policies should be improved prior to their implementation. OFFICE OF THE AUDITOR GENERAL OF CANADA, Report of the Auditor General of Canada, 2009 Fall Report, www.oag-bvg.gc.ca/internet/English/parl_oag_200911 _e_33252.html, accessed January 29, 2012.
138 OFFICE OF THE AUDITOR GENERAL OF CANADA, Report of the Auditor General of Canada, Fall 2009.
139 OFFICE OF THE AUDITOR GENERAL OF CANADA, Report of the Auditor General of Canada, Fall 2009.

sector, the federal government is still in the development phase, which raises doubt as to the efficiency of the implementation of measures relative to CI protection and national cyber security.

Nevertheless, in the midst of these findings and recommendations, on December 10, 2009 the federal government implemented the Federal Policy for Emergency Management.[140] The objective is "to promote an integrated and resilient whole-of-government approach to emergency management planning, which includes better prevention/mitigation of, preparedness for, response to, and recovery from emergencies."[141] Even though the policy is largely a copy of the Emergency Management Act of 2007, it can be credited with having introduced the notion of resilience into the official discourse. Moreover, the policy is part of an integrated and all-hazards approach, where PSC is in charge of the development, implementation, and coordination of emergency management.[142] The policy can thus be expected to play a crucial role in the development of an integrated approach in cyber security. Moreover, to this effect, the government has also developed learning tools to promote cyber security. The first tool explains the principal dangers existing on the Internet and proposes diverse recommendations to the citizens[143] and businesses.[144] This awareness-raising was prompted in part by the fact "that in 2008,

---

140 This policy is tied to the Emergency Management Act of 2007 and the National Security Policy of 2004. PUBLIC SAFETY CANADA, Federal Policy for Emergency Management, December 2009, www.publicsafety.gc.ca/prg/em/_fl/fpem-12-2009-eng.pdf, accessed January 29, 2012.

141 This replaces the Federal Policy for Emergency Management of 1995.

142 PUBLIC SAFETY CANADA, Federal Policy for Emergency Management, pp. 2.

143 Cyber security threats to citizens include hacking and malicious logic, offensive material, traditional offences, unsolicited emails, the protection of privacy, and risks to children. To this online fraud, threats, and harassment are added. Moreover, PSC disseminates information on identity theft and the sexual exploitation of children, the latter through the Cyberaide.ca site, Canada's national tip line for reporting the online sexual exploitation of children. This tool allows us to optimize the fight against cyber crime. THE ROYAL CANADIAN MOUNTED POLICE, *Internet Security*, www.rcmp-grc.gc.ca/qc/pub/cybercrime/cybercrime-eng.htm, accessed January , 2012. PUBLIC SAFETY CANADA, *Cyber Security Information for Canadians*, www.publicsafety.gc.ca/prg/em/cbr/csi-fra.aspx, accessed January 29, 2012. Cyberaide.ca "received and analyzed almost 30,000 tips about potential cases of online child exploitation since September 2002". PUBLIC SAFETY CANADA, *Cyber Security Information for Canadians*.

144 Cyber security threats to businesses include the theft of confidential information and intellectual property. The federal government informs businesses of the measures to take, in particular, for improving the monitoring of threats or reporting of cyber incidents. Threat monitoring is performed through CCIRC and the reporting of cyber incidents through RECOL. PUBLIC SAFETY CANADA, *Cyber Security Information for Canadian Businesses*, www.publicsafety.gc.ca/prg/em/cbr/csb-fra.aspx, accessed January 29, 2012.

businesses from all over the world declared losses of over a billion dollars in intellectual property rights due to data theft and cyber crime."[145]

This finding undoubtedly incited the federal government to engage in other actions. At the legislative level, two bills were introduced at the end of December 2009 in view of the [translation] "fight against crime and terrorism in a high-tech environment."[146] The bills introduced were C-46, on the Investigative Powers for the 21st Century Act,[147] and C-47, on the Technical Assistance for Law Enforcement in the 21st Century Act.[148] These developments are significant in the fight against cyber crime.

At the administrative level, we point to the implementation of the FERP in March 2010.[149] The plan was developed by the Federal Policy for Emergency Management and structures interventions in the case of emergencies. It has the objective of improving coordination between all the participants, in addition to promoting optimal decision-making within the government.[150] FERP subscribes to integrated intervention, which it defined as follows: "All involved federal government institutions assist in determining overall objectives, contribute to joint plans, and maximize the use of all available resources".[151] From then on, the integrated approach in emergency management was based on the collaboration of the participants in the preparation of the intervention. This 'all-hazards' plan covers national or international emergencies that have an impact on Canada.[152] In this way,

---

145   MCAFEE, *Unsecured Economies: Protecting Vital Information*, www.dorsey.com/files/upload/mfe_unsec_econ_pr_rpt_fnl_online_012109.pdf, accessed January 29, 2012. PUBLIC SAFETY CANADA, *Cyber Security Information for Canadian Businesses*.

146 PUBLIC SAFETY CANADA, *Cyber Security Information for Canadian Businesses*.

147 Bill C-46 [translation] "modernizes certain offences and creates new investigative powers to efficiently combat crime in the modern computers and telecommunications environment." PUBLIC SAFETY CANADA, *Cyber Security Information for Canadian Businesses*.

148 Bill C-47 [translation] "will oblige service suppliers to install equipment facilitating the interception of their networks." PUBLIC SAFETY CANADA, *Cyber Security Information for Canadian Businesses*.

149 The publication date of the official document is December 2009. Nevertheless, the press release was issued on March 15, 2010. The plan had been announced as early as 2004. Marketwire, *Le Gouvernement du Canada Annonce le Plan Fédéral d'Intervention d'Urgence*, www.marketwire.com/press-release/Le-gouvernement-du-Canada-annonce-le-Plan-federal-dintervention-durgence-1131647.htm, accessed January 29, 2012. GOVERNMENT OF CANADA, Federal Emergency Response Plan, December 2009, www.publicsafety.gc.ca/prg/em/_fl/ferp-2011-eng.pdf, accessed January 29, 2012.

150 The principal participants are federal, provincial, and territorial governments, non-governmental organizations, and the sector private.

151 GOVERNMENT OF CANADA, Federal Emergency Response Plan, December 2009, pp. 2.

152 FERP considers certain specific situations as requiring the integrated intervention of the Canadian goverment. Among these are the request for help from a province or a territory or

FERP contributes to improving the intervention dimension of emergency management, and by extension the intervention in attacks on cyber security.

Nevertheless, FERP reaffirms the current priority, or at least the state of current developments, in terms of implementation. Even though the Emergency Management Act and the Federal Policy for Emergency Management specify four pillars of emergency management, FERP has limited powers of intervention. This raises doubt as to the efficiency of developments in national and cyber security. Moreover, even though the Federal Policy for Emergency Management and FERP seek to improve emergency management in Canada, their performance is lacking in specifics as to the developments being effected in Canadian cyber security.

As for national defense, there is no specific military doctrine with regard to information warfare in Canada. The Canadian military doctrine of 2009 indicates that it "has yet to fully account for the rapidly developing space and cyber domains, and the operational and strategic level operations and systems within which all these are nested. Nevertheless, their doctrinal foundation, and the driving CF [Canadian Forces] principles within which these will emerge are found herein."[153] In summary, the doctrinal foundations are in essence the main principles of the Canadian armed forces. In Canada, the notion of IOs thus appears to encompass information warfare.

Despite this finding, at the level of domestic security the improvement in CI protection was delivered in 2010 with the adoption of the National Strategy for Critical Infrastructure, as well as with the adoption of Canada's Cyber Security Strategy.

1.5. The adoption of the current strategies for CI protection and cyber security

Adopted in March 2010, the National Strategy for Critical Infrastructure defined CI as referring "to processes, systems, facilities, technologies, networks, assets and services essential to the health, safety, security or economic well-being of Canadians

---

any emergency situation requiring the intervention of several departments and where the coordination of intervention is necessary. The integrated intervention of the government of Canada has also provided for any emergency situation that directly [translation] "concerns the assets, services, employees, powers conferred by the law, or responsibilities of the federal government, that compromises the trust in the federal government, [...or that] affects other elements of national interest". GOVERNMENT OF CANADA, Federal Emergency Response Plan, pp. 3, http://tvanouvelles.ca/lcn/infos/national/archives/2010/03/20100315-162149.html, accessed 29 January 2012.
153 NATIONAL DEFENCE, *Canadian Forces Joint Publication, Canadian Military Doctrine (CFJP 01)*, 2009, www.cfd-cdf.forces.gc.ca/sites/page-eng.asp?page=10770, accessed January 29, 2012.

and the effective functioning of government."[154] The strategy is part of an integrated and 'all-hazards' approach that promotes Canada's resilience in 10 sectors: energy and public services; finances; food; transportation; the Government, ICTs; health; water; safety; and the manufacturing sector.[155] It aims to optimize partnerships, information sharing and data protection in these sectors, mainly in that "responsibilities [...] are shared by federal, provincial and territorial governments, local authorities and critical infrastructure owners and operators"[156] and the general public. In compliance with the law, the four pillars of emergency management are considered according to the modalities stipulated in the Action Plan for Critical Infrastructure.[157] Finally, the strategy and action plan are significant developments for increasing Canada's CI protection, and by extension its national cyber security.

Moreover, the federal government adopted on Canada's Cyber Security Strategy October 3, 2010, which – responding to the growing number of cyber attacks – has the overall objective to "protect our economic prosperity, national security and quality of life."[158] To reach these goals, the federal government is mandated to detect, prevent and defend, if need be, the general public and its infrastructures against cyber attacks.[159] In other words, the strategy consists of a "plan for meeting the cyber threat"[160] and, with that in view, "securing our cyber systems".[161]

---

154 We are reminded that this strategy was implemented almost six years after the Government of Canada Position Paper [...], published in November 2004. PUBLIC SAFETY CANADA, National Strategy for Critical Infrastructure.

155 PUBLIC SAFETY CANADA, National Strategy for Critical Infrastructure.

156 PUBLIC SAFETY CANADA, National Strategy for Critical Infrastructure, www.publicsafety.gc.ca/prg/em/ci/ntnl-eng.aspx, accessed January 22, 2010

157 This plan is based on three components: partnerships, risk management, and information sharing. To this effect, diverse activities are foreseen. PUBLIC SAFETY CANADA, Action Plan for Critical Infrastructure, www.publicsafety.gc.ca/prg/ns/ci/index-eng.aspx, accessed January 29, 2012.

158 GOVERNMENT OF CANADA, Canada's Cyber Security Strategy. *For a stronger and more prosperous Canada*, 2010, pp. 14; PUBLIC SAFETY CANADA, *Government of Canada launches Canada's Cyber Security Strategy*, October 3, 2010, www.publicsafety.gc.ca/media/nr/2010/nr20101003-eng.aspx?rss=false, accessed January 29, 2012.

159 "The Government is entrusted with safeguarding some of our most personal and sensitive information in its electronic databases. It provides services to Canadians and the private sector through its websites and electronic processing systems. And the Government transmits highly classified information essential to our military and national security operations via its classified communications systems." GOVERNMENT OF CANADA, Canada's Cyber Security Strategy [...], *pp.* 9.

160 GOVERNMENT OF CANADA, Canada's Cyber Security Strategy [...], pp. 7.

161 GOVERNMENT OF CANADA, Canada's Cyber Security Strategy [...], pp. 14.

The main goal of the strategy is to assess the cyber threat, namely by identifying and exposing the connection between cyberspace, cyber attacks, and cyber security:

> "*Cyberspace* is the electronic world created by interconnected networks of information technology and the information on those networks. [...] *Cyber attacks* include the unintentional or unauthorized access, use, manipulation, interruption or destruction (via electronic means) of electronic information and/or the electronic and physical infrastructure used to process, communicate and/or store that information. The severity of the cyber attack determines the appropriate level of response and/or mitigation measures: i.e., *cyber security.*"[162]

The strategy furthermore exposes the context in which the main cyberspace-related risk vectors exist, in particular:

– cyber espionage and military activities supported by governments,

– the use of the Internet by terrorists, and

– cyber crime.[163]

The presence of these risks entails the need to improve national cyber security, in particular through the present national cyber security strategy. This strategy is based on three pillars:

– protecting the government systems;[164]

– building partnerships to protect the essential non-government cyber systems; and

– helping Canadians protect themselves online.

Each of these relies on the implementation of initiatives.

First, the protection of government systems is being pursued through the sharing of clear roles and responsibilities between the federal entities concerned, the increase in the security of the federal cyber systems, and awareness-raising among officials about existing measures to ensure cyber security.[165] This effort also seeks to

---

162 GOVERNMENT OF CANADA, Canada's Cyber Security Strategy [...], pp. 2-3.

163 GOVERNMENT OF CANADA, Canada's Cyber Security Strategy [...], pp. 5-6.

164 The protection of government systems involves the development and implementation of structures, tools and personnel to ensure cyber security.

165 An increase in the security of federal cyber systems will require new investments, allowing the emerging risks to be addressed. In this context, the expertise, systems, and existing frameworks will also have to be improved. The awareness-raising component

engage all levels of government, namely by optimizing cooperation and increasing human and financial resources.

The sharing of responsibilities for national cyber security merits further attention. Concretely, PSC "will provide central coordination for assessing emerging complex threats and developing and promoting comprehensive, coordinated approaches to address risks within the Government and across Canada."[166] Moreover, PSC disseminates information and performs activities in order to increase Canadians' awareness of the current and emerging risks coming from cyberspace and to allow them to better protect themselves. PSC is thus mandated to prevent the threat of cyber attacks and to coordinate intervention, if necessary, in particular through CCIRC, which is in charge of monitoring cyber threats, communicating advice on tackling them, and directing national interventions in the case of cyber incidents.

In terms of analyses and investigations, CSEC works to enhance "its capacity to detect and discover threats, provide foreign intelligence and cyber security services, and to respond to cyber threats and attacks against Government networks and information technology systems."[167] CSIS has the mandate to analyze "and investigate domestic and international threats to the security of Canada".[168] Moreover, the RCMP "will investigate [...] suspected domestic and international criminal acts against Canadian networks and critical information infrastructure".[169]

In addition, new players are called on to contribute to national cyber security. The "Treasury Board Secretariat will support and strengthen cyber incident management capabilities across Government, through the development of policies, standards and assessment tools. The Treasury Board Secretariat is also responsible for information technology security in the Government of Canada."[170]

Certain departments also have responsibilities at the national and international level. "Foreign Affairs and International Trade Canada will advise on the international dimension of cyber security and work to develop a cyber security foreign policy that will help strengthen coherence in the Government's engagement abroad on cyber security."[171]

---

consists of the effective application of the main protection measures in the field of cyber security.
166 GOVERNMENT OF CANADA, Canada's Cyber Security Strategy [...], pp. 9-10.
167 GOVERNMENT OF CANADA, Canada's Cyber Security Strategy [...], pp. 10.
168 GOVERNMENT OF CANADA, Canada's Cyber Security Strategy [...], pp. 10.
169 GOVERNMENT OF CANADA, Canada's Cyber Security Strategy [...], pp. 10.
170 GOVERNMENT OF CANADA, Canada's Cyber Security Strategy [...], pp. 10.
171 GOVERNMENT OF CANADA, Canada's Cyber Security Strategy [...], pp. 10.

Lastly, in addition to defending their own networks, collaborating with other federal departments in identifying threats, and determining possible interventions, the DND and the Canadian Forces collaborate with international allies in order to share information on best practices and "to develop the policy and legal framework for military aspects of cyber security".[172] Moreover:

> "Canada and our allies understand that addressing these risks requires modernizing our military doctrines. It is for this reason that the North Atlantic Treaty Organization (NATO) has adopted several policy documents regarding cyber defence, and like the militaries of our closest allies, the Department of National Defence and the Canadian Forces are examining how Canada can best respond to future cyber attacks".[173]

On this matter, the strategy is revealing in many respects. First, it shows the effective implication of the national defense in national and international cyber security. Second, by modernizing the military doctrine to improve its capacity to either respond to cyber attacks or, if need be, to orchestrate an offensive strategy, DND is aligned with the RMA, which confirms the above-mentioned trend.

The second pillar of the strategy consists of establishing partnerships with provincial and territorial bodies or with participants from private sectors, the CI, universities and non-governmental organizations. Though not mentioned as a goal, the strategy could also benefit from effective collaborations at an international scale. In compliance with the preferred integrated approach, the initiative aims to strengthen Canada's cyber resilience, in particular with regard to the CI. Even though collaborations are already in place in this domain, further efforts must be made to strengthen public–private partnerships, training and exercise programs, and the participation of Canada in international forums.[174] To this effect, the federal government implemented the Defence Research and Development Canada's Public Security Technical Program, which seeks "to better support cyber security research and development activities."[175] The program is a tangible example of how the integrated approach has been implemented with regard to national cyber security.

The third pillar of the strategy, which focuses on assisting Canadians with cyber security, emphasizes the fight against cyber crime and the protection of the general public online. To combat cyber crime, "the Royal Canadian Mounted Police will be given the resources required to establish a centralized Integrated Cyber Crime

---

172 GOVERNMENT OF CANADA, Canada's Cyber Security Strategy [...], pp.10.
173 GOVERNMENT OF CANADA, Canada's Cyber Security Strategy [...], pp.5.
174 GOVERNMENT OF CANADA, Canada's Cyber Security Strategy [...], pp.13.
175 GOVERNMENT OF CANADA, Canada's Cyber Security Strategy [...], pp.11.

Fusion Centre,"[176] by means of an approach based on risk analysis. Moreover, legislative amendments are being proposed and adopted. For example, a law against identity theft has been adopted and bills are being drafted to "enhance the capacity of law enforcement to investigate and prosecute cybercrime".[177] Lastly, even though members of the public have the responsibility to ensure their personal cyber security, the government promotes awareness-raising by disseminating information and safety tips on improving online protection. For example, "[t]he Government's ultimate goal is to create a culture of cyber safety whereby Canadians are aware of both the threats and the measures they can take to ensure the safe use of cyberspace".[178] The wish to develop a culture of cyber security is a new aspect of the strategy.

Following a slow take-off, Canada's Cyber Security Strategy was finally adopted. As pointed out earlier, the time prior to the adoption of this strategy was characterized by the "coexistence of many strategies, without a real coordination for facing the computer threats,"[179] which limited efforts to optimize national cyber security and the development of the integrated approach in that field. The adoption of this strategy thus represents significant progress in the effort to improve national cyber security.

The strategy was tested under a true trial-by-fire circumstance through the cyber attacks of March 2010 on the servers of three major Canadian departments.[180] The investigations were conducted by Canada national cryptologic agency, a unit of DND. Still largely classified, these investigations give evidence to the great extent to which the computer systems of the departments concerned have been penetrated.

---

176 GOVERNMENT OF CANADA, Canada's Cyber Security Strategy [...], pp. 13.
177 The Bill has objectives that include "Making it a crime to use a computer system to sexually exploit a child; Requiring Internet service providers to maintain intercept capable systems, so that law enforcement agencies can execute judicially authorized interceptions; Requiring Internet service providers to provide police with basic customer identification data, as this information is essential to combatting online crimes that occur in real time, such as child sexual abuse; and Increasing the assistance that Canada provides to its treaty partners in fighting serious crimes." GOVERNMENT OF CANADA, Canada's Cyber Security Strategy [...], pp. 13.
178 GOVERNMENT OF CANADA, Canada's Cyber Security Strategy [...], pp. 13.
179 B. GAGNON, *Informatique et Cyberterrorisme*.
180 G. WESTON, "Foreign hackers attack Canadian government; Computer systems at 3 key departments penetrated", *CBC News*, February 17, 2011, www.cbc.ca/news/politics/story/2011/02/16/pol-weston-hacking.html, accessed January 29, 2012.

1.6. Conclusion

A link exists between the preferred approach to national security and the development of cyber security. In fact, the transformation of the perception of risks following 9/11 influenced the development of an integrated approach to national security, which subsequently guided the development of Canadian cyber security.

Significant developments took place concerning national security, resulting in amendments to the legislative and administrative frameworks. At the legislative level, there were amendments, the drafting of bills, and the adoption of acts relative to the fight against terrorism, emergency management, and the fight against cyber crime. At the administrative level, the mandates of some federal organizations were further elaborated and their budgets adapted accordingly. The coordination of national security was improved through the creation of PSC, followed by the adoption of the national security policy, which promotes the development of the integrated approach in particular.

The sum of these developments to national security has been a determining factor for Canada's national cyber security. It began with the development of an integrated approach to ensure protection of CI, followed by efforts to combat first cyber crime and then cyber security. This manifested in the gradual development of position papers, followed by the adoption and implementation of two strategies – one on CI protection and the other on expanding the national cyber security. We underline that the development of these strategies is the tangible realization of two of the three main pillars of the national security policy for improving the national cyber security.

Even though these developments are significant, their actual implementation probably represents their greatest challenge. For example, according to an analysis and evaluations, the implementation of the cyber security strategy can be expected to face delays similar to those of the emergency management policy and the CI protection strategy. This assessment sheds doubt on the efficiency of the integrated national security system, and thereby on Canadian cyber security.

As for emergency management, intervention is largely focused on the other areas of risk management, despite the existence of a legislative framework that promotes an integrated and all-hazards approach. The same can therefore be expected to apply to cyber security, despite the fact that the strategy is designed to prevent cyber threats and ensure intervention in the case of cyber attacks.

Finally, even though tangible realizations have been achieved with regard to cyber security in Canada, they nevertheless remain preliminary and there is a lack of the required speed in their development and implementation. For example, a considerable delay exists between the emergence and development of cyberspace and the recognition of the risks associated with cyberspace and the development, adoption and implementations of policies, acts and concrete administrative amendments to reduce those risks. This lack of speed impedes the effort to efficiently secure cyberspace and to prepare responses to the risks experienced by members of the public, businesses and institutions in this virtual space.

The arrival of a majority federal government in 2011 and the recognition of Canada's vulnerability with regard to cyber security will most likely accelerate the process of securing the CI. Moreover, in August 2011 the Canadian government announced the creation of Shared Services Canada. This federal organization is dedicated to bringing together centers of data storage, email services and the streamlining of the 3,000 computer networks within the Canadian government.[181] The implementation of this federal agency is the latest initiative of the Canadian federal government with regard to cyber security and can be expected to deliver results by 2015.

1.7. Bibliography

[ARE 00] AREND S. and RABIER C., *Le Processus Politique. Environnement, Prise de Décision et Pouvoir*, Les Presses de l'Université d'Ottawa, 2000.

[BEC 01] BECK U., *La Société du Risque. Sur la Voie d'une Autre Modernité*, Paris, Flammarion, 2001.

[BOR 08] BORRAZ O., *Les Politiques du Risque*, Presses de Sciences, PO, 2008 .

[BRU 07] BRUNET S., *Société du Risque: Quelles Réponses Politiques?* Paris, L'Harmattan, 2007.

[CARR 10] CARR J., *Inside the Cyber Warfare. Mapping the Cyber Underworld*, O'Reilly, pp. 234, 2010.

[DAV 02] DAVID C.-P. *et al.*, *Repenser la Sécurité. Nouvelles Menaces; Nouvelles Politiques*, Fides, 2002.

[FOR 02] FORAND A.R., "Les Forces armées canadiennes et le verglas de 1998," in CONOIR Y.and VERNA G., *L'Action Humanitaire du Canada. Histoire, Concepts, Politiques et Pratiques de Terrain*, Ste-Foy, Les Presses de l'Université Laval, pp. 338-351, 2002.

[GAG 04] GAGNON B., La révolution dans les affaires militaire au Canada: une erreur stratégique?, Master's thesis, UQAM, 2004.

---

181 GOVERNMENT OF CANADA, Public Works and Government Services Canada, *Fiche de renseignements: Services partagés Canada,* www.tpsgc-pwgsc.gc.ca/apropos-about/fi-fs/its-sct-fra.html, accessed January 29, 2012.

[GAG 09] GAGNON B., "Informatique et cyberterrorisme" in LEMAN-LANGLOIS S. and BRODEUR J.-P., *Terrorisme et Antiterrorisme au Canada*, Les Presses de l'Université de Montréal, 2009.

[GOD 02] GODARD O., HENRI C., LAGADEC P. and MICHEL-KERJAN E., *Traité des Nouveaux Risques. Précaution, Risques, Assurances*, Paris, Gallimard, 2002.

[HAN 08] HANSON E. C., *The Information Revolution and World Politics*, Lanham, Rowmann and Littlefield Publishers, 2008.

[HAS 02] HASSAN-YARI H., "Perspectives de changement pour la défense et les forces armées du Canada" in DAVID C.-P. and RAOUL-DANDURAND C., *Repenser la Sécurité: Nouvelles Menaces, Nouvelles Politiques*, Montreal, Fidès, pp. 233-250, 2002.

[LIB 07] LIBICKI M. C., *Conquest in Cyberspace. National Security and Information Warfare*, New York, Cambridge University Press, 2007.

[LEM 10] LEMAY L., La gestion publique des risques de sinistres au Québec: Analyse du développement des cadres législatif et administratif de sécurité civile de 1996 à 2009, University of Sherbrooke, Masters thesis, 2010.

[MAC 08] MACLEOD A., DUFAULT E., DUFOUR F. G. and MORIN D., *Relations Internationales. Théories et Concepts*, 3rd edition, Outremont, Athéna Editions, 2008.

[NOS 07] NOSSAL K. R., ROUSSEL S. and PAQUIN S., *Politique Internationale et de Défense au Canada et au Québec*, Les Presses de l'Université de Montréal, 2007.

[ORG 03] ORGANIZATION FOR ECONOMIC CO-OPERATION AND DEVELOPMENT (OECD). *Les Risques Émergents au XXIe Siècle, Vers un Programme d'Action*, Paris, OECD, 2003.

[PAQ 09] PAQUIN S. and DESCHENES D. *Introduction aux Relations Internationales: Théories, Pratiques et Enjeux*, Montreal, Chenelière-Éducation, 2009.

[PEL 09] PELLETIER R. and TREMBLAY M, *Le Parlementarisme canadien*, 4th edition, Quebec, Les Presses de l'Université Laval, 2009.

[RAC 02] RACICOT J.-P., "La lutte antiterroriste et les guerres de quatrième génération" in DAVID C.-P. *et al.*, *Repenser la Sécurité. Nouvelles Menaces; Nouvelles Politiques*, Fides, pp. 111-133, 2002.

[ROU 03] ROUX-DUFORT C., *Gérer et Décider en Situation de Crise. Outil de Diagnostic, de Prévention et de Décision*, 2nd edition, Paris, Dunod, 2003.

[TAG 04] TAGUIEFF P.-A., *Le Sens du Progrès. Une Approche Historique et Philosophique*, Paris, Flammarion, 2004, 2004.

1.7.1. *Scientific and media articles*

[DES 04] DESCHENES D., "La politique de sécurité nationale du Canada à la lumière des enjeux contemporains en sécurité publique", *Sécurité Mondiale*, vol. 12, pp. 2, 2004.

[FLE 08] FLEURY G., "Internet comme vecteur de pouvoir", *Études Internationales*, vol. 39, no. 1, pp. 83-104, 2008.

[JAC 07a] JACOB S. and SCHIFFINO N., "Docteur Folamour apprivoisé? Les politiques publiques du risque", *Politique et Société*, vol. 26, no. 2-3, pp. 45-72, 2007.

[JAC 07b] JACOB S. and SCHIFFINO N., "Les politiques publiques du risque", *Politique et Société*, vol. 26, no. 2-3, pp.1-6, 2007.

[LEM 06] LEMAN-LANGLOIS S., "Question au sujet de la cybercriminalité, le crime comme moyen de contrôle du cyberespace commercial", *Criminologie*, vol. 39, no. 1, pp. 63-81, 2006.

[LOI 09] LOISEAU H. and LEMAY L., "L'hégémonie coopérative et le cyberespace: le défi de la coopération multilatérale", Paper presented at the annual meeting of the Canadian Political Science Association, Carleton University, Ottawa, May 27-29, 2009.

[WES 12] WESTON G., "Foreign hackers attack Canadian government Computer systems at 3 key departments penetrated", *CBC News*, 17 February 2011, www.cbc.ca/news/politics/story/2011/02/16/pol-weston-hacking.html, accessed January 29, 2012.

1.7.2. *Primary Data*

CANADIAN LEGAL INFORMATION INSTITUTE, *National Defence Act*, www.canlii.org/en/ca/laws/stat/rsc-1985-c-n-5/latest/rsc-1985-c-n-5.html, accessed January 29, 2012.

CANADIAN LEGAL INFORMATION INSTITUTE, *Police Act*, RSQ, c. P-13.1, www.canlii.org/fr/qc/legis/lois/lrq-c-p-13.1/derniere/lrq-c-p-13.1.html, accessed January 29, 2012.

CANADIAN LEGAL INFORMATION INSTITUTE, *An Act respecting the ministère de la Sécurité publique,* RSQ. c. M-19.3:www.canlii.org/eliisa/highlight.do?text=s%C3%A9curit%C3%A9+publique&language=fr&searchTitle=Qu%C3%A9bec&path=/fr/qc/legis/lois/lrq-c-m-19.3/derniere/lrq-c-m-19.3.html, accessed January 29, 2012.

COMMUNICATIONS SECURITY ESTABLISHMENT CANADA, *National Security*, http://www.cse-cst.gc.ca/home-accueil/nat-sec/index-eng.html, accessed January 29, 2012.

COMMUNICATIONS SECURITY ESTABLISHMENT CANADA, *An Overview*, www.cse-cst.gc.ca/home-accueil/about-apropos/overview-survol-eng.html, accessed January 29, 2012.

COMMUNICATIONS SECURITY ESTABLISHMENT CANADA, *Cryptographic Services*, www.cse-cst.gc.ca/its-sti/services/crypto-services-crypto/index-eng.html, accessed January 29, 2012.

COMMUNICATIONS SECURITY ESTABLISHMENT CANADA, *The Anti-Terrorism Act and CSEC's Evolution*, www.cse-cst.gc.ca/home-accueil/nat-sec/ata-lat-eng.html, accessed January 29, 2012.

CANADIAN SECURITY INTELLIGENCE SERVICE, *Role of CSIS*, www.csis-scrs.gc.ca/bts/rlfcss-eng.asp, accessed January 29, 2012.

CANADIAN SECURITY INTELLIGENCE SERVICE, *History of CSIS*, www.csis-scrs.gc.ca/hstrrtfcts/hstr/brfcssndx-eng.asp, accessed January 29, 2012.

CANADIAN SECURITY INTELLIGENCE SERVICE, *Integrated Threat Assessment Centre*, http://www.itac.gc.ca/index-eng.asp, accessed January 29, 2012.

CANADIAN SECURITY INTELLIGENCE SERVICE, *Examples of Electronic Attacks*, http://www.csis-scrs.gc.ca/prrts/nfrmtn/xmpls-eng.asp, accessed January 29, 2012.

DEPARTMENT OF HOMELAND SECURITY, *The National Strategy to Secure Cyberspace*, February 2003, p.1, http://www.dhs.gov/xlibrary/assets/National_Cyberspace_Strategy.pdf, accessed January 29, 2012.

DEPARTMENT OF JUSTICE, *Constitutional Documents*, http://laws-lois.justice.gc.ca/eng/const/, accessed January 29, 2012.

DEPARTMENT OF JUSTICE, *Canadian Charter of Rights and Freedoms*, http://lois.justice.gc.ca/eng/Charter/1.html, accessed January 29, 2012.

DEPARTMENT OF JUSTICE, *Canadian Human Rights Act*, http://laws-lois.justice.gc.ca/eng/acts/H-6/, accessed January 29, 2012.

DEPARTMENT OF JUSTICE, *Criminal Code*, http://laws-lois.justice.gc.ca/eng/acts/C-46/, accessed January 29, 2012.

DEPARTMENT OF JUSTICE, *The Anti-terrorism Act*, http://canada.justice.gc.ca/fra/antiter/loi-act/index.html, accessed January 29, 2012.

DEPARTMENT OF JUSTICE, *The Anti-terrorism Act. Context and Rationale,* http://canada.justice.gc.ca/antiter/contextandrational-contexteetraisondetre-eng.asp, accessed January 29, 2012.

DEPARTMENT OF JUSTICE, *The Anti-terrorism Act; The ATA in Perspective*, http://canada.justice.gc.ca/antiter/actloi/perspective-perspectives-eng.asp, accessed January 29, 2012.

DEPARTMENT OF JUSTICE, *Emergency Management Act*, http://laws.justice.gc.ca/PDF/Loi/E/E-4.56.pdf, accessed January 29, 2012.

DEPARTMENT OF JUSTICE, *Emergency Preparedness Act,* http://laws-lois.justice.gc.ca/eng/acts/E-4.6/, accessed January 29, 2012.

DEPARTMENT OF JUSTICE, *Royal Canadian Mounted Police Act,* http://lois-laws.justice.gc.ca/eng/acts/R-10/index.html, accessed January 29, 2012.

DEPARTMENT OF JUSTICE, *Canadian Security Intelligence Service Act*, http://lois.justice.gc.ca/PDF/Loi/C/C-23.pdf, accessed January 29, 2012.

DEPARTMENT OF JUSTICE, *Privacy Act*, http://lois-laws.justice.gc.ca/eng/acts/P-21/index.html; accessed January 29, 2012.

DEPARTMENT OF NATIONAL DEFENCE, *CanadaFirst Defence Strategy* p. 6, www.forces.gc.ca/site/pri/first-premier/June18_0910_CFDS_english_low-res.pdf, accessed January 29, 2012.

GOVERNMENT OF CANADA, *Securing an Open Society: One Year Later; Progress Report on the Implementation of Canada's National Security Policy*, April 2005, p. IX, http://pco-bcp.gc.ca/docs/information/Publications/secure/secure-eng.pdf, accessed January 29, 2012.

GOVERNMENT OF CANADA, Public Works and Government Services Canada, *Fiche de Renseignements: Services Partagés Canada*, www.tpsgc-pwgsc.gc.ca/apropos-about/fi-fs/its-sct-fra.html, accessed January 29, 2012.

GOVERNMENT OF CANADA, *Federal Emergency Response Plan*, December 2009 www.publicsafety.gc.ca/prg/em/_fl/ferp-2011-eng.pdf, accessed January 29, 2012.

GOVERNMENT OF CANADA, *Communications Security Establishment Canada*, www.cse-cst.gc.ca/index-eng.html, accessed January 29, 2012.

GOVERNMENT OF CANADA, *National Defence and Canadian Forces*. http://www.forces.gc.ca/site/home-accueil-eng.asp, accessed 29 January 2012.

OFFICE OF THE AUDITOR GENERAL OF CANADA, *Report of the Auditor General of Canada*, December 2009, www.oag-bvg.gc.ca/internet/English/osh_20091202_e_33489.html, accessed January 29, 2012.

OFFICE OF THE AUDITOR GENERAL OF CANADA, *Report of the Auditor General of Canada*, March 2004, http://oag-bvg.gc.ca/internet/English/parl_oag_200403_03_e_14895.html, accessed January 29, 2012.

OFFICE OF THE AUDITOR GENERAL OF CANADA, *Report of the Auditor General of Canada*, April 2002, http://oag-bvg.gc.ca/internet/English/parl_oag_200204_03_e_12376.html, accessed January 29, 2012.National Defence. *Canadian Forces Joint Publication, Canadian Military Doctrine (CFJP 01)*, 2009, www.cfd-cdf.forces.gc.ca/sites/page-eng.asp?page=
10770, accessed January 29, 2012.

NATIONAL WHITE COLLAR CRIME CENTRE OF CANADA, *Reporting Economic Crime On-Line*, www.rcmp-grc.gc.ca/scams-fraudes/recol-eng.htm, accessed January 29, 2012.Privy Council Office. *Securing an Open Society: Canada's National Security Policy*, April 2004, p. 16, www.pco-bcp.gc.ca/index.asp?lang=eng&page=information&sub=
publications&doc=natsec-secnat/natsec-secnat_e.htm, accessed January 29, 2012.

PUBLIC SAFETY CANADA, www.publicsafety.gc.ca/index-eng.aspx, accessed January 29, 2012.

PUBLIC SAFETY CANADA, *Canada's Cyber Security Strategy. For a Stronger and more Prosperous Canada*, p. 2, www.publicsafety.gc.ca/prg/ns/cbr/_fl/ccss-scc-eng.pdf, accessed 29 January 29, 2012.

PUBLIC SAFETY CANADA, *National Strategy for Critical Infrastructure*, http://www.publicsafety.gc.ca/prg/ns/ci/ntnl-eng.aspx, accessed January 29, 2012.

PUBLIC SAFETY CANADA, *Action Plan for Critical Infrastructure*, http://www.publicsafety.gc.ca/prg/ns/ci/index-eng.aspx, accessed January 29, 2012.

PUBLIC SAFETY CANADA, *Canada-United States Action Plan for Critical Infrastructure*, www.publicsafety.gc.ca/prg/ns/ci/cnus-ct-pln-eng.aspx, accessed January 29, 2012.

PUBLIC SAFETY CANADA, *Critical Infrastructure Partners,* www.publicsafety.gc.ca/prg/ns/ci/prtn-eng.aspx, accessed January 29, 2012.

PUBLIC SAFETY AND EMERGENCY PREPAREDNESS CANADA, *Government of Canada Position Paper on a National Strategy for Critical Infrastructure Protection,* www.acpa-ports.net/advocacy/pdfs/nscip_e.pdf, accessed January 29, 2012.

PUBLIC SAFETY CANADA, *Federal Policy for Emergency Management,* December 2009, www.publicsafety.gc.ca/prg/em/_fl/fpem-12-2009-eng.pdf, accessed January 29, 2012.Public Safety Canada. *About CCIRC,* http://www.publicsafety.gc.ca/prg/em/ccirc/abo-eng.aspx, accessed January 29, 2012.

PUBLIC SAFETY CANADA, *Government Operations Centre,* http://www.publicsafety.gc.ca/prg/em/goc/index-eng.aspx, accessed January 29, 2012.

PUBLIC SAFETY CANADA, *Security Publications,* http://www.publicsafety.gc.ca/prg/em/ccirc/anre-eng.aspx, accessed January 29, 2012.

PUBLIC SAFETY CANADA, *Cyber Security. Cyber Security Matters to Everyone, Everyday,* www.publicsafety.gc.ca/prg/em/cbr/csi-fra.aspx, accessed January 29, 2012.Public Safety Canada. *Information Security Threats,* www.csis-scrs.gc.ca/prrts/nfrmtn/index-eng.asp, accessed January 29, 2012.

PUBLIC SAFETY CANADA, *Working Against Information Security Threats,* www.csis-scrs.gc.ca/prrts/nfrmtn/wrkng-eng.asp, accessed January 29, 2012.

PUBLIC SAFETY CANADA, *Sharing Information with the Public,* www.csis-scrs.gc.ca/bts/shrngpblc-eng.asp, accessed January 29, 2012.

PUBLIC SAFETY CANADA, *Backgrounder No. 11 – Information Operations,* www.csis-scrs.gc.ca/nwsrm/bckgrndrs/bckgrndr11-eng.asp, accessed January 29, 2012.Public Safety Canada. *International Counterparts,* www.publicsafety.gc.ca/prg/em/ccirc/inc-eng.aspx, accessed January 29, 2012.

ROYAL CANADIAN MOUNTED POLICE, *Technological Crime,* www.rcmp-grc.gc.ca/tops-opst/tc-ct/index-eng.htm, accessed January 29, 2012.

ROYAL CANADIAN MOUNTED POLICE, *Integrated Technological Crime Unit,* www.rcmp-grc.gc.ca/on/prog-serv/itcu-gict-eng.htm, accessed January 29, 2012.

ROYAL CANADIAN MOUNTED POLICE, *National Child Exploitation Coordination Centre,* www.rcmp-grc.gc.ca/ncecc-cncee/index-accueil-eng.htm, accessed January 29, 2012.

ROYAL CANADIAN MOUNTED POLICE, *Internet Security,* www.rcmp-grc.gc.ca/qc/pub/cybercrime/cybercrime-eng.htm, accessed January 29, 2012.

SECURITY INTELLIGENCE REVIEW COMMITTEE, *About SIRC,* www.sirc-csars.gc.ca/abtprp/index-eng.html, accessed January 29, 2012.

STANDING COMMITTEE ON PUBLIC SAFETY AND NATIONAL SECURITY, *Evidence,* April 2, 2009, www.parl.gc.ca/HousePublications/Publication.aspx?DocId=3801940&Mode=1&Parl=40&Ses=2&Language=E, accessed January 29, 2012.

STATISTICS CANADA. *Cyber-Crime: Issues, Data Sources, and Feasibility of Collecting Police-Reported Statistics*, 2002, p. 6, http://dsp-psd.pwgsc.gc.ca/Collection/Statcan/85-558-X/85-558-XIE2002001.pdf, accessed January 29, 2012.Sûreté du Québec. *Cybercriminalité*, www.sq.gouv.qc.ca/cybercriminalite/cybercriminalite-surete-du-quebec.jsp, accessed January 29, 2012.

1.7.3. *Websites*

AUSTRALIAN GOVERNMENT, *GovCERT*: www.ag.gov.au/www/agd/agd.nsf/page/GovCERT, accessed January 29, 2012.

CHAIRE EN DROIT DE LA SECURITE ET DES AFFAIRES ÉLECTRONIQUE, *Cybercriminalité. Lois Canadiennes*, Université de Montréal, www.gautrais.com/Cybercriminalite, accessed January 29, 2012.

ELECTRONIC WARFARE ASSOCIATES (EWA), *CanCert Overview.* www.ewa-canada.com/cancert/index.php, accessed January 29, 2012.

GOVERNMENT COMMUNICATIONS SECURITY OFFICE OF NEW ZEALAND, *Centre for Critical Infrastructure Protection*, www.ncsc.govt.nz/, accessed January 29, 2012.

MARKETWIRE, *Le gouvernement du Canada annonce le Plan Fédéral d'Intervention d'Urgence*, www.marketwire.com/press-release/Le-gouvernement-du-Canada-annonce-le-Plan-federal-dintervention-durgence-1131647.htm, accessed January 29, 2012.

MCAFEE, *Unsecured Economies: Protecting Vital Information,* www.dorsey.com/files/upload/mfe_unsec_econ_pr_rpt_fnl_online_012109.pdf, accessed January 29, 2012.

RADIO-CANADA, *Archives*, http://archives.radio-canada.ca/guerres_conflits/conflits_moyen_orient/dossiers/581/, accessed January 29, 2012.

UNITED KINGDOM GOVERNMENT, *Centre for the Protection of National Infrastructure*, www.cpni.gov.uk, accessed January 29, 2012.

US DEPARTMENT OF HOMELAND SECURITY, *United States Computers Emergency Readiness Team*, www.us-cert.gov, accessed January 29, 2012.

Chapter 2

Cuba: Towards an Active Cyber-defense

Democratic states do not wage war on one another. Certain of the universal scope of this theory, democracies put pressure on authoritarian regimes to change their very nature. To steer states down the path of change, there are a number of tools that are required.

One rests on the theory of economic democratization, which incites developed, democratic states to provide financial aid to underdeveloped states, and involve them in the dynamics of the global economy. The economy would have democratic value.

Another is based on the theory of the democratizing power of information and information technologies. They have the capacity to bring individuals together, enable them to think collectively, bring an end to isolation, and expose connected communities to the influence of ideas and information from the rest of the world. These information technologies would therefore be a powerful tool or weapon, in the service of global democratization, enabling us to overthrow authoritarian political regimes. This technological determinism is reminiscent of the convictions of military men and their revolutionary strategies: it assigns technology a central role, conferring the power to change the world on its user, enabling them to achieve goals by means other than confrontation and armed conflict.

Since the early 1990s, it has been widely accepted that information technologies represent a genuine challenge for authoritarian regimes [KO 09], posing grave

Chapter written by Daniel VENTRE.

danger to their existence. The revolts of the Arab Spring, whose success is largely attributed to the mobilizing power of digital networks, seems to support this belief: the Internet has become an arena for political contest, a place of opposition between civilian society and the State, enabling dictatorships to be brought down.

Authoritarian regimes, for their part, are faced with the "dictator's dilemma" [PRE 97]: they may be tempted to profit from the global economy, but do not wish to lose control over their society. Hence, they need to balance this double strain – the risk of democratizing pressure through the economy and through opening the door to the worldwide information society. It must be recognized, however, that a number of authoritarian regimes in the world remain strong, and are able to get around this dilemma. China and Saudi Arabia are not democracies, but have been able to integrate themselves into the movement of globalization, and integrate networked communication technologies. Yet these States have difficulty in accepting total information openness. They want the technologies, but also want to manage their development, monitor their users and control their uses, applications and content. Thus, this is a conditional opening, with rules aimed towards protecting the political regime and putting a stop on the pressure towards democratization.

Given the resistance of certain authoritarian regimes to the democratizing force of the Web, which is supposed to sap the resistance of all dictatorships in the world[1], this postulate was called into question [HIL 98, DRA 00, ROH 00, BOA 00], meaning not that this capacity was denied, but rather that its automatic effectiveness was debated. This is because various conditions have to be satisfied and brought together for this force to be able to operate, such as (and this is by no means an exhaustive list):

– a significant Internet and telephone penetration rate;

⁻ the opening of networks to the global Internet; and

– social actors capable of transforming the ideas carried over the Web into action.

Evgeny Morozov's thesis [MOR 11], which is a reappraisal of the postulate, underlines that authoritarian regimes can exploit these technologies and networks in order to strengthen their own position. (The Internet facilitates surveillance and propaganda; it is preferable not to censor, block, close or prohibit it, but rather to play the game and launch yourself on the Web, to prove your innovativeness at State

---

1 On March 8, 2000, US President Bill Clinton declared: "In the new century, liberty will spread by cell phone and cable modem. We know how much the Internet has changed America, and we are already an open society. Imagine how much it could change China. Now, there's no question China has been trying to crack down on the Internet. Good luck. That's sort of like trying to nail Jell-O to the wall". Quoted in [DRA 00].

level, set up Twitter accounts, have a presence on social networking sites, and adopt the same tools and methods as your opponents.) The idea of democratization through networks is thus not automatically and universally applicable. The Internet cannot only serve the interests of the proponents of democracy, freedom of expression or political change. All parties have learnt to exploit the potential of cyberspace. Even very early on, authoritarian regimes became aware of the potential menace of cyberspace to their own equilibrium. The balance of strength established between the various forces may still swing in favor of the claimants of democracy or in favor of authoritarian regimes.

Cuba's policy of managing the Internet and, more generally, access to information – seems one of the most anti-libertarian on the planet. The country has one of the worst rankings in the world in terms of Internet access [MOL 11, FRE 09][2]. Opposition to the regime, organized from abroad, is not weakening, but has not yet found the tool it needs to accomplish its objectives in cyberspace. Cuba decries the United States' (US) strategy, which aims to destabilize the regime by action.

In this chapter, we offer an analysis[3] of this Cuban policy – an illustration of the strategic role the Internet can play in a state governed by an authoritarian political system capable of keeping part of cyberspace under its thumb.

2.1. Cyberspace: statistics and history

2.1.1. *The marginalization of Cuba*

South America has a population of 570 million people[4], of which a little over 182 million are Internet users[5]. Thus, with 8% of the world's population Latin

---

2 Scoring 15 countries from 0 (with the most freedom) to 100 (with the least freedom), Cuba comes in last place, with a score of 90, preceded, in descending numerical order, by Tunisia and China (78), Iran (74), Russia (51), Egypt (45), Turkey, Malaysia and Georgia (40). Estonia, in first place, scores 10. Those countries scoring lower than 30 are considered "free"; those whose score is over 70 are deemed "not free".
3 This analysis is based on cross-referencing the information available on the Web, bearing in mind that documents produced by external observers and official information published by the Cuban authorities alike are often biased, and we lack the means of validating the data thus collected. The limitations of research on Cuba lie in the difficulty in accessing official sources of information, and the impossibility of carrying out studies of the strategic factors on the ground (a practical difficulty that, it should be noted, is not necessarily peculiar to authoritarian regimes). The main source of information on Cuba comes not from Cuba but from abroad.
4 These statistical data were established for 2009.
5 http://www.internetworldstats.com/stats10.htm.

America is home to around 10% of Internet users on the planet. The country with the greatest number of "surfers" (nearly 72 million) is Brazil, followed by Mexico (27 million), Colombia and Argentina (20 million each). This list includes the countries with the highest gross domestic product (GDP) in the region (Brazil, Mexico and Argentina) and those with the largest populations (Brazil, Mexico, Colombia and Argentina). The countries where the Internet penetration rate is greatest are Chile (50%), Argentina (49%) and Colombia (48%) [IWS 12a].

The current population of Cuba is around 11.4 million. The number of Internet users is not known to any degree of certainty. Official statistics from Cuba claim there were 1.6 million in 2009 [ONE 09]. Data from the CIA gives the same figure [CIA 11], which represents a little over 14% of the population. Other studies (e.g. the Freedom on the Net report [FRE 11]) estimate the Internet penetration rate in Cuba as less than 1%, which is equivalent to the most backward countries in the world in terms of technological development. According to these figures, 2.9% of Cubans regularly have access to the Internet; 5.8% irregularly use e-mail; and only 200,000 residents have access to the World Wide Web [FRE 11].

At any rate, Cuba comes in far below the average in South America in terms of Internet access: with its 11.4 million inhabitants, it represents 2% of South America's population, but only 0.87% of Internet users in that same population (this figure is calculated based on the highest estimate of 1.6 million Internet users in Cuba). The Internet penetration rate in the South American population is over 32%.

The population of the Caribbean is 41.4 million, including 11.4 million Internet users (a penetration rate equal to 27.5%)[6] [IWS 12b]. Cuba is the most densely populated island. It is also the island where the Internet penetration rate is lowest, along with Haiti (10%). Overall, it could be said that the Caribbean islands occupy their correct place in world Internet rankings, because with 0.6% of the global population, they are also home to 0.6% of the world's population of Internet users. Hence, Cuba stands out clearly in this geographic ensemble, by its accumulated lack of progress; with nearly 27% of the region's population, it represents only 13% of its Internet users. By comparison, the Dominican Republic represents 24% of the region's population, but 35% of its Internet users.

Cuba is also the country with the lowest penetration proportion of people owning cell phones, in spite of the increase in subscriptions in recent years (75,000 subscribers in 2004; increasing to 443,000 in 2009). The market is monopolized by a single operator, Cubacel [ONE 09], a subsidiary of ETEC S.A. However, at the end of 2011 the number of cell phone users had increased significantly, reaching 1.2 million

---

6 Statistical data from 2011.

active lines, i.e. 300,000 more than in 2010.[7] Yet there remains a lot of room for improvement.

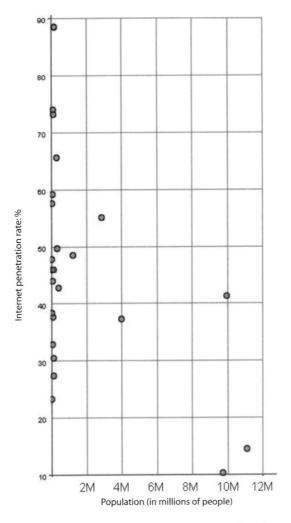

Figure 2.1. *The number of people with access to the Internet in Caribbean countries (each country is represented by a dot). Most of these countries are small and their Internet penetration rate ranges between 23 and 88%. The two countries represented in the bottom right of the graph, on their own, have the highest populations and the lowest Internet penetration rate (Haiti and Cuba)*

7 *Comenzaron a Aplicarse hoy las Nuevas Tarifas de los Celulares*, Granma Internacional, Havana, Cuba, 1 February 1, 2012, (Today, the new cellphone tariffs came into force), http://www.granma.cu/espanol/cuba/1febre-Comenzaron%20a.html.

There are two networks in Cuba – a national intranet and the Internet, access to which is strictly limited. The content offered on the national network consists of an encyclopedia, government-run information sites (such as Granma[8]), educational sites, and official press and e-mail services. A small blogosphere is being organized around platforms that necessarily share in the spirit of the revolution, such as *Blogueros y Corresponsales de la Revolución*[9], or *Blogs Periodistas Cubanos.*[10]

On June 1, 2011, there were some 124,158 Internet protocol (IP) addresses registered in Cuba, equating to 0.003% of the worldwide total (in 109th position on a list of 242 countries).[11]

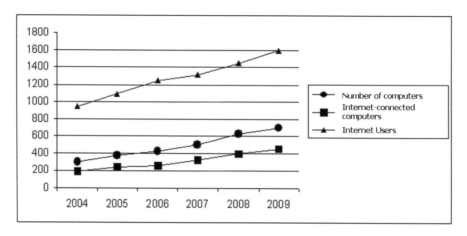

Figure 2.2. *Number of computers and internet users (in thousands) according to statistics published in [PRE 11]*

2.1.2. Cuban cyberspace as the target of attacks

Probably due to its low degree of connectivity to the Internet, Cuba has thus far been spared from malicious activities (malwares). However, it is surrounded by countries (Brazil, Mexico, Colombia and Venezuela) where there is a great deal of this activity. It is probable that the island's newfound connection to high-throughput networks should in time result in the exposure of Cuba to this surrounding security

8 http://www.granma.cu. This site is translated into six languages, its aim clearly being to reach a wide global audience.
9 http://bloguerosrevolucion.ning.com.
10 http://blogcip.cu/.
11 http://www.domaintools.com/internet-statistics/country-ip-counts.php?f=total&o=asc.

risk. The countries with the highest rate of malicious activity (viruses, spam, phishing, bots, etc.) recorded, both as the originators and the targets of attacks[12], are Brazil (44% of South America's activities), Mexico (12%), Argentina (10%) and Colombia (7%). Venezuela, one of Cuba's closest allies, accounts for 3%. The attacks aimed at South America, according to reports from Symantec, come mainly from the US (50%), Mexico (14%) and Brazil (7%), followed by China (2%) and Argentina (2%) [SYM 10].

We can conclude from this that the attacks affecting the continent (except those from China) come from the American continent itself. In South America, Brazil looms not large but gigantic. For years, it has been considered a significant source of online security risks on a global scale, and as a country possessing well-qualified and underemployed computer scientists who are likely to sell their services to the criminal element.

In terms of cyber-crime and cyber-security, we do not have enough data to allow us to evaluate the situation on the island. However, the country appears relatively unaffected by site-defacing attacks, as the statistics compiled based on the data published on zone-h.org would seem to suggest. The low number of available sites is undoubtedly a contributing factor to this.

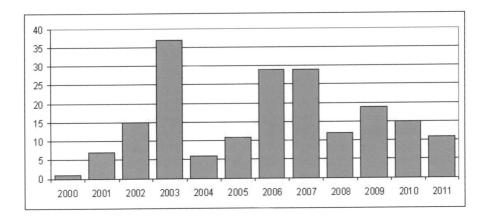

Figure 2.3. *Histogram of defacements of sites with the domain name ".cu", according to data published on zone-h.org (accessed June 14, 2011)*

---

12 Symantec report 2010 [SYM 10].

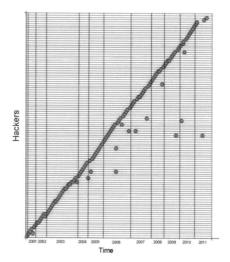

Figure 2.4. *Number of ".cu" sites defaced from 2000 to 2011. Several points on the same horizontal line signify that the hacker attacked the domain on dates $x_1, x_2, ... x_n$. The diagram shows that the hackers' actions are not long-lasting. It is not even possible to affirm that the Cuban sites were specifically targeted – these statistics simply illustrate the fact that the attacks are collateral effects of operations aimed at other online actors*

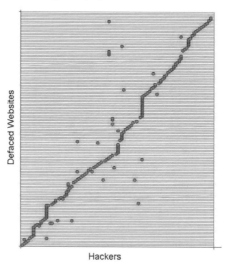

Figure 2.5. *The number of hackers defacing websites in the 2000–2011 period. Horizontally: a single point on the line denotes the site was defaced by one hacker and multiple points relate to multiple hackers. Vertically: the hacker attacked a site (a single point on the vertical line) or several sites (multiple points on the same virtual line). Overall, no one site appears to have been the target of a large-scale aggressive operation from multiple hackers*

These same statistics show that over the past 12 years, the servers whose sites have been defaced are founded, in equal part, on private and free systems.

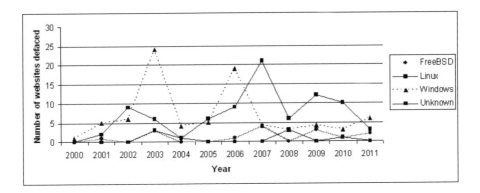

Figure 2.6. *The systems that have been the target of attacks over the 2000–2011 period (according to site defacement data published on the zone-h.org database)*

However, let us not forget that a project to develop a national open source solution for all governmental systems is officially under way[13]: the system Cuba Nova Linux is to be installed on nearly all government workstations. This policy, which consists of ensuring a State's technological sovereignty and independence from the US, is an approach that is increasingly widely being used the world over.

The part played by free software in Cuba, however, remains modest, even though according to a recent study it seems that Cuba has the highest proportion of machines running Linux. (In Cuba, 6.3% of machines operate on Linux; by comparison, in France only 1.72% of computers have that platform installed.[14] In Italy, the market share is 1.54%; and in the UK and the USA it is only 0.73%; the global average is 0.76%.)[15]

---

13 Cuban minister "Fighting cyber-attacks is matter of national security", *Cubaheadlines*, on February 25, 2011, http://www.cubaheadlines.com/2011/02/25/29755/fighting_cyber_attacks_is_matter_of_national_security_cuban_minister_said.html.

14 *Cuba, premier pays utilisateur de Linux*, May 16, 2011, (Cuba the world's main user of Linux). http://www.webimag.com/2011/05/cuba-premier-pays-utilisateur-de-linux/.

15 http://royal.pingdom.com/2011/05/12/the-top-20-strongholds-for-desktop-linux/.

2.2. Theoretical and practical considerations on information warfare and cyber-warfare

2.2.1. *Development of capabilities*

The history of computer science in Cuba goes back to the 1950s, when two first-generation American computers were installed there. After the revolution of 1959, trade with the US ceased. New computers arrived, particularly from France [MES 92], but after this time they were mainly imported from the Soviet Union. Cuba even invested in a program to develop its own computers in the 1970s. Specialists were trained in East Germany and the Soviet Union. An embryonic computer industry was formed at this time, but mainly involved assembling computers from imported components.

It was in 1991, a time when the economic situation was very difficult for Cuba (the Berlin Wall had come down, the Soviet Union had dissolved and a close ally had disappeared) that the first UUCP[16] connection was established between CENIAI (*Centro de Intercambio Automatizado de Información* – Center for Automated Information Exchange) and Web/NIRV in Toronto.

Since the 1990s, Cuban cyberspace has developed very little, not taking advantage of the Cuban Democracy Act passed in the US in 1992, exempting international telecommunications from the scope of the American embargo. The strategic measure was aimed at promoting democracy in Cuba by technological means [BOA 00]. The CENIAI is now one of only two Internet service providers in Cuba, the other being ETEC SA (*Empresa de Telecomunicaciones de Cuba S.A* – Cuban Telecommunications Company Ltd) [17]; both companies are under State control because of their strategic value. ETEC S.A. in which Telecom Italia had a 27% capital share until late January 2011, has since then been under total control of the State. The shares were bought out by the finance institution Rafin S.A., said to belong to Raul and Fidel Castro themselves[18], and to finance the Cuban army. In May 2010, Rafin S.A is thought to have created a joint venture with South Pacific Holdings Ltd, controlled by Russian money[19]. According to the Cuban authorities, the low level of infrastructural development is due to the American policy which has maintained a trade embargo against the island since 1962. This has forbidden US companies trading with the Castro regime, preventing Cuba from tapping into the

---

16 Unix-to-Unix Copy Protocol.

17 http://www.etecsa.cu/.

18 *The Internet is a Question Mark in Cuba*, Cuba Verdad, May 18, 2011, http://www.cubaverdad.net/weblog/2011/05/the-internet-is-a-question-mark-in-cuba-laritza-diversent/.

19 Rafin, S.A, Raul & Fidel Inc., 5 February 5, 2011, www.capitolhillcubans.com/2011/02/raul-fidel-inc-rafin-sa.html.

ARCOS-1 cable (the constructor and main shareholder of which is the American company New World Network Ltd.)[20], as well as depriving the country of good connections to the World Wide Web, forcing it to develop its own intranet relying on costly, low-throughput satellite connections.

The new undersea fiber optic cable that was deployed in early 2011, linking La Guaira (Venezuela) to Santiago de Cuba, is intended to increase the capabilities for communication with the rest of the world. Another segment links Santiago de Cuba to Jamaica. The project was carried out in part by the Franco-Chinese consortium Alcatel-Shanghai Bell[21], at a cost of around $70 million, financed by Venezuelan banks and Cuba's own money. The operator of the system will be Telecomunicaciones Gran Caribe S.A, which will then sell bandwidth to other countries. The installation of the cable, begun on January 22, 2011, was greeted by inflamed discourse from journalists[22]. The Cuban media emphasized the new opportunities offered, to both Cuba and the region, for a free world, with the chance to realize José Marti's vision.[23]

The country is financing new projects to develop, in particular, a software industry. It was to this end that the University of Computer Sciences (UCI – *Universidad de las Ciencias Informáticas*)[24] in Havana was created, and opened in September 2002. This institution's mission is to train thousands of software developers, capable of supporting the project, in order to bring the country into the information age in the years to come [HAA 05]. The following mission statement is displayed on the institution's homepage: "UCI is a productive university, whose mission is to produce software and computing services based on the link between study and work as a training model"[25]. A technological park must also be created in this context, in order to produce software to meet both national and international demands. The outfit was built on the site of the old military listening station, Lourdes, developed by the Soviets in 1964.

At its opening in September 2002, the university took in more than 2,000 students, taught by 300 professors. Four years later, the university had enrolled some

---

20 *Acceso a Internet en Cuba* (Access to the Internet in Cuba), September 17, 2010, http://www.pcacordoba.es/?p=1326.
21 *En busca de independencia, cable Cuba-Venezuela para el 2011*, October 31, 2009, (In search of independence – Cuba-Venezuela cable for 2011). http://www.cubadebate.cu/noticias/2009/10/31/en-busca-de-independencia-cable-cuba-venezuela-para-el-2011/.
22 See the video at http://www.cubadebate.cu/noticias/2011/01/22/comienza-instalacion-del-cable-submarino-venezuela-cuba/.
23 1853-1895, Cuban politician, poet, founder of the Cuban Revolutionary Party, veritable national hero and martyr for independence.
24 http://www.uci.cu/.
25 http://www.uci.cu/?q=node/46.

10,000 students. The work carried out there is aimed to create a large-scale site accommodating 20,000 people, in what is known as the Digital City of the Future (*Ciudad Digital Avanzada*). The means invested and the scope of the Cuban project, are not sufficient to envisage anything on the scale of the gigantic technological parks found in the US or in Asia.[26] However, it does bear certain similarities to some of them. Cyberjaya, in Malaysia, is a digital city opened in July 2003, 25 km south of the capital, Kuala Lumpur. These projects, which were thus begun in the aftermath of 9/11, are focused on new technologies and are geographically close to the political capital in order to underline their strategic nature. The major differences are that the digital city in Malaysia houses thousands of national and foreign enterprises.

2.3. Cyber-warfare theories and practices

In Cuba, the questions of information warfare and cyber-warfare are not (as yet) asked in the same terms as in industrialized countries where, it must be remembered, the discourse and strategies are concentrated around:

– dedicated military forces;

– cyber-attacks against the systems managing countries' essential infrastructures;

– cyber-espionage; and

– attacks mounted by non-state actors of terrorist, anarchist, anti-globalization or libertarian etc. persuasion, which may not have much of an impact individually but can, by cumulative effect, create an atmosphere of disorder, significantly destabilize the function of national economies and in particular, global systems.

For the Cuban regime, the question of cyberspace-based attacks is an even bigger part of the natural extension of the protection of its information space. Hence, we are dealing with the field of psychological operations, propaganda, the manipulation of opinions, the battle of ideas, interception of communications (electronic warfare) and intelligence – areas which are likely to undermine national unity. For the Cuban authorities, control of cyberspace and the ideas communicated therein is deemed necessary for the survival of the political model. Cuba decries the American strategy of cyber-warfare – which consists not of using networks as a tool but actually as a weapon to attack enemy cyberspace, to destabilize states – and one of its declensions, the setting up of a blogosphere that appears to be independent but which is in reality subjugated to Washington. Egypt and Libya have been victims of this strategy. Cuba is another major target, according to official Cuban media [MEX 11a]. This American strategy must rely on recruiting cyber-mercenaries, ersatz bloggers in Washington's pay particularly exiled Cubans, charged with

---

26 http://www.cyberjaya-msc.com/.

propagating untruths, misinformation, subversive ideas, etc. Here, Facebook, Twitter, YouTube, Flicker, etc., are vehicles for this destabilizing propaganda. Cubans would be approached, even within the country, to organize networks of cyber-dissidents. (Operation Surf, organized by the CIA and financed by USAID[27], with the involvement of Freedom House, is yet more proof of the US strategy against Cuba [MEX 11b].)

Thus, the Cuban Internet is controlled – under the thumb of the State – and nothing favors the emergence of an open Internet society: the information space has to be controlled.

However, it is not beyond the realms of possibility for Cuba to carry out more offensive cybernetic operations (virus attacks and invasions) against countries that are better connected than it is. It is that asymmetry which now constitutes the strength of small States. However, in the short term, we have to wonder about the consequences of the new high-capacity connection between Cuba and the global Internet, from which it has hitherto been isolated. This new technological capability could be a harbinger of other consequences that are more offensive, in the same vein as occurs in the rest of the world. For the Cuban government, cyberspace must be the instrument of its power strategy – the government must help to reinforce it, extend it, and officially pursue the revolutionary goals in the long term.

2.3.1. *Fidel Castro's discourse*

The various interventions by Fidel Castro over the past few years help to shed some light on Cuban policy in terms of the Internet, which is directly linked to the State's vision of using the media in the Cuban socialist society.

As regards the freedom of the media, Fidel Castro is intransigent. On the one hand, he states that the Cuban media have to learn the art of constructive criticism, in the spirit of the revolution; yet on the other hand he does not allow total freedom of the press, which would involve opening up the floor to the anti-revolutionary press (which, it is understood, would infect Cuba with subversive ideas, Western culture, capitalism and the call to revolt). The critical spirit is therefore restricted. The country would be unable to withstand another counter-revolutionary influence.

> "Our press organs are not in the hands of the enemies of the revolution, nor of the agents of the United States. They are in the hands of revolutionaries. Our press is revolutionary, our radio and television journalists are revolutionary. [...] We have discovered that

---

27 US Agency for International Development, http://www.usaid.gov/.

in the struggle against negative facts, the work of the press is very important. And we have stimulated critical spirit. We have come to the convinced conclusion that it is necessary to develop critical spirit a great deal further" [RAM 06].

This approach should not be seen as an indication of willingness to introduce total freedom of the press as Western media understands the term. Indeed:

"If by 'freedom of the press' you mean the right of counter-revolution and the right of Cuba's enemies to speak and write freely against socialism and against the revolution, to slander, lie and create conditioned reflexes, I would say to you that we are not in favor of that 'freedom'. As long as Cuba remains a country blocked[28] by tyranny, the victim of iniquitous laws such as the Helms-Burton Act[29] or the Cuban Adjustment Act[30], a country threatened by the very President of the US, we cannot give that freedom to the allies of our enemies, whose objective is to fight against socialism's very *raison d'être*" [RAM 06].

In addition, there can be no 'free' press in the sense that it cannot be a question of private property for the media, which are all State run.

The main points of argument lie in blaming the embargo situation, the total lack of freedom of the press and the little development in terms of Internet infrastructures primarily on the US, and more generally on the wider capitalist world. Cuba views itself as the victim of 'media terrorism' on the part of large international groups, who paint Cuba in an erroneous, untrue, negative light that is damaging to the nation[31].

"Today there are means of communicating with the world which make us less the victims of, or dependent on, any large-scale, mass-distributed media, be they private or State run, because today, with this worldwide Internet, all those who have an aspiration, a goal, will work together, be they from a rich or a poor country" [CAS 03].

---

28 The Cubans speak of a "block" and the Americans of an embargo.

29 Cuban Liberty and Democratic Solidarity, Helms-Burton Act, 1996, http://www.treasury.gov/resource-center/sanctions/Documents/libertad.pdf.

30 The 1966 law which, like the Helms-Burton Act, forms part of the US policy of maintaining an economic embargo against Cuba.

31 *Cuba llama a la "ciberdefensa activa" en la red y la "blogosfera"*, December 1, 2011, (Cuba calls for "active cyberdefense" on the web and in the "blogosphere"). http://elcomercio.pe/tecnologia/1341987/noticia-cuba-llama-ciberdefensa-activa-red-blogosfera.

Fidel Castro emphasizes the liberating dimension of the Internet, the revolutionary potential of the Internet the world over. He underlines the capacity of that tool to reinforce the power of collective popular action; however, he cannot envisage or take the risk of that being so in Cuba. This is probably because, from his point of view, Cuba is more of a model of revolution for others, rather than a model to be rethought. The official position is to give no ground at all in terms of media freedom, in the name of preserving the gains of the revolution. The State wishes to be able to exert an influence on the international stage without being influenced in return.

2.3.2. *The concept of active cyber-defense*

The Cuban State perceives a threat in cyberspace and thus calls on a form of protection which it calls 'active cyber-defense'; this would involve first defining a political strategy in cyberspace, which is thus far lacking[32]. In December 2011, the Cuban Foreign Minister, Rodríguez Parrilla, called for social networking platforms that pose a danger to peace in the country to be seized. This strategy involves the occupation of cyberspace. This does not necessarily imply an aggressive dimension in terms of cyber-attacks, but rather a position in the blogosphere, on social networks, in media space, and a strategy of influence. "It is fundamental that revolutionary movements will find their expression in cyberspace"[33].

Are the authorities envisaging supporting foreign revolts? The primary objective is to counter the presence of detractors and opponents of the Cuban regime. This active cyber-defense does not (officially, at least) display a military aspect. It is not (yet) a question of military cyber-units for Cuba, as is now the case in many countries. A document published on the CubaDebate[34] site transcribing the proposals put forward during a conference organized in Havana on November 29, 2011 shows the outline of this concept of active cyber-defense:

– Cyber-warfare is reserved for military action.

– Active cyber-defense is a new concept, which the Cubans must use in the struggle against the model imposed by capitalist tyranny, to complement the action

---

32 *Cuba llama a la "ciberdefensa activa" en la red y la "blogosfera"*, 1 December 2011, http://elcomercio.pe/tecnologia/1341987/noticia-cuba-llama-ciberdefensa-activa-red-blogosfera

33 Reported proposals, attributed to the Foreign Minister, *Cuba llama a la "ciberdefensa activa" en la red y la "blogosfera"*, December 1, 2011, http://elcomercio.pe/tecnologia/1341987/noticia-cuba-llama-ciberdefensa-activa-red-blogosfera.

34 *De la ciberguerra a la Ciberdefensa activa*, November 30, 2011, (From cyber-warfare to active cyber-defense), http://www.cubadebate.cu/opinion/2011/11/30/de-la-ciberguerra-a-la-ciberdefensa-activa/.

of those who oppose the postmodern folly of digital evangelization, which tries to make us believe that a computer program is a social network, that a thing is a human being.

– Revolutionary action must be built up: we must identify the enemy's actions, imagine alternatives and provide revolutionary movements with scientific instruments to enable them to adopt an offensive strategy.

– This effort must guarantee the security of the revolutionary movements on networks and establish synergies with computer experts, ever more given to crime and who will form part of the global government and its systems of surveillance and control.

– We must study the experiments of resistance on the Internet; develop strategies of visibility, of cooperation, of alliances; we must know what to do in the case of an attack or censure against a blog, a website or an account on social networks; we must know how to defend ourselves; how to free ourselves from technological dependence on a few global actors who bow to the decisions of the capitalist empire.

– Active cyber-defense must be the top priority.

– It must not be forgotten that, though there may be major inequality between those who have materialistic power and proclaim the need for war and the moral forces that reclaim the right to peace, only the will of men can conquer the will of other men.

"Ideas are and always will be the most important weapon", proclaimed Fidel Castro in a speech given on December 2, 2001 in Santiago de Cuba [CAS 01]. Hence, cyberspace can no longer be ignored by the authorities: active cyber-defense is presented first and foremost as taking account of the capacities of the medium to stage a veritable battle of ideas.

2.4. Regulations and ways around them

The Cuban authorities have many tools at their disposal to maintain control over the information space. Internet access is regulated by legal, technological and financial constraints. Content control is ensured both inside and outside the country. The immediate consequence is the limitation in the number of Cuban internet users; in addition, the impossibility of staying connected for a long time reduces the risk of any opening to the outside world, thereby reducing the influence of foreign ideas.

Cuba's strategy consists of developing and favoring collective access, but in actual fact still favors clearly-defined social classes.

2.4.1. *The State's influence over cyberspace*

Internet access is rendered difficult. It is authorized in hotels for foreign tourists (at prices that are prohibitive for most Cuban citizens), and at official access points that are monitored (in particular the cybercafés that the Cuban postal service has been able to set up following Law No. 99/2009). Domestic Internet connections are not yet authorized, except for a handful of citizens (doctors, professors and government officials). Outside of hotels, only a privileged few actually have special authorization and are allowed to connect to the international network. Thus, a person has to provide a valid reason in order to obtain accreditation facilitating access to the Web. The level of merit of the requester is assessed by a committee for the defense of the revolution. The authorities rely as much on making it difficult to access the Internet as on actually filtering the contents to limit contact with the outside world and with ideas deemed subversive.

Limitations are also imposed by the legal framework. Thus, anyone posting articles deemed to be counter-revolutionary faces 20 years in prison, whether or not the content is distributed via foreign sites or platforms. This sanction is written into the Penal Code and in Law 88. Decree 209 of 1996, Access from the Republic of Cuba to the global information network[35], stipulates that the Internet cannot be used in violation of the moral principles of the society or the laws of the country. Internet access is defined according to the country's interests, which are defined by the authorities. In 2007, Resolution 127 reminded us, as if it were necessary, that it is forbidden to use networks to broadcast information contrary to society's interests, to the norms of good behavior, to the integrity of individuals or to national security. The Internet service providers are obliged to put checks in place that are capable of detecting and preventing illicit activities; they are obliged to inform the authorities of any infraction of the law of which they are aware. Connecting to the Internet without authorization carries a sentence of five years in prison. Expressing yourself

---

35 *Acceso desde la República de Cuba a Redes Informáticas de Alcance Global, Gaceta Oficial de la República de Cuba*, no. 27, September 13, 1996 (Access from the Republic of Cuba to Computer Networks of Global Reach), http://www.ordiecole.com/cuba/209-1996.pdf. The text specifies the conditions of State control over Internet access: an inter-ministerial commission – made up of the Ministers of Science and Technology, Communications, the Interior, the Revolutionary Armed Forces and Justice, presided over by the Minister of the Steel and Electronic Industry – is charged with regulating the development of networks in the country, and the use of information coming from global networks. Contributions as regards the Internet are the preserve of the new Ministry of Computer Sciences and Communications, set up on 11 January 2000 (Decree-Law 204). In order to coordinate the institutional strategy on computer security, the Bureau of Security for Computer Networks (*Oficina de Seguridad para les Redes Informáticas*) was created on May 21, 2002 by Resolution 64. Cuba's legislation as regards the regulation of the Internet is relatively abundant: http://www.informatica-juridica.com/trabajos/Resena_de_la_legislacion_informatica_Cuba.asp.

online is risky. In the past few years, a number of journalists/bloggers have been imprisoned, with sentences from a few months to several years for subversive propaganda that is menacing to society.

Limiting technological development is an additional tool of the policy of keeping society under control. Technologies are being introduced gradually: up until 2008, citizens were prohibited from owning a computer. This explains the low level of technological development on the island, where there are 3.3 computers per 100 inhabitants. VoIP[36], a new form of technology, is forbidden, except at certain duly authorized and controlled access points in Havana. Besides the aforementioned technical constraints and the legal restrictions on access, the prohibitive costs of communication greatly restrict the number of Internet users. It should be borne in mind, by comparison, that the average monthly income in Cuba is $20. An hour's connection at an Internet access point costs $1.50, and $7.00 in hotels for tourists. A computer (distributed by the State-controlled importer Copextel Corporation) costs roughly $800 (or $600 on the black market). While 30% of Cubans claim to have access to a computer, it is usually either at work or at school [ONE 09]. Mobile telephony, whose network does cover 70% of the territory, is no more accessible in financial terms. In May 2011, Cubacel reduced the fees for initiating and activating cell phone subscriptions to $30.[37] The cost of international calls varies between $1.40 and $1.85 per minute. On February 1, 2012, the costs of SMS messaging were cut by 44%[38].

In order to ensure control of the information space, the authorities have put processes in place that allow them:

– To occupy blogspace: the authorities have to be present in cyberspace, however little of that space they occupy. To this end, an official association of Cuban bloggers has been created.

– To pirate Cuban websites abroad: Cuban websites and blogs hosted abroad have been victim to pirating. In May 2008 during the trial of the economist Martha Beatriz Roque, proof came to light that the government was pirating dissidents' Yahoo! accounts[39].

---

36 VoIP Voice over Internet Protocol.

37 *Cuba rebaja servicio de celulares en busca de mas usuarios*, May 24, 2011 (Cuba lowers its cellphone tariffs in search of more users), http://www.cubaverdad.net/weblog/2011/05/cuba-rebaja-servicio-de-celulares-en-busca-de-mas-usuarios/.

38 *Comenzaron a aplicarse hoy las nuevas tarifas de los celulares*, Digital Granma International, Havana, Cuba, 1 February 1, 2012, http://www.granma.cu/espanol/cuba/1febre-Comenzaron%20a.html.

39 Cuba, Freedom on the Net, Cuba Verdad, May 2, 2011, http://www.cubaverdad.net/weblog/2011/05/cuba-freedom-on-the-net-2011-freedom-house/.

– Software applications, such as Avila Link, enable communications to be monitored (communications are routed via proxies, and the authorities can obtain the usernames and passwords of surfers) at the level of the multiple public Internet access points [FRE 11]. As much as by the installation of tools for filtering and censure, because of the poor quality of the networks filtering takes place almost naturally: international sites, such as that of the BBC and *Le Monde* are officially accessible, but too-low throughputs prevent them from being consulted. Sites judged to be anti-Cuban, blogs written by Cuban residents themselves but hosted abroad may be blocked. Censure is certainly present on Cuban networks.

– In 2007, access to portals such as Yahoo!, MSN and Hotmail was systematically blocked [FRE 11]. The blocks remained in place for several months, including on blogger platforms. Facebook and Twitter were periodically available. For this reason, even those few citizens who could access the Internet rather than content themselves with the Cuban intranet could not surf the Web entirely at their leisure.

Thus, Cubans only have cyberspace, Internet, mobile telephony benefits and modern information and communication technologies (ICTs) in the broader sense, with limited and partial vision, access and usage.

2.4.2. *Getting around the restrictions*

Owing to Cuban politics, which is restrictive of fundamental liberties, Reporters Without Borders qualify the regime as an enemy of the Internet (a country that violates the freedom of expression online), similar to Saudi Arabia, Myanmar, China, North Korea, Egypt, Iran, Uzbekistan, Syria, Tunisia, Turkmenistan and Vietnam.

The socio-political climate in Cuba (a set of measures and conditions that limit both access to cyberspace and free expression) is clearly not very favorable to the emergence of a true information society, and of an Internet culture. The barriers and limitations, as always, drive individuals to come up with ways around them.

A black market appears to have taken root in Cuba, based on the trade in access to the Internet. Thus, those who have authorizations sometimes hire out their access. The cost proves high – around $65 per month, i.e. two to three times the average salary. Content that cannot circulate freely on the Web is exchanged on USB sticks or CD-ROMs. Similarly, a market for counterfeit DVDs and software packages has developed on the island to get around the US embargo and for simple reasons of cost (the original products are beyond the reach of Cuban consumers because they are too expensive). Thus, although Microsoft is not authorized to sell its products in Cuba, almost all computers run Windows. In a study published in 1992 [MES 92], the authors pointed out the existence of a counterfeiting system organized by the State in Cuba: a national center copied foreign software to distribute it to Cubans free of charge. The rate of software piracy in the country is estimated at 80% by the Business Software Alliance [ISR 10]. Cuba ignores the copyright system (although, paradoxically, copyright is imposed on some of its official websites).

In this environment so unpropitious for free expression, a small community of bloggers has nevertheless been able to take root. There are roughly 150 blogs that are hosted abroad. The contents are sent via e-mail from Cuban hotels to friends or family members living abroad, who then post the messages on the blogs, which most often talk about local, day-to-day life. The bloggers generally avoid politicized subjects that may be sensitive (auto-censure). However, some of them have acquired a reputation that extends beyond Cuba's shores, for their frankness. For instance, we can cite:

– Yoani Sanchez, who lives in Havana, and whose blog Generación Y[40] hosted on the *Voces Cubanas* (Cuban Voices) platform, describes daily life. The political dimension of her posts has brought her international renown, and in 2008 *Time* magazine dubbed her as one of the 100 most influential people. The Cuban authorities then attempted to discredit her, calling her a mercenary in the pay of foreign forces[41].

– Luis Felipe Rojas, a blogger who has been arrested many times, and was placed under house arrest in 2009.

These individuals form part of the elite circle of bloggers who, in their respective countries, have become mediatized personalities on an international scale for their opposition to the regime and their participation in revolutions. Notably, such bloggers include Slim Amamou and Lina Ben Mehni (Tunisian revolutionary bloggers), Zouhair Yahyaoui (Egyptian), Hassan al-Djahmi[42] (a Libyan political exile in Switzerland, who on January 28, 2011 on Facebook called for a nationwide day of anger (day of celebration) to be organized) and even Mohamed Nabous[43] (an anti-Gaddafi blogger who was killed by a sniper on March 19, 2011)[44]. The appearance of emblematic figures, or you might even say 'heroic' figures, is significant of the evolution of information warfare, which up until now have not yet

---

40 http://www.desdecuba.com/generaciony/.
41 *Cuba says blogger Yoani Sanchez part of "cyberwar"*, March 22, 2011:
http://uk.ibtimes.com/articles/125216/20110322/cuba-says-blogger-yoani-sanchez-part-of-cyberwar.htm.
42 http://www.facebook.com/hassan.aldjahmi.
43 http://en.wikipedia.org/wiki/Mohammed_Nabbous.
44 http://www.facebook.com/MartyrMohamedNabous);
http://www.streetpress.com/sujet/2161-libye-mohammed-nabbous-est-mort (Libya – Mohammed Nabbous dead).

found genuine combatant icons. Cyber-conflict is not merely dominated by anonymous hackers or state cyber-warriors, who are all nameless and faceless. The hacktivists of Web 2.0 give cyber-conflict a human face. It is no longer solely a question of shadowy hackers, viruses, virtuality and immateriality.

2.5. Capabilities of control, surveillance and interception

Cuba has had electronic surveillance systems (SIGINT)[45] at its disposal ever since the Soviet Union helped it build the Lourdes listening post near Havana, two years after the Cuban Missile Crisis. The station had 12 antennae[46] and 1,500 Soviet engineers and technicians. The base was shut down following the 9/11 attacks in New York, when Russia officially and unilaterally decided to withdraw from the project. The UCI was rapidly built on the site the following year. Classes began taking place, although the military equipment from the old base had yet to be removed[47].

The Cuban government, who did not have use of the Lourdes base, which was reserved for the Soviets and later the Russians, wanted to have its own SIGINT infrastructure. The base at Bejucal, not far from Lourdes, was then constructed between 1995 and 1998 with the participation of Russia. The equipment left for Cuba from the port of Riga in Latvia. In 1998, the US Department of Defense picked up on a significant increase in the amount of illegal importation of American computing material into Cuba. The military base at Bejucal, a militarized zone near to DAAFAR (*Defensa Anti-Aerea y Fuerza Aerea Revolucionaria* – Anti-Aerial Defense and Revolutionary Air Force) and the Rescate de Sanguily base includes 10 Satcom antennae[48]. Besides the interception systems, the bases have systems for interfering with satellite communications (GPS, Satcom, et.) designed and based on equipment bought from the Russian enterprise Aviaconversa. The systems enable Cuba to intercept US telecommunications, international satellite communications satellites, Internet communications and communications within the embassies.

According to the unconfirmed information provided by Manuel Cereijo[49] (a Cuban-born engineer teaching at the University of Miami in Florida, who publishes a great many articles on the situation in Cuba, and particularly on issues relating to

---

45 SIGINT – SIGnal INTelligence.

46   http://bbs.keyhole.com/ubb/ubbthreads.php?ubb=showflat&Number=521637&site_id=1# import. Accessed in October 2011.

47 http://www.uci.cu/?q=node/48. Accessed in October 2011.

48   http://bbs.keyhole.com/ubb/ubbthreads.php?ubb=showflat&Number=521637&site_id=1#i mport Accessed in October 2011.

49 CEREIJO M., *Cuba and Information Warfare*, undated, www.amigospais-guaracabuya. org/oagmc207.php.

the Internet, telecommunications and electronic warfare), an agreement was signed between Cuba and China in 1999, relating in particular to the development of these SIGINT capabilities. Thereby, China contributed to the development of the Bejucal base (not far from the UCI), where a cyber-warfare unit is active in monitoring data traffic. Chinese military personnel use the Bejucal base, using the Chinese communication satellites rather than the Russian ones. In addition, large SIGINT systems have been installed at Wajay (not far from UCI) and Santiago de Cuba as part of the Titan project, the fruit of Sino-Cuban collaboration.

Such information, which is near-impossible to verify, paints a picture of a nation that is active in the field of surveillance, control, data interception, cyber-warfare and electronic warfare. It is dependent on foreign capabilities, first Russian and now Chinese. Other, more recent articles suggest that Cuban security forces provided the Venezuelan government with the transmitters used in the new identification cards and passports, thus facilitating the surveillance of individuals [CRU 11].

More important than the (unprovable) veracity of the information provided by the various sources cited here is the image which emerges: Cuba appears to be a 'Big Brother'-type of island, with wide-reaching international influence, infiltrated by allied powers and which in turn infiltrates its allies.

2.6. Enemies

Cuban policy as regards security and defense is spearheaded by the struggle against American imperialism. The enormous military exercise in Bastion 2009, held between November 26 and 28, 2009, was the first on such a scale since the political transition in 2008. It was aimed at preparing Cuban forces to defend against a military invasion by the US. The exercise involved tactical maneuvers, ground-troop exercise and aerial maneuvers.

However, the threat is not limited to the conventional military dimension. As Boris Moreno, Minister for Computer Sciences and Communications, pointed out in 2008, "the use of the Internet [should serve to] defend the Revolution and the principles in which Cuba has believed for years". Information space and cyberspace are also perceived negatively, as being vectors of foreign misinformation, a danger, a weapon that could be used against the interests of the Cuban people and the Revolution. "A cyber-war is a war fought not with bombs and bullets, but with communication, algorithms and bits. Cyberwarfare is a new form of invasion, dreamt up by the developed world"[50].

---

50 *Ciberguerra*, March 21, 2011, http://idanialacubana.blogcip.cu/2011/03/21/ciberguerra/. idanialacubana is a blog that conveys the ideology of the Cuban authorities.

Cuba is not alone in this anti-imperialist stance. Hugo Chavez's government is one of the most virulent actors. Let us not forget the Asian giant China, which may resort to similar rhetoric. In a speech in Shanghai in June 2000, the son of Jiang Zemin, Jiang Mianheng, Vice-President of the Chinese Academy of Sciences, trained as an engineer in the US, declared that China must fight against one of the negative aspects of internationalization: cyber-imperialism [LAM 00]. Internet technologies are controlled by the US, and he believes China's integration into the economy dominated by cyberspace presents the danger of subjugating the country to the fealty of capitalist, neo-imperialist Western powers. This threat justifies the construction of a national network independent of the Internet, the elaboration of new protocols and technologies on which it is to be based. Anti-communist values are penetrating Chinese society by way of the Internet. The intrusion of these Western ideas represents a threat to the Chinese Communist Party's power. The other danger lays in the existence of "back doors" in Windows applications, which could lead to the leaking of secret State documents. The West's technological domination is perceived as a colonial menace. This is a question not only of technological dependence, but also of influence and remote control by ideas and cultures. The West uses globalization, utilizing cyberspace as a tool through which to exploit the third world, the second world and developing countries.

After opium, which subjugated China to the West's influence, there now appears to be the 'electronic heroin' of bourgeois-liberal websites [LAM 00]. The Chinese Communist Party is becoming addicted to this Marxist rhetoric. The Chinese people must steel themselves to fight against foreign cyber-invaders. The only solution to preserve national security is therefore to develop national technologies, to escape from any possible dependence on foreign powers. Of course, all this must go hand-in-hand with filtering of the Internet. Thus, the following is at stake:

– preserving the prerogatives of the Chinese Communist Party;

– preserving Chinese sovereignty;

– assimilating foreign technologies and developing China's own technologies; and

– adopting international standards while retaining control on the home front.

Cuba is a long way from having the same industrial, human, financial and military capabilities as China that enable China to envisage maintaining this posture in relation to the American giant. However, in spirit, the Cuban discourse of struggle against American imperialism tends to converge with the arguments developed by Jiang Mianheng.

The new concept of Cuban active cyber-defense is borrowed from these anti-imperialist arguments and could be considered to stem from this struggle against American cyber-imperialism.

Since the 1990s, Cuba has been concerned about the enemy using the Internet to subversive ends. In this context, international associations (NGOs) were identified as potentially subversive. In his speeches at the time, Raul Castro spelled out the nature of that threat in no uncertain terms[51]:

> "The enemy make no secret of their intention to use a number of NGOs recently installed in Cuba as Trojan Horses to foment division [...] it would be idiotic of us to pretend not to see the manipulation instrumented through the NGOs, whose only objective is to subject our country to slavery once more..."

The concerns voiced by Cuba are borne out by the projects carried out in the US. In a study published in 1992, David Ronfeldt recommended the adoption of a US policy of communication to help open up the Cuban system and speed up the emergence of an independent civil society [GON 92].

The adversary takes the form of a spy, an American entrepreneur attempting to smuggle telecommunication materials into Cuba. The US industrialist Alan Gross, 61, was arrested in December 2009 in Cuba and sentenced to 15 years' imprisonment in March 2011 for having attempted to illegally import communication materials [MIR 11]. These materials would have enabled Internet access to be provided to individuals by unlimited satellites (he was particularly looking at helping Cuban Jewish associations), thereby creating platforms beyond the control of the Cuban authorities. Havana, in turn, considered these attempts as manifestations of the American strategy to destabilize the existing regime, based on the model of the Orange Revolution in the Ukraine in 2004 or the Green Revolution in Iran in 2009. In late December 2011, the Cuban government announced the liberation of nearly 3,000 prisoners (including 86 foreigners from 25 countries)[52]. Alan Gross was not among them.

The enemy is also anyone who, in the eyes of the Cuban authorities, is on the side of foreign powers. According to the Cuban authorities, the US pays individuals to carry out informational operations (propaganda, anti-Cuban comments on Cuban blogs, etc.) aimed at tarnishing the image of the country, its government and its people. Cyberspace is no longer the vector of globalization, but one of globalization

---

51 Cited in http://som.csudh.edu/fac/lpress/devnat/nations/cuba/cubassy.htm.
52 "Cuba, libération prochaine de près de 3000 prisonniers", *Le Monde*, December 24, 2011, (Cuba: forthcoming liberation of nearly 3,000 prisoners). http://www.lemonde.fr/ameriques/article/2011/12/24/cuba-liberation-de-pres-de-3-000-prisonniers_1622576_3222.html

based on incessant plots or maneuvers for destabilization, conceived by capitalist regimes.

The statements of speaker Eduardo Fontes Tato Suarez[53] and the points made in the documentary "Razones de Cuba"[54] (Cuban Reasons) broadcast on March 21, 2011 on Cuban television provide some information on the Cuban perspective on cyber-warfare, and particularly the role played by the American giant in the counter-revolutionary propaganda conveyed in cyberspace. It is clearly in the field of rhetoric that the cyber-conflict between Cuba and its adversaries is played out, rather than the field of hacking *per se*. These statements affirm that:

– Technology itself is not a threat – it is the usage made of it that poses a danger.

– The enemy is American. The situation worsened under the Bush administration, which put more means in place to monitor Cuba. The G. Bush Institute organized a conference to draw up a strategy for cyber-warfare against countries the US considers to be their enemies, including Cuba. Freedom House[55] is an organization supported by the American government to finance the subversion of Cuba. The first cyber-war waged by the US army that we know of took place in Yugoslavia.

– Cyber-warfare against Cuba began when the US decided to keep the island under 24-hour surveillance, similar to that with China and Iran.

– The US is master of the Internet; it has technological domination but, paradoxically, maintains an information block against Cuba.

– The majority of the content of the cyber-war against Cuba consists of demonizing socialism. Within these statements, we can distinguish the theme of an international plot, with multiple ramifications. Communication companies are financed by the US; the Spanish newspaper *El País* maintains an incessant press campaign against Cuba; all the foreign press appears to be allied against Cuba, refusing to tell the truth about the pressure, the war waged by the US against the Cuban people; the deletion of CubaDebate from Facebook[56] was an example of an act of cyber-war. Thus, the speaker assimilates cyber-war and information war, news war, media war (lack of debate, lack of truth, truncated reality, etc.).

---

53 This talk is available on video at the following addresses: http://observers.france24.com /fr/content/20110218-cours-magistral-cyber-contre-revolution-agent-secret-cubain-fidel-Castro -raul-twitter-fuite or http://vimeo.com/19402730.

54 See the "Ciberguerra" episode in the *Las Razones de Cuba* series broadcast on March 21, 2011: http://www.cubadebate.cu/noticias/2011/03/21/vea-el-capitulo-ciberguerra-de-la-serie-las-razones-de-cuba-video/.

55 http://www.freedomhouse.org/.

56 http://www.facebook.com/cubadebate.en.

– The threat is not merely an external one – the enemy is within as well, in the person of the counter-revolutionary bloggers. The action of these cyber-mercenaries consists of sowing discord within the country using ICTs. They are paid by the US by way of diverse forms of recompense and bonuses. Yoani Sanchez is the figurehead of these mercenary bloggers in the pay of the foreign foe. According to Eduardo Fontes Tato Suarez, the Generación Y blog[57] wishes to prove that its discourse comes from within the country although it is entirely dreamt up abroad. He reproaches the blog for conveying a false image of social reality in Cuba: the blog gives the impression that the populace is on the point of revolt, the country on the point of imploding, its quest is to destroy a project rather than consolidate it. The majority of Cuban bloggers are ones who respect the spirit of the revolution and receive no funding from abroad. The 'mercenary' Ernesto Hernandez Busto, Suarez claims, proposed an invasion by the US Army as a solution for Cuba.

The 'cyber-warfare' referred to in Cuban political discourse essentially stems from psychological warfare. It concerns the use of ideas space by foreign forces[58] (the American enemy, channeled through its vassals the world over), attempting to place and maneuver their pawns (mercenaries, traitors to the revolutionary project) within a system (Cuban society) in order to destabilize it. It mentions that Cuba is subject to surveillance by the ECHELON network (which has a base in Guantanamo) [STR 09].

2.7. Conclusion

Cuba's policy for the management of cyberspace answers to a logic which has been in place from the very dawn of the Internet in Cuba. Fidel Castro stepped aside for his brother, Raul, to take power in February 2008. The transition was not accompanied by far-reaching reforms in terms of freedom of access to information, which would lead the country a fair way down the road to democracy promulgated by its American neighbor. The new high-capacity link does not guarantee an increase in the number of access points, or the relaxation of the policy of control and surveillance. Hence, restrictions are still in force, as are limitations on the number of access points, control of access by the identification of Internet users and high access costs. Usage restrictions open up the Web to categories that are politically favorable to the regime, and access is mainly limited to public places and institutions, as was the case more than 10 years ago [DRA 00], even from the time of the application of Decree 209 in June 1996, stipulating that Internet access would

---

57 http://www.desdecuba.com/generaciony/.
58 A particularly good example of this strategy of influence can be seen in the setting up of Radio Marti in 1985, aimed at the Cuban population. A study conducted in 2009 shows that 2% of Cubans listen to this station. A report on the subject was published by the GAO in 2009 [GAO 09].

be selective, and that priority would be given to institutions that were useful to the country's development [KAL 01].

State control remains complete: the official political line is opposed to total freedom of the press, in the sense that we understand it in Western countries. The State still holds control over industrialists in the domain of new ICTs; and the development of infrastructure and content is guided by the State and not by the law of the market. The Cuban regime is standing in the way of what could constitute a factor of democratization by the introduction of the Internet[59].

In fact, the Cuban authorities manage to get around the dilemma: they stay away from economic globalization; they do not fully enter into the digital society, and are instrumentalizing technology by way of centralized control (*instrumentalist approach*), although this approach is not as radical as that of North Korea, which forbids the public any access to the Web [KO 09]. Cuba has adopted an intermediary position on the scale of control of the Internet in authoritarian countries: North Korea imposes total blockage of the Internet, China has opened up its Internet although control and surveillance are the order of the day; Cuba is positioned between the two, and may be qualified as a moderate model [KO 09]. We also see in the Cuban model that a State's Internet strategy is not formulated independently. Beyond technological dependence, which most of the world's countries share in, economic and political considerations are such that they will influence choices made in the very long term. Is the Cuban strategy not ultimately an expression of a lack of confidence in the actual stability of the regime?[60] Clearly, the administration does not think itself able to withstand the ideological assaults of the outside world. As long as this uncertainty persists, Cuban cyberspace will remain under-dimensioned and under State control.

---

59 Note, finally, that State interference in the functioning of the Internet, control of the flow of information, cut-off of networks, etc., are not – and have never been – characteristic only of authoritarian regimes. A recent study [HOW 11] indicates that 39% of such 'incidents' can be attributed to democracies, 6% to emerging democracies, and 52% to authoritarian regimes and unstable States, over the period 1995–2011. Over an extended period, it seems that all types of regimes are increasingly tempted to interfere. The reasons proposed are many: protection of political authorities (i.e. of political leaders, institutions, national security, etc.), preservation of the public good (religious morale, culture, social/racial harmony, protection of minors, defense of privacy, fight against crime, etc.). This does not have the effect the authorities had hoped – in fact it results in the strengthening of links between the local and global society, and innovation in the means of getting around the restrictions.
60 Kyngmin Ko *et al.* [KO 09] hypothesize that when a country is confident in the solidity of its regime and its ability to hold power, and displays genuine economic ambitions, it does not deprive itself of Internet, it controls and profits from it. On the other hand, when a country is concerned for its political stability, it takes reactive and defensive measures, to the detriment of economic potential. The first scenario would seem to correspond to China, and the second to Cuba.

The relatively aggressive American discourse about the strategy of democratizing the world using the Internet [CLI 10] would not tend to incite authoritarian regimes to open up further. However, like any restrictive strategy, Cuba's is faced with an inventive or a confrontational spirit from people dreaming up means to circumvent the tools of control and censure, and all forms of limitations (costs and lack of access to technology). In addition, the State is under considerable outside pressure:

– the embargo imposed by the US;

– limiting technological dependence in the absence of any national industry in the field of new ICTs likely to produce genuine solutions of substitution[61];

– active opponents abroad;

– influential and critical bloggers, even on Cuban soil; and

– accusations of anti-American plotting and of alliance with States that are undesirable in the eyes of democracies.

The international tensions that are becoming increasingly manifest in cyberspace do not spare Cuba, which is accused of participation in the planning of terrorist actions. In early December 2011, the American press[62] hinted at Cuba's involvement in a vast network including Iran, Mexico and Venezuela, intended to carry out cyber-attacks against the US (nuclear installations, the CIA, the White House, the FBI, etc.). The theory of the Iranian Islamist plot, using South America to create a terrorist network, may be part of the new order in international politics, in which the

---

61 Most nations on the planet are now dependent on the technologies, protocols and applications developed in the US, and that form the backbone of cyberspace. For a number of States this situation of dependence is critical, because it involves giving up parts of their national sovereignty. Those States that have not been able to equip themselves with industries they control, both at the levels of software and hardware, find themselves at an *impasse* if they refuse to open their markets to foreign companies to compensate for what they lack. Cuba does not totally refuse, but the decision to open its market is taken grudgingly, and it is at a very slow pace that the country is gaining access to cyberspace. This State strategy, however, has the result of confining the populace a little more to the past. Its leaders admire the virtues of the Internet in the world, but refuse to accept the risks in their own back yard. Yet, as we have seen, this slow advance into the global society of Web 2.0 is not synonymous with a lack of capability in the field of information warfare and cyber-warfare. While Cuba does not actually have all the capabilities and skills, it could undoubtedly acquire them or sub-contract part of the task, e.g. as North Korea does with China. Power in the cybernetic domain can be found in a country's alliances, however, this always entails a degree of dependence.
62 A documentary aired by the Hispanic-American channel Univision on December 8, 2012, which describes the organization of an international network headed by Iran, and connecting parties in Mexico, Cuba and Venezuela. Cyber-attacks, according to the documentary, were to be launched from Mexico. The main parties in the plot would be diplomats and university students. Fact or fiction?

cybernetic dimension will have a not insignificant part to play. Is Cuba sufficiently well armed against this new form of conflict facing states in cyberspace?

The concept of active cyber-defense is not ground-breaking in terms of Cuba's defense strategy. Should the training of a new generation of experts (courses at the UCI, the Ciudad Digital Avanzada, etc.) be viewed as the project constituting new defensive forces, or technological emancipation with a view to participating more actively in cyberspace? It should be noted that the army seems to be absent from the debate on cyber-warfare. We are not aware of any official project to create a military cyber-unit, or a strategy or doctrine of cyber-defense.

2.8. Bibliography

[BOA 00] BOAS T.C., "The dictator's dilemma?", in: *The Internet and U.S. Policy toward Cuba, Center for Strategic and International Studies*, MIT, The Washington Quarterly, pp. 57-67, summer 2000, USA.

[CAS 01] CASTRO F., *Las armas son y siempre serán el arma más importante, speech*, Santiago de Cuba, Cuba, December 2, 2001, available at: http://usuaris.tinet. cat/mpgp/amigos953.htm.

[CAS 03] CASTRO F., *El símbolo de la globalización neoliberal ha recibido un colosal golpe, speech*, Faculty of Law, Buenos Aires, Argentina, May 26, 2003, available at: http://www.smaldone.com.ar/documentos/docs/fidel_argentina.html.

[CIA 11] CIA, World Factbook 2011, available at: https://www.cia.gov/library/ publications/the-world-factbook/geos/cu.html, 2011.

[CLI 10] Clinton H., speech, January 21, 2010, US Department of State, Washington, USA, available at: http://www.state.gov/secretary/rm/2010/01/135519.htm.

[CRU 11] CRUZ A., *Cuban Hackers Working for Venezuela's Hugo Chavez*, Blog, November 29, 2011, available at: http://babalublog.com/2011/11/cuban-hackers-working-for-venezuelas-hugo-chavez/.

[DRA 00] DRAKE W.J., Kalathil Sh., Cargenie T.B., "Dictatorships in the digital age: some considerations on the Internet in China and Cuba", *The Magazine on Information Impacts*, October 2000.

[FRE 09] FREEDOM HOUSE, Freedom on the Net: A Global Assessment of Internet and Digital Media, Report, Freedom House, USA, April 1, 2009

[FRE 11] FREEDOM HOUSE, *Freedom on the Net 2011*, Freedom House, USA, 2011, available at: http://www.freedomhouse.org/images/File/FotN/FOTN2011.pdf.

[GAO 09] GENERAL ACCOUNTING OFFICE, Actions are needed to improve strategy and operations, Report GAO-09-127, GAO, February 5, 2009, available at: http://www.gao. gov/assets/290/284998.pdf

[GON 92] GONZALEZ E., RONFELDT D., *Cuba Adrift in a Post-Communist World*, RAND R-4231-USDP, 1992.

[HAA 05] HAASTER K. V., *Circling around secrets of Cuba's software industry, Research Report*, July 2005, available at: http://networkcultures.org/wpmu/weblog/2005/07/05/circling-around-secrets-of-cuba%E2%80%99s-software-industry/

[HIL 98] HILL K.A., HUGHES J.E., "Is the Internet an Instrument of Global Democratization?" in HILL & HUGHES, *Cyberpolitics: Citizen Activism in the Age of the Internet*, Langham MD, Rowman and Littlefield, 1998.

[HOW 11] HOWARD Ph. N., AGARWAL Sh. D., HUSSAIN M. M., "The Dictators' Digital Dilemma: when do States Disconnect their digital networks?" *Issues in Technology Innovation*, no. 13, October 2011.

[ISR 10] ISRAEL E., *Despite Embargo, Cuba a Heaven for Pirated U.S. Goods*, Havana, Cuba, September 2, 2010, http://www.reuters.com/article/2010/09/02/us-cuba-usa-piracy-idUSTRE6814IM20100902.

[IWS 12a] INTERNET WORLD STATS, available at: http://www.internetworldstats.com/stats10.htm

[KAL 01] KALATHIL Sh., BOAS T.C., "The Internet and State control in authoritarian regimes: China, Cuba, and the counterrevolution, Carnegie endowment for international peace", *First Monday*, vol. 6, no. 8, pp. 1-17, 2001.

[KO 09] KO K., LEE H., JANG, S., "The Internet dilemma and control policy: political and economic implications of the Internet in North Korea". *Korean Journal of Defense Analysis*, vol. 21, no. 3, pp. 279-295, 2009

[LAM 00] LAM W. W.L., "Combating Web Imperialism", *South China Morning Post*, June 14, 2000, available at: http://archive.scmp.com/showarticles.php.

[MES 92] MESHER G.M., BRIGGS R.O., GOODMAN S.E., PRESS L.I., SNYDER J.M., "Cuba, dommunism and computing", *Communications of the ACM*, fol. 35, no. 11, pp. 27-29, 1992.

[MEX 11a] MEXIDOR D.F., "Ciberguerra: mercenarismo en la red", *Digital Granma Internacional*, Havana, Cuba, March 22, 2011, available at: http://www.granma.cu/espanol/cuba/1febre-Comenzaron%20a.html.

[MEX 11b] MEXIDOR D.F., MENENDEZ M., ALLARD J.G., "Operacion Surf", *Digital Granma International*, Havana, Cuba, March 8, 2011, available at: http://www.granma.cu/espanol/cuba/8marzo-operacion.html.

[MIR 11] MIROFF N., "A simmering cyberwar with Cuba", *Globalpost*, February 14, 2011 available at http://www.globalpost.com/dispatch/cuba/110213/cyberwar-alan-gross-internet.

[MOL 11] MOLONEY FIGLIOLA P., ADDIS C.L., LUM T., U.S. Initiatives to promote global Internet Freedom: Issues, Policy, and Technology, CRS Report for Congress n° R41120, FAS, US, January 3, 2011, available at: http://www.fas.org/sgp/crs/row/R41120.pdf.

[MOR 11] MOROZOV E., *The Net Delusion: the Dark Side of Internet Freedom*, Allen Lane Pub., January 2011.

[ONE 09] OFICINA NACIONAL DE ESTADISTICAS DE CUBA, *Tecnologías de la Información y las Comunicaciones (TIC) en Cifras*, ONE, Cuba, 2009, available at: http://www.one. cu/ticencifras2009.htm.

[PRE 97] PRESS L., KEDEZIE Ch.R., *Communication and Democracy: Coincident Revolutions and the Emergent Dictator's Dilemma*, Santa Monica, California, USA, Rand Corporation, 1997.

[PRE 11] PRESS L., *The State of the Internet in Cuba*, January 2011, available at: http://som.csudh.edu/fac/lpress/cuba/chapters/lpdraft2.docx.

[RAM 06] RAMONET I., *Cien Horas con Fidel, Conversaciones con Ignacio Ramonet*, Oficina de Publicaciones del Consejo de Estado, Havana, Capítulo 25, Cuba hoy, 2006

[ROH 00] ROHOZINSKI R., "How the Internet did not transform Russia", *Current History*, pp. 334-338, 2000.

[STR 09] STRAUSS M.J., *The Leasing of Guantanamo Bay*, Praeger Security International, Praeger, 2009.

[SYM 10] SYMANTEC, Symantec Internet Security Threat Report - Trends for 2010, Symantec, no 16, Mountian View, USA, 2010: available at: http://www4.symantec.com/mktginfo/downloads/21182883 GA REPORT IST R Main-Report.pdf

Chapter 3

French Perspectives on
Cyber-conflict

Discoursing on how a State comprehends the cybernetic dimension of a conflict amounts to asking yourself how this entity reconsiders its role and position on the international scene. Through theoretical, political and strategic reflections on cyber-conflict, cyber-war, cyber security, cyber defense, information warfare or information operations, this consists of viewing the power of this State through the lens of relatively new criteria and environments. These are different from those already known and used up until now by nations in order to secure their positions. The cybernetic dimension appeared during the second half of the 20th Century and has forcefully established itself at the beginning of the 21st Century, while greatly influencing political, economic and strategic decisions. Cyberspace is no longer solely the subject of economic growth or cultural development, nor even the target of crime. It has become a potential vehicle of confrontation, crisis and conflict, and a facilitator of revolts.

On the international scene, the balance of power is likely to be modified by the use of cyberspace. There is the commercial use of the space, but also the economic, political, security and military dimensions. States do not position themselves only in relation to one another via economic warfare; there are strategies for influence, soft and hard power. Intelligence is at the heart of the activities conveying this competition and this constant balance of power between States. There are also more violent relations, with more aggressive conflicts in times of crisis and, of course, of open conflict.

Chapter written by Daniel VENTRE.

Henceforth, governments have to be afraid of the internal as much as the external. Revolts forcing out governments, large-scale protests, etc., all this seems possible thanks to means of telecommunication, networks, the Internet and Web 2.0.

Destabilization movements can come from the inside and be encouraged or supported from the outside. States have very few really efficient means by which to prevent or counter these risks. Part of the information can be filtered and controlled. Not all of it can be controlled, except if we accept complete systemic paralysis.

In this context, all States and governments, including the most democratic ones, can fear for their existance. The United States (US), China and other great powers continue to pursue the mastery of this new dimension. Smaller nations with limited capacities must, however, do everything they can in order to stay in the game and play a significant role in this space.

French reflections on matters as important as the mastering of information and the information space are topical in this context of a changing environment.

France, and all the connected countries on Earth, must face up to several challenges. They must secure their own cyberspace and ensure that spies or novice spies are not hacking into their computers to uncover their secrets, which can sometimes be just a few clicks away. They must ensure that crime does not significantly destabilize their economies and they must ensure the protection of their values within their borders. They must also foresee possible attacks, which would be more open, aggressive, disruptive and sometimes more destructive – attacks that would strike insidiously at the fundamental values (via the exchange of ideas) and attacks against the functioning of the systems themselves, which would disturb companies, critical and sensitive facilities. The worst scenarios we could imagine are the layoff of the armies or the start of large industrial disasters.

The State, administration, the police, the army, security and defense agencies cannot guarantee the control of all these issues by themselves. They cannot control all areas. Internet crime does not necessarily come from inside a country's borders. Contents are shared nationally and yet they can come from abroad. The most direct attacks, such as espionage (which can sometimes be very invasive), from individual's to destabilize, via attacks against the systems themselves, are often instigated abroad. We thus cannot tackle these problems at the source. International cooperation is, however, not very effective. It is, for example, illusory to counter the effects of cybercrime in a State, when the same activity can immediately be moved onto another area.

The States thus do not know how to think of solutions other than putting restrictive rules and authoritarian laws on their own populations, in the name of the defense of freedoms and their sovereignty. We build digital, physical and legal strongholds; we create new rules that are added to the previous ones and we strengthen the norms, principles, laws, constraints and restrictions. But this is apparently not enough, as we can see every day. Attacks – which we are still hesitant to call acts of war – keep on happening, one after another. Nothing seems to be reversing the rising curve of the global statistics of acts of cybercrime or intrusions for purposes of espionage. Attacks aiming to disturb the functioning of institutions and to question them contributes to the creation of insecurity. Managers, major companies and institutions are targeted. This creates lawlessness, a sense of disorder, specters of chaos, etc.

These fears and constraints are shared by all States. France is no exception. Its authorities maintain a discourse on all the forms of insecurity. Its security and defense forces are structured in order to address new threats and maintain and strengthen the position of France in a constantly evolving international context. Economic crises and the new global balances appearing after the revolutions in North African countries are new challenges in which cyberspace now plays a major role.

As has happened in several nations, awareness increased in France that cyberspace had become a space of conflicts following the cyber attacks on Estonia in 2007. We need to go back further in time, however, to find the sources of this awareness in France.

The first Gulf War, the development of information highways, the start of the Internet era and the end of the Gulf War were major events and founding moments that have led to reflections in France and everywhere else. Such reflections have covered the revolution of military affairs, the computerization of the armies and the importance of cybernetic space – and more broadly the information space – in conflicts, in the field of war and in international competition (economic, political, diplomatic and cultural). Digital information, in the era of the Internet and new telecommunications, (again) became a tool in the service of power.

3.1. Cyberspace

Cyber-conflict is a conflict that is entirely or partially expressed in cyberspace, whether it is carried out in it or whether it uses this space as a vehicle. The mastering of various forms that cyber-conflict can take, then, presupposes a good comprehension of the space in which they will occur: cyberspace.

The online *"Trésor de la Langue Française Informatisée"*[1] thus recalls that from a philosophical point of view, the space designates an "ideal undefined environment in which all our perceptions are located and which contains all the existing or conceivable objects" or else that it is "an imaginary body, as time is a fictive motion". The "space" can also refer to the idea of a defined area (urban and littoral spaces, etc.), however, or an undefined one (extra-atmospheric space). It can still refer to the concept of living space and be a synonym of territories. It can be a partition (between two moments, a duration). It can also be measured (a memory space is measurable in bytes, bits, Kbits, Gbits, etc.).

Cyberspace is a compound word ("cyber" + "space") that was invented by William Gibson in 1982. In France, the philosopher Pierre Lévy defined cyberspace as "a computer whose center is everywhere and whose circumference is nowhere; a hypertext, dispersed, living, proliferating and unfinished computer" [LEV 97].

Even if it is considered as the symbol of the modern world, cyberspace was prefigured in 17th Century literature. This was the case when Francis Bacon [BAC 27] was describing scientists working for the collection of information and who had invented a machine transporting sounds in conduits on long distances, without being disturbed by reliefs in *New Atlantis*. We can see a machine foreshadowing phone networks here, and maybe even the Internet. The scientists manipulate information and create databases.

Inventions such as telegraphy and then telephony have led to the birth of images from a new world, a technicized world that prefigured our contemporary representations of a high-tech means of communication.

In 1883, Albert Robida[2] published *Le Vingtième Siècle* [ROB 83], a book in which he imagines the future. In Chapter V, called "Les merveilles du téléphonoscope"[3], he imagines an advanced phone that would show images of vehicles:

> "The former telegraph allowed us to understand at a distance a correspondent or an interlocutor, the phone enabled us to hear them and the 'téléphonoscope' enabled us to see them at the same time. What more could you want? When the phone was universally adopted, even for long distance correspondences, everyone could

1 http://atilf.atilf.fr/.
2 1848–1926, A. Robida was a columnist on the society of the future. He also illustrated Jules Verne's books. Many of his works are available on the Internet. Let us point out the journal devoted to him, *Le Téléphonoscope*, which has been going since May 1998 and can be found at http://www.robida.info/telephonoscope.htm.
3 [ROB 83] p. 54.

subscribe for a very small price. Each house had its ramified wire, with section, local and regional offices. Therefore, for a small sum, we could communicate at any time, any distance and without any difficulty or having to go to any office. [...] The invention of the 'téléphonoscope' was very favorably welcomed; by paying a higher fee, the device was adapted to the phone of all of those asking for it. Drama found in the 'téléphonoscope' the elements of a great prosperity. [...] New and significant source of income [...] what would you have said to the dreamer announcing to you that one day fifty thousand people, scattered all over the planet, could, from Paris, Beijing or Timbuktu, follow one of your plays shown in a Parisian theater... The device consists of a simple crystal plate, which is built-in the wall of a flat or put down as a mirror above any chimney. The show devotee sits in front of this plate, chooses the theater, establishes the communication and the show starts instantly [...]. While staying home, we are part of the international audience [...] and those at home can send applauses as well".

This text is extraordinary because of its power of anticipation:

– it imagines the economic model of telecommunications and the Internet;

– it imagines personalized, *a la carte* (the future Web) and real-time services;

– it imagines a computer connected to networks (a crystal plate on which we can see a device that we just need to connect to in order to choose the content);

– it imagines a communication of contents without border;

– it outlines the concept of affiliation to a virtual community, which will be the fundamental principle of the Internet and of telecommunications at the end of the 20th Century;

– it outlines the principle of the group and interactions between members of the group (applause). It then imagines actors with deviant behaviors or with behavior considered deviant, that disturb the good functioning of the communication. "Could we also transmit boos if needed? Ah no, said M. Ponto, this is forbidden. You will understand that if it was allowed to do so, practical jokers could, from their homes, disturb the performances"[4]. Prohibiting rules are thus written and a form of censorship is implemented. Practical jokers are feared, as hackers pirating the system solely for their own entertainment. Nothing that is not in accordance with the rules should be included. The audience can boo the show, but in their homes, without disturbing the community. Thus, the concept of regulation, of right (the necessity to impose rules for the use of this new media) and of disturbing behaviors

4 [ROB 83] pp. 59.

is already implicitly present. From simply failing to respect the etiquette that does not require any police control, the behaviors over time will become a failure to respect laws and will thus lead to delinquency and crime; and

– the description also recalls video-on-demand via television by cable or satellite, according to the same diffusion principle and facilitated access to numerous contents.

In 1892, Emile Gautier published *Les Étapes de la Science: Chroniques Documentaires* [GAU 92]. The chapter on "Téléphoneries" gives us a reflection on the phone.

> "In reality, the phone is from yesterday [...] However, in less than fifteen years, it has incorporated so intimately our lives and we are so used to it without realizing it and with such a mechanical silliness, that it seems nowadays as a very natural institution or even as something due, something that has always existed. At least, we have some difficulty to remember the ancient time [...]. This is nothing less than a revolution [...] and we can only imagine with difficulty now, the regular operating of trade, industry, finance, journalism, politics or diplomacy without the help of this small ordinary device [...]. We are already starting to find imperfections, disadvantages and vices in the phone... Finally, do we need to add that it has the serious disadvantage of not leaving any traces and of not being able to keep or fix the transmitted speech."

The themes tackled in these few lines can be found in almost identical words in the Internet era:

– this technology has established itself very quickly;

– it has become essential, vital;

– there is a before and an after: before the appearance of this technology, humanity was living in a "prehistoric" period;

– this implies that going back to what was before is impossible; and

– it is a revolution.

By referring to the 1888 book by Edward Bellamy, *Looking Backward*[5], describing the life of the next century, he takes up the following ideas:

---

5 In 1888, Edward Bellamy published the novel *Looking Backward* in the US [BEL 88]. This novel was very successful and was translated into several languages. The main character, Julian West, an American from Boston, falls asleep in 1887 and wakes up in 2000. Critical

"In this blessed time, where State socialism had definitely triumphed, all the professions will be experimented, the smallest details of life will be scientifically organized and regulated, all the citizens will be unburdened from the concern of their own happiness and will become many passive wheels of the great machine; telephone will naturally play a significant part."[6]

The author proceeds with a description of principles that are quite similar to the future Internet:

"I know here indeed a teacher [...] who suggests nothing less than to organize [...] music lessons – music theory and piano – by phone! [...] And Mrs Garnier-Gentilhomme does not intend to limit her ambitions to piano only. She dreams of also teaching everything by electrical wire, including drawing, speech and languages [...]. Here is now an inextricable electric wire cast net of human voices promising to wrap the entire world with the tight mesh of its 'pipes'..."[7]

We can see here how Internet and more generally cyberspace result from telephony.

In 1923, with *Je vous offre la santé, la gaieté, l'économie, le bien être, je suis la fée Electricité*, Henri Letorey [LET 23], an electrical engineer, offers an analysis of the contribution of electricity to our society:

"Immediately, the following question comes to mind: what is electricity? The answer is still fleeting. We precisely know what are air, water, fire and earth; their chemical composition is fixed by our scientists. But electricity? Vibrations or waves? No proper material answer has yet been made to this astounding question."[8]

These are some ideas that we still use when talking about the Internet:

– All the hopes we have from technology are found in the title of the book. All of society relies on it: its happiness and its economy. Here the promise of a society completely dependent on technology is roughly described. The contemporary leitmotif on the dependence of our societies on communication networks is an idea that is already known. Here we talk about the "nervous system", but the image is the

---

towards the contemporary society, Bellamy takes the excuse of a simple plot and time travel to state his ideas about socialism and to describe the ideal future society.
6 [GAU 92] pp. 255.
7 [GAU 92] pp. 256.
8 [LET 23] pp. 2. Translated from the original French.

same. Electricity will be distributed by cabled networks. These cables are bringing happiness and the economy is developing based on them.

– Questions on the nature of the object considered that are similar to the recurrent contemporary questions on the nature of cyberspace or information. What is cyberspace? What is information? The answer is still fleeting. Let us note how paradoxical it was even at this time to pretend that the development of a society relies on a technology, when we do not understand its essence.

– Cyberspace is put into perspective in comparison to the four known dimensions (earth, air, sea and space); in Letorey's work, electricity was put into perspective in relation to the four elements.

– Electricity seems to escape any description relying on known (chemical) elements. Cyberspace escapes a satisfying description, because we lack some elements to do so.

– The author here is an engineer. He describes electricity and he is the one who can open the doors of knowledge and understanding of the phenomena, as nowadays the computer engineer is the one who has the keys to the knowledge of cyberspace.

– We need to use metaphors to spread a concept. Resorting to metaphors is a mode of description for cyberspace. The latter is no longer personified and we prefer to talk about a machine. But we are still resorting to the world of dreams.

– Here, in the "astounding question" we are even finding a hint of the "hallucination" that William Gibson used to describe cyberspace in 1982.

Beyond words, cyberspace iconography also has an origin in the engravings from the end of the 19th Century and of the beginning of the 20th Century.

In 1883, *Le Vingtième Siècle*, written and illustrated by Albert Robida, shows representations of the height of cities where buildings are topped by electrical pylons, between which are hundreds of cables forming a tangle of lines. We see communication networks, which are already taking the appearance of a spider's web. Representations of the Internet often rely on this image, which is that of its basic infrastructure, i.e. the telephone network. It seems to be difficult for the authors of short stories, graphic designers, illustrators or even engineers to move away from this basic structure: the lines are the cables and the points of interconnections are the machines and the users. If such pictures announce the large modern cities under construction at the beginning of the 20th Century, is the height of the cities also prefiguring the contemporary representations of cyberspace, as will be shown in cinema for example? Thus, engravings of cities topped by cables transmitting data are the picture of cities from the 20th Century yet to come, but also the ancestor of the virtual cities that we find in movies such as *Hackers* and *The Matrix*.

Cyberspace, as we know and describe it nowadays, is thus broadly borrowed from representations of previous centuries.

Nevertheless, it remains a mysterious and unknown space that is under construction and, above all, a space to explore or conquer.

In 2002, during a speech, the secretary-general of the ITU (International Telecommunication Union), Yoshio Utsumi, declared that "cyberspace is a new land, without borders and for now, without government. Cyberspace is not a parallel universe: it interacts with our own world and raises many new challenges for politicians"[9].

Cyberspace is firmly perceived as a space in its own right, which we need to explore (with the help of tools, such as Internet Explorer), as if we were on our way to discover new territories. The conquest of cyberspace recalls the history of the great conquerors of continents and lands unknown to Europeans: but whereas these spaces, often new from an ethnocentric point of view (America was new for Europeans in 1492 but not for those already living there), cyberspace is truly new. At least it was for the first designers.

In 1995, Joël De Rosnay[10] wrote that: "Cyberspace is an unlimited ocean, a *Terra Incognitae* in which we venture with basic maps" [DER 95]. He was referring to the legendary wide-open spaces. Cyberspace is a "digital Wild West" according to him; alluding to the individuals running wild there (pirates and crooks). Cyberspace is a place of adventure but also of danger, where the fittest rules: "cyberspace is still a jungle, rustling of many dangers". He mentions the geopolitical vision of the world (the world is a jungle for States) and the hostile jungle in which 19th Century colonists were venturing at their own risks.

Jacques Attali[11] in an article published in the French newspaper *Le Monde* on August 7, 1997 [ATT 97], described the Internet (cyberspace?) as a new continent. He was using metaphors: the Internet is a continent, on which we need to land, because it possesses treasures that we should not leave for the others. Cyberspace becomes a living space and we must have a conquering spirit. The Internet is a:

> "virtual continent, the seventh continent, where we will soon be
> able to install everything already existing in the real continents, but
> without any materiality [...] Inside this continent devoid of real

---

9 Quoted in Caslon Analytics Guide, *Cyberspace Governance*, http://www.caslon.com.au/governanceguide2.htm.
10 French biologist, specialist on the origins of the living and of new technologies.
11 French economist, writer, high-ranking civil servant, and former adviser to the French President (François Mitterrand).

inhabitants, a huge trade will be developed between the virtual agents of a pure and perfect market economy, without any intermediary, without taxes, State, payroll, unions, political parties, strikes or social minima. Internet thus becomes nowadays, in the world of imagination, what America was in 1492 for Europeans: a place undamaged by our shortcomings, a space free from our legacies, a haven of free trade, where we could finally build a new and clean man, free from what corrupts and limits him, an insomniac consumer and a tireless worker".

Then, speaking of the American hegemony on this new territory, he adds that:

"it is urgent and vital to discuss this problem as we would face the discovery of a new continent. Let's set up a large conquest program! Five centuries after America's discovery, will Europe have the strength to do it? [...] The growth of the seventh continent will be the main drive of growth of the 21th century. We have to seize this opportunity and transform a virtual utopia into a conquering reality. Europe is staking here its survival."

Behind this conquering will, there is naturally a necessity of confrontation. The Internet is open to all and thus imposes a confliction.

The military domain offers several definitions of "cyberspace". In *Concept d'Emploi des Forces de l'Armée Française*, published in January 2010 [PIA 10], cyberspace is designated as:

"[the] global network which virtually connects human activities through the interconnection of the computers, and helps the fast circulation and exchange of information. Cyberspace, as electromagnetic space, supports many civil and military applications which are necessary for entire sections of national activity. It has become a fully-fledged ill-controlled field of activity and thus a potential space of conflict for armed forces. They must protect themselves at any time from an attack aiming to destroy the functioning of the networks, their throughput and their security level, but they must also be able to prevent their misuse by potential opponents, by leading offensive actions."

From this definition, we retain the following:

– the term cyberspace first designates a network and thus an infrastructure;

– cyberspace is distinct from the cognitive layer, since the field of perceptions is considered separately;

– cyberspace is a network on a planetary scale, but would a local network be part of a global network, even if it is disconnected from it?;

– this network establishes a virtual connection. This concept of "virtuality" is, however, undefined;

– the fast data exchange recalls the American wording, mentioning the propagation of information at the speed of light;

– cyberspace is not electromagnetic space;

– cyberspace is neither civil nor military, but both at the same time. The report does not mention whether soldiers should only take part in the military section of cyberspace and leave to the private/public sector the civilian part of cyberspace;

– cyberspace is 'ill-controlled' as it is modeled on territories avoiding State control. The consequences of such poor control will then be the same as for ill-controlled States ('poor' does not mean 'too little' or 'too much');

– the poor quality of the control of cyberspace is in fact a military confrontation space;

– the poor quality of control, understood as a lack of technical security, creates security breaches endangering army networks;

– armies must protect themselves from attacks aiming to disturb the functioning of their networks, and there must be OCW[12] operations against their adversaries;

– in this definition, we are not speaking of national, international or transnational spaces; and

– this approach is for the most part negative and does not show the possible advantages of the use of the capacities offered by cyberspace.

As the American discourse on the nature of the threats and of cyberspace, the French army considers this new dimension as a confrontation place. The new *Concept d'Emploi des Forces de l'Armée Française* (PIA-00.100)[13] highlights that "other threats are coming to light nowadays in new fields, such as the attacks in cyberspace and in extra-atmospheric space". Thus, we must know how to position ourselves within this space, in order to remain a world-ranking military power. The document indicates that military forces must "intervene in new confrontation fields, such as the space, cyberspace and information".

---

12 OCW: offensive cyber-war.
13 [PIA 10].

3.2. Assessments, view on the world and awakening

As with most States in the world, France has been aware of the major events of the past 20 years: the first Gulf War; the introduction of the Internet; the development of the information society; the growing dependence of society on cyberspace; the new wave of cyber-attacks; the rise of the feeling of insecurity rapped out in political speeches and media; and terrorism. All these factors have significantly modified the perception of the world and have triggered new defense and security policies, strategies and doctrines, in which cyberspace is playing an increasingly decisive role.

3.2.1. *Attacks*

During the past decade, many official reports have put the emphasis on modification of the international environment under the influence of cyberspace development and on the stakes involved in terms of security and defense of the nation, which have developed with this new space. These reports have often highlighted the nature of the threats and have taken the cyberattacks that France and industrialized countries have been the victims of as examples.

Among these official reports, we can mention:

– *La Sécurité des Systèmes d'Information – un Enjeu Majeur pour la France*, a report signed by Deputy Pierre Lasbordes[14] that was published in 2005 [LAS 05];

– the *Report of Information* created for the Committee on Foreign Affairs, Defense and Armed Forces on cyber-defense and published by Senator Roger Romani in 2008 [ROM 08][15]; and

– the White paper on security and national defense published in 2008 [LIV 08].

Depending on their release dates, these reports refer to the major incidents that have occurred over the past few years:

– the Estonian affair (spring 2007);

– cyber-attacks on the US since the middle of the 1990s;

– the wave of cyber-attacks in 2007 that affected many countries, such as New Zealand, Germany and the UK; and

---

14 Pierre Lasbordes is a French politician, deputy, born in 1946.
15 Roger Romani is a French politician, senator, born in 1934.

– attacks suffered by France: the hijacking of the CEA "*Commissariat à l'Energie Atomique*" (French Atomic Energy Commission) servers in 2006[16]; hacking into the e-mail accounts of French diplomats.

These incidents have "very concretely materialized a threat which was still not well identified on our continent and especially in France" [ROM 08]. Since 2007, France has not ceased to suffer from more or less visible and discrete or mediated attacks. There were notably the impacts of the malware Conficker[17]; and, more recently in March 2011, the hacking into the French Ministry of Finance computers.

The report of the deputy (politician) Pierre Lasbordes [LAS 05] specified that cyber-attacks aim to "destroy, alter and access sensible data, in order to modify them or to harm the good operation of the networks".

French cryptology expert Eric Filiol[18], meanwhile, defines a cyber-attack as an attack aiming at the real sphere:

– either directly by going through an information and communication system (ICS). In that case, the computer field is only a tool or a means (attack against people for example); or

– indirectly by attacking an ICS, on which one or more components of the real sphere depend (attack against a network of electronic voting machines)[19].

Cyber-attacks can threaten national defense in peacetime.

---

16 http://www.zdnet.fr/actualites/internet/0,39020774,39363088,00.htm.

17 A computer worm that appeared at the end of 2008, using a breach in Windows. The worm is also known as Downup, Downandup and Kido. Almost 10 million of machines would have been infected across the world, including those of several defense ministries (notably the UK, France and US). The Conficker virus has affected hundreds of thousands of computers in the world. The French army, as well as many companies, has paid the price for it. Newspaper articles stated that some Rafale fighters were kept on the ground because of this virus attack [JOS 09]. The virus has probably affected the unsecure French Intramar network. The French army has declared that the virus did not have any effect on the availability of the forces.

18 French expert in computer security, specializing in cryptology and operational computer virology. Lieutenant-colonel of the French Army, director of the laboratory of virology and cryptology of the ESAT (*Ecole Supérieure d'Application des Transmissions*, military university with a technical emphasis), he is now director of the the ESIEA research center (*Ecole Supérieure d'Informatique, Electronique, Automatique*, engineering school in computer science, electronics and automatics). He has written books on virology and cryptanalysis, as well as on cyber-criminality. He has contributed to the collective work *Cyberguerre et Guerre de l'Information* published in 2010 [VEN 10]. Eric Filiol declares himself as a cyberspace "corsair".

19 Eric Filiol, in [VEN 10]

"We have agreed to call 'attacking' any individual or corporate body (State, organization, service, reflection group, etc.) deliberately harming or seeking to harm an information system and whatever their motives" [LAS 05]. This broad definition of the attacker thus includes offenders, cybercriminals, hacktivists, terrorists, mafia networks, military attackers and any State or non-State actor. The decisive character is *a priori* not the identity of the individual or the group, but rather:

– the action was carried out intentionally; and

– the objectives of the attacker: deliberately misinforming, preventing access to a resource, taking control of the system, fetching information and using the system for "bounce" attacks. The attack can be motivated by ludic, grasping, terrorist and strategic interests (States and groups).

Senator Romani [ROM 08] draws the profile of the attackers. According to him, it would be individuals or groups that are:

– professionals: "evidently the current computer attacks cannot be imputed to simple amateurs" because they are highly targeted and use more sophisticated techniques;

– acting in networks;

– "organized groups or even [...] intelligence services";

– motivated by money, since they would sell back their services to States;

– cyber-terrorists[20] resorting to cyber-criminality services, even if "we know [...] that terrorist organizations have acquired a significant mastering of computer tools";

– mastering the use of the computer as a "weapon";

– well-identified by the international press; and

– located in China[21] and Russia.

Each line of this description is debatable.

– Would only "professionals" be able to use "sophisticated technologies"? Should the mark of professionals be the use of sophisticated methods and acting via networks?

– Who has proof showing the States resorting to mercenary networks, showing a connection between governments, terrorist groups and their armed forces? Could the

---

20 Eric Filiol, in [VEN 10].
21 [ROM 08] pp. 18.

press have some proof, since it has "stated the existence of such groups in Russia" [ROM 08]?

– Do the motivated States not have the means to develop their own devices of aggression and should they resort to a form of criminal subcontracting?

– Why is the concept of the computer as a weapon not defined even if it has serious consequences on how to comprehend the security measures and the means by which to face such threats? When does the computer as a tool become a threat?

– Isn't the view of the distribution of the threat in the world conditioned by media and American speech, which designate China and Russia as major attacking States? Is the attacker no longer American? Are the large antennas intercepting the communications of satellites turned off? Are the submarines intercepting communications from submarine Internet cables remaining at port? Do the most respectful States not know how to use these technologies, which are "so little detectable as intelligence weapon" [ROM 08]?

There are many types of threats aimed at parts of the State. In *Les Nouveaux Visages de la Guerre: vers le Champ de Bataille Virtuel* [HOU 08], Colonel Jean-Michel Houbre suggests a classification of actors in four categories: ludic, greedy, strategic or terrorist. *A priori*, we can subscribe to this rough typology. The first two categories are part of the cyber-criminality field and the last two are more closely connected to the aspect of conflict in cyberspace.

An article published in the French journal *Défense Nationale* in March 2009 [BUC 09], was suggesting a classification of the various actors and actions in function of the threat they represent for society. And yet, there is not here strictly speaking any measurement of the threat level, but simply a subjective judgment.

Threat spectrum	Threat level
Isolated pirate	Low
Small crime	Low to average
Use of the Internet for terrorist purposes	Low to average
Cyber espionage	Average
Organized crime	Average to high
Cyber-attack by a State	High
Invasion of a State after a cyber-attack	Dangerous

Table 3.1. *List of the types and levels of threat that may affect States [BUC 09]*

These past few years, the two main types of attacker have been the spy (a foreign intelligence services agent) and the terrorist.

Most of the time, the spy is Chinese, on the evidence of the declarations of many victims worldwide. The Chinese spy is quite familiar to us. In 1765, Ange Goudar[22] published a book in six volumes called *L'Espion Chinois, ou L'Envoyé Secret de la Cour de Pékin, pour Examiner l'État Présent de l'Europe* [GOU 65]. This is also found in a book by Georges Weulersse, published in 1902, called *Chine Ancienne et Nouvelle, Impressions et Réflexions*, which contains a few revealing chapter titles such as: "*Le problème chinois*"[23] (the Chinese problem), "*Le Péril chinois*" (the Chinese danger), "*Le nationalisme chinois*" (Chinese nationalism), "*Les hommes d'Etat de la Chine – La jeune génération – La nouvelle armée chinoise*"[24] (China statesmen – The young generation – The new Chinese army) or "*Le péril économique chinois*"[25] (the Chinese danger to economics).

This is in almost identical terms what we can speak nowadays of the "Chinese threat": the Chinese threat is always a "problem", a "danger", notably because of the rise of strong "nationalism" in the "younger generations", without forgetting the ghost of the threat of the "Chinese army's growth", which is really worrying the US and without forgetting the extent to which the Chinese industrial renewal is a danger for the West[26]. From one century to the next, we still have the same images, the same themes, the same vocabulary, the same threat, the same victim (the West) and the same denunciation and alert attitude[27].

Judging by the official reports, including the report by Europol on terrorism in Europe covering 2004, "no case of cyberterrorism has been listed in the Member States." We speak of cyber-terrorism but, "we need to highlight the fact that it has never been reported" [LAS 05]. Cyber-terrorism is therefore the subject of scenarios. The *Livre Blanc du Gouvernement sur la Sécurité Intérieure face au Terrorisme* [LIV 06], a doctrine text in the continuation of the law of January 23, 2006 on the fight against terrorism, proposes a scenario entitled "Attentats diversifiés transfrontaliers" which registers attacks on its program: one of the terrorist team involved in attacks tries to disrupt rescue operations by attacking the computer systems.

More simply, the terrorist is perceived as an Internet user profiting from its anonymity. To fight against terrorism, "intelligence services must be able to identify

---

22 French adventurer and literary figure, 1708–1791.
23 [WEU 02] chapter 5, pp. 333.
24 [WEU 02] parts of chapter 5.
25 [WEU 02] chapter 1, pp. 191.
26 [WEU 02] chapter 1, pp. 191.
27 http://intelligencenews.wordpress.com/2011/11/10/01-863/.

and select interesting information from all the available information on the open part of Internet. They also must be able to access information under certain conditions on the closed part of the Internet" [LIV 06].

These measures, which some describe as 'liberty killers', perfectly fit within the broader construction of a surveillance system whose purposes are officially justified: authorizing intelligence services access to files from home offices (identification documents, passports, residence cards, car registration papers, driving licenses), airlines, shipping and railway companies. They also authorize the exchange of data between each organization or the capture of biometric data and video surveillance data and helping preserve them in a single file for greater efficiency, etc. The war against terrorism encompasses the control of information.

To these two main threatening figures, we must add hackers with unequal skills from all origins and nationalities that are able to disturb the economy by their actions. There are actors with projects or political demands, such as hacktivists or networks of anonymous hackers. For the authorities, the threat comes from protest from the street organized via cyberspace. The threat landscape is evolving.

3.2.2. The feeling of insecurity, the threat

The feeling of insecurity and the fear of attacks and of social destabilization were exacerbated by the cyberattacks against Estonia in 2007. This affair has become the symbol of the threat hanging over cyberspace. Although the threat seems enormous according to the official position, it is not completely new. For about 15 years, cyber-criminality has introduced a feeling of insecurity towards the networks. This threat is used by politicians to justify a more formalized control of the use of networks and was predicted in a visionary text by Anatole France published in 1905:

> "Telegraphy and wireless telephony were then used all over Europe and were so easy to use that the poorest man could talk, when and how he wanted to someone anywhere in the world. [...] This was the abolition of the borders. A critical hour amongst all! [...] The French, German, Swiss and Belgian Republics [...], each express by a unanimous vote of their Parliament and in huge meetings, the solemn resolution to defend the national territory and industry against any foreign aggression. Energetic laws were promulgated, [...] strictly regulating the use of wireless telegraphs [...] Our borders are protected by electricity. There is a lightning area around the federation. A small man with glasses is sitting somewhere in front of a

keyboard. He is our only soldier. He just has to put a finger on a key
to crush an army of five hundred thousand men." [FRA 05]

Of course this text is not describing information warfare or cyberspace, but we
can already see the formulation of concerns on security that we sometimes think to
be modern. The attitude of the government in order to control the information
sphere is also described in this text.

Several key ideas can be found in these few lines that also structure the positions
of our contemporaries on matters of security or insecurity in relation to cyberspace:

– This is about the dissemination of a technology on all the continents.

– It is about governments worrying when facing a technology that leads them to
lose control of people's opinions and ideas. Individuals who are connected have
access to a new freedom of expression, which ignores the borders. This freedom is
also made possible thanks to the extreme facility of use of the media.

– Facing this loss of control, which would be a danger for all States, there is only
one solution: regulating, supervising, controlling and limiting access to information.
This legal prospect was outlined and foreseen in *Le Vingtième Siècle* by Albert
Robida, as we have seen. And what are we doing nowadays besides putting these
premonitory thoughts in practice?

– A technology is seen as a national defense tool: electricity protects the borders.

– The small man with glasses is equivalent to our 21th Century hacker: he has
become a soldier and he is almighty.

– The asymmetry is presented to the advantage of the solitary individual, who
can, from his keyboard, slaughter half a million people. This is the fight of David
against Goliath, but a high-tech David, who has swapped the sling for modern
weapons resulting from new technologies.

'Attacks are a reality' [LAS 05] and the threat hanging over information systems
and national security is 'evident' [ROM 08]. The daily attacks on information
systems will increase and it is highly probable that there will be more 'major cyber-
attacks' in the 15 years to come against national information systems [ROM 08].
These major cyber-attacks are registered in the six illustrative scenarios proposed by
the 2008 White paper [LIV 08]. They are subject to the same consideration (and
worries) as the threats that can involve NATO, massive high-lethality pandemics,
natural disasters, crises in overseas departments, and the engagement of France in a
major regional conflict. The scenario on the threats or conflicts that could involve

the Atlantic Alliance[28] considers cyber-war as one of the means of attack enabling the classic defenses of the Allies to be circumvented.

On a hierarchical scale of the risks and threats, major cyber-attacks are supposed to be 'highly probable' (on the same level as terrorist attacks and organized crime) and of 'low to high amplitude' (thus never reaching the 'critical' level on this classification, which is usually kept for terrorism, pandemics, natural disasters and ballistic weapons) [LIV 08]. Attacks on information systems can thus be considered acts of aggression and subject of crises and/or major conflicts.

Do we have to fear the threat of chaos? Chaos, as François Bernard Huyghe[29] recalled in his book *L'Ennemi à l'Ère Numérique* published in 2001 [HUY 01], are:

– the final stage of disinformation or informational aggression;

– the result of infectiousness: an incident causes another and a chain of events could lead to chaos. We can also talk of avalanche effect [HAS 05]; and

– one of the aims of information warfare and cyber-war[30].

In science-fiction literature, chaos is the result of a disaster, and humans are always the cause of it: post-nuclear apocalyptic area and natural disasters that are the consequences of human activity, pandemics caused by biological manipulation, etc.

Chaos can be illustrated in the following terms:

> "Accompanied with the airplanes of the Coalition strike force and escorted by a fleet of highly armed destroyers and frigates, the aircraft carrier boat has been sent to demonstrate to China that Great Britain is determined to protect its shipping lines. But before a single shot was being fired, the aircraft carrier and all the other boats were suddenly stopped by a general electricity failure. Motors and computer systems failed to operate [...] In only one shot, the British battle group was overpowered by gifted hacker teams working for the Chinese army.

---

28 [ROM 08] Chapter 5.
29 Researcher at the IRIS (*Institut des Relations Internationales et Stratégiques* – the French Institute of International and Strategic relations), specialized in information and communication sciences. He is the author of many books on information, on the relations of information towards war and on the role of the media in war times. http://www.huyghe.fr/biographie.htm.
30 Here reminding us of the title of the book by Winn Schwartau: *Information Warfare, Chaos on the Electronic Superhighway* [SCH 94].

At the same time, Chinese cyberwarriors were launching a 'clickskrieg' against United Kingdom."

These few lines are an excerpt from a short article published in 2010. The action takes place in 2025 [COU 10].

The various phases of this scenario can be examined in parallel with the events happening in *Ravage*, the novel by René Barjavel published in 1943 [BAR 43]. The story unfolds in Paris. "You don't know what happened yesterday? All the plane motors stopped yesterday at the same time, just when the electric current was giving out everywhere. All the planes which had started their approach fell like hail". In the disaster scenario, planes are crashing, all the machines cease to operate and the lights are turned off plunging the city into the darkness, because electricity seems to have disappear from Earth. Electricity is a vital resource for all mankind (mankind in the city mankind, because the countryside seems less affected by the disaster) and there are immediate consequences of its disappearance:

– People are panicking, crowds are fighting and humans act like animals and kill each other.

– Politicians ask themselves who is guilty:

  - they do not have an answer;

  - soldiers speak about war and affirm that the culprit is France's arch enemy (this enemy is not identified); and

  - scientists say that it is nature, but nobody really knows. They need time to understand. And yet society does not have time: mankind needs to know immediately because their lives are suddenly disrupted. A shock has occurred. The social body is destabilized. Will it survive this ordeal?

– The crowd is wondering: what is happening to us? The crowd is ignorant, murderous and violent.

– There is a return to the age "before electricity": the army take out weapons that they manufactured based on the models of those from the past centuries. Men are going into the countryside and they must fight, make fire, etc. It is a return to the Stone Age.

– Cascading disasters: the disappearance of electricity has immediate consequences, such as lack of access to cash (the financial system is based on electricity), lack of access to water, etc.

In this picture of a mankind confronting its demons (dependence on technologies, end of the civilization), we find a few similarities with the positions, representations and behaviors of our contemporaries:

– Scientists and engineers are seeking explanations for extensive electricity failures (example: as in Brazil and North America), but cannot give any conclusive answers. The argument of the effect of nature on the system malfunctioning has been put forward (trees falling on electrical wires, human error in maintenance, snowfalls, heat, etc., explaining failures, fires and power outages of electric distribution systems). Others speak about cyber-attacks.

– Observers and other experts in security and defense put forward the argument of attack by hackers (the enemy) in order to explain general power outages. But as the engineers, they do not provide convincing proof. The army takes up the argument to justify the existence of threats and the necessity of preparation to fight against this unknown enemy (we speak about the Chinese, Russians and other cyber-terrorists without ever precisely identifying this enemy).

– The consequences of attacks on critical infrastructures are found in the same fields as those of the novel: no more computer networks would mean no more financial system and the stoppage of water, electricity, etc., distribution systems and transport (airplanes and trains).

"I don't know yet if we are dealing with sabotage, strikes, acts of war or accidents." [BAR 43]

These questions raised by a fictional character are the same as those that we hear nowadays when significant cyber-attacks occur. It is always difficult to say who is behind these cyber-attacks: saboteurs, armies, terrorists; or whether it is just technical hitches. The case of electricity failures in Brazil and in North America is a good example: are they due to intervention by hackers, hacktivists or foreign armies? The Stuxnet affair is another example: was it about destroying nuclear power plants (sabotage) or about committing an act of war (against Iran, for example)? It was impossible for the characters in *Ravage* to narrow down the act to any culprit in an acceptable timeframe; the situation is exactly the same nowadays in the case of cyber-attacks (it is sometimes difficult to distinguish accidents from attacks).

In Barjavel's book, electricity is a vital resource, on which all facilities (transports, communication, water, etc.), and thus the entire society, depend. Let us replace 'electricity' with 'computer networks' and we might have a similar scenario, with consequences similar to those of the novel. The best way to paralyze computer networks would still be to cut off electrical distribution circuits. Electricity remains one of the most important resources. It is even more essential than cyberspace because cyberspace cannot exist without electricity. To durably affect the operation of computer networks, the best bet is to target electricity production and distribution systems. Most of the time, the threat is comprehended the other way around: as a cyber-attack against electricity distribution systems.

3.2.3. *Potential vulnerabilities of States*

France, in this information space, is according to some in a vulnerable situation[31]. There are several reasons for this:
– France would be unprepared to face these threats: France appears to be behind and neighboring countries seem to be better prepared and defended;

– in France the culture of security is supposed to be lacking;

– France does not have a national industry for hardware or software. France thus depends too much on technologies that it does not control;

– these policies, even if started early (from 1986[32]) with a series of statutory texts organizing the security of information systems, and then in March 2004 with the adoption of a three-year plan of enhanced security of the State information systems[33] and finally with the creation of the ANSSI (*Agence Nationale de la Sécurité des Systèmes d'Information*, the French Agency for Information System Security)[34] in 2009 did not until now have the expected efficiency[35];

– a lack of means. This was the main argument of the report written by Senator Romani. However, the number of structures, actors, programs and operations dealing with the security of the information systems on various levels is quite large and the national security structure is relayed or coordinated through international initiatives: the works of the UN, the ITU, OECD, G8, NATO, EU, coordination of the CERTs via FIRST (forum of incident response and security teams) or ENISA[36].

By a lack of coordination of the existing means "Ensuring our defense and our security requires perceiving and then understanding dangers and threats". Yet, despite this plethora of actors, it seems that "France is nowadays devoid of all the necessary tools to comprehend, analyze and deal with everything entailed by the expression "global security" [BAU 08].

---

31 These arguments are found in reports on the security of information systems and on cyberdefense published since 2006.
32 Decree no. 86-316 of March 3, 1986 creating the directory of the information system security; decree no. 86-318 of March 3, 1986 creating the central service of information system security, and then Decree no. 87-354 of May 25, 1987, Decree no 87-864 of October 26, 1987, and Decree 87-865 of October 26, 1987.
33 http://www.ssi.gouv.fr/site_documents/PRSSI/PRSSI.pdf.
34 http://www.ssi.gouv.fr/.
35 Recent cyberattacks against French ministries servers, including those of the Finance Ministry in 2011, recall the difficulty of this task.
36 The European Network and Information Security Agency, which was created in 2004. www.enisa.europa.eu/.

The Romani report on Cyber-defense [ROM 08] establishes an inventory of the reasons common to all modern States:

– interconnection of systems;

– their relation to the Internet;

– the contaminant nature of the Internet (everything in contact with the Internet becomes fallible);

– dependence of society on information systems;

– permeability of information space because of mobile equipment (threat to network integrity);

– weaknesses of the Internet protocol;

– use of applications (off-the-shelf software) that add to the complexity and security breaches;

– contamination of the most solid bricks by the weakest ones;

– etc.

3.2.4. *Evolution of the international environment*

The White Paper on Defense and National Security, published in June 2008 [LIV 08], largely gives way to digital information and information systems[37]. With a new era comes a new vision of the world, a new context and new constraints. A new world began with globalization that "does not create a better or a more dangerous world" but "a more unstable one" (hence the financial crash of 2008). This world remains controlled by the power of the US, but with a balancing to the benefit of Asia. This new period is also characterized by:

– The multiplication of threats (terrorism, ballistic missiles, attacks against information systems, espionage, organized crime networks and natural risks) that has also made the difference between internal and external security disappear and makes a global approach to this phenomena necessary.

– A higher degree of complexity and uncertainty that make our environment and its threats quite difficult to apprehend.

– The increase in military expenditure.

This new world is also the world of the affirmation of cyberspace as a vital system, as the nervous system of our model of society. In cyberspace, information is

---

37 This was not the case in the previous White Paper in 1994 [LON 94].

more broadly and quickly diffused. The consequences of this are an acceleration of action, an increase in the power of the media[38], an uncontrolled flow of ideas (notably ideas of ideological, religious and radical protest), an increased power of private actors and a reduction in the expression of the State's ability to control things and a reduction in the sovereignty of States. "The sudden increase of the information flow [...] weakens the autonomous intervention capacity of States" [LIV 08].

3.3. Reaction, position of France and choice: theories, political strategies and military doctrines

Caught in the turmoil of cyber-attacks over the past five years, France has elevated information system security to a national defense and security issue. Threats, as they are identified and perceived, justify a strategy based on the control of information, the systems and the implementation of computer means. This security strategy contributes to specifying the outlines of a French concept of information warfare.

On the basis of all the aforementioned statements, France thus adapts its reactions, position on the international scene, political strategies in terms of cyber-security and cyber-defense and military doctrines. The dimension of cyberspace relating to conflict is a new challenge for States and France is facing it by maintaining a defensive posture.

3.3.1. *Information: a powerful weapon for those controlling it*

Those controlling technology can, from their keyboard or their screen, control the opponent and lead to its destruction. The fact that only one individual or a small group can defeat an 'army' or a 'State', can destabilize or destroy it without seeing it, take it by complete surprise, ignoring the distances and with the sole power of technology, is one of the threat scenarios weighing on States. Fears of major attacks against critical systems are not of the ordinary cyber-criminality field but are acts of aggression. The Department of Defense has decided to describe operations to sabotage computers as acts of war and reserves the possibility to retaliate with conventional military force. The control of information space is thus a priority matter, since this control decides the state of the world: whether it is at peace or war.

---

38 The White Paper speaks about the "CNN effect" (pp. 24).

3.3.2. *Media information: beneficial if controlled*

The position given to the concept of 'information' in the White Paper on Defense in 1994 [LON 94] is quite representative of French thought at the time. Information is indeed:

– placed at the center of the evolution of the world and at the core of the globalization of the exchanges, i.e. perceived as an economic tool;

– a tool at the service of decision processes;

– a tool at the service of republican values: "the position of information has beneficial effects for the transparency in decision-making and in the implementation of these decisions. It is an essential factor in the fight for human rights, in order to prevent conflicts and defuse tensions" [LON 94];

– But this is mainly in its 'media' dimension (more accurately we would say the 'news') which is "at the heart of any defense policy" where information is attacked and is worrying. The predominant information influencing public opinion "is henceforth at the heart of the functioning of our democracies". Diffused by media, it can have a negative impact on society and the risk of misinformation is quite high. Henceforth, "it seems difficult to strike a balance between total freedom and information restriction" [LON 94].

3.3.3. *Economic information as power, if controlled*

The *Intelligence Économique et Stratégie des Entreprises* report[39], also published in 1994 [MAR 94], states in its preface that "the strategic managing of economic information has become one of the main drives of the overall performance of the businesses and nations". This 'economic' information will be one of the main elements of the debate from now on (regarding business intelligence and economic warfare). We can find the same concerns for the control of economic information in the Carayon report[40] *Intelligence Économique, Compétitivité et Cohésion Sociale* published in June 2003 [CAR 03]. Business intelligence campaigns for a defense of the economic fabric through better control of information.

---

39 The report was written by a work group presided over by Henri Martre. Born in 1928, he was general delegate for Armament (DGA) from 1977 to 1983, then CEO of the Aérospatiale society from 1983 to 1992 and President of Afnor from 1993 to 2002.
40 Bernard Carayon is a French politician born in 1957 in Paris. He has written many reports on industrial policy, business intelligence, intelligence services and information technologies. He advocates a certain form of economic patriotism.

3.3.4. *Information warfare*

The new information society built around computer science, telecommunications and a newly born Internet just after the Cold War, was accompanied by an awakening: information, whose diffusion is now global in real-time and whose manipulation is easier than ever, is opening new prospects in terms of conflicts and confrontations. Following the works and reflections carried out on economic conflicts in the information society[41], other works were published in 1996 on information warfare at the instigation of the Stratco/Intelco group [42] on behalf of the DGA (*Délégation Générale à l'Armement*, the French General Delegation for Armament). The Cold War has just ended and the First Gulf War imposed American power. We progressively become aware of the possibilities of the defensive and aggressive use of information, notably in the economic and commercial fields. Information warfare was then defined by a formula that was quite successful in France: this is the war "by, for and against information"[43]. This expression was taken up again in 2008 in the report on cyber-defense [ROM 08]. The French approach attempts to distance itself from the American approach. French information warfare then focuses on knowledge warfare, attacks on information (for example misinformation operations aiming to destabilize rival companies), in line with the theories developed within the EGE (*Ecole de Guerre Economique*, the Economic Warfare School) directed by Christian Harbulot, a French business intelligence specialist. This prospect is different from the American one; the latter putting computer piracy at the center of 'infowar' [HAR 99]. A conference on the theme of information warfare was organized in March 1999 at UNESCO by the EGE[44].

France does not have a reference document in terms of information warfare, which would define the concept, the issues, the tools and the respective roles of the civil and/or military actors at the same time. Therefore, everyone is using it at will. It is sometimes a synonym of economic warfare or business intelligence, information manipulation dealing with the role of the media, information in times of war, cyber-war and cyber-attacks, espionage, information operations, influence operations, or even cyber-criminality.

François Bernard Huyghe defines this concept as follows:

---

41 Particularly the works of a group presided over by Henri Martre between 1992 and 1993.
42 Stratco is a French consulting and auditing company that is involved in matters of defense and security. It was created in 1991.
43 War 'by' information uses new ICTs as vehicles of propaganda and misinformation. War 'for information' consists of penetrating the systems to recover the information. The war 'against' information aims to disturb the operation of the systems.
44 http://www.infoguerre.fr/evenements/colloque-la-guerre-de-l-information-a-l-unesco/.

"Information warfare consists of hiding, destroying and corrupting information, from intellectual knowledge to computer data. Its aim is to produce damage or to win hegemony. Its motto: 'Information, predation, destruction'. It also rallies symbols and affects in order to build a consensus and control passions. Information society would thus be subjected to a double danger: that of the always recurrent archaic violence, tormenting the bodies, and a new violence, ill-treating or altering brains, humans' or computers'" [HUY 05].

In France, information warfare was for a long time a symbol of economic warfare. Also caught up in the turmoil of cyber-attacks in the past five years, France now more carefully considers the question of the "hacker war" and of the "cybernetic war". They are two of the seven forms of information warfare, as defined by Martin Libicki [LIB 95].

3.3.5. *Information warfare or information control*

In January 2000, General Loup Francart proposed an exploration guide of the vast field of information control [FRA 00]. Information control is "a tool of knowledge, governance, influence and action, whose efforts we need to direct and whose activities we need to plan". "On the strategic level, we can talk of a real information war, which conditions and is at the center of the other aspects of the conduct of conflicts: war for the mastery of the spaces, war of capacities and war for the decision". This control or mastering is also defined as "the capacity... to access in due course information and to use it operationally and efficiently" [LIV 08][45].

Information control could be the miracle recipe for power: it would guarantee the advantage, superiority, transparency, anticipation, speed, action and knowledge. But the theory is written as if we were alone in the game. Nowadays, some other variables must be taken into account: the actions suffered, the relative inefficiency of the fortress paradigm, the possibilities of bypass, are all obstacles for control. A rule-of-law State does not have the initiative of aggression and thus cannot have the advantage. It can only act in reaction to an aggression. Therefore, maybe it would be better to develop a theory of the mastering of reaction?

From the French point of view, 'control' enables us to supply useful information to decision-makers, to "have at our disposal reliable information at the right time and place"[46]. This control also helps us to protect ourselves from the risk of not

---

45 Page 147 of the 2008 White Paper [LIV 08]. We must note that the expression 'information warfare' appears only once in this voluminous report.
46 Les fiches du CESA. Fiche n°18. Armée de l'air. April 2006. "La maîtrise de l'information dans l'armée de l'air".

seeing, not knowing or not having the reliable information, of taking a decoy for reality, building wrong representations from exact information, etc. This form of control[47] is not from the field of the dream of absolute domination of information space that the US calls 'info dominance': the supremacy over the information space makes the world transparent and guarantees control of the world.

French information control is as much of the 'hard power' dimension of information warfare (defensive and offensive cyber-war, electronic warfare, physical attacks against the information systems, etc.) as of 'soft power' dimension (war of words, images, political and diplomatic discourse, control of the media, representation of France abroad, etc.).

3.3.6. *The ANSSI*

The matter of cyber-defense has been quite topical ever since the events that occurred in Estonia in 2007. Evidently, this affair has relaunched debates and raised some questions within the authorities and general staff. Since this time, we have witnessed the implementation of new national strategies, which are also accompanied by the creation of cyber-defense and cyber-security agencies and units. This no longer consists of just having monitoring and warning tools, but of organizations that are able to go further: for example to carry out investigations, be ready for aggressive actions in times of conflict, crisis or even simply of peace.

States are thus developing their capacities; officially from a strictly defensive aspect. For many years, the US has had specialized information warfare units within its armies. Cyber-war, or whatever name we give to the conflict or confrontation in cyberspace, is only a subset of information warfare. It is thus natural that American forces develop capacities in this new field. Americans then prefer to talk about units devoted to cyber-operations rather than cyber-war units.

The US Cyber Command was launched in May 2010. Within the US Cyber Command, the Army Cyber Command (ARCYBER) was created in October 2010. It employs 21,000 soldiers and civilians[48]. The 24th Air Force was created in August 2009 and has been fully operational since October 2010. It is in charge of protecting the Air Force networks against cyber-attacks[49].

---

47 Also see http://www.cesa.air.defense.gouv.fr/DPESA/FCG/Fc18.pdf.
48 [KEN 10].
49   http://www.signonsandiego.com/news/2010/oct/01/air-force-declares-cyberwarfare-unit-operational/#.

Germany created a cyber-defense unit in 2009, which is located in Rheinbach[50]. In February 2011[51], it introduced a national cyber-security council, which is in charge of the coordination of the operations of a national defense center located in Bonn.

In March 2009, the UK announced the creation of a unit devoted to cyber-war[52], the Cyber Security Operations Centre (CSOC) within the GCHQ (Government Communications Headquarters). Less than 20 people were said to be working in this center. In January 2011, General Sir David Richards expressed his wish to create a cyber-command, taking inspiration from the American model, in order to protect the country from cyber-attacks and to be able to launch its own cyber-attacks. This process is in line with the conclusions of the Strategic Defense and Security Review published in the UK in October 2010[53].

The Netherlands published a new cyber-security strategy and announced the creation of a National Cybersecurity Center in February 2011.

In 2010, South Korea created a center for cyber-war, in order to counter the possible North Korean and Chinese attacks[54]. According to South Korean intelligence services, North Korea is reportedly equipped with specialized cyber-attack units.

In 2010, Switzerland was planning the creation of two cyber-war units within the *"Centre des Opérations Electroniques de l'Organisation de Soutien au Commandement des Forces Armées"* [CAV 10][55].

In January 2011, the Estonian Defense Ministry proposed the creation of cyber-defense units on the basis of expertise of the country computer scientist

---

50 http://benmazzotta.wordpress.com/2009/02/11/new-german-cyber-warfare-unit/.

51 Cyber Security Strategy for Germany, Federal Ministry of the Interior, http://www.cio.bund.de/SharedDocs/Publikationen/DE/IT-Sicherheit/css_engl_download. pdf?__blob=publicationFile.

52 http://www.theregister.co.uk/2009/11/12/csoc_date/.

53 [SEC 10].

54 http://www.theregister.co.uk/2010/01/12/korea_cyberwarfare_unit/.

55 Units with a defensive role. The first unit must take the form of a military CERT and must be coordinated with the GovCERT. But the *Centre des Opérations Electroniques* must also implement a CNO (computer networks operations) unit. From a legal point of view, CND are lawful, but CNA and CNE are only lawful in an aggression state. This means that Switzerland forbids itself to use CNA other that in war times, if these systems are attacked.

communities. The activities of this unit will be carried out in consultation with the NATO center of excellence in Tallinn[56].

Israel is said to be equipped with Unit 8200, based in the Negev desert.

Iran will also be equipping itself with cyber-war capacities.

Australia announced the creation of a specialized unit within its intelligence services in March 2011[57].

China has reportedly had specialized units in this field for more than 10 years, according to several American reports. In May 2011, China declared that it had created a cyber-defense unit in the Guangzhou province. Beijing has also accused Taiwan of leading cyber-attacks with the help of dedicated military units.

NATO has 15 centers of excellence on this level, including one cooperative cyber-defense center of excellence in Tallinn (Estonia). In this international context – where States are strengthening their cyber-security and cyber-defense capabilities – France created by a decree on July 7, 2009 a national agency for cyber defense: the ANSSI. Its mission has then been strengthened by the decree of February 11, 2011. Some media have not hesitated to wrongfully compare the ANSSI to the US Cyber Command[58]. Yet, the ANSSI is not a military organization with a mission to carry out acts of aggression. It ensures the security of the country's information systems and is in charge of protecting them from all sorts of cyber-attacks.

3.3.7. *Cyber-security and cyber-defense*

The security of the information space is a political, strategic and national defense and security question. According to the Lasbordes report, information system security is "an issue on the scale of the entire Nation […] For the State, this is a national sovereignty issue. Its responsibility is indeed to guarantee the security of its own information systems, the continuity of the functioning of the institutions and facilities vital for the socio-economic activities of the country and the protection of the companies and citizens" [LAS 05][59].

---

56 http://www.defensenews.com/story.php?i=5556484.
57 Australian Security Intelligence Organization.
58 *ANSSI, Naissance du CyberCommand Français*, February 15, 2011. http://www.linformaticien.com/Actualit%C3%A9s/tabid/58/newsid496/10342/anssi-naissance-du-cybercommand-francais/Default.aspx.
59 [LAS 05] The report: 1) identifies the threats towards information systems; 2) the current security devices; 3) and the critical points in order to; 4) conclude with a lack of coordination between public and private actors.

In France, the report by Senator Roger Romani [ROM 08] defined cyber-defense as all the means enabling us to protect ourselves from the attacks on information systems; these attacks are likely to question the security and defense of the country.

For the ANSSI, cyber-security is a "sought after state for an information system, helping it to resist events coming from the cyberspace; these events are likely to compromise the availability, the integrity or the confidentiality of the data, stored, discussed or transmitted and of the connate services that these systems offer or make available. Cybersecruity uses techniques of the information system security and relies on the fight against cybercriminality and on the implementation of a cyberdefense". The latter is the set of technical and non-technical measures helping a State to defend the information systems that are considered essential in cyberspace [ANS 11].

The achievement of the French policies and strategies is accompanied by a development plan of its capacities. In addition, these projects comply with a system of logic, which is not specific to mainland France.

The research and development group within the prospective and technology sub-commission of the *Commission Interministérielle de la Sécurité des Systèmes d'Information*, itself placed under the SGDN (Secrétariat Général de la Défense Nationale), published the update of a first report from 2006, entitled *Orientation des Travaux de Recherche et de Développement en Matière de Sécurité des Systèmes d'Information* in April 10, 2008[60]. From this report, we note the issues that seem essential to the authorities in terms of information system security:

– accountability of the accesses (who is the attacker, how to go back to them);

– nomadism;

– evolution of the fortress security paradigm towards the living paradigm, with a wish to abolish all the borders; and

– the control of all the bricks constituting information systems.

The possibility of a dual use of security techniques for purposes other than strictly defensive ones: "knowing how to detect such steganography devices or conversely how to make them hardly detectable are thus the two complementary aspects of the sword and the armor".

---

60 http://www.ssi.gouv.fr/fr/sciences/fichiers/rapports/rapport_orientation_ssi_2008.pdf.

3.3.8. *Army: Information operations, NEB (numérisation de l'espace de bataille/digitization of battlespace), info-development*

3.3.8.1. *The temple of information operations*

If in the French military vocabulary the expression 'information warfare' does not appear, this is to the advantage of the expression 'information operations' (IOs), following the American model and that of the terminology adopted by NATO. *IOs*, (inter-army function) *are influence operations* and are not in this approach part of the coercion field, which is strictly exercised in the physical field. The French IOs doctrine strongly relies on the psychological dimension and the power of influence; the objective is always to limit the recourse to force by as much as possible, to limit violence by a weakened resistance, to shorten the duration of the conflicts and limit losses.

Doctrinal reflections on IOs began at the end of the 1990s. They consist of transmitting a coherent message and having a better reactivity, i.e. of endowing France with an efficient influence strategy. This focuses on the 'soft power' field than on the 'hard power' one.

The *Concept Interarmées des OI* (PIA 03.152) was published on March 11, 2005 and an inter-army doctrine of the IOs (PIA 03.252) on May 29, 2006. IOs are defined in the text of March 11, 2005 as a "set of actions carried out by forced armies, defined and coordinated on the highest level, aiming to use or defend information, information systems and decision processes, with the constant support of an influence strategy, and contributing in operations to the attack of the EFR[61], in the respect of the values". IOs are thus:

– military operations;

– actions with a purpose: to disturb the will to act against adversary. This purpose is pursued by aiming at two targets:

   - the information collected by the adversary in order to alter their knowledge, and

   - the adversary sensors, to alter, modify and disrupt their information acquisition capacities;

– operations fitting into a continuum, in coordination with the use of force and civil-military actions (CIMIC[62] and COMOPS[63]).

---

61 EFR (Effet Final Recherché), final sought-after effect.
62 CIMIC (Civil-Military Cooperation).
http://www.giacm.com/index_fichiers/Page316.html.

– "indirect strategies offering another path or an additional choice to the modes of action founded on the destruction"[64].

The components of information operations are generally represented in the form of columns supporting a temple. These components are as follows:

– *Military influence operations (MIOs)*, an equivalent of the psychological operations (PSYOPS), are the key function of the IOs:

- they fit in the military continuum: intervention – stabilization – reconstruction. Their relevance is higher and higher as the kinetics operations decrease;

- they must be carried out in prevention, during and after the conflicts;

- they are exerted on info-targets, which are only adversaries[65] and are individuals or groups of individuals whose behaviors, attitudes, perceptions and will we want to modify and influence. The national public opinion is not the target of the MIO, but of the COMOPS;

- they rely on communication methods;

- they are only efficient if they are able to overcome the operations carried out by the adversary, to defeat counter-psyops operations if the conflict has a significant ideological dimension or if the info-targets operate as good receivers and do not oppose any resistance by unpredictable reactions, that could possibly turn the psychological maneuver against its instigator.

- military disappointment.

– *Cyber-war* is defined in the *Glossaire Interarmées* of 2004 as "In the computer field, actions carried out in order to paralyze the systems of an adversary, to disturb the data transmission flow and to deform them or take note of these data". This field was still recently considered as 'emergent'[66] and defined as 'a guerilla of the information warfare'[67]. This task is 'exclusively defensive'[68] within the armies. The control of defense should also enable us to counter these attacks, but the aggressive

---

63 COMOPS (Operational Communication of Armies).
64 Fiche no. 217/DEF/EMAA/GMG/CESAM. October 19, 2006. Les opérations d'information et l'armée de l'air.
65 Generally, we consider that "psychological warfare" is directed against the enemy and 'psychological actions' towards friendly troops.
66 " Opérations d'information dans la troisième dimension" by the work group Air 2 of the XIII° clas of the Collège interarmées de défense. www.cesa.air.defense.gouv.fr/ DPESA/PLAF/PLAF_N_11?pdf October 2006.
67 Ibid. Page pp. 70
68 Ibid. Page pp. 70.

use of cyberspace seems delicate because of the possible collateral effects, which are difficult or impossible to control, but also because of the legal issues. Finally, a new vulnerability appears: that of communication satellites. Eventually, the space will probably be fought over. We have to prepare ourselves to this fact. At the Ministry of Defense, the piloting of the information systems is ensured by the DGSIC[69] and the defensive cyber-war leans on its actions, while relying on OPVAR (organization of the watch, alert, and response) functions.

– *Activities of information protection (OPSEC/INFOSEC)*: security of operations (protection of the force) and information. We need to ensure the good circulation of information within the armed forces, to offer efficient protection from the possibilities of attacks against information systems and to protect ourselves against the risks related to the vulnerability of the systems and personnel.

– *Attitude and behavior* of the forces. By their behavior, soldiers are conveying the representation of France and its determination.

– *Electronic warfare.*

These six pillars are the "dedicated domains" of information operations. We can add to them the *CIMIC* and *COMOPS*, which are the 'associated domains' and the *destruction*, which is "the use of force".

These nine pillars thus support the "temple" of information operations[70].

There is no real hierarchy of the tasks between these pillars, which are the foundations of IOs. However, the psychological dimension is essential. IOs and the influence strategy support the six IOs pillars, but also the recourse to force and CIMIC and COMOPS operations.

3.3.8.2. *Battlespace digitization*

Battlespace digitization is in line with the process of transformation of the French armies. Digitization[71] is an efficiency factor: it helps to accelerate the pace of operations and to improve the decision cycle[72], to point where information is controlled (information of quality). Issuing this quality information on all levels of responsibility and in any place relies on the organization of a 'system of systems', which is a complex structure that must be interoperable with the systems of allies.

---

69 Created in 2006.
70 "Les opérations d'information: mythe ou réalité ?", *Penser les Ailes Françaises*. no. 17, April 2008, pp. 114.
71 Also see the *Principes d'Emploi de la FOT Numérisée de Niveau 3*, July 8, 2004. http://www.cdef.terre.defense.gouv.fr/doctrineFT/doc_trans/FOT_niv3.pdf.
72 "Place de la fonction SIC dans les crises actuelles et futures", *Doctrine Numéro Spécial*, May 2008, pp.37.

This stage is still under development and we mention the impact of this new information structure on the doctrines and organization of general staffs in the future tense[73].

Battlespace digitization is organized around the networks, C4ISR systems, and implementation of the famous network-centric warfare and still goes on nowadays with the introduction of futuristic solutions (drones, robots, infantry equipment, etc.). It is not the only aspect of the introduction of new information communication technologies (ICTs) in the army. Internet, on the side of secured networks, is used by the armies and is taken right into the field of confrontation. Soldiers have access in their everyday life to the same technologies and the same communication means as any other member of the public. Soldiers express themselves, communicate with each other and exchange ideas. Soldiers are members of the public but they are exposed to prying eyes. Soldiers can come out of their "reserve" and talk openly online and then there are risks for the institution, army, State and for soldiers themselves, since they are not always aware of the importance of what they are saying and reporting.

The relationship of the soldiers to means of communication must be questioned. If we can find virtues in the freedom of expression of soldiers within the army [BIH 10], data theft, expression on blogs open to the general public, chat rooms or other social networks, are however debatable. The relationship of the military authorities to the freedom of expression of their soldiers, or even of the media, varies from one country to another. The French Code of Defense (*Code de la Défense français*) stipulates in article 4122-2 that soldiers must be 'discrete', which by default forbids any publication on the Internet likely to disclose military information.

3.3.8.3. *Info-valorization*

Information control and its simultaneous sharing on all levels gave birth to the concept of info-valorization, an equivalent of the American concept of NCW (Network Centric Warfare)[74]. The model of the info-valorized maneuver is thus presented as the ideal solution, enabling us to integrate everything, deal with everything, see and know everything and to assess knowledge described as "a form of intelligence", which "covers also the estimation of the strictly necessary lethality level"[75].

---

73 Ibid. pp. 38.
74 See the special issue of *Doctrine* journal, February 2005. pp. 17.
75 See the special issue of *Doctrine* journal, February 2005. pp. 18

Info-valorization has been defined as one of the three fundamental concepts structuring the future land forces (info-valorization, operational versatility and synergy of the effects):

> "Info-valorization aims at an optimal exploitation of the informational resources enabled by the new information and communication technologies"[76].

3.3.8.4. *Cyber-war*

The French inter-army glossary of operational terminology [MDF 07] (PIA 0.5.5.2.) of 2007 associates 'cybernetic war' with 'cyber-war'. The two concepts are synonyms. Cyber-war corresponds to the set of "actions carried out in order to paralyze the systems of an adversary, to disturb data transmission flows and to deform these data or take note of them". [MDF 07] The targets are the systems.

The White Paper on Defense and National Security published in June 2008 [LIV 08] introduced two major concepts: defensive cyber-war (DCW)[77] and offensive cyber-war (OCW)[78]. Some States are significant threats because they have strategies of aggressive information warfare. Open or concealed attacks are in the realm of possibility. To face these threats, France is changing its strategy from a passive defense to an active in-depth one, which affects equally civil society and the military domain.

Passive defense consists of implementing automatic protection systems (firewalls, antivirus software). This consists of an essential protection level, which is insufficient because we can go around it. Active defense (DCW) consists of implementing surveillance systems and of adapting to the evolution of threats. For this mission, the White Paper of 2008 [LIV 08] predicts the creation of a detection center (in order to monitor the sensitive networks). The Romani report [ROM 08] notes that this protection level is not either a sufficient security despite this protection, the Pentagon is subjected to incessant attacks.

To this necessary but insufficient layer, the White Paper of 2008 [LIV 08] was thus suggesting to add a new one, "OCW", which relies on the conviction that "in the computer domain more than in any other one, we will have to know how to attack in order to defend ourselves" [LIV 08]. This layer will probably enable us to contradict the assertion according to which "the defender must imagine everything without being able to respond… because there is no legitimate defense in ISS[79],

---

76 http://www.air-defense.net/Forum_AD/index.php?topic=4945.20;wap2.
77 In French *lutte informatique défensive* (LID).
78 In French *lutte information offensive* (LIO).
79 Information system security.

whereas the attacker seems entitled to do everything possible" [LAS 05]. The development of these OCW capacities is not an innovation of the 2008 White Paper, since they were already present in the Law of Military Planning 2003–2008[80]: "The model of the armies 2015 [...] also includes the recognition of defensive and offensive cyberwar".

According to the Doctrine of the Use of the forces of 2003[81]:

> "The threats relying on the computer systems are quite unpredictable in their origin, their nature and their aims. The consequences of cyber-aggressions appear simultaneously in numerous places, because the networks are accessible by many points of entrance.
>
> By taking into account the very specific nature of these threats, which are diffused, sometimes clandestine, often undetectable and unpredictable, cyberwar obeys to the following principles:
>
> - permanence, reactivity, anticipation: cyberwar consists of "mastering time" by a surveillance function and a significant reactivity to computer events;
>
> - interactions with the other fields: cyberwar is directly related to electronic warfare, of which it is probably only one aspect. The use of weapon systems is related to a computer science of action and research. The computer infrastructure which does not depend on weapon systems notably includes decision support computing, administrative data processing, etc.

The mastering of the OCW capacities must ensure the superiority of the engagements. The objectives are ambitious: identify the adversaries (and thus have the means of identification), know the operating processes of the adversaries, be equipped with capacities to neutralize the adversary (i.e. to be able to paralyze the opposite operation centers), implement retaliatory measures, develop specialized tools (notably digital network tools), and formulate a doctrine for the use of OCW capacities. The doctrine will notably reflect on the legal framework of the use of these new weapons (whose targets are authorized, which power of destruction can be used), on the threshold of actions of this new external intervention capacity (intelligence services, soldiers), and on the question of the proportionality of the possible retaliatory measures.

---

80 http://www.legifrance.gouv.fr/affichTexte.do?cidTexte=JORFTEXT000000234154
&dateTexte=.
81 [DIA 01] Chapter 7.

This project of offensive capacities is causing some significant problems in terms of feasibility:

– Using these capacities in a legitimate defense context or to apply retaliatory measures, after an act of aggression, implies knowledge of the precise identity of the attackers. Nowadays, the level of the technique does not enable us to do this. On a battlefield, the adversary is identified. When a cyber-attack aims at incapacitating a vital infrastructure, the perpetrators generally forget to sign their action, and assumptions are not proof enough.

– The time taken to carry out the investigation can be quite long. Legitimate defense can only be exerted in a short time. The time constraint in the context of an aggression is the same as in an investigation concerning an act of cyber-criminality.

– Respect of the proportionality principle of retaliation or of the response implies that we have an exact view of the extent of the damages suffered by our own side by an attack. What could the metric of these losses be?

– What will be the consequences of the use of network weapons? How can we control, for example, the collateral effects?

– OCW first assumes that we know about the attack. Detection capacities are not, however, ensuring that we can see everything. Attacks can be very discrete. Some sensitive machines seem to have been pirated for years before we realize it[82]. A DCW/OCW coordination is thus essential.

– If "the use of violence in war has never any other aim than producing psychological effects"[83] (an assertion that generally refers to physical violence), what level of violence will we authorize in cyber-war operations, which would give them the necessary force to convince, terrorize or dissuade the adversary?

3.3.8.5. *Military point of views*

In the absence of revolution, if some evolutions can be found in official texts and doctrines, they are foremost carried out by men, with their convictions and their approval. Yet, if the digitization process is progressing, caution, reluctance and resistance are often present in the technological race and the temptation is to yield to the influence of the American doctrine.

---

82 The Moonlight Maze and Titan Rain affairs in the United States, nominative data thefts that are sensible in the servers, etc.

83 "La violence psychologique dans la guerre au XX° siècle". *Revue Historique des Armées*, no 238, 2005. http://www.servicehistorique.sga.defense.gouv.fr/04histoire/articles/articles_rha/violencepsychologie.htm

Thus, General Vincent Desportes wrote the following about the NCW concept [DES 08]:

> "In the dream of the RMA (revolution in military affairs) [...] is born this idea that war, the true war, must henceforth be 'network-centered' [...] these operations in network should enable us to make the myth of the quick war become a reality [...] This technical evolution, much more based on the wonder of new capacities than on the observation of the conflictuality, was soon going to show its limits [...] the British [...] have abandoned the idea of NCW to put technology back where it belongs, and speak about NEC, for Network Enabled Capacities [...] After a first phase of wonder in front of NCW, the French doctrine has fortunately followed the British example and adopted the quite awful but realistic neologism of 'infovalorisation' ('infovalorization')".

"Technology would not know how to change or transform the war. We will soon make war in space, but it will not be 'the space war'", continues General Vincent Desportes [DES 07]. Techno-skepticism (or salutary caution) is appropriate in many environments, including the military one. This position is a brake to that of the supporters of the technology, who see in technology the future, promising the perfection and solution to all our problems.

If there is a reticence or a strong caution within the army. This is mostly because:

– Chiefs are not trusting chimeras[84]: "the predominant position of information and communication systems and the use of dematerialized information must not lead us to the trap of the virtual, which is completely disconnected from reality"[85].

– Chiefs do not always trust new technologies: "For a while, innovation remains a foreign body that disturbs an existing balance"[86]. We should not yield to the "technological illusion" or to the "fascination with the new gadget and to the temptation for technophiles to exploit it at the maximum of its possibilities"[87].

– Chiefs do not always see the benefit of digitization, virtualization, computerization and of theories that have been developed on their basis:

---

84 Also see "Les opérations d'information: mythe ou réalité?", *Penser les Ailes Françaises*, no. 17, April 2008. pp. 112.

85 "Place de la fonction SIC dans les crises actuelles et futures", *Doctrine*, Special issue, May 2008, pp. 39.

86 "Des électrons et des hommes", "Nouvelles technologies de l'information et conduite des operations", Cahier de la recherche doctrinale. CDEF/DREX. June 2005. pp. 4

87 Ibid. pp. 26

- How will NICTs save the chiefs from reproducing the mistakes they have systematically made for centuries; and if it is not possible to avoid all these mistakes, how can they make fewer errors?

- How can NICTs help them to understand and act[88] (and especially not one without the other)?

- How will we be able to avoid the vulnerability resulting from the dependence of human actors on information systems? The attacks against Estonia are often taken as an example of vulnerability and dependence[89]. The systems are subjected to the risk of attacks: for example cyber-attacks against NATO sites and the American defense department machines preparing the offensive in Kosovo in May 1999 [CDE 05][90].

- An army must be strengthened and not weakened by the introduction of weak links.

– American doctrines cannot be the object of a simple copy and paste within the French model. The NCW concept has raised many questions and critiques.

– Systems do not always become a reality and fulfill all hopes because on the operational field, "the control of the information space" does not ensure the fluency and the success of operations:

- We have put in new information communication technologies (NICTs) and hope to see the enemy without being seen, to see them and reach beyond the horizon, etc. But on the field, the monitoring of enemy forces never seems to be as good as the monitoring of its own forces.

- The systems enable us to access more information more quickly. But we have to deal with the various speeds: an order can be given, transmitted and received with very short delays. However, the implementation of the order will still not be accelerated.

- Many communication technologies are relatively inefficient nowadays in the field of urban guerilla warfare.

- The capacities offered by NICTs enable us to always produce more documents and thus to complicate and slow down the processes: "a Wehrmacht battalion was taking at least about 30 minutes to conceive and diffuse an order. In

---

88 See some reflections on the art of command on the *Collège Interarmées de Défense* webpage: http://www.college.interarmees.defense.gouv.fr/spip.php?article917.
89 "Place de la fonction SIC dans les crises actuelles et futures", *Doctrine* Special issue, May 2008. pp. 39.
90 Also see the CNN article "Cyberattacks spur talk of third DOD network", June 22, 1999, http://edition.cnn.com/TECH/computing/9906/22/dodattack.idg/.

1994, the 3rd British Division made an estimate of 12 hours for the duration necessary for the deployment of an order of operation"[91].

- "The increase of the acquisition and processing capacities has not proportionally reduced the uncertainties of the battlefield since it has also created other needs"[92].

General Desportes matches the certainties that were built at the turn of the 1990s on utopias (beliefs in the powers of technology) to the uncertainty appearing nowadays. "The adversary seems to be less and less detectable and thus less and less easily spotted. Henceforth, the only situations which are often asymmetrical, are characterized by the 'surprise'; the chief on the field must thus quickly decide and react" [DES 07]. The fast decision can only count on the speed of the information processing by computer and telecommunication systems. More simply, the decision cannot rely on the technology alone. To partly compensate for the uncertainty, chiefs[93] must thus use their experience and knowledge. A military chief can partly rely on military history but chiefs of military cyber-operation have only a very short history and a limited experience at their disposal. In terms of cyber-war, for example, what is taught nowadays in defense universities and military schools? This teaching should train chiefs in the practice of uncertainty. The command is partly based on the knowledge of known realities from the past. In terms of cybernetics, the situation is a bit different. History is still young and remains to be written. Almost everything has to be invented. Chiefs must thus have invention and innovation capacities. But the conduct of cyber-war will partly be built on reasoning that is not specific to it but is borrowed from conventional war.

General Desportes is very critical of the position of ICTs within the field of military operations. "The battlefield 'transparency' seems more and more like a false good theoretical idea. Previously, we wanted to decide and fight 'by' information; we realize nowadays that we are condemned to fight in addition 'for' information before even deciding." Information must be sought after, acquired, processed and analyzed. There is a great deal of information (even if the adversary is becoming less easy to spot), but it is not necessarily relevant and does not especially contain information enabling us to better know and understand the adversary and anticipate its actions. Information must thus be protected. The adversary also knows how to use it and how to attack ours. Information is a fully-

---

91 Ibid. pp. 40.

92 Ibid. pp. 44.

93 The command by objective considers that war is unpredictable: it is a reign of uncertainty. It favors trust in the adaptation capacities of individuals, their initiative, the decentralization of communications and networks. The command by order considers that war is predictable. This mode of command is more rigid, averts initiative and opts for a centralized approach and a vertical mode of communication from top to bottom.

fledged subject that is fought over. The efficiency of ICTs is at fault due to the nature of the 'disputed areas', where land engagements are conducted[94]. "Informational supremacy is there reduced and communication systems have their limits as well in these areas" [DES 07]. The field and the reality of the fight remain major factors of the military fight that information technologies cannot ignore. How we make war and how we fight in the field will influence the strategy:

> "tactics is taking again an increasing importance in comparison to strategy; [...] this will be all the more true in the future with digitization possibilities inexorably leading to a 'distribution' of the fight in small distributed teams inserted within the adversary system: no more continuous front and thus no more continuous control"[95].

Conventional command (planning and a hierarchical system from top to bottom) is questioned, to the benefit of adaptability and flexibility: "therefore, the important element is not the planning and conception capacity, but the adaptation capacity"[96]. This capacity must partially reduce the effects of uncertainty, which overly rigid organizations' systems and structures cannot face.

Thus, we will need to be able to conduct wars of reaction (permanently knowing how to react); to quickly adapt equipment, methods, doctrines and decisions; to favor cultural and structural evolution; to increase the flexibility of men and systems (digitization must be a great help for this aspect); to trust men, because it seems that now more than ever "the science of action becomes first the science of decision in uncertainty situations"[97]. Clausewitz is speaking of chance: nothing is completely predictable during war.

In cyber-conflict, one of the main uncertainties results from the difficult attribution of the attacks: it is very difficult or even almost impossible to know who has really perpetrated the attack (who is the attacker). This is a phenomenon inherent in cyberspace that goes totally against dreams of transparency (knowing and seeing everything about the world). If we do not know who we are fighting against, the duel (a characteristic aspect of war) is no longer possible. All the rhetoric of Clausewitz or of General Desportes relies on one main principle: to fight, we need to have an adversary who is known, seen and identified. Chance, the lack of information and, reactivity are all problems that can only appear if war is possible. When we have identified or seen an adversary, we cannot always predict

---

94 [DES 07] pp. 3.
95 [DES 07] pp. 4.
96 [DES 07] pp. 8.
97 [DES 07] pp. 7.

its behavior, and we need to foresee its decisions and foil its plans. But when we do not see or know anything, there is no certainty.

Will the scenarios developed in response to cyber-attacks, tested during multiple exercises carried out each year, be able to encompass all the possible situations, configurations and combinations? Will the real attack catch defenders unprepared? Will they have all the necessary aptitude and flexibility to adapt to the unexpected? Nobody can be sure that the scenarios tested are the right ones and that the events will occur as imagined. The fate remains unsolved.

The cautious or even reticent attitude of some military chiefs with respect to RMA or even NEB is not specific to this technology (ICT).

The birth of aviation was a complete revolution for soldiers. This technological breakthrough took time to establish itself as a significant advance, which became useful in the art of war.

> "The first aerial exploits of the Wright brothers were almost not known and we were only starting to consider them as real, when we started to be concerned in France of the possible use of airplanes as weapons of war. [...] It was logical to examine if these new devices, with special operating and all different conditions, could be used in the future wars, either as fighters, or as scouts" [NAN 11][98].

These few lines are from a text by Max de Nansouty published in 1911 and relate to the use of airplanes in war. This extract raises two questions:

– conditions of acceptance and of introduction of a new technology, whatever it is in military affairs and its conditions of transformation into an instrument of war; and

– the impact and position of this new technology among the existing weapons.

Skepticism, reluctances, indecisions, shy adoption of the technology, acceptance, discourse on the breakthrough, on the revolution in military affairs… the process is sometimes long and complicated from one extreme to the other. Confronted with the emergence of aviation, soldiers were very cautious and reserved. They had a technology in front of them that they did not know what to do with. The airplane was first seen as a pastime and not as a strategic military instrument. The use of this technology as tool of war was not obvious at first and came up against great resistance, as if the military machinery was so precise a clock that the introduction

---

98 Utilisation des aéroplanes à la guerre, p. 15.

of a new cog would disturb it. This explains all the reluctances and caution that were exercised.

The Italian Giulio Douhet was one of those who contributed in making aviation a strategic instrument of war. At the beginning of the 1910s, he was assuring people that a new battlefield had opened: the sky[99]. This position recalls that of French experts in contemporary military issues who think that cyberspace is a new field of battle and confrontations. At the beginning of the 20th Century, the technological breakthrough of aviation seemed to open the doors to a revolution of the art of war. It was henceforth possible to imagine attacking the adversary beyond the front line, in-depth, in their own land (to hit where the civilians are). We can find this idea again nowadays in the new dimension: by resorting to cybernetic weapons, it is possible to strike a society at its core (to see and hit beyond the horizon). The capacities offered by cyberspace enable us, for example, to aim at the critical infrastructures that are quite sensible targets – such as banks, services of power distribution and vital industries. This strategy of striking the capacities of an adversary at their sources fits with the information warfare and cyber-war theories[100].

3.3.9. *Cyber-war and other modalities of the cyber-conflict*

3.3.9.1. *Cyber-war*

Sometimes not well adapted to the objects it is supposed to describe, this concept leads to many mix-ups. The attack of a few state or company servers by hackers – who are not always "Chinese" – is often classified as cyber-war. This is the same for some waves of defacement of sites, which can occur during specific events, such as a major crisis or an armed conflict. There are ordinary-time defacements and those during intense political periods. This is often described as cyber-war. We just have to browse international media websites to realize it.

In *Cyberguerre et Guerre de l'Information: Stratégies, Règles, Enjeux"* [VEN 10], we suggest a restrictive definition of cyber-war, by affirming that it is the technical dimension of information warfare; resorting to cybernetic capacities to carry out aggressive operations in cyberspace against military targets, a State or its society; a conventional war of where at least one of the components

---

99 Quoted in *Aux Origines de la Stratégie Aérienne*, Histoire et Stratégie, La puissance aérienne, no. 2, Paris, France, September 2010
100 International law is then undermined and the attacks against critical infrastructures have direct consequences on civilians.

relies on the computer or digital field, in its implementation, motives and tools (weapons in the broad meaning of the word)[101].

In accordance with this definition, acts of cyber-war are thus much less numerous than it seems. When the Georgian Ministry of Foreign Affairs had to ask foreign countries to host its official websites that have been victims of cyber-attacks, should we then have talked about cyber-war because of the context of the operation? Or simply have considered that it was the actions of opportunists with no link to the war in progress, and shifted the question on the field of confrontation in the information dimension or even of simple cyber-criminality?

The French inter-army glossary of operational terminology (PIA 0.5.5.2.) defines war as an "armed fight between social groups and especially between states, which is considered as a social phenomenon", specifying that "it results in the confrontation zone in a state or a situation of war". The state of war is specifically defined as a legal state "which results from a declaration of war or from an ultimatum with conditional declaration of war". Cyber-war thus cannot be a war, according to this conventional approach.

"The war is born and with it the necessity to quickly transmit from afar the orders of the command and important news" [BEL 94]. Many essential principles, which are now applicable to the use of cyberspace in war, were already present in the implementation of telegraphy and telephony during war, as we can see, for example, in the study by Léon Poinsard published in 1894 [POI 94]:

> "In times of war, the situation is quite different. The specific needs of the time, the frequent situation of a foreign authority which is an enemy of the sovereign, alter all the while the state of things. Here, as for Transport and Post, the state of war results in a condition in law and new legal relations. It is essential that we talk a little bit about this aspect... In times of war, the situation is characterized by these two principles which each are an urgent necessity for all the adversaries: firstly, we need to have at our disposal the telegraph and the phone as means of attack or defense, depending on the case; secondly, it is very useful to cut off as much as possible the telegraphic or telephonic communications of the enemy. This double requirement is very important and all the armies worthy of the name have therefore nowadays specialized troops for these actions: part of these troops are specialized in the destruction of the enemy lines, and the others in the restoration of these same lines or in the fast construction of temporary

---

101 Definition proposed by Eric Filiol in his chapter in [VEN 10], entitled *Aspects opérationnels d'une cyberattaque: renseignement, planification et conduite.*

communication ways. Besides, it is not very useful to stress this aspect, because everyone knows more or less nowadays about the military role of the telegraph and telephone. Therefore, every belligerent will think of impeding enemy communications by all possible means; for example by seizing their lines or if needed by destroying them, or by intercepting their dispatches by all possible means. Therefore, belligerents will have no scruples if necessary to cut the wires, to destroy the devices, to scatter the staff or take them as prisoners... Sometimes, depending on the circumstances, the enemy seizes and uses the lines and installations, and this while always acting in the fullness of their right [...]. In all cases, acts of war leading to the destruction of the lines or at least the stopping of communications, have very bad consequences for civilians. The transmission of communications is stopped and belligerents are also suffering from it: the private correspondence can be paralyzed on all the territory or can still partially survive. Let us observe that this break, result of the state of war, can be ordered by the local sovereign for the interest of their military preparations; this was the case in France in 1870. Moreover, when the service is stopped because of destruction, this break can last a long time because of the time necessary for repairing. It stands to reason that the movement of the business is also deeply affected and this, still a long time after the restoration of peace. The nationals of belligerent states are not the only ones suffering from this condition of things and neutral states are also suffering from it".

The points discussed in this text are almost all topical nowadays in the developments relative to the use of cyberspace in conflicts:

– What is practiced in times of war is necessarily different from peacetime. War is a specific time. For example, legal relationships between the parties are deeply modified in war times.

– All means of communication must remain operational for offensive and defensive operations.

– Offensive operations mainly consist of attacks against facilities, but also against contents (interceptions).

– There are some specialized troops to carry out offensive and defensive operations in the field of communications. These troops are the forerunners of military cyber-units.

– Belligerents are authorized to carry out almost everything in offensive actions. The rule dictates its law. Nowadays, the legal framework is not defined in terms of cyber-war and it is quite likely that in the situation of war, belligerents are then authorized to do almost everything.

– The attacks carried out against telecommunications have consequences on the general public and on the economy.

– The authorities can decide to cut off communications, in the interest of war, even if the consequences may be detrimental for civilians. We can find this method for imperatives of security and defense of vital interests, which consists of cutting off the Internet, in some States.

– Offensive operations and all the defensive measures can have an impact on the neutral actors and neutral parties.

The text also discusses the legal dimension of telecommunications in times of peace and war. From this observation, it emerges that there were many questions that were not answered.

> "Concerning land telegraphs, we must first set out that, in principle, war is a *force majeure* which releases administrations from the transmission obligation; an obligation resulting from international conventions. The State remains free in that case to exclusively use as long as it wants all the lines, even if they belong to private companies [...] During the fall of 1869, the government of Washington took the initiative to organize a diplomatic conference with the aim to study the condition of the telegraphic transmissions in peace and war times. But other events attracted the attention of the public and the conference did not happen. Several years later, a congress organized in Brussels with the aim to write some rules of practices during war times, alluded to the condition of telegraph lines and their equipment, while comparing them to railway tracks. At that point, it was only about land installations and this was not studied in detail. They were simply proposing to set the rule that telegraphs could only be sequestrated and not confiscated in case of occupation. In 1871, during a conference in Rome of the Telegraph Association, the question was brought up again by the Norwegian delegate and the famous American financier Cyrus Field. The Norwegian delegate suggested that a committee was appointed within the conference, in order to prepare a project of convention with the aim to settle the condition of telegraphy in war times. The American financier was asking that the conference took the initiative to forbid, by a provision of the Act of Union, the destruction of the lines and of the equipment, by admitting the transmission of harmless dispatches notwithstanding the acts of war. The conference did not have the capacity to discuss

these propositions and limited itself to send them for discussion to the various governments, by recommending them to their kind attention. Since then, things have not changed. This inertia of the governments can be explained by the difficulty of regulating such a delicate matter. Will we for example forbid a belligerent to send runners to cut off the telegraphic and telephonic wires of its adversary, in order to paralyze as far as possible the mobilization and the concentration of its troops or supplies? In addition, how will we convince the involved armies to allow the transmission of dispatches through their lines? Who does not know that the most insignificant telegram at first can have a hidden meaning and be used to transmit excessively valuable information for the enemy? [...] Concerning submarine cables, the situation is not quite the same. First, the destruction of a cable is much more serious than that of a land wire, because of the material damage and of the significance of the cut off of communications. Indeed, the repair costs are much more significant and repairing requires more time. Moreover, there are fewer submarine than land cables and therefore one submarine cable serves a much larger area. In such conditions, we can easily imagine how the consequences of the destruction of a cable can have more repercussions than that of the cut off of a land line, including for the neutrals. Still, on the other hand, we can affirm that the cables are generally less completely in the hands of the belligerents than land wires. [...] To simplify, they are to a lesser extent in the field of operations [...] a cable establishes between a given country and its colonial possessions or between two points of its territory [...] the enemy will be able to destroy it if they think this destruction would be useful for them [...] the cable can still be established between the coast of a belligerent and that of a neutral State [...] the interests of a country not engaged in the war are often challenged [...] it seems that the enemy only acquires rights on the cable at the moment when they manage to block or occupy the landing point... It only remains the case where the cable is established between two neutral territories. In that case, the belligerents cannot say anything about the line, which is rightfully placed completely outside the scene of hostilities. Besides, the neutrals are the owners of the cable and have the duty to avoid any transmission with a visible aim to assist one of the fighting States".

Ending his chapter with the rules that should be imposed on the States in order to salvage communication systems (i.e. a neutralization of the cables), forbidding the States to cut or destroy them in case of war, the author concludes: "This is not in a period of 'armed peace', i.e. in the preparation period of the war, that we should think to ask the countries to sacrifice one of their best attack and defense means".

This very long quotation showed – if needed – the significant similarities between the way of comprehending problems with cyberspace nowadays and the problems of telecommunication space at the end of the 19th Century:

– Question of the legal status that should be given to facilities in war times.

– Question of the law applicable to belligerents and neutral countries.

– Question of the protection of the interests of everybody, even in war times (we are not always in situations of total destruction, but are usually involved in conflicts that remain controlled by the law).

– Question of the relationships established between belligerents and between belligerents and neutral states.

What the armies can do:

– Get involved in international relations and the negotiation of international treaties and agreements, while facing the inertia of States.

– Address the issues surrounding the relationships between civilians and soldiers in war times: can the army requisition all the national facilities, including civilians for war purposes?[102]

– Look at how to process the information flows: how can we distinguish the important information, intelligence services actions, etc?

The fragility of the physical facilities is probably the core of the problem of the use of telecommunication tools in war times. Cyberspace permanently gives us the image of a completely virtual world and probably makes us forget that it also relies on some facilities and that it is the first target in war.

So many questions that still are quite topical!

---

102 For this specific question of the relations between civilians and the army, we also refer the reader to a previous text by Victor Flamache published in 1882 [FLA 82]: "The application of electricity to the art of war is establishing itself more and more every day. Since the example of the Civil War in 1862, which used electrical agent in the lighting of passes, in the firing of submarine mines, of torpedo, above all in telegraphy, military science has registered to its curriculum the perfect knowledge of the multiple uses of electricity. [...] The study of electricity applied to the art of war is divided in four parts..." The first part includes "a) telegraphy; b) telephony; c) optical telegraphy [...] The question of the type of wire to use is quite important: indeed, we are seeking to hide them from the enemy, and thus the army whose bodies will be in continuous contact, will evidently put more chance of victory on its side. For this, there are two means: establishing a permanent secret communication in peace times or using flying telegraphy even organized in times of war. The first means would be excellent if we could operate without the public knowing it; but the situation is unfortunately not like that..."

3.3.9.2. *CID*

> "By (wrongfully) thinking of all the conflicts as wars, we suppose
> a bellicose nature for the entire social existence" [ARO 76].

Not all conflicts are wars. Yet, we are lacking words to describe some operations or events, borrowing the methods from the art of war. Such operations include conflicts in cyberspace, confrontations between individuals or groups, against or sometimes between States, but that are not wars, or even cyber-wars.

We are introducing the concept of confrontation in the information dimension (CID), which will designate conflicting acts carried out in cyberspace, without being completely in the domain of cyber-criminality.

CID encompasses all sociopolitical, ethnic and religious movements[103]:

– the use of social networks by citizens who are opposed to the political regime. We could speak of cyber-revolts, cyber-demonstrations, cyber-revolutions, or simply of the cybernetic dimension of protest movements;

– site defacements or virus attacks for political purposes, involving nationalist hackers or hacktivists;

– any form of political activism, whatever the subject, cause, and targets attacked (businesses and institutions).

Intelligence operations carried out by the States or by private parties are also CIDs. There are numerous intrusions into information systems by major industrial groups, who contribute through the information they enable us to draw. This also includes the industrial and economic power of the actors (we speak about economic warfare). Interference in State systems (e.g. the French Ministry of Finances in 2011 and European Commission in 2011) for political, economic or industrial purposes will also be CIDs.

CIDs are often quite close to cyber-criminality. Their actors can be sued in the States where they act and this falls within the scope of the law. Let us think here about the hacktivists who, although motivated by political objectives, remain cryber-criminals in the eyes of the law; let us again consider the 'anonymous' hackers, who although self-proclaimed or declared warriors, revolutionaries, antiglobalists, alterglobalists or anarchists, are still cyber-criminals because of the methods they use.

---

103 Athina Karatzogianni [KAR 06] identifies two main types of cyberconflicts: sociopolitical and ethno-religious.

3.4. Conclusion

Cloud computing, social networks, anarchist and terrorist threats on the Internet and cyberspace weaponization are all challenges that States (including France) must face in order to hold their position on the international scene. This is because it is from cyberspace that powerful and unexpected actors and destabilizing actions can emerge. We can also notice, however, that although technology leads to new behaviors and game rules, it also follows logic that has already been tried out. Not everything is new in the field of cybernetics, as we have been able to show during this chapter: the questions asked now are sometimes similar to those of the 19th Century, with men confronted with challenges and the hopes of a new communication technology.

French thought thus does not consider cyberspace as a distinct element, but as a subset of the information space; digital data as a subset of all data. Digitized or not, information is still information. This thought also puts men at the center of the questions, the space and the processes. This is one of the reasons why the psychological dimension has such an important position in military doctrine, for example.

The French doctrine on information warfare is thus mainly contained in the military concept of 'information operations'. But to the columns of the temple that are IOs, we must probably add civilian approaches (to control the economic warfare and the media), the concepts shared between civilians and soldiers (DCW/OCW), or even the fight against cyber-criminality in order to build a civilian–military protection continuum in the information space. In this approach, France still remains faithful to its defensive position. However, despite everything, we see the difficulty of a rule of law that we can use to protect and defend ourselves while forbidding ourselves from committing the same acts as our attackers and, facing new difficulties such as the invisibility of the attackers, the absence of a designated enemy, the permanent bypassing by the attackers of some of the security fortresses.

Will the cyber-war strategy be able to fit within the deterrence strategy of France, as stated by Senator Romani [ROM 08]? Let us moderate this argument, because deterrence works in only one condition: if the adversary is aware and convinced of the risks. The message contained in the last White Paper [LIV 08] seems clear: doctrine of information warfare or not, France is ready to fight to defend its information space. Maybe then France should refine its model? Because despite resistances, reluctances and critiques of American thought, the French model has sometimes some difficulty in distancing itself and hiding its references: the columns of the temple of information operations are still very similar to the stacking of the bricks of Libicki.

Thinking about cyber-conflict, cyber-security, cyber-defense amounts to rethinking the role and definition of the State. The Internet modifies the way in which the State should be managed. It has imposed new rules that citizens have appropriated faster than public administrations and leaders, in France and everywhere else. Mentioning the transparency brought by the Internet (everything is immediately known, information can cross the planet in a heart beat), during the opening of the e-G8 meeting in Paris on May 24, 2011 Nicolas Sarkozy declared: "[transparency] changes the management of our States and governments and in particular the reactivity. I am convinced that a head of State from 10 years ago would not recognize nowadays the control panel of their function"[104]. Governments are also realizing the importance of the influence of the street via the Internet and the pressure it can have, even if this influence is not exactly measurable (what is the share attributable to the Internet or social networks in the eviction of some heads of State; and why do others resist despite the so-called importance of these tools in revolts and popular movements?).

Leaders, such as Nicolas Sarkozy during the e-G8, seem to be convinced of the importance of the role of Internet in the expression of democratic movements. "This is not because it did not work and this is not because M. Ahmaninedjad has not been overthrown by the street that the Internet did not have a major role (Iran)"[105]. But these leaders must also wonder about the possible control of the same tools by non-democratic movements. Democracy does not have the monopoly when it comes to the use of Web 2.0.

According to the French president during e-G8, the Internet and the fate a State gives to its cyberspace conditions the position of this State on the international scene. States can be evaluated by the yardstick of the level of liberty given to the Internet: are they democratic or not? "In the name of stability, we have tolerated two German states and dictatorships. From now on, the freedom of Internet measures the scale of credibility of a democracy and of shame of a dictatorship. I add that henceforth it is difficult or even impossible for a dictator to muzzle the people in the silence of the international community"[106]. The Internet alone cannot be a good way to measure freedom and democracy or even to decide on the positioning of a State internationally. As there are operational cyber-attacks, i.e. that simply come to accompany (preparation, continuation) the operations carried in the field in all other

104 Mentioned in http://www.linformaticien.com/actualites/id/20737/n-sarkozy-l-internet-libre-est-un-marqueur-d-une-societe-democratique.aspx.
105 Nicolas Sarkozy, Paris, e-G8, 24 May 2011, mentioned in http://www.linformaticien.com/actualites/id/20737/n-sarkozy-l-internet-libre-est-un-arqueur-d-une-societe-democratique.aspx.
106 Nicolas Sarkozy, Paris, G8, 24 May 2011, quoted in http://www.linformaticien.com/actualites/id/20737/n-sarkozy-l-internet-libre-est-un-marqueur-d-une-societe-democratique.aspx.

dimensions (land, air, sea, space, political, diplomatic, economic, etc.), there is an operational dimension of the Internet whose use by any actor, in a conflicting context, can support democratic (or non-democratic) movements. The levels involved in this are not yet well-defined or controlled. Any conflict can manifest itself in cyberspace, but this dimension alone is not sufficient for a conflict. A call to demonstrate supposes that individuals then go into the streets to physically demonstrate; launching cyber-attacks against critical systems supposes that the actors involved do not have any resiliency; launching cyber-attacks with the purpose of extending them to the real and tangible world, in order to give them meaning and to make the effects concrete. Cyber-conflict encompasses combinations of actions, strategies and tactics, whether it is a civilian or military conflict.

The balance of powers between the States seems to be partially conditioned by their respective levels of cyberspace control.

During a conference in October 2010, Patrick Pailloux, director of the ANSSI declared: "In the real world, States have the monopoly of the weapons and control their diffusion via anti-dissemination treaties or via the interdiction of sales of weapons, in order to keep an advantage over citizens. In the virtual world, this is exactly the contrary: citizens have developed weapons and States are for the most part helpless. And this without thinking that the control of their diffusion is almost impossible"[107]. Rules are thus reversed. States are no longer major actors and it is difficult for them to preserve the monopoly on the use of violence. They no longer control it.

This prospect is of course debatable, because the rule is not absolute. It is quite probable that they are aware of the stakes and with respect to the measures taken in many countries (notably the creation of cyber units, cyber-forces and entities dedicated to cyber-war; deployment of significant capacities; public-private, civilian–military cooperation) States are regaining control. If there is a cyber-war, there will be cybernetic confrontations between State actors. We therefore need to know whether the States are able to regain control and keep it during cyber-conflict, or if they will be overwhelmed by actors and capacities they are unable to control and whose reactivity, adaptability and flexibility they cannot equal. (Here we are thinking about the networks built spontaneously or in the background, such as anonymous networks, hacktivist groups or other movements of the public using social networks to demonstrate against the State.)

Through the words of Pailloux, we can see a vision of the world appearing: there are States in inferior positions in comparison to other States or non-State actors.

---

107 Quoted in http://www.securityvibes.fr/cyber-pouvoirs/la-geopolitique-de-la-ssi-selon-patrick-pailloux-anssi/, October 4, 2010.

Asymmetry seems to be the rule and would by default be quite unfavorable to powerful States. This consideration also raises the question of the definition of the State: what is its area, what is a State, and what does the notion of power mean in this context?

The American Richard Clarke in his last book raised the same question. According to him, the current situation would be advantageous for States that are less dependent on cyberspace, those less developed in terms of technology and those that we would describe as weak. In this way of thinking, the most fragile, sensible, weak actor is the one that is seen as being the most dependent on cyberspace, the most economically powerful, i.e. the US. Roles are reversed. America and other great powers of this world, which are able to master technologies and cyberspace – i.e. the advanced cyber states – are the first targets for cyber-attacks. The most deprived have so little to lose that they are not very dependent on cyberspace and offer very few points of entrance for cybernetic attacks. For Jeffrey Carr [CAR 10], powerful States are also the most fragile ones and the favored targets and to find salvation, they must cooperate with the public who, with their actions, have the means to be the 'guardians of the temple'. We must not let the responsibility for national cyber-security and cyber-defense (two critical infrastructures) weigh on State actors alone. The State must finance private actors so that they can contribute to securing and strengthening national sanctuary. The logic imposed by the nature of cyberspace thus seems to oppose the rules of the real world: the strong have become the fragile ones and the weak the most powerful ones. Logic, balance of power, everything seems to be reversed and cyberspace would thus be like a negative of the real world, reversing the basic principles of geopolitics.

The basic premise of geopolitics is not questioned: the world is a jungle and the States fight each other to survive but the premise that makes States the main actors of this jungle is discussed. The relationships are not only reversed between the States. Non-State actors seem to be able to challenge the States and to compete with them. The power of cyber-citizen communities is overcoming borders, challenging the outlines of the nation-state (border and sovereignty) and bringing about new variables: cooperation, communities, shared values beyond the borders, empathy, etc.

To face these new challenges, some are calling to reconquer a fragment of technological autonomy. This attitude maintains its conventional positions: the State is defined by its borders; it can only be defended by a return of the control of its boundaries and it needs national production and industry. This introversion strategy, designed to be protective and ideal, denies the realities of the present time: technologies are dominated by the US and the control of new solutions would require financial and human investment, which are unfortunately not accessible to European countries taken separately, or possibly even Europe as a whole.

Finally, we still have to affirm the presence and power of the State within cyberspace. "The time of a finite world is starting", wrote Paul Valéry. This meant that everywhere where human settlement was possible, the State was already there. Thus, there was nothing to share and distribute to the States. It has all changed since then. Now there are spaces (extra-atmospheric space and cyberspace) that give the world the perception of infinite space again. They require us to consider the relations between the States and their positions. Nowadays, we wonder about the space: will it be American, if this is not already the case? We can ask the same question concerning cyberspace. The existence of a State is determined by three factors:

– a territory defined by fixed borders;

– a population established on this territory; and

– an organized and stable political power.

This does not exist in cyberspace, but we need to ensure its presence and mark its existence. The stakes are high. For now, it seems that the global State actors are above all concerned with the defense of their traditional borders.

3.5. Bibliography

[ANS 11] ANSSI, *Défense et Sécurité des Systèmes d'Information. Stratégie de la France*, ANSSI, Paris, France, February 2011

[ARO 76] ARON R., *Penser la Guerre*, Clausewitz, Gallimard, Paris, France, 1976

[ATT 97] ATTALI J., Le Septième Continent, August 7, 1997, available at: http://www.attali.com/ecrits/articles/nouvelle-economie/le-septieme-continent.

[BAC 27] BACON F., *New Atlantis, 1626*, Pennsylvania State University, USA, 1998, available at: http://www2.hn.psu.edu/faculty/jmanis/bacon/atlantis.pdf.

[BAR 43] BARJAVEL R., *Ravage*, Editions Denoël, France, 1943.

[BAU 08] BAUER A., "Déceler – Étudier – Former: une nouvelle voie pour la recherche stratégique, Rapport au Président de la République", *Les Cahiers de la Sécurité*, no. 4, Paris, France, March 2008, available at: http://www.iris-france.org/docs/pdf/rapports/2008-03-bauer.pdf.

[BEL 88] BELLAMY E., *Looking Backward*, William Ticknor Publ., USA, 1988.

[BEL 94] BELLOC A., *La télégraphie historique*, Librairie de Firmin-Didot Paris, France, 1894, available at: http://gallica.bnf.fr/ark:/12148/bpt6k621150/f3.image.pagination. r=guerre+t%C3%A9l%C3%A9phonie.langFR.

[BIH 10] BIHAN B., *Liberté d'Expression et Efficacité Stratégique*, Défense et Sécurité Internationale, Paris, France, no. 63, October 2010.

[BUC 09] BUCCI S., POULAIN G., *L'Alliance du Terrorisme et de la Cybercriminalité,* Défense Nationale et Sécurité Collective, Paris, France, March 2009.

[CAR 03] CARAYON B., *Intelligence Économique, Compétitivité et Cohésion Sociale, Rapport au Premier Ministre,* La Documentation Française, Paris, France, June 2003, available at: http://lesrapports.ladocumentationfrancaise.fr/BRP/034000484/0000.pdf.

[CAR 10] Carr J., *Inside Cyber Warfare,* O'Reilly, USA, 2010.

[CAV 10] CAVELTY M.D., *Cyberwar: Concepts, Status Quo, and Limitations*, CSS Analysis in Security Policy, no. 71, Zurich, Switzerland, April 2010

[CDE 05] CENTRE DE DOCTRINE D'EMPLOI DES FORCES, "Des Électrons et des Hommes. Nouvelles Technologies de l'Information et Conduite des Opérations", *Cahier de la Recherche Doctrinale,* CDEF/DREX, Paris, France, June 2005, available at: http://www.cdef.terre.defense.gouv.fr/publications/cahiers_drex/cahier_recherche/electro ns_hommes.pdf.

[COU 10] COUGHLIN C., *Gearing up to Face the Cyber Threat,* October 22, 2010, available at: http://gulfnews.com/opinions/columnists/gearing-up-to-face-the-cyber-threat-1.699920.

[DEN 01] DENNING D., *Is Cyber Terror Next?* SSRC, November 1, 2001,   available at: http://www.ssrc.org/sept11/essays/denning_text_only.htm.

[DER 95] DE ROSNAY J., *L'Homme Symbiotique. Regards sur le Troisième Millénaire,* Paris, Seuil, pp. 166-167, 1995.

[DES 07] DESPORTES V., *Décider dans l'Incertitude*, Editions Economica, 2007.

[DES 08] DESPORTES V., *La Guerre Probable*, Editions Economica, Paris, France, 2008.

[DIA 01] CICDE, *Doctrine d'Emploi des Forces, Doctrine Interarmées, DIA-01*, CICDE, Paris, France, November 2003.

[FLA 82] FLAMACHE V., *L'art de la Guerre à l'Exposition d'Électricité de Paris en 1881*, Imprimerie A. Lefevre, Brussels, Belgium, 1882, available at: http://gallica.bnf.fr/ ark:/12148/bpt6k56985449.r=guerre+t%C3%A9l%C3%A9phone.langFR.

[FRA 00] FRANCART L., *La Maîtrise de l'Information*, Paris, France 2000, available at: http://www.infoguerre.fr/doctrines/la-maitrise-de-l-information-par-le-general-loup-francart/.

[FRA 05] FRANCE A., *Sur la Pierre Blanche*, L'Humanité, Paris, France, 1905.

[GAU 92] GAUTIER E., *Les Étapes de la Science.* Chroniques Documentaires, Paris, France, 1892.

[GOD 02] GODELUCK S., *Géopolitique d'Internet*, Editions la Découverte, Paris, France, 2002.

[GOU 65] GOUDAR A., *L'Espion Chinois, ou L'Envoyé Secret de la cour de Pékin, Pour Examiner l'État Présent de l'Europe*, Cologne, volumes 1 to 6, 1765.

[GUI 95] GUISNEL J., *Guerres dans le Cyberespace*, Editions La Découverte, Paris, France, 1995.

[HAR 99] HARBULOT C., *Intelligence Économique et Guerre de l'Information*, Les Cahiers de Mars, Revue des anciens de l'Ecole Supérieure de Guerre et du Collège Interarmées de Défense, Paris, France, 1999.

[HAS 05] HASSID O., *La Gestion des Risques*, Paris, Dunod, 2005.

[HOU 08] HOUBRE J.M., Les Nouveaux Visages de la Guerre: vers le Champ de Bataille virtuel, *Télécom*, no. 152, Telecom ParisTech, Paris, France, pp. 44-48, 2008.

[HUY 01] HUYGHE F.B., *L'Ennemi à l'Ère Numérique. Chaos, Information, Domination*, PUF, Paris, France, 2001, available at: http://fr.calameo.com/read/000005 128e245e296d11c?editLinks=1.

[HUY 05] HUYGHE F.B., *Qu'est-ce que la Guerre de l'Information?*, Paris, France, 2005, http://www.huyghe.fr/dyndoc_actu/4451ebfb7de54.pdf.

[JOS 09] JOSHI S., *French Naval Rafales Grounded by Virus*, March 2, 2009, http://www.stratpost.com/french-naval-rafales-grounded-by-virus.

[KEN 10] KENYON H., *Army Cyber Unit Guards Computer Networks*, Defense Systems, October 14, 2010, available at: http://www.defensesystems.com/Articles/2010/10/15/ Cyber-Defense-Army-Cyber-Command.aspx.

[LAS 05] LASBORDES P., *La sécurité des Systèmes d'Information - un Enjeu Majeur pour la France*, 26 November 2005, available at: http://www.lasbordes.fr/IMG/pdf/rapport_ Pierre_Lasbordes.pdf.

[LET 23] LETOREY H., *Je vous Offre la Santé, la Gaieté, l'Économie, le bien être, je suis la Fée Électricité*, Le courrier de l'Oise, Imprimeries réunies de Senlis, 1923.

[LÉV 97] LÉVY P., *La Cyberculture. Rapport au Conseil de l'Europe*, Paris, Éditions Odile Jacob, 1997.

[LIB 95] LIBICKI M., *What is Information Warfare*, Strategic Forum Number 28, United States, May 1995, available at: http://ics.leeds.ac.uk/papers/pmt/exhibits/ 1660/Libicki_What_Is.pdf.

[LIV 06] Livre Blanc du Gouvernement sur la Sécurité Intérieure Face au Terrorisme, La Documentation Française, Paris, France, June 2006, available at: http://lesrapports.ladocumentationfrancaise.fr/BRP/064000275/0000.pdf.

[LIV 08] Livre blanc sur la Sécurité et la Défense Nationale, La Documentation Française, Paris, France, June 2008, available at: http://lesrapports.ladocumentationfrancaise.fr/cgi-bin/brp/telestats.cgi?brp_ref=084000341&brp_file=0000.pdf.

[LON 94] LONG M., BALLADUR E., LÉOTARD F., *Livre Blanc sur la Défense*, La Documentation Française, Paris, France, June 1994.

[MAR 94] MARTRE H., *Intelligence économique et stratégie des entreprises*, La Documentation française, Paris, France, 1994, available at: http://lesrapports.ladocumentation française.fr/BRP/074000410/0000.pdf.

[MDF 07] Glossaire Interarmées de Terminologie Opérationnelle, Etat-Major des Armées, Ministère de la Défense, March 8, 2007, Paris, France, available at: http://www.cicde.defense.gouv.fr/IMG/pdf/PIA/CPIA/PIA_0-5-5-2.pdf

[NAN 11] NANSOUTY M., *Actualités Scientifiques*, Paris, France, Librairie Schleicher Frères, 1911, http://gallica.bnf.fr/ark:/12148/bpt6k5684032v/f000023.

[NOR 78] NORA S., MINC A., *L'Informatisation de la Société*, Seuil, Collection Points, Paris, France, 1978.

[PIA 10] PIA-00-100, *Concept d'Emploi des Forces*, Etat-major des armées, CICDE. No. 004, DEF/CICDE/NP, January 11, 2010, Paris, France, available at: http://www.cicde.defense.gouv.fr/IMG/pdf/PIA/PIA-00.100.pdf.

[POI 94] POINSARD L., PICHON F., Etudes de droit international conventionnel, Paris, France, 1894. available at: http://gallica.bnf.fr/ark:/12148/bpt6k56295720/f000333. tableDesMatieres.

[ROB 83] ROBIDA A., *Le Vingtième Siècle*, Georges Decaux, Paris, France, 1883.

[ROM 08] ROMANI R., Rapport d'Information Fait au nom de la Commission des Affaires Étrangères, de la Défense et des Forces Armées, sur la Cyberdéfense, Senate, report no. 449, Paris, France, July 8, 2008. The report is available at: http://www.senat.fr/rap/r07-449/r07-4491.pdf.

[SCH 94] SCHWARTAU W., *Information Warfare: Chaos on the Electronic Superhighway*, New York, Thunder's Mouth Press, 1994

[SEC 10] Securing Britain in an age of uncertainty: the strategic defence and security review, Presented to Parliament by the Prime Minister, October 2010, London, UK, available at: http://www.direct.gov.uk/prod_consum_dg/groups/dg_digitalassets/@dg/@en/documents /digitalasset/dg_191634.pdf?CID=PDF&PLA=furl&CRE=sdsr

[VEN 07] VENTRE D., *La Guerre de l'Information*, Hermès-Lavoisier, Paris, France, 2007.

[VEN 09] VENTRE D., *Information Warfare*, ISTE, London, John Wiley & Sons, New York, 2009.

[VEN 10] VENTRE D. (ed.), CHAUVANCY F., HUYGHE F.B., FILLIOL E., HENROTIN J., *Cyberguerre et Guerre de l'Information. Stratégies, Règles, Enjeux*, Hermès Lavoisier, Paris, France, 2010

[VEN 11] VENTRE D., *Cyberespace et acteurs du cyberconflit*, Hermès-Lavoisier, Paris, France, 2011.

[VEN 11_b] VENTRE D., *Cyberattaque et Cyberdéfense*, Hermès-Lavoisier, Paris, France, 2011.

[WAU 98] WAUTELET M., *Les cyberconflits, Internet, autoroutes de l'information et cyberspace: quelles menaces?*, Editions GRIP, Brussels, Belgium, 1998, available at: http://www.technolytics.com/Technolytics_Cyber_Warfare_Training.pdf.

[WEU 02] WEULERSSE G., *Chine Ancienne et Nouvelle, Impressions et Réflexions*, Armand Colin, Paris, France, 1902.

Chapter 4

Digital Sparta: Information Operations and Cyber-warfare in Greece

The intense scholarly debate about information operations and cyber-warfare tends to be dominated by the American experience. This is to some extent justified; but the reality is that national doctrines of information operations and cyber-warfare are as varied as human fingerprints. Countries do not enter the sphere of the information society in a vacuum. Instead, they carry their particular historical experiences and strategic concerns with them. These are instrumental in shaping national cyber-warfare doctrines with distinct features, reflecting the geopolitical identity of each nation.

Such varied doctrines combine the military and civilian dimensions of information operations. The formal origins of information operations are undoubtedly military [VEN 09]; yet it would be an error to limit our understanding of the broader concept of information operations to the context of war, or even to the military realm altogether. Although they include traditional military components, such as deception or psychological warfare, information operations extend to areas more closely associated with intelligence and network warfare – that is, offensive and defensive information operations implemented in times of peace [VEN 09]. Examples of such operations range from the 1982 explosion of the Urengoy-Surgut-Chelyabinsk natural gas pipeline in Siberia due to defective computer systems supplied by the United States (US) Central Intelligence Agency (CIA) to unsuspecting Soviet engineers [WEI 96], to the 2010 Stuxnet computer virus that targeted the technical infrastructure of the Iranian nuclear energy program [FAL 10].

Chapter written by Joseph FITSANAKIS.

The connections between military and civilian information operations are critical for the full comprehension of cyber-warfare, which is a relatively new concept that tends to blend conventional distinctions between domestic and international security, military and civilian targets, and even warfare domains. It is also important for understanding the doctrinal framework within which countries other than the US, with more limited defense postures and strictly peripheral security concerns, approach cyber-warfare. Greece is a case in point.

4.1. Geopolitical significance

Arguably, Greece may not be the first nation that comes to mind when considering national conceptions of cyber-warfare and information operations. The country's small size and weak economy inevitably place it among the more marginal of Western states. Moreover, there appears to be consensus, even among Greek scholars [KON 88], that Greece's geopolitical weight has diminished in the post-Soviet environment. Additionally, it may be argued that the recent implosion of the Greek economy has severely constrained the country's strategic maneuvering [ANO 11b]. This section aims to show that dismissing Greece's relevance in the domain of cyber-warfare would be myopic – indeed dangerous. If anything, the country's geopolitical significance is such that Greece's international stature far exceeds the narrow parameters of its small armed forces and relatively weak economy. In other words, dismissive views of Greece's structural and economic weaknesses ought to be tempered by the elevated geopolitical framework of the country's wider region, in which even nations of diminished regional importance remain significant in the global domain.

Although an integral part of the Balkans, Greece's geopolitical standing rests on its geographical position in the immediate periphery of the Middle East. Its 16,000 km coastline, which is dotted with indispensable military outposts on islands like Crete, Rhodes and the Republic of Cyprus, allows it to monitor – and often directly engage in – the prolonged crisis in the Middle East [DEM 99]. The Balkan Wars of the 1990s, the rise of Islamic fundamentalism and the wave of popular revolts that swept Arab countries in 2010 and 2011 serve as reminders of Greece's continuing geopolitical relevance in the post-Cold War environment. Moreover, its crucial position at the transcontinental crossroads of Europe, Asia and Africa provides it with strategic proximity to the Dardanelles and the Suez Canal, two critical transportation junctures that link the Mediterranean with the energy-rich regions of the Black Sea and the Persian Gulf, respectively [DEM 99].

Though severely hampered in recent times, Greece's economy is important, too. The international weight of the Greek economic sector should not be underestimated. In the 14 years immediately preceding 2008, the country's gross domestic product rose by between 3% to nearly 6% annually, making the Greek economy one of the world's fastest-growing [LIV 10]. Even in times of economic crisis, its economy is listed among the world's 30 wealthiest [BAK 10, LIV 10], only 15 times smaller than that of China and four times smaller than that of India – whose population sizes exceed Greece's by a factor of up to 160 [BAK 10]. Greece's employee sector, one of the world's most highly educated and multilingual [BAK 10], is largely responsible for the Greek economy's impressive peripheral role in recent years [TAY 03]. This allows the country to regularly influence patterns of political interaction in the Balkans and southern Europe [MOU 07]. Greek-registered companies active in the Balkans have invested over $20 billion in the fields of telecommunications, energy, food production and distribution, and banking [BAK 10, TAY 03]. Greece's role is particularly notable in the latter: as of 2010, 30% of bank headquarters in the Balkan region (including Turkey) belonged to Greek companies, which operated as many as 3,500 bank branches throughout the region [BAK 10, LIV 10]. The regional role of the Greek finance sector, coupled with Greece's absorption of over a million laborers from Balkan countries, can be partially credited for helping stabilize the economies of the Balkan region during the crucial post-1991 transitional period [BAK 10].

The peripheral weight of Greece's finance sector is coupled by the country's formidable seafaring power. In 2010, Greece boasted the world's second-largest merchant naval fleet, with ownership of nearly 20% of the world's total fleet[1] [LIV 10]. Greeks own over half the European Union's (EU) merchant navy, making the country's role in European civilian naval transportation comparable to Germany's role in the area of heavy industry. In 2010, nearly 60% of the EU's total exportation of goods and products to China, and 35% of its exports to the US, was facilitated though Greek-owned ships [BAK 10].

The country is also gradually transforming itself into a telecommunications hub for the Eastern European and Balkan regions [TAY 03], fulfilling an infrastructural function similar to that of Cyprus in the Near East. The Athens-based Hellenic Telecommunications Organization (OTE) and its subsidiary, CosmOTE, own majority or minority shares in telecommunications providers in Armenia, Ukraine, Romania, Serbia, Bulgaria, Albania, Turkey and elsewhere [TAY 03]. Furthermore, Greece's strategic location positions it at the heart of some of the Internet's most crucial fiber optic "choke-points" [ANO 10c], which facilitate undersea digital traffic patterns from the Middle East, to Europe, Central Asia and beyond.

---

1   See United Nations 2007 Review of Maritime Transport: http://www.unctad.org/en/docs/rmt2007_en.pdf and also British Embassy in Athens' publication Marine Sector Report in Greece" (2009), section 1.2: available at http://www.britishmarine.co.uk/pdf/Marine%20Sector%20Report%20Greece%20May%2020 09.pdf.

Last, though certainly not least, Greece's geopolitical significance can be expected to increase due to its inclusion in planned energy distribution routes connecting Europe to Russia and Central Asia [KER 04, DEM 99]. In 1994, Russia, Bulgaria and Greece drafted plans to construct the trans-Balkan oil pipeline, which would enable Russia to transfer oil from Novorossiysk to the Aegean Sea while bypassing the Turkish Straits [DEK 03]. The project, known as the Burgas–Alexandroupolis pipeline, has been stalled, but if completed it will facilitate an alternative oil route to the Western-sponsored Baku–Tbilisi–Ceyhan pipeline, and will constitute the first-ever Russian-controlled pipeline on EU territory [LUF 09, GRA 09]. Since 2007, a new natural gas pipeline has connected Turkey and Greece, allowing the latter to receive some Azerbaijani gas, which marks the first-ever gas supply from the Caspian region to the EU. If plans to extend the supply into Italy through the proposed Interconnector Turkey–Greece–Italy pipeline materialize, the route will provide two – and potentially more – EU Member States with natural gas from a source other than Russia [NIC 11]. There are also plans for an extension to the Nabucco pipeline, which would carry Iraqi and Central Asian natural gas supplies to Greece and Italy [TAG 09].

The above analysis demonstrates that Greece's international stature far exceeds the narrow parameters of its small size and relatively weak economy. Despite its diminutive standing within the Western context, its geopolitical position is anything but trivial. A severe Greek crisis, whether sociopolitical, economic or military in nature, would bear immediate, extensive and multifaceted consequences for southeast Europe, the Balkans, the Middle East, and several international organizations, including the EU and the North Atlantic Treaty Organization (NATO), for which Greece serves as "a sensitive strategic outpost" [TSA 04] across several troubled regions [KOF 03].

Greece's geopolitical importance is inevitably reflected in the information environment. Should the country be threatened or otherwise destabilized by coordinated cyber-attacks on its information networks, similar to those experienced by Estonia in 2007 and Georgia in 2008 [ANO 10b], spillover effects could massively impact on international shipping patterns, energy transportation networks, global banking, NATO military and communications assets, and regional telecommunications systems, to name but a few. Perhaps more importantly, Greece's geopolitical attributes are decisive in helping formulate the country's conception of information operations and cyber-warfare, as will become evident further on in this chapter.

4.2. Strategic concerns and internal balancing

Another factor in shaping Greek conceptions of information operations and cyber-warfare is the country's immediate and long-term strategic concerns, particularly in relation to the age-old Greek–Turkish rivalry. The latter, in its ethnic/religious dimension, or as part of imperial policies during the Byzantine and Ottoman periods, has been a feature of regional politics for over 10 centuries [KER 04]. Since its independence in the first half of the 19th Century, the Greek state has never made a major strategic policy decision without considering its potential impact on its balance of power with the Ottoman Empire/Turkey [TAY 03]. This includes the period of the Cold War – particularly after 1974, when Greek strategic thinking reflected relations with Turkey to a far higher degree than relations with the Soviet Union or countries aligned to it [TSA 04].

Throughout modern times, the Greek–Turkish bilateral relationship has been one "of low-intensity conflict disrupted by shorter or longer détentes [periods of relaxation]" [GÜN 05]. Periods of the absence of war have usually been tense and viewed on both sides of the Aegean as opportunities to prepare plans for future wars [KON 88]. This prolonged tension is driven by mutual suspicion and the perception that the other side is actively "harboring aggressive designs" [AYD 04], even when discernible evidence points to the contrary. Spiraling suspicion has helped solidify a bilateral framework of conflict-oriented power-politics, in which preemption and domination often supersede balancing behavior or the establishment of mutual security objectives [AYD 04]. Today, individual issues of contention between the two nations typically blend into a unified system of recrimination and retort. Such issues include the political independence of Greek religious institutions in Turkey, the ethnic character of the Muslim minority in northeastern Greece, and the control of territorial waters, mineral rights, airspace and even small islets in the Aegean Sea [NAC 03]. In 1996, the two countries came dangerously close to war over one such disputed pair of uninhabited islets. Known as the Imia/Kardak crisis, the heated episode cost the lives of three Greek military officers, when their helicopter crashed over the islets – some argue due to live fire shot from a Turkish warship [HAD 99]. The crisis led to the eventual dismissal of the Chief of the Hellenic National Defense General Staff at the time (the commander of all Greek armed forces), Admiral Christos Limberis.

By far the most dominant issue, however, in terms of impact on Greek strategic thinking, is the Turkish military occupation of northern territories in the Republic of Cyprus. Before 1974, when Turkey invaded the majority Greek-speaking island in response to a coup led by Greek ultranationalists, Greece had implemented a policy of appeasement against Turkey, while maintaining a "modicum of [...] autonomy and independence" [KOF 03] from the US. Its entry into NATO in 1952, along with Turkey, was a major component of that policy, which rested on the belief that the

US would protect Greece from perceived Turkish aggression, in order to maintain the stability of NATO and direct unified Member State resources against the Warsaw Pact [KER 07, NAC 03]. Washington's failure to prevent Turkey's invasion of Cyprus, however, shattered Greek strategic thinking almost overnight. Athens faced the reality of violent conflict, and experienced a potentially direct threat to its territorial integrity by a fellow-NATO Member State. This highly traumatic experience led Greek planners to redirect their strategic resources to internal balancing [TSA 04], namely strengthening Greece's armed forces in direct competition with its eastern neighbor [TSA 04, KER 04]. As a result of this policy, by 1992 the Greek state was the industrialized world's second-largest weapons purchaser [MOU 07]. Greece's internal balancing trajectory, which has been sustained in recent years by regional instability in the Balkans and the Middle East, remains high in defiance of declining average defense spending rates among NATO and EU countries [TSA 04, NAC 03].

The process of internal balancing in Greek strategic thinking, which encompasses the country's information operations doctrine, rests on visions of technological superiority. The latter are viewed as the key to counteracting Turkey's geopolitical advantages, as perceived by Greek defense planners [FIT 10a]. These perceptions include Greece's lack of strategic depth, which exposes virtually all of its major population and military production centers to the reach of Turkish artillery, as well as its physically fragmented territory, composed largely of thousands of hard-to-defend islands and islets. They also incorporate what is known in Greece as 'the demographic problem', namely the growing population disparity between Greece's 10 million aging inhabitants and Turkey's youthful populace, which is widely expected to reach 100 million by the year 2020 [KON 88, NAC 03]. More importantly, modern Greece is seen as lacking what some theorists call a 'geopolitical dynamic' [KON 88], namely a set of historical and political regional ambitions that can, under certain conditions, unify its population and motivate it to constantly rise above its insecurities and inhibitions [KON 88]. It can be argued that this view ignores the multitude of Turkey's internal limitations and inconsistencies, such as its often schizophrenic relationship with Europe and the Middle East – including Israel – as well as its fragmented religious, ethnic and class composition, which can be said to lie behind the country's prolonged political instability [DEM 99]. Nevertheless, the view of Turkey's geopolitical dynamic as somehow more vigorous compared to that of Greece is a driving perception among Greek defense planners [FIT 10a]. The latter view Turkey's internal inconsistencies as potentially empowering Ankara's regional ambitions, by acting as a discharging mechanism for impulsive expansionist tendencies harbored among ultranationalist military circles [KON 88].

4.3. Formative experiences in information operations: the Ergenekon conspiracy

Conceptions of information operations in Greece reflect the dominant views of defense policy experts about Turkey's vigorous and impulsive geopolitical dynamic. They are also shaped by defining moments in information operations experienced by Greek planners since the late 1990s. One such defining moment centers on revelations in Turkey of what has come to be known as the Ergenekon affair – an alleged alliance of military and intelligence officers in pursuit of secular and ultranationalist objectives. The Ergenekon conspiracy, which was partly neutralized by the Turkish government in the years following 2007, appears to have been part of what observers describe as Turkey's 'deep state'. The term signifies a covert network of influential individuals operating within the country's security state apparatus, who view themselves as custodians of Turkey's secularist and nationalist traditions [ANO 10a]. The Ergenekon conspiracy involved, among other things, a series of coup plots, terrorist acts and other sophisticated criminal schemes, some dating as far back as 2001. These were all aimed at destabilizing, or altogether terminating, the government of the pro-Islamic Justice and Development Party. Since 2007, an ongoing legal investigation into the affair has involved the detention of over 200 prominent figures involved in Ergenekon's civilian, paramilitary and intelligence wings [ANO 10a].

According to the public indictment drafted by the Turkish state prosecutor, several of Ergenekon's plots involved information operations – particularly black propaganda and false flag operations – directed against Greece and Greek national and regional interests. They included the planned assassination of Ecumenical Patriarch Bartholomew I of Constantinople, the prelate of the Eastern Orthodox Church, which would be subsequently blamed on Kurdish paramilitaries [ANO 10a]. Another plot involved "the shooting down of one of Turkey's own F-16 fighters over the Aegean Sea, which was to be blamed on the Greeks" [ANO 10a], presumably in an attempt to destabilize bilateral relations between Greece and Turkey and unify the Turkish population in support of the country's military. Thankfully, Ergenekon was penetrated by the Turkish authorities before these activities were carried out.

One of Ergenekon's information operations did, however, materialize. In October 2009, an anonymous letter from a whistleblower revealed the existence of a detailed sub-operation under a broader political destabilization program entitled "Action Plan to Fight Reactionaryism" – a term used by the Turkish military to refer to non-secular political views. The sub-operation proposal had initially been drafted by Turkish Army Colonel Dursun Çiçek, following explicit directives in 2000 by the Office of Prime Minister Bülent Ecevit. Brigadier General Hıfzı Çubuklu, legal adviser to the Turkish Armed Forces General Staff, which took control of the operation, handed it over to its Third Information Support Unit. The latter implemented it under direct supervision by Deputy Chief of General Staff General Hasan Iğsız. According to Istanbul's 13th High Criminal Court, which began pursuing the case in March 2010, General Iğsız provided regular updates about the operation to the Chief of General Staff, General İlker Başbuğ [YEN 10].

The court indictment explains that the operation had a two-fold mission, centering on information collection and active propaganda. On one hand, the Third Information Support Unit was tasked with systematically monitoring the activities of over 400 Turkish and foreign-language websites. The latter were carefully targeted for allegedly supporting "reactionaryist" politics, "separatist" causes, the Justice and Development Party views, as well as voicing criticism of the Turkish armed forces. The more sinister aspect of the operation involved the clandestine creation of 42 websites aimed at disseminating fabricated information against groups and individuals deemed as adversaries by the Turkish military. According to court documents, the ultimate goal was to "gain public support regarding a possible military coup and mislead public opinion in line with the alleged coup plotters' aims" [YEN 10].

The websites and Internet domains, which were provided by Middle East Software Services Inc., a now-defunct internet provider with links to the Turkish military, were maintained for several years by active and retired Turkish military personnel. Many of these online propaganda outlets acted as far-reaching vehicles of psychological warfare directed specifically toward destabilizing Greece, a goal that appears to have been perceived by Ergenekon's members as somehow advantageous to Turkish national interests. The websites included cameria.org, which openly promoted irredentist claims against northwestern Greek territories in pursuit of the creation of a "Greater Albania". They also included greekmurderers.net that, according to the Ergenekon public indictment, was created and maintained using IP addresses belonging to the Turkish Ministry of National Defense [YEN 10]. At the time of writing, the case remains under examination by Turkish government prosecutors. Ongoing investigations have led to the arrest of at least one retired Turkish military officer, Ataman Yildirim, who was indicted in 2009 for creating and maintaining 35 of the propaganda websites [ANO 09b].

4.4. Formative experiences in information operations: intensifying cyber-attacks

Greek defense planners have been evaluating the Ergenekon revelations in the wider context of computer hacking and cyber-espionage operations against Greek government information networks and databases, which have intensified since 2007. Until that time, most cyber-attacks detected against the Greek state involved symbolic defacements of websites, perpetrated by individuals or groups using crude methodology and boasting ideological, but no operational, allegiance with foreign governments. The three-day attack by a group of Turkish self-described 'Patriotic Hackers' in 2006, which defaced and later disrupted the operations of several websites owned and operated by the Greek Ministry of National Defense, was typical of the pre-2007 period [ANO 10g, FIT 10b]. Since that time, cyber-attacks against Greek civilian and military networks have increased exponentially in frequency, technical sophistication and operational scope [FIT 10b]. In the last few months of 2010 alone, Albanian hackers disabled the Hellenic Centre for Marine Research network in Heraklion, Crete. This network operates POSEIDON, a leading maritime weather forecasting system that is consulted by merchant and civil transportation vessels transiting through Greek territorial waters [ANO 10e]. The Greek Ministry of National Defense also reported a 'very skilled' [ANO 10f] cyber-espionage attack against its online network, during which intruders managed to get into the code-protected part of the system and appeared to be specifically pursuing access to classified documentation. The Ministry's cyber-defense system experts reportedly managed to repel the intrusion, but not without resorting to shutting down the entire network, causing severe operational problems across online defense systems nationwide [ANO 10g].

4.5. Formative experiences in information operations: the Öcalan affair

Several instances of cyber-attacks against Greek networks arguably go unreported or even undetected. Those that are reported would seem to indicate that Greek cyber-defense planners are gradually overcoming the naïveté that until recently plagued Greek conceptions of information operations. This naïveté was publicly displayed in February of 1999, when Turkish government forces captured Kurdish separatist leader Abdullah Öcalan.

Until 1998, Öcalan, founder of the Kurdistan Workers' Party (PKK), which campaigns for the creation of a Kurdish State incorporating territories in Turkey's southeastern Anatolia region, was based in Damascus, Syria. Due to concerted diplomatic pressure by Turkey and other NATO Member States, Öcalan was forced to abandon his Syrian command center and seek political asylum in a number of European countries, including Italy and Russia. Traveling clandestinely around Europe, he was eventually transported to Greece on January 30, 1998 on a private plane owned by a retired Greek military officer.

Despite the fact that Öcalan was wanted in Turkey for participating in armed attacks and for fomenting a bloody 15-year civil war that cost the lives of nearly 40,000 people [ANO 99b, KER 07], the Greek government chose to shelter the Kurdish separatist, eventually smuggling him into the compound of its Embassy in

Nairobi, Kenya. The decision was unfortunate on numerous levels, not least in ignoring Washington's active interest in seeing Öcalan captured [WEI 99], and in overlooking the massive presence of over 100 US intelligence personnel in Nairobi in the aftermath of the bombing of the US Embassy there the previous August [FAL 09].

Soon after Öcalan's arrival in Nairobi, on February 2, US intelligence officers placed the Embassy's landline and cellular communications under surveillance, before tipping off Turkish and Kenyan authorities about the PKK leader's whereabouts [FAL 09, WEI 99]. A few days later, a team consisting of members of Turkish Special Forces and officers of Turkey's National Intelligence Organization (MİT) arrived secretly in Nairobi and were deployed around the Greek Embassy compound, guided by constant human and technical intelligence from the US side [NOM 10]. On February 15, a two-car convoy left the Greek Embassy for the Jomo Kenyatta International Airport in Nairobi, where Öcalan was scheduled to board a plane *en route* to Amsterdam, Holland. Unbeknownst to Greek officials, however, the Kenyan acting as Öcalan's driver that day was secretly collaborating with American and Turkish intelligence. Shortly before reaching the airport, he suddenly changed course and drove Öcalan to Wilson Airport, a smaller airfield for light aircraft located at the southern outskirts of the Kenyan capital [FAL 09]. At Wilson Airport, Öcalan was delivered into the hands of Turkey's MİT and was immediately flown, handcuffed and blindfolded, to Turkey, prompting a wave of national jubilation [WEI 99].

For Greece, the diplomatic and political fallout of Öcalan's abduction by the MİT from the hands of Greek officials is difficult to overstate. The Turkish government's public response to the capture appeared to have been prepared prior to Öcalan's arrest. In scope and intensity it resembled the propaganda victory scored by the Soviet Union against the US following the 1960 U-2 Incident. Ankara supplied information to the Kurdish community implying that the Greek authorities had surrendered Öcalan to Turkey, prompting an unprecedented Kurdish wave of anti-Greek demonstrations and attacks against Greek embassies and consulates worldwide. On the international front, Turkey publicized intelligence showing details of the way in which the Greek authorities had smuggled the Kurdish leader into Greece and Kenya. The intelligence included a copy of a Cypriot diplomatic passport bearing Öcalan's picture, confiscated from Öcalan's by MİT officers following his arrest. The passport allowed the PKK leader to travel around the world under the assumed name of Lazaros Mavros. Interestingly, the Cypriot government later denied that the passport was diplomatic, but it did not address the question of its issuance [ANO 99a]. The stunning revelations led directly to a political crisis in Athens and the resignation of three senior Greek government ministers, while relations between Greece and Turkey plummeted to what was arguably their lowest level since the 1974 invasion of Cyprus [KER 07].

More importantly, the Öcalan affair displayed astonishing inexperience and staggering innocence about communications surveillance – and information operations in general – on behalf of Greek officials and Greece's National Intelligence Service (EYP). Greek diplomats appeared to be unaware of the importance of forbidding the Kurdish leader to use his unencrypted cellular telephone while under their protection. They also failed to comprehend the degree to which their diplomatic communications were vulnerable to outside penetration. Remarkably, Athens' instruction to its diplomats in Nairobi to transport Öcalan to the airport came via a call over an unprotected telephone line, in which a Greek government official used 'code-words' to tell the diplomats that Öcalan had to leave the embassy [THO 09].

The operational role of the Greek and Turkish intelligence services in the Öcalan affair appears to have been minimal, compared to that of the US [FAL 09]. The episode, however, showed Greek defense and intelligence planners that they had severely underestimated the degree to which Greece's defensive info-dominance – that is, its ability to defend the integrity of its information and communications systems – had been compromised by the US, and possibly other countries. Contrasting Greece's handling of Öcalan with that of Italy in this context is revealing: the Italians – though uneasy – chose to publicly reveal Öcalan's presence in their country, even though the Kurdish leader had entered the country seemingly undetected, under an alias, using forged travel documents. Realizing the ominous merging of America's strategic interests in Turkey and the Near East, and the panoply of the superpower's technical collection capabilities, the Italian government consciously chose to handle Öcalan's case via relatively open diplomatic and judicial channels. In contrast, Greece opted for a conventional secretive methodology that took no notice of the country's informational vulnerabilities and landed Greek diplomacy one of its most damaging operational fiascos in recent history, while also exposing the Greek state to national and international condemnation [FIT 99].

4.6. Formative experiences in information operations: the Greek wiretapping case of 2004–2005

Shortly after the Öcalan fiasco, Greece may have once again become the target of America's information operations arsenal. In the spring of 1999, US President Bill Clinton reportedly authorized the CIA to hack into the bank accounts of Slobodan Milosevic in Greece, Cyprus and Russia, and 'waste' the Yugoslav President's personal funds [VOS 99].

Using computers to hack into a personal or corporate bank account and transfer funds by manipulating the SWIFT (Society for Worldwide Interbank Financial

Telecommunications) global financial messaging network is theoretically possible. The technical complexities involved in such an operation, however, raise doubts as to whether the action actually occurred [SIN 00]. Moreover, depending on the particular banks in Greece where the late Yugoslav President kept his private funds, such actions could constitute cyber-espionage against assets administered by the Greek state, which at the time was informally supporting Serbia's position in the Yugoslav wars [HEN 06]. In any case, Greek, Cypriot and American officials have never directly commented on the CIA computer-hacking allegations.

A far more significant and damaging case of cyber-espionage erupted in Greece a year and a half after the 2004 Summer Olympic Games in Athens. On February 2, 2006, the Greek daily newspaper *Ta Nea* published allegations of a major security breach at the digital telephone exchanges of Vodafone Greece, the Greek subsidiary of London-based Vodafone Group, which is the world's second-largest cellular telecommunications provider. Later on that same day, the Greek government publicly admitted that it had been aware of the breach for almost a year, but had kept it secret. It also acknowledged that the breach first occurred sometime before the 2004 Olympic Games and that it continued uninterrupted until it was uncovered on March 7, 2005 [SAM 10]. According to the information presented by the government, unknown culprits had surreptitiously installed complex software from inside Vodafone's central traffic handling system, which compromised the privacy of over 100 cellular telephone numbers belonging to current and former Greek civilian and military officials and public figures. Telephone numbers affected by the breach included those of the prime minister, his wife, the foreign minister and his deputy, the ministers of justice, public order, and public works, the mayor of the city of Athens, most of the country's senior police officers, the former minister of defense, the former head of EYP, as well as dozens of parliamentarians, journalists and other public figures [SAM 10, NOM 10].

What made the interception scheme so extensive and effective was that the software that facilitated it had been installed directly on four AXE (automatic cross-connection equipment) telephone exchanges manufactured and supplied to Vodafone by its chief hardware vendor, Ericsson Telecommunications, in collaboration with Athens-based Intracom Telecom [PRE 07, LEY 07]. The software, which consisted of nearly 6,500 lines of code, was essentially a rootkit, enabling its creators to access the system without being detected. Once installed and activated, most likely by a person inside Vodafone or Ericsson [SAM 10], the rootkit seamlessly duplicated and redirected cellular voice traffic to 14 prepaid and unregistered mobile telephones [BLU 09, SAM 10]. In doing so, it relied on pre-established traffic redirection functionality that is used to enable lawful interception of targeted telephone communications by Greek law enforcement and intelligence agencies [BLU 09]. The interception would most likely have continued indefinitely, had it not been detected by Ericsson technicians following complaints about undelivered short message service (SMS) texts by Vodafone Greece customers [SAM 10, TSA 04].

The rootkit was written in the PLEX (Programming Language for Exchanges) source code, a specialized programming language only common among highly trained digital switch software writers [FRA 08]. This led most expert observers, including Vodafone Greece CEO Giorgos Koronias, to deduce that "the perpetrators of the phone-tapping belong to the secret service of a major power" [FRA 08, SAM 10]. A subsequent technical study revealed that the antennae that facilitated the redirections of intercepted communications were located inside apartments in the vicinity of the US Embassy in Athens, giving some credence to the dominant theory that the interceptions were orchestrated by the CIA, the US National Security Agency, or both [NOM 10, SAM 10]. Such accounts, however, remain unconfirmed and therefore speculative [SAM 10].

The operation's culprits aside, there has been fervent debate about the strong possibility that one or more technicians inside Vodafone or Ericsson were involved in the scheme. The debate intensified considerably after it was discovered that Vodafone executives first informed the government about the existence of the wiretaps on March 10, 2005, one day after Vodafone Greece network manager Costas Tsalikidis was found hanged in his Athens apartment [PRE 07, GAL 06]. Vodafone Greece has denied any connection between Tsakalidis' apparent suicide and the company's timing in informing the Greek government about the existence of the wiretaps [GAL 06]. Tsakalidis' family insist that he was killed because he accidentally discovered the wiretaps; but Brady Kiesling, a retired US State Department diplomat who was stationed at the US Embassy in Athens for a total of nine years, has put forward the theory that Tsakalidis may have actually been employed by US intelligence as a 'Trojan horse' to install and activate the rootkit from inside Vodafone's central traffic handling system [GAL 06]. Kiesling argues that Tsakalidis may have committed suicide once his role in the affair was discovered, "to protect his professional honor" [GAL 06].

Though important in a political sense, the identity of the culprits does not affect the operational significance of the wiretap conspiracy: its discovery marked the first known major infiltration of a cellular telephone system anywhere in the world; the entire scheme combined a degree of operational audacity and technical sophistication "rarely seen before or since" [PRE 07, SAM 10]. Furthermore, the exceptional nature and extent of penetration of Vodafone's computers caused the biggest cyber-espionage scandal ever to engulf a major cellular telecommunications provider [PRE 07], with far-reaching implications for communications security in the deregulated wireless environment [FRA 08, FIT 03]. It also had an 'immediate impact' [FIT 10b] on Greek cyber-defense planners' understanding of information security. For the first time in history, the Greek state publicly acknowledged that it had been subjected to a severe and protracted communications penetration affecting its executive, law enforcement, intelligence and military echelons [SAM 10]. By doing so, it also acknowledged its failure to protect its sensitive communications and the secrecy of internal decision-making processes about critical affairs of state at the highest levels of government [PRE 07, SAM 10].

Due to the technical methodology and the selected targets of the wiretapping case, Greek cyber-defense planners regarded it as a computer network exploitation operation, which had a direct and prolonged psychological impact on intelligence, military and civilian decision-makers in the country [FIT 10b]. Moreover, the series of computer forensic errors by Ericsson and Vodafone technicians, who essentially tipped off the perpetrators of the wiretaps before they could be detained [PRE 07], generated a new and ongoing process of technical negotiation between the EYP and the telecommunications industry in Greece, which remains classified, but which knowledgeable insiders describe as "fruitful [and] long overdue" [FIT 10b].

4.7. Emerging civilian information operations strategies

There is little doubt that the Öcalan affair, the 2004–2005 Vodafone wiretapping, and, more recently, the Ergenekon conspiracy caused great concern among Greek political decision-makers and defense planners alike. To some degree, this concern has proved constructive. This is because, though regrettable, the fallout from these experiences was both political and technological. It therefore vividly highlighted – even to non-experts – the need to reinterpret Greece's traditional geopolitical concerns and strategic interests through the all-encompassing prism of the information society. "For the first time [after the exposure of the 2004–2005 Vodafone wiretapping] we were able to explain to the political leadership the significance of defending the country against network warfare", says a Greek cyber-defense expert involved in national planning [FIT 10d]. "This was in the aftermath of the most serious espionage scandal in Greek history, so for the first time we had the impression that they were truly listening to us" [FIT 10d]. At the same time, a younger generation of technologically savvy political decision-makers is gradually taking control of Greek political institutions – a cathartic side-effect of the European sovereign debt crisis, which is washing away some of the old political power structures. These new leaders appear to be more aware of, and interested in, issues around information security and cyber-defense. A typical example is that of General Secretary of Telecommunications, Dr Socrates Katsikas, who joined the Ministry of Infrastructure, Transport and Networks in 2009 after having directed the graduate program on networked systems security at the University of Piraeus.

There is, therefore, a general sense among national planners in Greece's cyber-defense community that, through the experiences detailed above, the country's decision-making bodies have grown progressively aware of the country's vulnerability to cyber-attacks, as Greece becomes increasingly reliant on computer networks [GRI 08, MAT 02]. It is probably too early to speculate about the precise shape of Greek cyber-defense and cyber-security in the years to come; as of 2010, the country's civilian and military institutions did not subscribe to a common national cyber-security policy [ILI 10c]. This, however, is hardly unique in the field of cyber-security. Even the US, which is arguably among the global leaders in the field, did not operate on a formal concept of information warfare until 1992, while the three main branches of its military have only recently begun to explore the possibility of sharing a common information warfare doctrine [VEN 09]. Even after the tragic events of September 11, 2001, America's civilian and military security planners have proved largely unable to work in partnership in securing civilian computer networks [ANO 10c, GRE 09].

The Greek state is no stranger to turf warfare and bureaucratic infighting. Cyber-defense planners are however encouraged by the pending National Communications Security Strategy (ESAE), which is currently in the legislative committee stage in the Greek Parliament. When enacted, the legislation will provide a much-needed institutional framework for the security of civilian information networks on a national scale. It is also expected to streamline, modernize and synchronize the multitude of institutional actors that are currently tasked with civilian information security [KAT 10]. The latter issue is considered to be of paramount importance by technical experts and policymakers, who view the current institutional setting as unproductive and lacking planning [KAT 10].

There are currently as many as 15 distinct agencies engaged in various aspects of protecting the content and infrastructure of civilian communications systems – often with largely overlapping functions. They include independent agencies, subject only to parliamentary oversight, such as the Authority for the Security of Communications Privacy (ADAE) and the National Telecommunications Commission (EETT). The latter appears to be responsible for a host of highly disparate tasks, such as digital signature verification systems and the maintenance of telecommunications networks during national emergencies [GRI 08]. They also include a number of more flexible 'planning and action teams', such as the Digital Awareness and Response to Threats (DART), that is vaguely tasked with "preventing and combating dangers related to new electronic information and communications technologies" [ANO 09a]. Its mission partly overlaps with that of the more specialized Computer Emergency Response Team (CERT), which provides incident response and security services to Greece's National Research and Technology Network (GRNET). Greek cyber-security policy planners describe the current fragmentation of the country's information security infrastructure as "incoherent and ineffective [...], a remnant of Cold-War-era monolithic conceptions of analog communications security" [FIT 10c]. Many of these agencies will be "merged or altogether eliminated in the [ESAE] environment" [FIT 10c], while a new supervisory General Secretariat for Telecommunications Security will be created, which will act as a direct channel of communication between civilian cyber-defense agencies and the Office of the Prime Minister [GRI 08].

A central element in Greece's emerging civilian information security strategy is the EYP, the country's National Intelligence Service [ILI 10a]. The Service's counterintelligence component will constitute one of the cornerstones of the country's defense against network warfare in the ESAE environment. Operating under the Ministry of Interior, since 1992 the EYP has acted as the coordinating mechanism for securing the integrity of the government's encrypted and unencrypted information infrastructure. In 2003, the service assumed responsibility for the classification of government communication networks, as well as information security (INFOSEC) and emission security (EMSEC or TEMPEST) duties. In 2008, a little over two years after the 2004–2005 Vodafone wiretapping was exposed, the EYP's Fifth Directorate was designated Greece's official national CERT. Its duties include the coordination of cyber-defense mechanisms against network warfare and cyber-terrorism on a national scale [ILI 09a, MAR 10, GRI 08].

Under the ESAE plan, the EYP will maintain its national CERT designation, but its duties will be cross-linked with those of two other civilian cyber-defense agencies, which also operate under the Ministry of Interior. The first of these will be the Civil Defense and Emergency Planning Directorate (PAM-PSEA), which is tasked with peacetime coordination of all emergency planning operations, through its network of bureaus and stations located throughout the country. The second will be the Informatics Development Service (YAP), which is responsible for overseeing the application of networked information systems in the public sector. This tripartite collaboration will be closely linked with a network of academic research teams throughout the country, such as the Information Security and Critical Infrastructure Protection Research Group of the Department of Informatics at Athens University of Economics. This group, which has been operational since 2000, currently coordinates research from four Greek higher education research centers, and aspires to create the nation's first National Center for Excellence in Critical Infrastructure Protection [KAL 10].

The question, however, remains as to whether, in order to adequately fulfill its National CERT mission, the EYP will be made to undergo a painful period of internal reform. The EYP has undergone three substantial reorganizations since Greece's political changeover to democracy, after the military junta of 1967–1974, the most recent of which was in 2008, when it was assigned its national CERT duties [NOM 10]. In 2010, as part of its national CERT obligations, the EYP participated in a national cyber-defense simulation exercise for the first time, along with several academic, civilian and military agencies. Its contribution to the exercise was deemed positive [ILI 10a], though insiders criticized it as an instance of 'too little, too late', and accused it of exhibiting a "turf-war mentality against [Greek] law enforcement and [military] agencies", which are often "ahead of the game" in cyber-defense [FIT 10c]. More clouds appeared to gather on the horizon for the EYP in January of 2011, when British newspaper *The Guardian* published a confidential report sent from the US Embassy in Athens to the US Department of State, leaked though the international whistleblower organization WikiLeaks. In the communiqué, the US Ambassador to Greece, Daniel V. Speckhard, provided details of a January 22, 2010, closed-door meeting with Greece's Minister for Citizen Protection at the time, Michalis Chrysohoidis. According to Ambassador Speckhard, the Minister, then a member of the ruling Panhellenic Socialist Movement (PASOK) party, "severely criticized the state of EYP", saying bluntly that "EYP is nothing", and that "[i]t does not serve its mission of protecting Greece and in fact is dangerous to national security because of its many shortcomings, not the least of which is a unionized labor force". He continued saying that he intended to "collapse and rebuild [the service] via a draft law that is in the process of being drawn up" [SPE 10]. What is arguably even more interesting is Chrysohoidis' response to the WikiLeaks revelations. Speaking on the day after the revelations, the PASOK politician rejected the revelatory tone of the disclosure, saying that the opinions expressed in the leaked US Embassy communiqué constituted summations of opinions he had previously expressed in public. He went on to state that the EYP was in a "sad state of affairs" when he assumed his cabinet position in October 2009, and that the service "did not serve its [stated] function of protecting the country", but that "several things have improved since that time" [ANO 11a].

Chrysohoidis' statements about the EYP are characteristic of opinions held by many Greek parliamentarians and government executives. They stem from the EYP's less-than-honorable record prior to the country's political changeover to democracy in 1974, as well as from its chronic subservience to Washington during most of the Cold War. These two issues have stained the service's image among large segments of the Greek public and have raised doubts about its operational independence from Washington and NATO. These issues have thus placed an unfortunate ideological wedge between the EYP and the public-at-large, which is far from removed today despite over two decades of socialist rule since 1981. Consequently, inside observers maintain that government reforms aimed at enhancing the EYP's role in national cyber-defense must include concerted efforts to raise the service's public profile and to strengthen society's confidence in the EYP's institutional values and national mission [FIT 10d].

4.8. Emerging military information operations strategies

In contrast to the EYP, whose historical relations with Greece's political leadership and the broader civil society have been awkward and strained, the country's military forces enjoy a somewhat more positive image, which translates to superior funding opportunities and a greater degree of political influence. Consequently, Greek policy planners have been more receptive to the military's viewpoint on information operations, as opposed to its civilian counterpart in the form of the EYP [NAC 03, MAT 02]. At the same time, the susceptibility of policy planners to military views of cyber-warfare can be partly attributed to the ability of Greek defense experts to advocate such views within the context of the country's established foreign policy patterns and strategic concerns, as outlined in previous sections of this chapter.

Greece's emerging information operations doctrine, therefore, reflects the widely established notion of cyberspace as the fifth domain of warfare (after sea, land, air and space), but tends to focus on those features of cyber-warfare that are seen as having the potential to offer solutions to the country's strategic priorities, primarily in relation to Turkey. One such priority is maintaining Greece's vigorous defensive and – to a somewhat lesser extent – pre-emptive posture in the ongoing low-intensity conflict with its eastern neighbor, while simultaneously exploring political, diplomatic and economic avenues to rapprochement and reconciliation. Information operations or, in times of crisis, information warfare, entail the promise of clandestine preparations for war, or the conduct of clandestine war, in what Carl von Clausewitz called "conditions of civilization" [CLA 80]. More specifically, the development of a technologically robust information warfare arsenal does not preclude, nor does it prohibit, the gradual development of healthy bilateral relations between strategic rivals. In the particular context of Greek–Turkish strategic relations, the anticipatory (preventive or pre-emptive) aspects of information operations are in agreement with broader efforts by Greek military planners to steer the country's military thinking toward offense-oriented strategic concepts [FIT 10a].

The underlying technological component embedded in the concept of information operations is also attractive to Greek military planners, who view it as a vehicle through which Greece can reinvigorate its geopolitical dynamic and rise above its national insecurities and inhibitions. This view is further strengthened by the 'demographic problem', explained previously in section 4.2. The destabilizing impact of this crucial social indicator on the sheer size of the armed forces of tiny Greece, in relation to those of Turkey (NATO's second-largest) is both evident and drastic, and helps direct Greek defense planning toward the asymmetrical promise of technologically-based balancing solutions [FIT 10a]. One such example is the concept of 'information network war fighting', which allows a technologically enhanced "platoon of just thirty soldiers to effectively control and achieve superiority over a space that in the Napoleonic era would need a 1,200 men-strong regiment for its control" [DEL 07]. Greek military planners have been among the first in the world to engage in the practical aspects of this concept, which is viewed as critical in reforming the country's conscription-based territorial army into a permanent fighting force consisting mostly of professionals. Information network war fighting is the driving force behind the country's ongoing strategy to reduce its armed forces from 160,000 to around 80,000 in the next few years, of which over 75% will consist of professional combatants [MAT 02].

The merits of the strategic thinking informing the land forces reduction plan have been strengthened by the severe impact of the European sovereign debt crisis, which has placed near-unprecedented financial constraints on Greece's economy. Since 1974, which saw a drastic turn toward internal balancing in Greek strategic thinking, Greece has consistently maintained the highest proportional defense spending of any NATO Member State, and one of the highest in the world [GRA 09, NAC 03]. At the turn of the 21st Century, as much as 5% of the country's active labor force was employed in military and military-related industries [NAC 03]. Greece's economy has suffered from the high cost of military equipment imports, however, which account for 95% of its overall military equipment procurement. This highlights the difficulties involved in trying to maintain a "modern, efficient arms industry" in conditions of a "diminutive domestic market" [NAC 03]. As the financial crisis continues to exert a heavy toll on the Greek economy, and as the weight of the country's productive sector shifts from state-owned industries to the private sector, the reduction in the country's defense budget will have a direct impact on its strategic thinking. In 2010 alone, the government announced a 22% reduction in its non-discretionary defense budget, a trend that is expected to continue [DAL 10]. Under these financial constraints, Greek military planners are rapidly gravitating toward the concept of information operations as a method by which to maintain Greece's internal balancing requirements in conditions of sustained economic recession [FIT 10a]. Greek advocates of information operations as a strategic equalizing option point to the examples of regional powers, such as Israel and Estonia, who boast some of the world's most effective cyber-defense arsenals despite their relatively small size [ANO 10b].

The operational epicenter of Greece's military information operation strategies is the Cyberdefense Directorate (DIKYV), administered by the Hellenic National Defense General Staff [ILI 09a]. In 2000, when it was officially established as a unit, it was one of the first of its kind in the world [PAV 10]. In 2003, its status was upgraded to that of a department, and a year later it was upgraded again, this time to a directorate, operating under the research and informatics division (DEPLI) of the Hellenic National Defense General Staff. With a permanent staff of around 100, trained mostly in the US and Western Europe, DIKYV is responsible for maintaining and refining the technical capabilities that are necessary to protect the digital information and communications infrastructure of the Hellenic Armed Forces in times of peace and war. Its tasks involve both preventive and responsive components, in the form of network penetration tests and incident handling, conducted through a number of Cyberdefense Rapid Reaction Teams. Furthermore, it organizes and facilitates institutional training on cyber-defense for members of the Hellenic Armed Forces, and conducts web information intelligence activities with an eye to coordinating cyber-defense on a national scale, involving the participation of both military and civilian institutional actors [PAV 10].

In November 2009, DIKYV was among the participants of Cyber Coalition 2009 (NCDEx 09), NATO's second-ever Alliance-wide cyber-warfare exercise, which involved several simulated scenarios of multiple, simultaneous cyber-attacks against military and civilian facilities in NATO Member States. DIKYV also coordinated the participation of several Greek government ministries and academic research centers in the exercise. This participation was deemed highly successful, as Greece was one of only two NATO Member States to participate in all of the exercise's seven attack scenarios. The Greek team was crucial in helping deflect three of the attacks, while it was alone in successfully combating one of the scenarios [PAV 10]. This successful presence was largely replicated in November of the following year, during NCDEx 10, when Greece's EYP participated for the first time along with DIKYV [FIT 10d]. The NCDEx experience prompted DIKYV to organize and coordinate Greece's first-ever nationwide cyber-defense exercise, which took place in May 2010. Code-named PANOPTIS 2010, the exercise brought together a host of institutional actors from the Greek military, law enforcement and intelligence communities for the first time. Among the participants were 18 centers of higher education, several government ministries, the EYP, GRNET, most government agencies engaged in protecting the content and infrastructure of civilian communications, as well as the Office of the Prime Minster and the Technical Chamber of Greece [PAV 10]. Despite its largely experimental character, PANOPTIS 2010 was largely successful in repelling the majority of the attack scenarios [KAL 10]. It was also actively supported by the chiefs of staff of the Hellenic Armed Forces, including the chairman of the Joint Chiefs of Staff, who participated in a scheduled visit to the PANOPTIS operational headquarters [ILI 10c].

As with any other constituent of modern military bureaucracy, DIKYV has had to fight for its existence and justify its operational mission to both military and civilian leaders. In one anecdotal episode that took place some years after DIKYV's establishment, the directorate's technical experts had to argue against a report advocating for DIKYV's dismantling on the grounds of its 'strategic irrelevance' [FIT 10a]. Moreover, observers maintain that DIKYV remains underfunded and understaffed [ILI 09b, ILI 10b]. Judging by recent developments within the Hellenic National Defense General Staff, however, it seems safe to state that DIKYV's operational mission has been secured, and that the directorate's future is relatively promising. In January 2011, Greece's Ministry of National Defense announced the formation of a new National Cyberdefense Authority, based on the conclusions of a report commissioned by DIKYV [ILI 11a]. A month later, the Greek Minister of National Defense announced in parliament that DIKYV's operational role would be upgraded from a directorate to that of a command, and would "assume a central role in protecting the nation from cyberwarfare attacks" [ILI 11b]. The minister refused to provide further information, saying that the details of the pending upgrade were "highly classified". Knowledgeable observers, however, believe that the announcement is directly related to the planned formation of the National Cyberdefense Authority, and that DIKYV rather than the EYP had been selected to spearhead the new effort [ILI 11b]. What is more, the announced changes may open the door to further modernization, including increased funding for DIKYV, the hiring of larger numbers of technical specialists and the establishment of a cyber-defense training center, which has been a longtime request of Greek cyber-defense advocates [ILI 10c, ILI 11b].

4.9. The European Union dimension in Greek information operations

Greece's announcement of the formation of a National Cyberdefense Authority follows closely on the heels of organizational standards set by NATO [ILI 11a]. This should be viewed as indicative of the manner in which Greece's international alliances and obligations, whether civilian or military, affect its internal national strategy on information operations. In addition to NATO, the EU – of which Greece has been a full member since 1981 – is gradually emerging as an international force shaping Greek conceptions of information operations, both legislatively and operationally. An important aspect of this is Greece's central role in establishing, hosting and funding the European Network and Information Security Agency (ENISA). ENISA's establishment was first proposed by the European Commission in early 2003, and was officially adopted by the European Council in February 2004 [WES 04]. The Agency's existence remains tentative: it was initially given a five-year mandate, which was extended for a further three years in 2009 [UKH 10]. Its stated mission is to promote cyber-security standards and certification systems across the EU, and to operate as a rapid reaction mechanism against cyber-attacks across this area [WES 04].

The Agency's operational success can be described as limited, or, as one insider put it "not the biggest success story of all time" [UKH 10]. There are several reasons that critics cite this, including the differing levels of development in informatics across EU Member States, as well as ENISA's chronic understaffing, which some judge to be as much as 60% behind requirements [UKH 10, ANO 10b]. Despite this, Greek cyber-defense experts were thrilled when, in 2003, the European

Council voted to locate the Agency in Greece, in a move that some in the Greek cyber-defense community say recognized the country's constructive international presence in the field [FIT 10c]. It is worth noting, however, that some individuals in ENISA were disillusioned by the Greek government's decision to base the Agency's headquarters in Heraklion, the largest city in Crete, Greece's largest island. The idea behind the decision was to establish links between ENISA and the Greek Foundation for Research and Technology, which is also located in Heraklion [UKH 10]. The outcome of the move, however, was to give ENISA the ambiguous distinction of being the EU's most physically remote agency. Its headquarters is now located almost 2,500 km from Brussels, which some critics say has affected recruiting and keeps staff away from important research and policy centers in northern Europe [UKH 10]. In 2009, the Greek government responded to these criticisms by independently funding the establishment of an ENISA branch in Athens, which has somewhat pacified critics and has kept ENISA in Greece [UKH 10]. Despite its mixed record, ENISA's presence in Crete has elevated Greece's international cyber-defense presence and has enabled the country to assume a central role in facilitating inter-European cyber-defense collaboration. This was illustrated during Cyber Europe 2010, the EU's first-ever large-scale cyber-attack simulation exercise, which was conducted with the participation of all 27 EU Member States and several other nations. The exercise was organized by ENISA from Heraklion and Athens, placing both Greek cities on the cyber-defense map, in the same way that the efforts of NATO's Cyber Defense Center of Excellence in Tallinn have elevated Estonia's status in the cyber-defense universe [ANO 10d].

4.10. Conclusion

Greece's geopolitical importance is such that the country's approach to information operations and cyber-warfare matters within several international contexts, including those of maritime transportation, banking, energy, telecommunications, the Balkans, the Middle East, NATO and the EU. Although Greek conceptions of information operations and cyber-warfare are still emerging, it is safe to say that they will continue to be decisively shaped by the country's distinct historical experiences and strategic concerns, particularly in relation to its geopolitical archrival Turkey.

The asymmetrical promise embedded in the concept of information warfare appeals to Greek defense planners, who seek:

– ways of maintaining Greece's internal military balance;

– to combat the growing demographic gap between Greece and Turkey; and

– to reinvigorate Greece's geopolitical dynamic without directly antagonizing the Turkish military.

These broader strategic parameters have been revised through the prism of several formative experiences in information operations, including – but not limited to – the Öcalan affair, the Vodafone wiretapping of 2004–2005, and the Ergenekon conspiracy. Although damaging Greece's reputation in exposing substantial gaps in its defensive info-dominance, these experiences have also proved constructive in highlighting – even to non-experts – the urgent need to reinterpret Greece's traditional geopolitical concerns and strategic interests through the all-encompassing prism of the information society. These experiences have therefore helped make the country's decision makers progressively aware of the country's vulnerability to information operations.

This awareness has resulted in a two-fold reorganization of Greece's cyber-defense structure:

– the pending National Communications Security Strategy (coordinated by the EYP, Greece's National Intelligence Service); and

– the pending formation of a National Cyberdefense Authority (coordinated by DIKYV, the Hellenic Armed Forces' Cyberdefense Directorate).

These initiatives represent the civilian and military facets of Greece's new cyber-defense structure that, in times of crisis, will be directly coordinated by the Office of the Prime Minister through a new General Secretariat for Telecommunications Security. Judging by recent developments, it appears that the military has the upper hand in shaping Greece's doctrine of information operations, though the role and influence of the country's civilian intelligence agency, the EYP, should not be underestimated. Finally, Greece's NATO and EU membership does, to some extent, influence the country's conceptions of information operations, both legislatively and operationally. This is exemplified by Greece's central role in establishing, hosting and funding ENISA, the EU's network and information security agency.

At the time of writing, Greece is experiencing the most severe economic crisis in the country's postwar history. The path of this crisis, which is developing in the context of a wider, severe financial downturn for the economies of the West, is both unchartered and unpredictable. As such, its impact on Greece's security and cyber-defense doctrines is extremely uncertain and does not lend itself to any obvious conclusions. As late as February 2012, over two years after the onset of the economic crisis, Greece's spending on military infrastructure had remained largely intact, despite the severe austerity measures that were implemented to stabilize the country's substantial budget deficit. Moreover, the senior planning leadership of Greece's National Defense Department had remained largely intact, even following the collapse of George Papandreou's PASOK government in November 2011. It remains doubtful whether its replacement by a tri-party unity coalition, led by technocrat international banker Lucas Papadimos, will prove powerful enough to implement substantial changes – budgetary or otherwise – in the armed forces.

At the current juncture it would be unrealistic to expect drastic changes in Greek defense planning, especially when it comes to those aspects deemed strategically critical, such as air power. It has been noted that "Greece currently spends more on defense, as a percentage of gross domestic product than any other EU member, including the United Kingdom, which maintains a global defense reach, and Poland, which sees itself as needing to be ready to hold out against the vastly superior Russian army" [MES 10]. Despite severe economic and social pressures, there is currently little indication that this reality may be about to change. In April 2010, Athens attempted, for the first time since the onset of the economic crisis, to put forward an official proposal for bilateral defense cuts to Ankara. During a mini-summit held in Athens on May 14 of that year, Greek officials suggested a 25% mutual cut in defense spending. Perhaps predictably, the Turkish side – which is most definitely not under the pressure of a pending economic collapse – did not consent to the Greek proposal [MES 10]. This may change, however, depending on whether Turkey's regional ambitions prompt it to outgrow its rivalry with Greece, in pursuit of broader geopolitical interests in the Middle East, the Caucasus and beyond.

The spiraling economic pressures on Greek society may ultimately increase the government's role in economic planning. This could in turn transform the military into a political vehicle for alleviating high unemployment among the younger generations. In this case, Greek military and security planners are likely to turn toward low-technology, high-personnel models of defense posturing. On the diametrically opposite side of the forecasting spectrum, a rapidly imploding Greek economy could drive defense planners to seek highly innovative technological solutions to regional security challenges. This could gradually transform the Greek armed forces into an experimental hotbed of pioneering cyber-defense doctrines within existing NATO structures – similar perhaps to the case of Estonia after 2007. Greece's history, both ancient and modern, features numerous examples of groundbreaking warfare innovation. No serious student of history would be genuinely surprised if yet another groundbreaking military innovation was to come out of Greece in the next few decades.

4.11. Bibliography

[ANO 09a] ANONYMOUS, *What is DART?*, Digital Awareness and Response to Threats, Athens, 2009.

[ANO 09b] ANONYMOUS, Turkish General Staff Behind Anti-Hellenic Websites, Strategy Report, November 4, 2009 (in Greek).

[ANO 10a] ANONYMOUS, Turkey: Guide to Ergenekon, Open Source Center, Office of the Director of National Intelligence, Washington, DC, March 19, 2010.

[ANO 10b] ANONYMOUS, "Cyberwar", *The Economist*, July 1, 2010.

[ANO 10c] ANONYMOUS, "Cyberwar: war in the fifth domain", *The Economist*, July 1, 2010.

[ANO 10d] ANONYMOUS, "EU cyberdefence exercise mirrors US trials", *Security & Defense Agenda*, November 5, 2010.

[ANO 10e] ANONYMOUS, "Sustained hacker attack on the Hellenic Centre for Marine Research", *SecNews*, November 10, 2010 (in Greek).

[ANO 10f] ANONYMOUS, "Cyberattack on the Ministry of National Defense", *Strategy Report*, December 3, 2010 (in Greek).

[ANO 10g] ANONYMOUS, "Attack by unknown hackers on the Ministry of Defense", *Press Time*, December 13, 2010 (in Greek).

[ANO 11a] ANONYMOUS, "Michalis Chrysohoidis: WikiLeaks 'Revelations' are known public statements", *To Vima*, January 12, 2011 (in Greek).

[ANO 11b] ANONYMOUS, "No agreements under threat", *Eleftherotypia*, February 25, 2011.

[ANO 99a] ANONYMOUS, *Turkish Propaganda Against Cyprus is Rejected*, Press Office, Permanent Mission of the Republic of Cyprus to the United Nations, February 24, 1999.

[ANO 99b] ANONYMOUS, *Text of the Öcalan Verdict*, BBC, June 29, 1999.

[AYD 04] AYDIN M., K. IFANTIS K., "Introduction", in AYDIN M., IFANTIS K., *Turkish-Greek Relations: The Security Dilemma in the Aegean*, Routledge, London, 2004.

[BAK 10] BAKOYANNIS D., "Europe and Greece: The crisis as an opportunity", *Konrad Adenauer Stiftung Foundation*, Berlin, June 2010 (in Greek).

[BLU 09] BLUNDEN B., *The Rootkit Arsenal: Escape and Evasion in the Dark Corners of the System*, Worldware Publishers, Plano, US, 2009.

[CHA 11] CHAROUNTAKI M., *The Kurds and US Foreign Policy: International Relations in the Middle East since 1945*, Routledge, London, 2011.

[CLA 80] CLAUSEWITZ C., *Vom Kriege*, W. Hahlweg, Bonn, 1980.

[DAL 10] DALOUMIS I., "22% Reductions in defense spending", *Isotimia*, January 9, 2010 (in Greek).

[DEK 03] DEKMEJIAN R.H., SIMONIAN H.H., *Troubled Waters: The Geopolitics of the Caspian Region*, I.B. Tauris, London, 2003.

[DEL 07] DELIBASIS D., *The Right to National Self-Defence in Information Warfare Operations*, Arena Books, Bury St. Edmunds, UK, 2007.

[DEM 99] DEMESTICHAS G., "Greek security and defense policy in the eastern Mediterranean", in STAVROU N.A., *Mediterranean Security at the Crossroads: A Reader*, Duke University Press, Durham, NC, 1999.

[FAL 09] FALIK O., KROITORU H., "The internationalization of suicide terrorism", in MORGENSTERN H., FALK O., *Suicide Terror: Understanding and Confronting the Threat*, John Wiley & Sons, Hoboken, USA, 2009.

[FAL 10] FALLIERE N., *Stuxnet Introduces the First Known Rootkit for Industrial Control Systems*, Symantec, August 6, 2010.

[FIT 99] FITSANAKIS J., *Here's How We Lost Him*, Macedonia, March 14, 1999 (in Greek).

[FIT 03] FITSANAKIS J., "State-sponsored communications interception: facilitating Illegality", *Information, Communication and Society*, vol. 6, pp. 403-428, 2003.

[FIT 10a] FITSANAKIS J., *Interview with Hellenic National Defense General Staff and North Atlantic Treaty Organization Official*, October 2010.

[FIT 10b] FITSANAKIS J., *Interview with Digital Awareness and Response to Threats Member*, August 2010.

[FIT 10c] FITSANAKIS J., *Interview with Research and Informatics Division Official*, Hellenic National Defense General Staff, October 2010.

[FIT 10d] FITSANAKIS J., *Interview with Hellenic National Intelligence Service Official*, August 2010.

[FRA 08] FRANCESCHETTI G., GROSSI M, "Homeland security technology challenges", in *Sensing and Encrypting to Mining and Modeling*, Artech House, Boston, MA, 2008.

[GAL 06] GALPIN R., *Death Muddies Greek Spy Probe*, BBC, March 24, 2006.

[GRA 09] GRAMATIKOV P., "Bulgarian energetics management and environmental security", in STEC S., BESNIK B., *Energy and Environmental Challenges to Security*, Springer, Dordrecht, 2009.

[GRE 09] GREENBERG A., *Top Cyber Official Sounds Off*, Forbes, March 9, 2009.

[GRI 08] GRITZALIS D., MITROU N., SKOULARIDOU V., *Protection of Critical Information and Communication Infrastructure in Public Administration: Strategic Design*, eGovForum, Athens, 2008 (in Greek).

[GÜN 05] GÜNLÜK-ŞENESEN G., "An Analysis of the action-reaction behavior in the defence expenditure of Turkey and Greece", in ÇARKOĞLU A., RUBIN B.M., *Greek-Turkish Relations in an Era of Détente*, Routledge, London, 2005.

[HAD 99] HADJIDIMOS K., *The Role of the Media in Greek-Turkish Relations*, Robert Bosch Foundation, Stuttgart, 1999.

[HEN 06] HENTEA C., *Balkan Propaganda Wars*, Scarecrow Press, Lanham, MD, 2006.

[ILI 09a] ILIADES M., "Ankara shielded from cyberwar", *O Kosmos tou Ependiti*, September 26, 2009 (in Greek).

[ILI 09b] ILIADES M., "Paramilitary internet warriors", *O Kosmos tou Ependiti*, September 26, 2009 (in Greek).

[ILI 10a] ILIADES M., "National cyberdefense exercise in Greece", *O Kosmos tou Ependiti*, April 1, 2010 (in Greek).

[ILI 10b] ILIADES M., "Habemus cyberdefense", *O Kosmos tou Ependiti*, May 8, 2010 (in Greek).

[ILI 10c] ILIADES M., "Panoptes deflected the attack", *O Kosmos tou Ependiti*, May 29, 2010 (in Greek).

[ILI 11a] ILIADES M., "Green light for a National Cyberdefense Authority in Greece", *O Kosmos tou Ependiti*, January 21, 2011 (in Greek).

[ILI 11b] ILIADES M., "A Step Forward", *O Kosmos tou Ependiti*, February 19, 2011 (in Greek).

[KAL 10] KALYVIOTOU M., "A war in cyberspace", *Avgi*, July 31, 2010 (in Greek).

[KAT 10] KATSIKAS S., "Toward a national strategy of communications security", *Workshop on Coordinated Supervision and Administration of Security and Privacy in the Greek Territory*, Hellenic Ministry of Infrastructure, Transport and Networks, Athens, October 2010.

[KER 04] KERIDIS D., PERRY C.M., *Defense Reform, Modernization, and Military Cooperation in Southeastern Europe*, Brassey's Inc., Dulles, VA, 2004.

[KER 07] KER-LINDSAY J., *Crisis and Conciliation: A Year of Rapprochement between Greece and Turkey*, Palgrave Macmillan, New York, NY, 2007.

[KOF 03] KOFAS J.V., *Under the Eagle's Claw: Exceptionalism in Postwar US-Greek Relations*, Praeger, Westport, CT, 2003.

[KON 88] KONDYLIS P., *Theory of War*, Themelio, Athens, 1988 (in Greek).

[LEY 07] LEYDEN J., "Greek mobile wiretap scandal unpicked", *The Register*, July 11, 2007.

[LIV 10] LIVIERATOS D., "Greek capitalism today", *Kokkino*, no. 49, July 2010 (in Greek).

[LUF 09] LUFT G., KORIN A., *Energy Security Challenges for the 21st Century*, Praeger Security International, Santa Barbara, CA, 2009.

[MAR 10] MARINAKIS G., "Security of national communication and information systems: 5th Directorate, Hellenic National Intelligence Service", *Workshop on Coordinated Supervision and Administration of Security and Privacy in the Greek Territory*, Hellenic Ministry of Infrastructure, Transport and Networks, Athens, October 2010.

[MAT 02] MATHIOPOULOS M., "Greece ventures onto new ground: the new Greek security and defense policy, 2000-2015", in GYARMATI I., WINKLER T., *Post-Cold War Defense Reform: Lessons Learned in Europe and the United States*, Bassey's Inc., Washington, DC, 2002.

[MES 10] MESSINIS A., "Greece: Defense Spending and the Financial Crisis", *StratFor*, April 29, 2010.

[MOU 07] MOURITZEN H., WIVEL A., *The Geopolitics of Euro-Atlantic Integration*, Routledge, London, 2007.

[NAC 03] NACHMANI A., *Turkey: Facing a New Millennium, Coping with Intertwined Conflicts*, Manchester University Press, Manchester, 2003.

[NIC 11] NICHOL J., *Armenia, Azerbaijan and Georgia: Political Developments and Implications for US Interests*, Defense Technical Information Center, Ft. Belvoir, VA, USA, 2011.

[NOM 10] NOMIKOS J., LIAROPOULOS A., "Truly reforming or just responding to failures? lessons learned from the modernisation of the Greek National Intelligence Service", *Journal of Policing, Intelligence and Counter Terrorism*, vol. 5, pp. 28-41, 2010.

[PAV 10] PAVLIDES A., "Cyberdefense", *Cyberdefense in the Service of National Strategy Workshop*, Hellenic National Defense General Staff, Athens, December 2010.

[PRE 07] PREVELAKIS V., SPINELLIS D., "The Athens affair", *IEEE Spectrum*, July 2007 (online).

[SAM 10] SAMATAS M., "The Greek Olympic phone tapping scandal: A defenceless state and a weak democracy", in HAGGERTY K.D., SAMATAS M., *Surveillance and Democracy*, Routledge, Abingdon, 2010.

[SIN 00] SINAI T., *The New Security Threats - Cyberterror: An Assessment*, GRIN Verlag, Norderstedt, 2000.

[SPE 10] SPECKHARD D.V., *Citizen Protection Minister Upbeat on Reorganization, Cooperation*, Embassy of the United States of America in Athens, January 29, 2010.

[TAG 09] TAGARINSKI M., AVIZIUS A., "Energy security for the Euro-Atlantic region", in STEC S., BESNIK B., *Energy and Environmental Challenges to Security*, Springer, Dordrecht, 2009.

[TAY 03] TAYFUR M.E., *Semiperipheral Development and Foreign Policy: The Cases of Greece and Spain*, Ashgate, Aldershot, 2003.

[THO 09] THOMAS G., *Gideon's Spies: the Secret History of the Mossad*, Thomas Dunne, New York, NY, 2009.

[TSA 04] TSAKONAS P.J., DOKOS T.P., "Greek-Turkish relations in the early twenty-first century: a view from Athens", in MARTIN L.G., KERIDIS D., *The Future of Turkish Foreign Policy*, MIT Press, Cambridge, MA, 2004.

[UKH 10] UK House of Lords, "Protecting Europe against large-scale cyber attacks", *5th Report of Session 2009-10*, Government Stationery Office, London, 2010.

[VEN 09] VENTRE D, *Information Warfare*, ISTE, London, John Wiley & Sons, New York, 2009.

[VOS 99] VOSTICA G., "Cyberwar and Sabotage", *Newsweek*, May 31, 1999.

[WEI 96] WEISS G., "The farewell dossier: duping the Soviets", *Studies in Intelligence*, vol. 35, no. 5, pp. 121-126, 1996.

[WEI 99] WEINER T., "US helped Turkey find and capture Kurd rebel", *The New York Times*, February 20, 1999.

[WES 04] WESTBY J.R., *International Guide to Cyber Security*, The American Bar Association, Chicago, IL, USA, 2004.

[YEN 10] YENILMEZ C., "Propaganda websites used defense ministry IPs", *Today's Zaman*, May 1, 2010.

Chapter 5

Moving Toward an Italian Cyber Defense and Security Strategy

5.1. Information warfare and cyber warfare: what are they?

Nowadays armed forces are much more dependent on information networks and systems for command, control, intelligence, logistics and weapon technologies. At the same time, civilian infrastructures rely on information networks and technologies for their functioning. If we take into consideration the number of information systems and networks and their widespread vulnerabilities, it is not surprising that they have become targets for adversaries bent upon disrupting society, the economy and welfare of a nation. If we also consider the availability on the Internet of tools that allow everybody – not only those with IT skills – to automatically take advantage of security flaws for espionage and criminal or military purposes, we can gather a clear picture of the current situation. Sometimes, software security flaws are not even voluntarily exploited.

I wish to recall a personal experience of mine to enable you to see the full picture. One day, while surfing on the net looking for a scientific article, by clicking on a link in Google search I was redirected, quite oddly, to a United States (US) Navy Intranet webpage. This was strange because to get to the same page from the Navy website you need to log in. This page contained a list of high-ranking senior officers with their social security numbers – which are confidential for every US citizen. I was redirected to that page because the name of the article's author was in

Chapter written by Stefania Ducci.

that list – even if it was a case of homonymy – but what could apparently look like an innocuous webpage index-linked mistake, was instead a breathtaking vulnerability. It can easily be imagined what would happen if these names were to fall into the hands of criminal gangs, terrorist organizations, cyber warriors or non-allied intelligence services. New identities could be exploited for network-centric warfare to gather additional information since social security numbers are usually used for common identification throughout the military.

In Italy, the theme of cyber-security has been recently dealt with by military research centers[1] as well as by the Italian Parliamentary Intelligence Oversight Committee (Co.Pa.Si.R. – *Comitato Parlamentare per la Sicurezza della Repubblica*) [COP 10]. The purpose is clear: Italy needs to elaborate a comprehensive cyber-defense and cyber-security strategy in order to prevent and react in an efficient and coordinated manner to possible cases of information and cyber warfare.

However, apart from a comprehensive strategy, it seems that we first of all need a clear definition of the terms 'information warfare' and, especially, 'cyber-warfare'. Too often concepts such as cyber-terrorism and cyber-warfare are ill-used or are used as synonyms. This is also true for cyber-espionage. With respect to the first dichotomy, the danger of assimilating cyber-terrorism to an act of cyber warfare, which is an act of war carried out within the fifth domain, is quite evident[2]. It can be defined as "the unauthorized penetration by, on behalf of, or in support of, a government into another nation's computer or network, or any other activity affecting a computer system, in which the purpose is to add, alter, or falsify data, or cause the disruption of or damage to a computer, or network device, or the objects a computer system controls" [CLA 10].

Cyber warfare may be symmetric while terrorism, also in its cyber form, is asymmetric by definition. Moreover, assimilating cyber-terrorism with cyber warfare would mean that cyber-terrorists are 'legitimate combatants' – an assimilation that is firmly denied by the international community in the physical world. It is also interesting to note how cyber warfare is clearly not governed by the Hague Regulations of 1899 and 1907, or by the four Geneva Conventions of 1949, regulating *jus in bello*[3]. This aspect is not secondary, if we consider that cyber operations are often carried out in support of acts of conventional warfare – e.g. the

---

1 See, for example, the Center for Military Strategic Studies (CeMiSS), which published a paper on cyber warfare in 2008 [IOV 08], and a research on the risks for Defense's IT infrastructures [IOV 11] and another on the development of a national concept of "Information Assurance" [ANT 11] in 2011.
2 The other dimensions are land, sea, air and space [LIB 09].
3 For the debate about rendering the Geneva and Hague Conventions for governing cyber conflict, see [RAU 11].

Georgian case – and that they may have indiscriminate effects on the civilian population.

At the same time cyber-espionage is something totally different from cyber warfare, even if the former is aimed at stealing military information, such as new weapon systems.

It should also be noted that the techniques (tools and *modus operandi*) usually used for cyber-attacks are not univocal. For instance, those normally used in criminal activities are similar to those used for cyber-espionage, cyber-terrorism or cyber warfare. This leads us to another consideration: in most cases these attacks are carried out by private hackers, thus allowing plausible denial by the sponsoring State. This happened in the second half of the 1980s. An example is the cyber-espionage case involving the Chaos Computer Club hacker group and the KGB, described by Clifford Stoll in his book *The Cuckoo's Egg* [STO 00].

Cyber warfare attacks are not necessarily perpetrated by military hackers wearing a uniform. This sheds light on the difficulties related to the attribution of the attack source – not only the nature of warfare – especially when the attacker uses "triangulation" (a method where the attacker can disguise the origin of the attack), a technique very familiar to the intelligence community and relatively easy to use within the shadow domain of computer networks. This aspect poses another problem when State A engages private hackers to hack into the information and communication technology (ICT) systems of another country B – possibly an adversary of A – to use them as launch pads for cyber-attacks against an additional country that is its final target C – an adversary of country B and/or A. In the case where B and C are both adversaries of A, this technique permits A to gain a double advantage since it will be able to defeat two adversary countries with a single coordinated attack without being recognized as the originator of the cyber-aggression. It will also trigger a possible reprisal by C against B, giving rise to an escalation of the cyber-conflict between the two enemies. This may have been the scenario in which the Stuxnet cyber weapon was used.

Finally, while defining the notion of cyber warfare, we should also consider the effects of an attack against national stock exchange markets, which could produce an even more damaging outcome than those of conventional warfare.

China and Russia are currently trying to define and shape a legal framework and rules of engagement for cyber warfare [FRI 08]. What we need at the moment at a national and international level is a clear definition of what is meant by cyberspace and information warfare – especially cyber warfare – and, then, the identification of which actions are allowed or banned by the international community. The fact that the same attack techniques are used for criminal, military or intelligence purposes does not mean that these three areas should be treated equally (from a law-enforcement perspective), even if overlapping among the aforementioned areas is common, and considering that there could be State-sponsored attacks carried out by private attackers. This issue has been recognized by the Group of Governmental Experts on Developments in the Field of Information and Telecommunications in the Context of International Security (*UN General Assembly, Resolution A/65/201 of July 30, 2010*). This group is concerned about the involvement of individuals, groups or organizations, including criminal organizations, in "disruptive online activities on behalf of others" [UNG 10], both State and non-State actors. The above-mentioned document contains recommendations – formulated by Italian experts[4] together with a group of experts from other nations[5] – aimed at reducing the threat of attacks on each others' computer networks[6]. The group stated that "there is increased reporting that States are developing ICTs [information and communication technologies] as instruments of warfare and intelligence, and for political purposes. [...] Non-criminal areas of transnational concern should receive appropriate attention" [UNG 10]. Indeed, during the past decade, national efforts to work with global partners in cyberspace have centered on combating crimes online. This set aside the more sensitive issues of State involvement in, or responsibility for, cyber intrusions into critical computer systems. This requires a political rather than a judicial solution.

5.2. Understanding the current Italian geopolitical context

Even if a comprehensive cyber threat assessment has not been elaborated in Italy to date, either at an official or unofficial level, we can entertain some considerations beginning with the fact that Italy is a United Nations (UN), OSCE (Organisation for Security and Co-operation in Europe), North Atlantic Treaty Organization (NATO), Council of Europe and European Union (EU) member and that it takes part in several peacekeeping support operations. The Italian armed forces are currently employing 7,811 soldiers in 30 missions in 22 countries and two geographical areas, including the Balkans (NATO), India–Pakistan (UN Nations Military Observer

---

4 These experts were from the Communication Security Sector of the Presidency of the Council of Ministers.

5 Namely, Belarus, Brazil, China, Estonia, France, Germany, India, Israel, Qatar, Russia, South Africa, South Korea, the United Kingdom and the United States.

6 The group of governmental experts recommended: further dialogue among States to discuss norms pertaining to State use of ICTs; confidence-building, stability and risk-reduction measures to address the implications of State use of ICTs, including exchanges of national views on the use of ICTs in conflict; information exchanges on national legislation and national ICT security strategies and technologies, policies and best practices; identification of measures to support capacity-building in less developed countries; and elaboration of common terms and definitions.

Group in India and Pakistan), Sudan (UN African Union-United Mission in Darfur), Lebanon (UN Interim Force in Lebanon), Israel (UN Truce Supervision Organization), Gaza (EU), Iraq, and Afghanistan (International Security Assistance Force, EU Police Mission in Afghanistan or EUPOL) [MDD 10]. According to a Ministry of Foreign Affairs report [MAE 09], Italy is the first 'blue helmet' contributing country among the European G8 partners, the second EU country for the number of personnel engaged in missions abroad, and the ninth largest contributor – out of 117 countries – to UN military and police operations with its 2,864 peacekeepers. These facts and figures are indicative of Italy's well-defined role in the maintenance and enhancement of international governability with related burdens and risks. In this regard, Italy's alliance with the US[7] – which is one of the cyber-power nations together with China, France, Germany, Israel, Russia and the United Kingdom [CLA 10, AGY 09] – requires the protection of the nation from both State and non-State adversaries. In this connection, some important exercises were held in 2010 that were aimed at assessing the cooperation capabilities of participating organizations and improving the procedures for exchanging information within the national, pan-European and NATO scenario through "Cyber Shot 2010", "Cyber Europe 2010" and NATO "Cyber Coalition 2010", respectively [ANA 10, ENI 10a]. Moreover, the Italian armed forces, as in other developed nations, strongly rely on commercial off-the-shelf technologies rather than on government off-the-shelf ones, and this presents some vulnerabilities due to private foreign manufacturing of electronic components (hardware and software) that may contain security flaws, embedded malware, or loggers for stealing sensitive information.

Products produced for the defense market can be altered throughout the product lifecycle, "from the inception of the design concept, to product delivery, and to product updates and support" [USA 10]. Undoubtedly, the possibility of rogue microchips from China, for example, which is considered one of the main countries with information warfare capabilities [KRE 09], represents an important counterintelligence problem. Nowadays, computer chips and software are produced globally and an adversary can infect high-tech military equipment with computer bugs. This is particularly true for current military technologies: the more technological they are, the more vulnerable they will be, even if countermeasures are built up. This is why doctrines, policies and strategies on information and electronic warfare should be elaborated on and kept constantly updated to keep pace with ICT developments. From this perspective, Italy– together with France – is currently involved in the FREMM (*FRegate Europee Multi Missione*, i.e. the Multi-mission European Frigates) program and will acquire at least six of the 10 frigates

---

7 Italy participates in NATO's International Security Assistance Force with 3,815 soldiers, leading the mission in the western sector of the country – including the provinces of Ghor, Badghis, Herat and Farah [ISA 11].

initially envisaged, which will be also equipped with electronic warfare devices. Another example is given by the technologically-advanced stealth fighter F-35B Lightning II with which the Italian Navy and Air Force would like to renew their fleet, whose plans were stolen by hackers who could have implanted logic bombs in the code that manage the aircraft's wired brain [CLA 10].

However, cyber warfare attacks may have indiscriminate targets and effects. They can – either directly or indirectly – destroy or disrupt civilian infrastructures on which military networks and systems also depend. The more digitalized a country is the, more vulnerable it is to cyber attacks, as the Estonian case clearly shows. Many highly computerized nations are working on devising their own defense mechanisms. If we look at the 2010 UN e-Government Readiness Index, we can see that Italy is ranked 38th in the list of the top 50 countries in e-government development[8]. From this stand point, Italy is less vulnerable to cyber attacks against governmental ICTs than other European countries that ranked higher in the above-mentioned index, e.g. the United Kingdom (4th), the Netherlands (5th), Norway (6th), Denmark (7th), Spain (9th), France (10th), Sweden (12th), Germany (15th), Belgium (16th), Switzerland (18th) and Estonia (20th) [UNI 10, pp. 114].

It is extremely difficult to find reliable and complete data on cyber-attacks against a specific country, considering that not all attacks are easily detectable if they do not show their effects in the physical world. However, as far as Italy is concerned, we can mention two recent cases that have had tangible repercussions. On January 26, 2007, the Italian Air Force website was successfully defaced by four Turkish hackers claiming that it was "a protest against those who support the war". More recently, in November 2009, the Air Force and Ministry of Defense websites were infected by a malware that in an automatic and stealthy way reproduced itself through a download on visitors' machines without them noticing.

In the case of war, either kinetic or cyber, critical national infrastructures (CNIs) may be the first to be hit, together with traditional military targets. As with the cyber incident at the Iranian Bushehr's nuclear plant demonstrates, this kind of cybe-attack has increased to an unprecedented level of sophistication. The criticality is reflected by the fact that SCADA (supervisory control and data acquisition) systems that manage CNIs are connected to internet protocol (IP) networks or to the Internet[9], as reported in a recent survey conducted by McAfee interviewing 600 managers from 14 advanced countries, including Italy [MCA 10]. According to this

---

8 Scoring 0.5800 – compared to an average European score of 0.6227 and world average of 0.4406 – of which 0.0982 were online service components, 0.1622 were telecommunication infrastructure components, and 0.3196 were human capital components [UNI 10, pp. 114].
9 Precisely, they are connected to the company's Intranet, which is in turn connected to the Internet.

report, around 45% of Italian managers interviewed think that foreign governments are involved in attacks against CNIs [MCA 10] and the countries that generate primary concern are China (around 40%), the US (21%) and Russia (5%) [MCA 10]. Nowadays information and communication infrastructures (ICIs) govern CNIs and are themselves critical infrastructures on which defense and national security agencies also rely. Italy hosts the main exchange point between Central and Southern Italian internet service providers (ISPs) – the Nautilus Mediterranean eXchange point (NaMeX) in Rome – on which Southern European and Mediterranean carriers converge. Apart from ICIs, those that provide electric energy are the most sensitive among CNIs.

In this regard, two major challenges have been identified by the EU.

First, we are all increasingly dependent on ICTs in all areas of our daily life. Indeed, ICTs govern energy-critical infrastructures – normally managed by privately-owned companies – on which other critical infrastructures are in turn interdependent:

– ICTs themselves;

– other energy supply services (natural gas and oil);

– food and water supply;

– waste disposal;

– hazardous materials storage;

– government and public agencies in general;

– finance and insurance companies;

– healthcare, emergency and rescue services;

– transport, traffic and logistic services;

– postal services;

– mass media; and

– cultural and research institutions.

Such interdependence and the great complexity of CNIs mean that even small outages, failures and disruptions can produce dramatic consequences (the so-called "vulnerability paradox").

Second, the creation of a common and liberalized energy market in the EU has driven the development of regional networks that extend across national and even EU boundaries. This is true for both electricity and gas supplies provided through long distance pipelines. The gas supply system is considered the 'Achilles' heel' of the European energy supply security, since the supply chains start in other States –

often situated in difficult regions, such as the North Sea and the Maghreb and, in the future, also in the Arctic area, Caspian Basin, Persian Gulf, Middle East, and Central Africa. These pipes transport natural gas across several transit States before reaching their final destination [NER 09]. The growing EU dependence on gas and other energy imports from countries outside Europe – including unstable regions – determines an expansion of network interconnections that increase vulnerability to cyber-attacks. It is, however, outside the remit of this chapter to analyze Italian strategy for energy policies. In this framework it is sufficient to know that, according to the 2010 ENEA[10] report on energy and the environment, in 2009 the Italian level of foreign energy dependence remained virtually unchanged at around 85%, compared to the average of about 53% across the 27 EU Member States, There is a growing dependence on foreign markets for natural gas compared to a basic stable dependence on imported oil [ENE 10]. A comparison between Italy and some major EU countries – France, Germany, Spain, and the UK – shows that, as opposed to different levels of dependence on total energy, for all these countries there is a constant dependence on oil (close to 100%) required by the transport sector – except for the UK, which has a significant domestic production. The Italian case, however, is unusual considering its total dependence on the importation of solid fuels (like France) – in the absence of a significant domestic production – and of electric energy, which is historically constant [ENE 10].

Both ICIs' and CNIs' network security and resilience can be ensured through supranational coordinated strategies. Since the bulk of critical infrastructures, as we have just seen, are transnational, an international approach is required.

5.3. The Italian legal and organizational framework

The importance and strategic value of public information systems was first recognized by the Minister for Innovation and Technologies Directive in the January 16, 2002 document *Information and Telecommunications Security in the Public Sector*. However, the legal basis for the protection of CNIs from cyber-attacks can be found in Article 7bis (electronic security) of law no. 155 from July 31, 2005, which contains urgent measures for countering international terrorism. CNIs are those processes the destruction, disruption, or partial unavailability of which significantly weakens the efficiency and functioning of the vital services of a nation. Specifically [COP 10]:

– production and distribution of energy;

---

10 ENEA stands for *Agenzia Nazionale per le Nuove Tecnologie, l'Energia e lo Sviluppo Economico Sostenibile* and is the national agency for new technologies in the energy sector, facilitating a sustainable economic development.

- communications;

- transport;

- management of water resources;

- production and food distribution;

- health (hospitals, networks and interconnection services);

- banks and financial systems;

- security and civil protection;

- supporting networks of institutions and constitutional bodies;

- special services provided by some strategic organizations and companies.

A dedicated State police unit, the National Computer Crime Center for Critical Infrastructure Protection (CNAIPIC or *Centro Nazionale Anticrimine Informatico per la Protezione delle Infrastrutture Critiche*)[11], was established in order to apply law no. 155. It has been in operation since June 23, 2009, on a 24 hours a day, seven days a week basis, and supports the security efforts of the operators of computerized information infrastructures, listed in the Minister of the Interior's decree of January 9, 2008[12]. To ensure CNIs security, agreements have been entered into by the Ministry of the Interior's Department of Public Security and public/private companies providing critical services [VUL 10]:

- the Italian mail service (*Poste Italiane*);

- the national agency for air-traffic control (*Ente Nazionale Assistenza al Volo* or ENAV);

- telecommunications companies (*Telecom Italia*, Vodafone, Fastweb, Wind, H3G);

---

11 Foreseen by the State Police Chief Directive of August 7, 2008.

12 According to Article 1, section 1, computerized information infrastructures should be considered of national interest, as well as those systems and services that support the institutional functions of:

a) ministries, agencies and institutions that they supervise, that are active in the fields of international relations, security, justice, defense, finance, communications, transport, energy, environment or health;

b) Bank of Italy and independent authorities;

c) companies owned by the State, regions and metropolitan areas by municipalities with not less than 500,000 inhabitants, engaged in the communication, transport, energy, health and water sectors;

d) any other institution, administration, organization, public or private legal person whose activities, for reasons of law enforcement and public security, are recognized to be of national interest by the Minister of the Interior or the provincial public security authorities.

– energy producer and provider companies (Terna, Enel, ENI, ACEA);

– banks and financial institutions (CONSOB[13], ABI[14], Bank of Italy, and private banks);

– the Italian Railway Company (*Ferrovie dello Stato*);

– Alitalia; and

– mass media such as RAI[15,] ANSA[16] and Mediaset.

It should be noted, however, that the mission of CNAIPIC is to prevent and prosecute computer crimes of a common, organized or terrorist nature through intelligence capabilities and judicial police tasks. Therefore, cyber-attacks for information and cyber warfare purposes lie outside the mandate of the above-mentioned agency.

The Italian intelligence services are also actively involved in cyber-security activities. Within the Information Department for Security (or *Dipartimento Informazioni per la Sicurezza*) of the Presidency of the Council of Ministers, which is the coordinating body of the two intelligence agencies AISI (*Agenzia Informazioni e Sicurezza Interna* – Internal Information and Security Agency) and AISE (*Agenzia Informazioni e Sicurezza Esterna* – External Information and Security Agency), there is the UCSe (Central Office for Secrecy – *Ufficio Centrale per la Segretezza*). This office has expertise concerning the security of classified communications (COMSEC) and the physical security of facilities that handle classified information. UCSe also takes part in the work of the UN Group of Governmental Experts to study the consequences of cyber-attacks and evaluate possible countermeasures to protect critical information systems. Furthermore, an ICT counterintelligence section has recently been created within the counterintelligence department of the Internal Information and Security Agency, in accordance with Law No. 124/2007 that transferred internal counterintelligence tasks from the former SISMi (now the AISE) to AISI. This section operates in close cooperation with police forces and with strategic public and private national organizations. Its technical personnel participate in multilateral forums, such as the Working Groups on Electronic Attacks and the Working Group on Interceptions. AISE has an INFOSEC Division instead, which is responsible for identifying and neutralizing ICT attacks on the Agency's and country's information resources. It also achieves this through timely cyber-intelligence information-sharing with international partners.

---

13 CONSOB is the National Commission for Companies and the Stock Exchange Market.
14 ABI is the Italian Banks Association.
15 Italian public radio-television company.
16 The main Italian press agency.

In 2007, a board for the protection of CNIs (*Tavolo PIC – Protezione Infrastrutture Critiche*) was established within the Office of the Military Advisor of the Prime Minister to study and analyze CNIs. Representatives from major interested ministries are assigned to the board.

Moreover, pursuant to an EU Directive[17], in order to identify and list Italy's crucial infrastructures beginning with the energy and transportation sectors, a technical secretariat – functionally subordinate to the Military Advisor of the Prime Minister and inclusive of computing facilities – was formed in January 2010[18] to protect CNIs. It also fosters interdepartmental coordination of national activities also within international forums. This list is classified, since a well-coordinated attack against those infrastructures could seriously jeopardize the national security of Italy, even if their protection is mainly focused on accidents, such as natural disasters, rather than attacks[19]. This is confirmed by the creation of the above-mentioned secretariat within the Centre of Civil Protection/CBRN (chemical, biological, radiological and nuclear) of the Civil Protection Department.

In addition, the e-government 2012 information technology security plan foresees the stabilization and strengthening of the Computer Emergency Response Team (CERT) of the Public Connectivity Service created within the National Center for Information Technology in Public Administration (CNIPA or *Centro Nazionale per l'Informatica nella Pubblica Amministrazione*) – now called "DigitPA" – under Article 21, paragraph 5(a) of the President of the Council of Ministers Decree of January 4, 2008. In this context, a stronger integration between the central component (CERT-SPC, the CERT for Connectivity Public System) and Public Administration structures that are locally distributed is felt necessary. These bodies have the task of implementing measures to prevent and manage accidents that may occur on systems inherent to their domain, and follow the instructions and support provided by CERT-SPC[20]. The consolidation of the CERT-SPC provides the central government with the capability to:

– have an information network that is primarily focused on collecting data and information necessary for coordination in their frame of reference;

– use advanced tools for monitoring vulnerabilities and observing hostile behaviors on the network;

---

17 Council Directive 2008/114/EC of December 8, 2008, on the identification and designation of European critical infrastructures and the assessment of the need to improve their protection.

18 With Civil Protection Ordinance No. 3836 of December 30, 2009.

19 As noticed by the academician Salvatore Tucci, professor of computer engineering and co-founder of an Italian think tank promoting infrastructure protection [KIN 10].

20 The Defense has its own, independent CERT.

– develop a complex system of communication through alerts and reports of emergencies, addressed to personnel and facilities involved in the operational management of government information technology systems;

– use of standardized procedures for response and coordination on occasion of computer accidents;

– interact with a variety of analog bodies to ensure proper verification and correlation of information and data obtained; and

– improve the mechanisms and protection measures based on incident analysis.

Between 2002 and 2003, well before such major developments, two groups were created within the Department of Innovation and Technology of the Presidency of the Council of Ministers [ENI 10b]. The first was a National Technical Committee on Informatics Security, which is responsible for improving the information technology security of public bodies and for defining their nationwide ICT security plan. The second is a Working Group on Critical Information Infrastructure Protection, which is composed of representatives from government departments and agencies, as well as private sector actors involved in the management and control of CNIs.

Finally, it is interesting to note that last year Italy's Prime Minister issued a decree on the national organization for crisis management[21], which led to a reorganization of the crisis management system by creating a Political-Strategic Committee (*Comitato Politico-Strategico* or CoPS) and an Inter-ministry Unit for Situation and Planning (*Nucleo Interministeriale di Situazione e Pianificazione* or NISP). The CoPS is charged with addressing and managing national crises. It is chaired by the Prime Minister and its members are the Ministers of Foreign Affairs, Defense, Internal Affairs, Economy and Finance. The NISP, on the other hand, is a permanent body chaired by the Under-Secretary of the Presidency of the Council of Ministers–Secretary of the Council of Ministers. It aims to support the CoPS and the Prime Minister in the case of current or potential crisis as well preventing damage, planning countermeasures and preparing the country in the case a crisis should arise. The NISP, which replaces the Political-Military Unit (*Nucleo Politico-Militare*), a non-permanent body providing the CoPS with consultancies in times of crisis, systematically monitors the national and international security situation to foresee and prevent possible crisis. It relies on the early-warning system provided by the bodies represented within the NISP, namely the interested ministries and the intelligence community[22]. A common Secretariat for the CoPS and the NISP is

---

21 DPCM "Organizzazione nazionale per la gestione delle crisi", *Gazzetta Ufficiale*, vol. 151, no. 139, June 17, 2010.
22 The NISP is composed of:

foreseen within the Prime Minister's Military Consultancy Office [GER 10]. It is worthwhile noting that the above-mentioned bodies would play a strategic role in the event that an information- and cyber warfare-related crisis should arise.

This multiplication and proliferation of actors within the Presidency of the Council of Ministers creates a problem in the case of a real and not simulated cyber warfare attack or, more generally, information warfare activity, since it would be difficult to establish who should do what. This also represents a vulnerability of the system.

5.4. The need for a national cyber-defense and -security strategy

To date, Italy has successfully built up infrastructures to tackle cyber-crime and protect intellectual property, including trademarks and industrial patents. However, as stated in the Co.Pa.Si.R. report on the possible implications to national security of cyber threats [COP 10], what is lacking is a strategic plan to counteract the cyber-threat – as part of a national security strategy – that dictates the guidelines to all stakeholders, coordinating efforts and planning actions for security implementation of CNIs. The Italian Parliamentary Intelligence Oversight Committee, moreover, recognizes that appropriate countermeasures have to be adopted before the attack occurs, since success is directly proportional to the speed of implementation of countermeasures.

It is also evident that, considering the global dimension of the cyber-threat, intervention strategies involving all security bodies is necessary, including those beyond national boundaries. In this regard, the Parliamentary Committee has registered an absence of unique coordinated planning at a political level. To overcome this shortage in planning, Co.Pa.Si.R. recommends that the government adopts a strategic-organizational system to ensure appropriate leadership and clear policies for tackling the threat and coordinating stakeholders. The report stresses the fact that this could be achieved through a coordinating structure within the Presidency of the Council of Ministers, without the need to grant additional funds, but simply redefining the activities of existing facilities. This structure should perform specific tasks, such as:

---

a) two representatives designated by the Ministry of Foreign Affairs, Internal Affairs and Defense, respectively;
b) a representative designated by the Ministry of Economy and Finances, Health, the Department of Civil Protection, DIS, AISE and AISI, the fire department and the public medical emergency service;
c) an officer from the Prime Minister's press office and spokesperson, and an officer from the Prime Minister's Diplomatic and Military Consultancy Office.

– define the threat and provide a draft of a national security document dedicated to the protection of critical infrastructures;

– prepare an action plan outlining the perimeter of Italian cyber-security, defining the roles and responsibilities of those responsible for national cyber-security;

– draft strategic policies for cyber protection, resilience and security, in close coordination with public and private partners, starting with our intelligence services;

– promote public awareness-raising campaigns and common specialized training among various stakeholders at national and international level;

– prepare disaster recovery plans for data of strategic value for the security of the Republic; and

– coordinate the participation of Italian delegations to international cooperation boards, bilateral and multilateral, at EU and NATO level.

The Committee also recommends an insight, from a technical, legal and regulatory perspective, on the emerging practices of acquisition and retention of computerized data. This is particularly important with regard to phenomena such as cloud computing and the proliferation of virtual servers, as well as on the delicate profiles related to deep packet inspection operations, which has an undoubted effect on the protection of national security but requires proper regulation to ensure privacy and confidentiality. The delicate balance between privacy and national security requires the constant updating of laws in compliance with the constitutional right to privacy.

The same Co.Pa.Si.R. report highlights that the transnational nature of the threat requires a wider participation of Italian intelligence services to international coordination initiatives. This applies, in particular, to the need to identify a national focal point for the Network Security Incident Alert Mechanism established upon the decision of the EU Council Secretary General following the protracted cyber-attack against the unclassified IOLAN (intranet office local area network) network of the EU. This was before the establishment of the envisaged European bodies (including an EU-CERT) dedicated to the protection of critical information technology infrastructures. The above also applies to the process underway within NATO – and particularly within the Working Group on Information Assurance of NATO Security Committee, in which UCSe participates. This is probably intended to urge Member States to identify a national authority of reference on the matter. On both fronts, Co.Pa.Si.R. suggests to the government that the Information Department for Security, which already strategically and operationally participates in the coordination of activities to prevent and combat cyber-threats to national security, is the most appropriate institutional reference.

Specifically referring to information warfare, the report then concludes that Italy should promote consensus-building in multilateral forums and lead to the drafting of a treaty to counter State-originated cyber threats, such as the use of information and network technologies as unconventional military tools. It states that this could be achieved through the creation of an International Centre for the Repression and Control of the proliferation of offensive cyber tools. Indeed, the current militarization of the scenario by major geopolitical players is liable to degrade the political and strategic relations and undermine the search for a world order based as much as possible on stability and cooperation. In this context, Italy is called on to participate, politically and diplomatically, in NATO's joint action plan to respond to the threat posed by the military use of networks. It is also involved in the expansion of the scope of 'collective security' envisaged by Article 5 of the North Atlantic Alliance Treaty to cases of 'computer attack'[23].

In order to counter cyber-threats, policy-makers are currently discussing the creation of a cyber-defense command. In this regard, the Italian Parliamentary Intelligence Oversight Committee has consulted many experts from both the public and private sector on the best way to counter cyber-attacks on Italian national security, in order to deliver a packet of proposals to the Parliament. Currently, Italian cyber-security is managed by the armed and police forces and government departments but, as noted by one of the experts audited, there should be a common definition and vision of those threats. Decision makers are discussing whether to create one or two controlling structures, in the latter case one military with links to intelligence agencies and the other civilian. Italy has many cyber-crime units, some also dealing with cyber-terrorism, but what is missing is a structure that is able to tackle information warfare and, specifically, cyber-war-type attacks. To prevent and react to this kind of cyber-attack, a 2008 report commissioned by the Center for Military Strategic Studies [IOV 08] proposed the creation of a Centre of Excellence (CoE), which should be coordinated by a director who responds and is directly subordinate to the director of the intelligence apparatus, or other equivalent defense structure. Other than managing CoE activities, the director should coordinate CoE relationships with analogous centers of Italian and foreign intelligence services, as well as with other bodies such as research centers, universities, national and international companies. CoE shall be composed of four units: information systems; data analysis and processing systems; telecommunication systems; and identification and recognition systems[24].

---

23 In this sense, see [TIK 11, pp. 7].

24 Each unit should be further divided into sub-units. Specifically, Unit 1 is composed as follows: operating systems; protection technologies for attacks against critical information infrastructures; technologies and methodologies for rapid system recovery) and rapid system management in information crisis management activities. Unit 2: monitoring, control and

The report also suggests that, together with the CoE, a defense information infrastructure should be established and implemented, which should incorporate all defense networks – both classified and not classified – since such an effort would allow resource optimization at networking, security and core services level. It would also ensure interoperability with NATO, the EU and other international organizations' systems and services, through the Information Exchange Gateway.

Interoperability and coordination is also essential from a policy and strategic perspective. At the moment many EU countries have their own policies for critical information infrastructure protection, which are fragmented and not coordinated, and a coordinated emergency response between national governments and EU institutions is still lacking [REN 10]. Therefore, while thinking about a possible cyber-defense and -security strategy for Italy, we cannot leave the EU internal security strategy [EUC 10] out of consideration. Although this document is focused on cyber-crime, some considerations also apply to cyber warfare attacks, such as those contained in "Action 3: Improve capability for dealing with cyber attacks" of "Objective 3: Raise levels of security for citizens and businesses in cyberspace", and in "Objective 5: Increase Europe's resilience to crises and disasters". In Objective 5, the document expressly recognizes how the EU is exposed to an array of potential crises and disasters, such as those caused by cyber-attacks on critical infrastructures:

> "These [...] threats call for improvements to long-standing crisis and disaster management practices in terms of efficiency and coherence. They require both solidarity in response, and responsibility in prevention and preparedness with an emphasis on better risk assessment and risk management at EU level of all potential hazards" [EUC 10].

With the aim of enhancing prevention, detection and fast reaction in the event of cyber- attacks or cyber -disruption, by 2012 all EU Member States and EU institutions themselves should have established a "well-functioning CERT", which will be supported by ENISA. These CERTs should cooperate with law-enforcement agencies to prevent and react to cyber threats. By the same deadline, "Member States should network together their national/governmental CERTs [...] to enhance Europe's preparedness" [EUC 10]. Together with ENISA, Member States should develop national contingency plans and undertake regular national and European exercises in incident response and disaster recovery. Moreover, by 2013,

---

acquisition systems; data mining and harmonization; software engineering; bio-informatics. Unit 3: web methodologies and technologies; mobile, wireless, satellite and radiofrequency identification technologies; modeling systems and simulation of complex systems; advanced systems for pervasive computing. Unit 4: science and biometric technologies; methodologies and tracking technologies; multimedia technologies; advanced computing; artificial intelligence; advanced signal processing and analysis.

with the support of the European Commission and ENISA, a European Information Sharing and Alert System and a network of contact points between relevant bodies and Member States will be established [EUC 10].

In the framework of the European Program for Critical Infrastructure Protection (EPCIP), Council Directive 2008/114/EC of December 8, 2008, which identifies the ICT sector as a future priority sector (Section 5)[25], foresees that a security liaison officer should be established in every EU country who acts as a point of contact for security-related issues between the owner/operator of the European critical infrastructure and the relevant Member State authority (Article 6). Each Member State shall conduct a threat assessment and shall report to the Commission every two years (Article 7). They shall appoint a European Critical Infrastructure Protection focal point that shall coordinate European critical infrastructure protection issues within the Member State, with other Member States and with the Commission (Article 10)[26]. The EPCIP also includes a Critical Infrastructure Warning Information Network, created in 2005 by the Commission, which brings together the critical infrastructure protection specialists of Member States assisting the Commission in drawing up a program to facilitate the exchange of information on shared threats and vulnerabilities and appropriate countermeasures and strategies[27].

Of course, a cyber defense and security strategy should also take into account the new NATO Strategic Concept, adopted in Lisbon on November 20, 2010, which replaces the old one approved in Washington in 1999. During the discussion about the strategic concept, there had been divergences between the US and allied European countries. Among them, the US stressed the necessity to enhance the protection of the Internet and other networks and envisaged collective defensive and offensive cyber warfare operations. However, while allied European countries agree on the necessity of having collective defensive cyber warfare capacities, they do not support the proposal for establishing a corresponding offensive apparatus [CER 11].

Section 19 of NATO's new Strategic Concept clearly states that NATO has to develop further its "ability to prevent, detect, defend against and recover from

---

25 In 2011, the European Commission reviewed the Council Directive to include the ICT sector.

26 The provisions of the Directive have only recently been implemented in Italy with the Legislative Decree of April 11, 2011, No. 61, which assigns a central role to the NISP. It is responsible for the identification of Italian European critical infrastructures, the draft of the initial threat assessment and the biennial report to the Commission. Finally, it serves as the European Critical Infrastructure Protection contact point.

27 This system is similar to the US Critical infrastructure Warning Information Network, which has been operational since 2003.

cyber-attacks, including the use of the NATO planning process to enhance and coordinate national cyber-defence capabilities, bringing all NATO bodies under centralized cyber protection, and better integrating NATO cyber awareness, warning and response with member nations" [NAT 10]. In this regard, Italy is one of the sponsoring countries[28] that contributed to the creation of the Cooperative Cyber Defence Centre of Excellence in Tallinn, Estonia, on May 14, 2008. This Centre conducts research and training on cyber warfare in order to enhance NATO's cyber-defense capabilities. This body, which is responsible for further developing NATO cyber-defense doctrine and strategy, together with the Cyber Defence Management Board, which is the main consultation body for the North Atlantic Council on this subject and provides advice to Member States, should be kept in consideration while developing a national cyber-defense policy and strategy that is truly coordinated and consistent with the Alliance approach.

Since a clear, coordinated and coherent national strategy is still missing, we are going to consider a possible cyber-defense and security strategy for Italy. We are inspired to instigate a proactive rather than a reactive approach and that ensures operational flexibility and adaptability, taking into consideration what has been developed up to date on this subject in other countries and by supranational organizations such as NATO and the European Commission. Even if, for obvious reasons, information and cyber warfare policies and strategies are not publicly available, with some exceptions like the US where doctrines are publicly discussed, we can make reference to national cyber-security strategies that are all too often general. Most probably, this is currently due to policy-makers not having a full comprehension of this phenomenon. Starting from the assumption that there are no valid solutions for every country, and that national policies, strategies, theories and doctrines reflect the political background and organizational culture of interested agencies, we can draw some conclusions.

After having established who should participate in the drafting of a cyber defense and security strategy, it is important to consider the issues that such a strategic document must address. There is no doubt that, since the bulk of potential targets are owned by private entities – for example ISPs, telephone companies, electricity, water and gas suppliers, and nuclear power plant owners – they should be actively involved in the design and development of national doctrines, strategies and policies on cyber security and defense. They should work together with relevant institutional stakeholders – thus envisaging the necessity of public–private partnerships[29]. The aspects that this multidisciplinary team should address are

---

28 Together with Estonia, Germany, Latvia, Lithuania, the Slovak Republic and Spain [NAT 10, pp. 4].
29 A necessity that had been stressed in the White House's Cyberspace Policy Review [WHI 10, pp. i].

several and varied, ranging from technical to geopolitical, from organizational to legal ones. Let us observe the main points.

First, a clear chain of command and control seems to be needed. A possible solution is a one-stop coordination center for national cyber-security that deals with cyber-related threats whatever their nature: hackers, criminal, terroristic, military and so on. The coordination center should be established within the Presidency of the Council of Ministers – absorbing all the existing uncoordinated and dispersed structures – and should encompass three clusters: a political board, a research and development unit and a technical-operative body. These should be directed by a responsible individual, preferably an Under-Secretary of State, who must have deep knowledge of the subject – thus encompassing the political and technical stance in a single person. This person needs to mediate between the coordination center and the Prime Minister. Naturally, the Under-Secretary of State should rely on a secretariat that has the required personnel and capabilities to support the several and complex tasks required. The political board should represent all interested ministries – defense, internal and foreign affairs, economy and finances, infrastructures and transports. The order of business and the calendar of the sessions should be established by the Under-Secretary of State responsible for the coordination center and the chair of the political board. He/she should be responsible, also upon the suggestion of Ministries' representatives to invite audit experts and authorities from relevant public institutions, such as CNAIPIC, Information Department for Security and the Civil Protection Department, and from private companies, such as administrators or technicians from CNIs to the sessions. The board should have the task of developing national strategies and policies, with the support of the other two components of the coordination center.

The research and development unit should merge the knowledge coming from national intelligence services – civilian and military – and from university departments and think tanks, to draft studies, reports and analysis. The unit should act as an early-warning system, should draft strategic analysis and should foster technical solutions for enhancing resilience, cyber-defense and security.

Finally, the technical-operative body, exclusively composed of highly-skilled technicians, should keep the national networks and systems constantly monitored – keeping contacts and sharing information with national CERTs. Together with the research and development unit and the political board, we should have a full picture of strengths and vulnerabilities of our networks. The technical body can also act as an advisor for CNIs.

Both the research and development unit and the technical-operative body should be partly composed of personnel seconded from relevant national ministries, agencies and departments to ease information-sharing. The coordination center shall play a fundamental role also in the international arena, since it can act as the unique referent for the NATO Cyber Defence Management Board and ENISA. Moreover, the research and development unit can be in charge of drafting the threat assessment to be submitted to the European Commission every two years, while the technical-operative body can encompass the security liaison officer and the European Critical Infrastructure Protection contact point envisaged by the Council Directive 2008/114/EC, as well as the national focal point for the Network Security Incident Alert Mechanism.

The coordination center should have the power to reorganize the bodies currently operating within the Presidency of the Council of Ministers – rationalizing resources and avoiding useless duplications and redundancies – without changing the organization and mandate of external existing organizations, such as CNAIPIC and intelligence agencies' sub-units.

This reorganization will respond to two necessities. First, since cyber war happens swiftly, the effects of a cyber-attack can be immediate and unforeseeable. This leaves decision-makers with no time to think and take decisions, and stresses the importance of sharing almost real-time intelligence (within the research and development unit) and post-mortem forensic data (eased by the technical body) among relevant stakeholders, e.g. military and law-enforcement authorities. Second, this will allow the attribution problem to be dealt with properly and determine what action is needed and justified, proportionate and appropriate according to national and international law. This is because when enough confidence on the motives for an attack/incident is gained, the coordination center will be able to switch the case to the competent agency – civil protection, military, intelligence or law enforcement – or to a group of them according to the nature and complexity of the case. The attribution problem can be overcome through strong computer forensics capabilities and conventional intelligence: capacities that come from different agencies.

Many attacks are blurred, considering that cyber criminals can become "rental cyber warriors" and potential targets are often non-military but are indirectly involved in military infrastructure. As stated in the 2010 White House's Cyberspace Policy Review, "[...] this issue transcends the jurisdictional purview of individual departments and agencies because, although each agency has a unique contribution to make, no single agency has a broad enough perspective or authority to match the sweep of the problem" [WHI 10]. The US cyberspace policy envisages the appointment of a cyber security policy official responsible for coordinating the US's cyber security policies and activities. This official would chair the already established Information and Communications Infrastructure Interagency Policy Committee. The US Comprehensive National Cybersecurity Initiative is to put together law enforcement, intelligence, counterintelligence and military capabilities to address the full spectrum of cyber threats. Thus, an "integrated approach" is the best suitable solution.

As for the defense sector, since many nations – such as China, France, Russia, and the US, to name but a few – have already established cyber commands and cyber warfare units with offensive and defensive capabilities, Italy should develop a cyber command within the Ministry of Defense. The command should be able to integrate the capabilities of existing units, namely Unit II – Information and Security (the military intelligence service), Unit VI – C4I Systems and Transformation, and the Defense C4 Command, with information and cyber warfare capacities. While the protection of military networks and systems is granted by the Defense's CERT, which is a component of Unit II, armed forces should also protect civil networks as well as CNIs not only during conventional war but also in case of cyber warfare, since, otherwise, such infrastructures would remain without the State's protection, considering that CNAIPIC is a police entity and that the task would be outside its mandate. Therefore, a strict cooperation between cyber command, CNAIPIC and CNIs – directed and eased by the coordination center – should be taken into consideration. In this regard, the Cyber Shot 2010 exercise organized by the CERT-Technical Defense Centre has seen the participation of CNAIPIC and ENAV, among the others, and it is desirable that future drills will also involve the participation of other main CNIs to improve joint incident response and disaster recovery.

It is also important to note how, according to the Italian Constitution, "Italy repudiates war as an instrument of offence to other people's liberties and as a means to resolve international controversies [...]" (Article 11, see section 1). Therefore, an Italian cyber warfare strategy can only consider it from a cyber-defense perspective excluding Italy's being first in using cyber weapons in the framework of a pre-emptive attack. This does not exclude cyber-offence capabilities, especially those to be used as force multipliers, in the case of conventional or unconventional warfare. Rather, Italy should develop its own cyber war capabilities like other NATO Member States. The sole fact that every developed nation has its own information and cyber warfare capabilities should urge Italy to improve its own.

As already mentioned, public–private partnerships are also essential for designing and implementing a cyber-defense and -security strategy – since the private sector runs and manages most of the network and critical infrastructures used by government and private users. The PPP should establish the roles and responsibilities for each partner, such as industry, financial institutions and academia. Operators of critical infrastructures should engage with government officials and set up procedures and protocols in case of an attack. Thus, the chief executive officers and chief technology officers of major information technology/defense companies and critical infrastructures should meet regularly with the security liaison officer envisaged by the Council Directive 2008/114/EC. They should also meet with other officers from relevant ministries and agencies/departments within the proposed coordination center.

Public–private partnerships also facilitate trusted information-sharing among relevant EU stakeholders [REN 10]. Indeed, as urged by the European Commission, within the EU, Italy should share information through the European Public-Private Partnership for Resilience (EP3R) [EUC 10]. Cooperation with international partners through a structured exchange of information and good practices could considerably facilitate in fighting cross-border threats. A report by NATO's Parliamentary Assembly [NPA 09] encourages the cooperation and exchange of information between State authorities and crucial NATO cyber defense bodies, such as the CDMA[30].

It is also needed to coordinate national strategies, integrating them in a global dimension within the EU Common Security and Defense Policy, as envisaged in the Lisbon Treaty, which entered into force on December 1, 2009. Moreover, "the security strategies of the EU and NATO should not only be complementary but also convergent, each giving due weight to the potential of the other" [EUP 09: Section 10]. To this should be added the fact that Italy has recently supported the project for a common European defense within the EU through the renewed European Defense Agency [SEN 10].

National policies should also be in compliance with an international framework on information and cyber warfare that will establish which acts are lawful and which are not, in order to develop compliant rules of engagement. The purpose is to minimize collateral damage and to be in compliance with the fundamental customary International Humanitarian Law, including the principles of humanity, proportionality and distinction. Indeed, according to US Senator Carl Levin, Chairman of the Senate Committee on Armed Services, "cyber weapons are approaching weapons of mass destruction in their effect" [SIN 10]. Current international law does not explicitly address information and cyber warfare, and the possibility of an international treaty on cyber warfare was discussed at the 2010 World Economic Forum in Davos, Switzerland [HUG 10]. The main challenges that have to be faced are:

– finding a shared definition of what constitutes an act of cyber warfare;

– attack attribution;

---

30 CDMA stands for Cyber Defence Management Authority, which is managed by the Cyber Defence Management Board, and is responsible for coordinating cyber defense throughout the Alliance.

– dual-use weapons; and

– proxy attacks.

However, an international treaty on the war in this fifth dimension appears to be unfeasible due to several issues. If the States reach an agreement on what constitutes an act of cyber warfare and they sign and ratify an international convention on it, international law cannot – by definition – keep pace with technological developments and it would quickly become obsolete. Moreover, it does not apply to non-state actors and the verification of its implementation seems to be impossible with regard to limiting – and even monitoring – the proliferation of banned cyber weapons. In this regard, the idea proposed in the Co.Pa.Si.R. report to establish an International Centre for the Repression and Control of the proliferation of offensive cyber tools seems unfeasible due to the volatile and easily concealable nature of cyber arms. To overcome this issue and that of attribution, the more viable path seems to be that proposed in the US where States are considered accountable for malicious cyber activity generated in or passing through their cyber space, whether State-sponsored or not [ZET 10].

Another issue is the great importance of developing cyber-security higher education in order to prepare talented ICT experts for employment by institutions such as the defense and intelligence services, and to retain them through career incentives to prevent their leaving the public service for the private sector [WHI 10]. Directly linked with this aspect is the enhancement of awareness and skills to reduce the vulnerabilities and counter-threats in the cyber domain, from users to system and network administrators. One of the most successful and most frequently used attack tools should not be forgotten: 'social engineering'. The human factor continues to be the main point of vulnerability, therefore administrators must be held accountable for the security of systems and networks. Moreover, ICT security experts and system/network administrators in the public and private sectors should be trained in 'ethical hacking' which will allow them to identify computer flaws and vulnerabilities before they are exploited by an adversary[31]. At the same time, security controls over CNIs' employees are needed in order to prevent or at least to manage the threat from insiders.

At least one of the possible insider threats can be defeated granting that SCADA systems cannot be accessed through USB ports or other connections through which malware can be transmitted, as happened in the Stuxnet case. The problem of external memory devices should be borne in mind when designing hardware and software components for critical infrastructures. Controls over the hardware and software supply chain for military and other critical infrastructure networks and

---

31 This practice is already a reality for the Pentagon's network administrators [LYN 10].

systems should be also envisaged in order to prevent sabotage and the injection of malicious instructions in the source code.

Moreover, CNIs should remain disconnected from the Internet and unencrypted command and control radio transmissions should be avoided. Intranets should be kept distinct and not related to the Internet through web-portals. The access to critical information systems should only be granted through the satisfaction of multiple key authentication requirements. Furthermore, resiliency should be granted through secret intrusion prevention systems, deep packet inspection and a back-up of the command and control network. Since these practices may violate users' privacy and civil liberties, these should be granted by the Privacy Warrantor.

5.5. Conclusion

Italy needs a Cyber Security National Strategic Plan that envisages an integrated and coordinated approach among key stakeholders, which should be granted through the establishment of a one-stop coordination center for national cyber security. Up to date different official policy documents for each sector have been produced – defense, foreign affairs, internal security, intelligence – but never a common strategic document in which these different instances are represented, discussed and integrated in a synergic way. From the perspective of a center, redundancies of bodies and functions should be overcome and a clear chain of command and control should be established, according to the principle of rationalization, efficiency, efficacy and economy that inform Italian public administration. We also need to overcome a merely judicial and law-enforced approach to the problem, and become aware that information and cyber warfare are first and foremost national security problems or, in other terms, political matters. At the same time, the old post-Cold War and conventional warfare mindset of counter proliferation and disarmament does not make any sense if applied to the fifth domain. This realm of unconventional weapons and emerging threats requires the formulation of new solutions, rather than an adjustment of doctrines and policies that already exist.

5.6. Bibliography

[AGY 09] AGVEMANG F., "On the imminent cyber warfare, what's Ghana's preparedness?", *GhanaWeb*, December 2, 2009.

[ANA 10] ANALISI DIFESA, "Esercitazioni di cyber defence per la difesa", *Analisi Difesa*, vol. 11, no. 113, 2010. http://cca.analisidifesa.it/it/magazine_8034243544/numero113/article _756277855521088703734640406506_2683573816_0.jsp

[ANT 11] ANTINORI A., "Sviluppo nell'ambito Nazionale del Concetto di 'Information Assurance'", *Relativo alla Protezione delle Informazioni nella loro Globalità*, Rome, Centro Militare Studi Strategici (CeMiSS), 2011.

[CER 11] CERVONE G., "La sicurezza internazionale e il nuovo concetto strategico della NATO", *Specchio Economico*, no. 2, February 2011.

[CLA 10] CLARKE R.A., KNAKE R.K., *Cyber War. The Next Threat to National Security and What to Do About It*, Harper Collins, New York, 2010.

[COP 10] COPASIR, Relazione. Possibili Implicazioni e Minacce per la Sicurezza Nazionale Derivanti dall'utilizzo dello Spazio Cibernetico, Co.Pa.Si.R Rome, 2010.

[ENE 10] ENEA, Rapporto energia e ambiente. Analisi e scenari 2009, ENEA, November 2010.

[ENI 10a] ENISA, *Cyber Europe 2010 Exercise has Started*, ENISA, November 4, 2010.

[ENI 10b] ENISA, Italy Country Report, ENISA, January 2010.

[EUC 10] EUROPEAN COMMISSION, Communication from the Commission to the European Parliament and the Council. The EU Internal Security Strategy in Action: Five Steps Towards a More Secure Europe, COM(2010) 673 final, EC, November 2010.

[EUP 09] EUROPEAN PARLIAMENT, European Parliament Resolution of 19 February 2009 on The Role of NATO in The Security Architecture of the EU, (2008/2197(INI)), European Parliament, 2009.

[FRI 08] FRITZ J., "How China will use cyber warfare to leapfrog in military competitiveness", *Culture Mandala*, vol. 8 no. 1, pp. 43, October 2008.

[GER 10] GERMANI L.S., GORI U., *Verso un Nuovo Sistema di Gestione delle Crisi di Sicurezza Nazionale*, 2010.

[HUG 10] HUGHES R., "A treaty for cyberspace", *International Affairs*, vol. 86 no. 2, pp. 523-541, March 2010.

[IOV 08] IOVANE G., Cyberwarfare e Cyberspace: Aspetti Concettuali, fasi ed Applicazione allo Scenario Nazionale ed all'ambito Militare, Centro Militare Studi Strategici (CeMiSS), Rome, 2008.

[IOV 11] IOVANE G., I Rischi per l'Infrastruttura Informatica della Difesa. Individuazione delle risorse organizzative necessarie al contrasto dell'attacco informatico per l'attivazione di strutture dedicate all'anti-hacker intelligence, Centro Militare Studi Strategici (CeMiSS), Rome, 2011.

[ISA 11] ISAF, International Security Assistance Force (ISAF): Key Facts and Figures, ISAF, March 4, 2011.

[KIN 10] KINGTON T., "Italy weighs cyber-defense command", *Defense News*, May 31, 2010.

[KRE 09] KREKEL B., *Capability of the People's Republic of China to Conduct Cyber Warfare and Computer Network Exploitation*, Northrop Grumman, October 9, 2009.

[LIB 09] LIBICKI M.C., *Cyberdeterrence and Cyberwar*, RAND Corporation, 2009.

[LYN 10] LYNN W.J. III, "Defending a new domain. The Pentagon's cyberstrategy", *Foreign Affairs Magazine*, September/October 2010 issue.

[MAE 09] MINISTERO DEGLI AFFARI ESTERI, *Winning Italy*. Almanacco dell'eccellenza italiana, December 2009.

[MCA 10] MCAFEE, Nel Mirino. Le Infrastrutture Critiche nell'era Digitale, McAfee, 2010.

[MDD 10] MINISTERO DELLA DIFESA, *Missioni/attività Internazionali – Situazione*, Ministero Della Difesa, 2010.

[NAT 10] NATO, Strategic Concept for the Defence and Security of the Members of the North Atlantic Treaty Organisation, NATO, 2010.

[NAT] NATO, CCDCOE - Cooperative Cyber Defence Centre of Excellence Tallinn, Estonia, NATO, 2008.

[NPA 09] NATO PARLIAMENTARY ASSEMBLY, NATO and Cyber Defence, 173 DSCFC 09 E bis, NATO, 2009.

[NER 09] NERLICH U., UMBACH F., "European energy infrastructure protection: addressing the cyber-warfare threat", *Journal of Energy Security*, October 2009, http://www.ensec.org/index.php?option=com_content&view=article&id=219:european-energy-infrastructure-protectionaddressing-the-cyber-warfare-threat&catid=100: issuecontent&Itemid=352.

[RAU 11] RAUSCHER K.F., KOROTKOV A., *Working Towards Rules for Governing Cyber Conflic: Rendering the Geneva and Hague Conventions in Cyberspace*, EastWest Institute, January 2011.

[REN 10] RENDA A., Protecting Critical Infrastructure in the EU, CEPS Task Force Report, Centre for European Policy Studies, 2010.

[SEN 10] SENATO DELLA REPUBLICA, *Risoluzione Approvata dalla Commissione sull'affare Assegnato n. 502*, Doc. XXIV no. 14, 16ᵃ Legislatura, 4ᵃ Commissione permanente, Resoconto sommario no. 175, December 2010.

[SIN 10] SINGEL R., "Cyberwar commander survives senate hearing", *Wired News*, April 15, 2010.

[STO 00] STOLL C., *The Cuckoo's Egg. Tracking a Spy through the Maze of Computer Espionage*, New York, Pocket Books, 2000.

[TIK 11] TIKK E., "Ten Rules for Cyber Security", *Survival*, vol. 53, no. 3, pp. 119-132, June-July 2011.

[UNI 10] UNITED NATIONS, United Nations e-Government Survey 2010. Leveraging e-Government at a Time of Financial and Economic Crisis, United Nations, New York, USA, 2010.

[UNG 10] UN GENERAL ASSEMBLY, Group of Governmental Experts on Developments in the Field of Information and Telecommunications in the Context of International Security, Resolution A/65/201, United Nations, July 30, 2010.

[USA 10] US ARMY, Cyberspace Operations Concept Capability Plan 2016–2028, TRADOC Pamphlet 525-7-8, February 22, 2010.

[VUL 10] VULPIANI D., "La cyber threat alle infrastrutture critiche in Italia: punto di situazione ed azione di contrasto", *Convegno ICSA – La Protezione delle Infrastrutture Critiche in Italia*, Rome, 5 May 2010.

[WHI 10] WHITE HOUSE, Cyberspace Policy Review. Assuring a Trusted and Resilient Information and Communication Infrastructure, The White House, 2010.

[ZET 10] ZETTER K., "Countries should be held responsible for cyber attacks", *Wired News*, July 30, 2010.

Chapter 6

Cyberspace in Japan's New Defense Strategy

Since the end of the Second World War, Japan's policies on security and defense have progressively evolved, while still being based on the restrictive principles of the 1947 Constitution. Japan's accession to the rank of global economic power in the 1970s, the end of the Cold War, the first Gulf War and the aftermath of 9/11 were all milestones that offered Japan the opportunity to re-examine the fine points of its alliance with the United States (US), its role in the security of the Asia-Pacific region, and its involvement in military operations abroad.

While the international environment poses new challenges for the country's security (the pressure exerted by the growing Chinese military; the threat from North Korea; and the weakening of the US hegemony), Japan has very recently experienced a significant political change, with the rise to power of the DPJ (Democratic Party of Japan) in August 2009. The new government soon advanced a new strategy for defense, redefining its priorities. One of the characteristics of this evolution lies in the inclusion of the 'cyberspace' dimension in Japan's defense strategies and military doctrines from 2010 onwards. This chapter aims to add to the debate on the directions Japan's defense policies are taking, focusing on the contribution of the cybernetic dimension to the defense strategy. We shall examine the extent to which the treatment of cyberspace constitutes a major evolution in defense policy: does cyberspace call into question the way in which security and national defense should be viewed?

Chapter written by Daniel VENTRE.

6.1. Japan's defense policy

Japan's defense policy is often explained by the yardstick of two theoretical approaches: realist and constructivist [GRE 11]. When Japan published the *National Defense Program Guideline* (NDPG) in 1976, it was a case of the school of the realist theory – a power that is militarizing. However, this militarization is not optimal and is weak, even in relation to the country's economic resources [KAW 01]. It is therefore reasonable to wonder about the reasons for this imbalance. For the constructivists, the reasons for the State's stance on the international scene are internal (the legal, normative, and social contexts). Thus, the institutions, social norms (anti-militaristic sentiment deeply anchored in society and the State machinery), and the Constitution render the emergence of a militarily strong Japan impossible [BER 98, KAT 96]. In the realists' view, this imbalance has its origins in the Nippo-American alliance, with Japan relying on the US for protection from external military threats, and therefore concentrating on its economic development [KAW 01].

For the neo-realists, the reason lies in Japan's desire to reduce the intensity of the security dilemma in the region [ATA 10]. To this end, Japan maintains its alliance with the US and retains a modest military arsenal, so as not to send a strong negative signal to the other countries in the region [KAW 01]. Japan is essentially betting on the dissuasive power of the alliance with the US, making it unlikely that a military campaign will be waged against it. Its military weakness is relative, however, as Japan has once again become a military power [LIN 03], with numerous pressures having driven the country to go beyond the limits initially imposed by the 1947 Constitution [WAN 08]:

– the US' desire to make Japan a strong ally in the region;

– China's growing military might;

– the rise of Japanese nationalism, inciting the country to strengthen the defense of its sovereignty;

– Japan's desire to make its presence felt as a military actor and no longer merely as an economic or diplomatic player (international contribution).

Japan's strategic choices are constrained by the posture of the States in the region. China's sending of destroyers into the Gulf of Aden in Somalian waters in December 2008 confirmed that it has ambitions to project its forces far beyond its borders, to secure its own interests. In fact, China could threaten Japan [HUG 09] and destabilize the region, which justifies Japan's remilitarization. However, the realists' and constructivists' views on Japanese defense complement one another rather than being mutually exclusive [DES 98]. While civil society appeared hostile to the militarization of the country, it has come to be in favor of an affirmation of

Japan's role on the international stage, and its restoration to the status of a 'normal' country, 'like any other', thus supporting a new phase of militarization that is crucial to that position (thereby rejoining the principles of realism) [HUG 04, PYL 07].

Since the mid-1970s, consideration of the security dilemma and the economic stakes (i.e. how to remain an economic power) has characterized Japan's posture in terms of defense [KAW 01]. For instance, this results in the need for Japan to maintain its economic relations with China, in order to maintain its economic prosperity; and the need to monitor China's growing military power [CHE 11]. Security in the region is essentially guided by a logical balance between powers and not of regional integration [ATA 10].

At the end of the Second World War, the international community wished to impose conditions on Japan such that it would never again be able to become a threat to peace. To this end, its capability and any vague notion of waging war had to be completely obliterated. Restrictive principles were written into the 1947 Constitution. In 1950, the American troops stationed in Japan were deployed to Korea, forcing Japan to build up its own forces to ensure its defense (creating the National Police Reserve). The peace treaty signed in 1951, known as the Treaty of San Francisco, was a bilateral security agreement, formalizing a Nippo-American alliance, which was considered essential to Japan's security at the time. In the context of its alliance with the US, Japan has continuously been providing assistance ever since, particularly in the war efforts in Korea and Vietnam; then in the war on terror by deploying its naval forces in the Indian Ocean (November 2001) to provide logistical support to the American troops engaged in Operation Enduring Freedom; and later in Iraq and Kuwait, in reconstruction missions. The principles of Japan's defense were set out in the *Basic Policies for National Defense* in May 1957, which laid the foundations for the formation of the Self Defense Forces (SDF). Its military capabilities were expanded at the occasion of subsequent plans (1962, then 1967).

Up until the mid-1970s, Japan depended almost entirely on the US for protection. Then Japan reformulated its defense strategy. A military doctrine, the *National Defense Program Guidelines* (NDPG) was published in 1976 during the Cold War. In 1989 the cards had to be re-dealt, with the common enemy – the Soviet Union – disappearing. New challenges appeared: the North Korean threat and the emergence of China as a power. In 1992 the Japanese government passed a law authorizing the deployment of its national forces for peacekeeping operations.

This change was due to Japan's desire to contribute to international security, and also a way of getting around the limitations of the Constitution (which forbade the redeployment of Japanese troops abroad). This contribution was and still is significant, because it enabled Japan to exert military influence on the international stage, rather than just having economic or diplomatic sway. The NDPG was updated in 1995 (*New National Defense Program Guideline*); a new version was published in 2004, and the latest incarnation was published on December 17, 2010, with the title *National Defense Program Guideline for FY[1] 2011 and Beyond*. During the 2001–2006 period (under Junichiro Koizumi's government), Japan still firmly supported the US in its role to guarantee security in the Asia-Pacific region. Prime Minister Abe Shinzo's government resolutely subscribed to the strategy of reinforcing links with the US, as well as with NATO, Australia and India, with the implicit intention of counteracting China's rise [HUG 09]. Japan and the US perceived a common threat (from China and North Korea) and shared their beliefs as to what means should be used to respond to security threats [ATA 10].

Nippo-American cooperation in terms of defense was reinforced, with the American-designed program to install anti-missile systems between 2003 and 2007, which heightened the security dilemma in the region. This strengthening of links had the result of worsening Sino-Japanese relations, with Beijing viewing Japan as a spy for the US, and the Nippo-American alliance as a common enterprise intended to halt the growth of Chinese power in the region [ATA 10, HUG 09]. Although it was in line with that of the US, this Japanese international policy was also interpreted as a bid for a certain degree of independence, Japan aspiring to establish and consolidate a national identity on the international scene [GRE 01].

During the course of its evolution, the priorities of Japan's defense policy have been constantly changing. The 2003 White Paper on Defense deemed it necessary to concentrate efforts on the struggle against terrorism and ballistic missiles, and to adjust the budgets to these priorities – budgets that had thus far been aimed at defending against invasions, which had become an unlikely eventuality in any case because of the alliance with the US. In 2004, the new military doctrine (the NDPG)[2] was aimed at giving Japan the opportunity to contribute to international, rather than merely regional, security. On January 9, 2007, the Japan Defense Agency became the Ministry of Defense, although this did not mark a genuinely new departure in Japan's defense policy [WAN 08]. In 2008, in response to North Korea's launch of a missile two years earlier, Fukuda Yasuo's government passed a law authorizing Japan to use space for defensive means, and thus to launch missile detection satellites.

The political change of 2009 (with the DPJ entering office) marked a turning point in Japan's security policy. Hatoyama's government put an end to the presence of Japanese naval forces in the Indian Ocean, was reticent to involve the SDF in forceful operations and recalibrated the defense strategy towards protecting the

---

1 FY: Fiscal Year.
2 Prime Minister of Japan and his Cabinet, National Defense Program Guideline for FY 2005 and Beyond, 2004, http://www.kantei.go.jp/foreign/policy/2004/1210taikou_e.html.

national territory, reinforcing the antimissile defense program, commissioning the construction of new submarines, strengthening the defense of the Japanese islands in the south-west of the archipelago and increasing the capacities of the units deployed in Okinawa.

Japan's defense policy is greatly constrained by its regional environment, pressure from China whose military strategy is deemed to be opaque[3], and from North Korea, which has held a provocative stance since the 1990s. Sino-Japanese relations have improved since 2007, both in political and military terms. Prime Minister Fukuda made Japan's diplomacy in Asia a priority, and chose to strengthen links with China. This policy of reinforcing partnerships in the region also characterized the diplomacy of Prime Minister Hatoyama's government. However, despite the warming of relations, China is regularly identified as the source of cyber-attacks suffered by Japan in recent years.

The military doctrine evolved in terms of its priorities, particularly as regards the type of attacks Japan must be prepared for. The NDPG in 2011 abandoned the distinction between peacetime and wartime, estimating that threats will come from new forms of actions that are not necessarily related to wars or to major combats (e.g. China's invasion of Mischief Reef in 1995, placing the Philippines in a situation that could not be reversed without the danger of a significant conflict). In order to dissuade potential aggressors, Japan proposed to restructure the SDF, replacing the concept of basic defense capability with that of dynamic defense, placing the forces of the SDF on a permanent state of alert, with capacity for immediate intervention, and therefore more mobile and reactive forces. It is into this context of evolution of the security policy that the 'cyberspace' dimension is introduced.

6.2. Cyberspace in Japan's defense strategy

6.2.1. *The context*

6.2.1.1. *Cyberspace and Japan*

According to the questions raised at a conference held in Tokyo in 2010 [AIZ 10], Japan, by its isolated nature, would have difficulty finding its place in a globalized, multicultural, multilingual space, and therefore in cyberspace. The topology of the World Wide Web is US-centered. Networks run from Europe to the US via the Atlantic and from Asia to the US via cables in the Pacific Ocean, but there is no direct link between Asia and Europe. Thus, like Asia, Japan is primarily

---

3 Ministry of Defense, Defence of Japan (Annual White Paper), Tokyo, Japan, 2009, http://www.mod.gov.jp/e/publ/w_paper/2009.html.

connected to the US. Cyberspace is American-centered. Japan, which has long been a second world power, and has always had a moderate presence in cyberspace. In particular, this is for linguistic reasons, with the Japanese language being rarely found on the Web – a phenomenon that is currently increasing with the accession of a great many countries to the world of networks and communications. Having been centered in America, the center of gravity for cyberspace is gradually shifting towards China, condemning Japan to continue to play a small part. The Chinese market is so attractive, so powerful, that today the international community sometimes bows to China's wishes and constraints: the International Telecommunications Union has adjusted its standards to China [AIZ 10].

The Internet was introduced into Japan in the mid-1980s, in the form of the experimental network JUNET, which initially linked Tokyo's three universities to Usenet in the US [AIZ 98]. The development of the Internet in Japan is not limited purely to the military domain. Japan, a country that inspires science fiction writers (part of the action in W. Gibson's novel *Neuromancer*, which was published in 1984 and introduces the term 'cyberspace', takes place in Japan [GIB 84]), is not, however, one of the most dynamic when it comes to the development of this technology. The Internet's introduction into society took place relatively slowly: in 1999, only 25% of Japanese people owned a personal computer; only 20% of the population had access to a low-throughput and high-cost Internet [HAY 11]. In 2003 the situation had already evolved quickly, as 40% of the population had access to high-capacity Internet. This can be explained by the entry of the NTT (Nippon Telegraph and Telephone Corporation) operator into the arena. Today, Japan has the fastest Internet connections, benefiting from more up-to-date fiber-optic infrastructures or copper networks than in other countries, particularly the US. In 2011, the Japanese population stood at 126 million, including 101 million Internet users, equating to an Internet penetration rate of 80%, and 10% of users in the Asiatic region (for a population that only represents 3.2% of the region).

Japan, along with South Korea (which had an Internet penetration rate of 82.7% in 2011), Singapore (77%), Taiwan (70%) and Hong Kong (67%), is one of the countries most open to the Internet in the Asiatic region. With 200,147,823 Internet protocol (IP) addresses counted at the beginning of 2012[4], Japan is 4th in the world, behind the US, China and the UK, out of a total of 246 countries (5.7% of the worldwide total). The .jp domain is used by 2.1% of sites in the world – even more than .cn, which only totals 1.6%[5].

---

4 http://www.domaintools.com/internet-statistics/country-ip-counts.html.
5 Statistics accessed February 11, 2012 on http://w3techs.com/technologies/overview/top_level_domain/all.

The cell telephone penetration rate was 95% in 2010 (compared to 64% in China, 105% in South Korea, 119% in Taiwan, 145% in Singapore and 195% in Hong Kong)[6], which is only slightly higher than the global average of 90%.

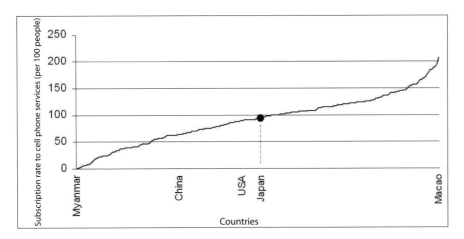

Figure 6.1. *Worldwide rate of subscription (per 100 inhabitants) to cell phone services. Japan, with 95%, is close to the average*

6.2.1.2. *Japan as a victim of cyber-attacks*

In July 2010, the company SecureWorks published the results of its investigations aimed at defining the countries most vulnerable to online cyber-attacks.[7] It emerged from this study (which classifies 16 countries) that Japan suffers a lower-than-average threat: 214 attempts at cyber-attacks per 1,000 machines (21.4%); when the average is 62.54%.

The recent, well-publicized cyber-attacks highlight that Japan, for many reasons, is a prime target for cyber-aggressors the world over:

– it is a high-tech country (and therefore its computers contain top-drawer technological, scientific and industrial secrets);

– it is a global economic power (altering its cyberspace would disrupt the function of that power);

– it is an ally of the US (itself the main international target of cyber-attacks);

– its networks are certainly no better protected than those of other nations; and

---

6   http://www.itu.int/ITU-D/ict/statistics/material/excel/2010/MobileCellularSubscriptions_
00-10.xls. Data collected February 11, 2012.
7 http://www.techdigest.tv/2010/07/secureworks_wor.html.

– it has economic and political adversaries who may resort to cyberspace to exert pressure upon it (China, North Korea, economic rivals, etc.).

Between 2000 and 2010, large enterprises and government agencies suffered multiple attacks and security incidents (losses and thefts of sensitive data):

– in 2006, NTT and KDDI lost nearly 6 million clients' data;

– also in 2006, confidential information was stolen from the computer of an officer in charge of communications on the destroyer Asayuki and distributed via peer-to-peer (P2P) platforms;

– confidential data (passwords to access secure areas) were revealed via the Internet from the machine of a subcontractor (Mitsui) at the Misawa air base (which houses a base of the Echelon network);

– in 2007 an employee of Dai Nippon Printing stole data from 43 of the company's commercial clients;

– in 2007 it was revealed in the press that details of police investigations in the Aichi prefecture had been stolen two years earlier from the computer of a police officer;

– the same kind of incident occurred in 2007 with the Tokyo police, with the theft from a police officer's computer of the names and addresses of members of the yakuza organization Yamaguchi-gumi, and the identifying data of 12,000 people involved in criminal enquiries[8].

During 2010, cyber-attacks were directed at Sony, resulting in the theft of the personal data of 77 million PlayStation Network users and 25 million users of its PC Network.

In September 2011, two industrial groups in the defense sector claimed they had been victims of cyber-attacks of (at least officially) unidentified origin:

– Mitsubishi Heavy Industries, which builds the F-15 and F-16 Mirages, the AIM-7 Sparrow air-to-air missile systems, and Patriot antimissile systems. The company is the foremost contractor for the Japanese Ministry of Defense, accounting for one-quarter of its expenses[9].

– IHI, a producer of engines for fighter planes and containment structures for nuclear reactors.

---

8 http://www.theregister.co.uk/2007/07/20/japan_p2p_leak_cop_fired/.
9 The budget of contracts given to Mitsubishi Heavy Industries is equivalent to $3.4 billion, according to the figures published in *Mitsubishi Heavy Industries Hacked: Japan Defense Industry's First Cyberattack*, September 19, 2011: http://www.huffingtonpost.com/2011/09/19mitsubishi-heavy-industries-hack_n_969427.html.

The Ministry of Defense launched an enquiry, demanding a severe sanction and the cancelation of the contracts with the companies affected, for a breach of security. Mitsubishi had already been the victim of similar incidents in 2003 and 2006, when information relating to hunter aircraft and nuclear power plant reactors were pirated. The Ministry of Defense enquiry showed that 83 of the company's computers and servers in 11 different locations were infected by 50 different viruses. As per usual, the company began by denying the loss of confidential information[10]; then, under pressure from the authorities and from the enquiry, had to admit that sensitive information had probably been accessed – particularly information relating to the development of hunter airplanes, helicopters, nuclear plants and anti-earthquake systems [WIL 11b][11].

Companies linked to defense are major targets, but the victims also include ministries, State agencies, official institutions and politicians. Several attacks against ministries have come to light[12]. The websites of the National Personnel Authority, the Cabinet Office and a video broadcasting service were affected [RYA 05]. In early November 2011, the press revealed that the Japanese Parliament (more specifically, the Upper House), had suffered cyber-attacks originating from servers in China [WIL 10] – the same type of attack as had affected the Lower House the week before. Numerous infected e-mails were circulating within that institution. Over the preceding months, lots of Japanese diplomatic posts the world over had been the object of cyber-attacks. According to police, a call was launched in China to attack Japanese sites on the occasion of the 80th anniversary of the Mandchoury incidents in 1931 (the invasion of China by Japan).

Thus, the authors of the attacks may just as well be hacktivists moved by nationalistic ideas, by an anti-Japanese sentiment; hackers searching for saleable information; or State actors (information gathering). Indications and suspicions point to China, without any evidence ever having come to light of the Chinese State's involvement in these actions. The defense industry is an obvious target. It is impossible to know whether the aggressors are specifically targeting Japan in these

---

10 *Cyberattaque contre deux groupes de défense japonais* (*Cyberattack against two Japanese defense groups*), Reuters, 20 September 2011: http://fr.news.yahoo.com/cyber-attaque-contre-deux-groupes-d%C3%A9fense-japonais-063833967.html.

11 The Ministry of Defense obliges its contractors to inform it promptly of any incidents they suffer (thefts, losses of sensitive data, and so on). However, it seems the Ministry learnt of the incident through the press, and not directly from its contractor. "Japan Cyber attack silence may breach arms contract", *India Times*, September 20, 2011: http://economictimes.indiatimes.com/news/international-business/japan-cyber-attack-silence-may-breach-arms-contracts/articleshow/10051787.cms.

12 "Japan Gov't websites hit by cyberattacks", *Inquirer Technology*, September 19, 2011, http://technology.inquirer.net/4327/japan-gov%E2%80%99t-websites-hit-by-cyberattacks%E2%80%94report/. Accessed February 23, 2012.

actions or whether they are aimed at all the world's armament industries; whether the objective is to destabilize Japanese-American relations or American interests worldwide by way of their industrial partners. The effects are many-splendored.

In July 2011, attacks against Toshiba compromised the details of 7,500 customers. During the night of July 10–11, 2011, the website of Japan's National Police Agency was subject to a DDoS (distributed denial of service) attack launched from China [HAY 11].

In November 2011, it was learnt that the Fujitsu Ltd. servers, which were connected to a network of over 200 regional governments in Honshu and Kyushu had been victims of cyber-attacks[13]. Online administrative services were paralyzed, as they became victims of DDoS attacks. Most of the IP addresses used in the attack were Japanese.

In January 2012, Japan's space agency was attacked[14]. Data relating to the international space station was the target[15]. The attacks sent data to servers located in China.[16]

The cyber-attacks that were publicized in the media have the political or industrial nature of their victims in common, and the often-international scope of those victims' activities. The implications of the attacks extend beyond Japanese territory. The image of the companies is tarnished and Japan's reputation for seriousness and quality is damaged. The idea of increased risk is associated with Japan.

While the history of security incidents in Japanese cyberspace is very eventful, paradoxically it was not until December 2010 that the government made it a crime to create and distribute viruses, carrying a prison sentence (three years of prison, and a ¥500,000 fine). The government has put structures in place whose mission is to work towards securing the State's information systems [ISP 06, ISP 09]. However, only recently has the 'cyber-defense' dimension *per se* become part of the defense policy – even though the SDF have integrated the concepts and tools of 'information warfare' and network-centric warfare into their strategies [YAM 05].

---

13 A two-wave attack, November 9, 2011.
14 http://www.ukfastnews.co.uk/internet-news/japanese-space-programme-hit-by-trojan.html.
15   http://www.infosecurity-magazine.com/view/23278/lost-in-space-japan-admits-to-breach-of-space-station-resupply-craft-data/.
16 http://www.physorg.com/news/2011-10-china-based-servers-japan-cyber.html.

6.2.2. *Cyberspace in security and defense policies*

One of the innovative characteristics of the defense policy of the new party that has been in power since 2009 is the introduction of the specific dimension of cyber-defense. Since 2010, cyberspace as a new problem has been a part of strategic thinking. The new defense policy is formalized in a number of texts:

– Information Security Strategy for Protecting the Nation[17] (published May 11, 2010).

– Japan's Visions for Future Security and Defense Capabilities in the New Era: Toward a Peace-creating Nation [COU 10][18], published August 27, 2010 by the New Council on Security and Defense, led by Shigetaka Sato, the CEO of Keihan Electric Railway.

– National Defense Program Guideline for FY 2011 and Beyond – NDPG 2011[19], published December 17, 2010.

– The Mid-Term Defense Program (FY 2011–2015)[20], published December 17, 2010, echoes the terms and outlines of the program defined in the National Defense Program Guideline for FY 2011, also validated December 17, 2010.

– Defense of Japan 2010 (Annual White Paper).[21] Before 2010 (see 2005[22], 2006[23], 2007[24], 2008[25] and 2009[26]) the successive versions of the White Paper on defense did not deal with cyberspace, cyber-security/cyber-defense and cyber-warfare. It was only in 2010 that the problem was introduced, discussed briefly in the chapter entitled "Trends concerning cyberwarfare capabilities" (Part I, Chapter I, section 3)[27]. The cybernetic issue appeared as third on the list of priorities, after weapons of mass destruction and terrorism.

– Defense of Japan 2011 (Annual White Paper).[28] It is in the 2011 publication that cyberspace is given its full dues. The White Paper opens directly with considerations relating to cyberspace. In the first part, entitled "Security

---

17 http://www.nisc.go.jp/eng/pdf/New_Strategy_English.pdf.
18 http://www.kantei.go.jp/jp/singi/shin-ampobouei2010/houkokusyo_e.pdf.
19 http://www.mofa.go.jp/policy/security/pdfs/h23_ndpg_en.pdf.
20 http://www.mod.go.jp/e/d_act/d_policy/pdf/mid_termFY2011-15.pdf.
21 http://www.mod.go.jp/e/publ/w_paper/2010.html.
22 http://www.mod.go.jp/e/publ/w_paper/2005.html.
23 http://www.mod.go.jp/e/publ/w_paper/2006.html.
24 http://www.mod.go.jp/e/publ/w_paper/2007.html.
25 http://www.mod.go.jp/e/publ/w_paper/2008.html.
26 http://www.mod.go.jp/e/publ/w_paper/2009.html.
27 http://www.mod.go.jp/e/publ/w_paper/pdf/2010/07Part1_Chapter1_Sec3.pdf.
28 http://www.mod.go.jp/e/publ/w_paper/2011.html.

Environment Surrounding Japan"[29], section 1 is "Trends Concerning Cyberspace", in Chapter 1 on "Issues in the International Community".[30] This time, cyberspace is dealt with before the issue of weapons of mass destruction, international terrorism and regional conflicts.

The major axes of Japan's defense strategy, set out in the White Paper and the *Mid-Term Program Defense* are threefold:

– developing means of dissuasion (to deter any aggressor from attempting to launch an attack on Japanese territory);

– reinforcing security in the Asia-Pacific region (security dilemma); and

– contributing to international security (by preserving the alliance with the US)[31].

Cyberspace, its security and its use in a military context must serve these three objectives. Cyberspace is found at each of these three levels. The means for satellite observation, telecommunication networks, the rate of data transmission and the quality of data processing, must lend themselves to Japan's intelligence, surveillance and reconnaissance capabilities.

The security of the region is endangered by cyber-attacks that disturb Japanese, Korean and Chinese (and other countries') cyberspace, and by the aggressive nature of China, to which the attacks are often attributed. Securing Japanese cyberspace should contribute to the security of cyberspace as a whole, given that a weak link presents a danger for the other links.

The strategy for security and defense is techno-centered: more investment is set aside for the development of new submarines and for intelligence, surveillance and reconnaissance capabilities (satellites, modes of communication, data processing, etc.). The results of research and technology need to be integrated, and in parallel, it is a question of reducing costs, particularly in terms of personnel.

---

29 http://www.mod.go.jp/e/publ/w_paper/pdf/2010/07Part1_Chapter1_Sec3.pdf.
30 http://www.mod.go.jp/e/publ/w_paper/pdf/2011/04_Part1_Chapter1.pdf
31 "The Japan-U.S. Alliance remains vital for the peace and security of Japan, and the presence of the U.S. armed forces in Japan is essential to maintaining peace and stability of the region. Japan will enhance bilateral consultations and other cooperation to deepen and develop the Alliance to adapt to the evolving security environment, while actively taking measures for the smooth and effective stationing of the United States armed forces in Japan". *Mid-Term Defense Program*, 2011, pp. 2.

Action	Date
National Defense Program Guideline - NDPG	1976
NDPG	1995
North Korea: missile launch	1998
Launch of four spy satellites and decision to install American-designed anti-missile defense systems	2003
Japan's Defense Agency becomes Ministry of Defense	January 9, 2007
Cyber-attacks against Estonia. Supposed origin: Russia	*March 2007*
Deployment of anti-missile systems: Patriot Advanced Capability 3 (PAC-3)	March 2007
Publication of the **Medium to long-term Defense Technology Outlook report**[32], Ministry of Defense	2007
Creation of NATO's Cooperative Cyber Defense Centre of Excellence (CCDCOE)	*October 2008*
The Democratic Party of Japan (DPJ) gain electoral victory over the Liberal Democratic Party, who have held office since 1955	August 30, 2009
Yukio Hatayama, Prime Minister of the new government following the DPJ's electoral victory	September 19, 2009
Publication of **Defense of Japan 2010**	2010
Publication of the **Information Security Strategy for Protecting the Nation**	May 11, 2010
Naoto Kan, leader of the DPJ, named Prime Minister, succeeding Yukio Hatayama	June 8, 2010
Law criminalizing the creation and distribution of computer viruses	December 2010
Publication of **Japan's Vision for Future Security and Defense Capabilities in the New Era; Toward a Peace-Creating Nation**	August 27, 2010
Publication of the **National Defense Program Guidelines (NDPG) for FY 2011 and Beyond**, the first defense policy document of Naoto Kan's new government	December 17, 2010
Mid-Term Defense Program FY 2011-2015	December 17, 2010
Publication of **Defense of Japan 2011**	2011
Earthquake, tsunami	March 11, 2011
Cyber-attack against Sony's PlayStation Network	April 2011
Yoshihiko Noda, new Prime Minister, succeeding Naoto Kan	September 2, 2011
Revelation of the attacks against Mitsubishi Heavy Industries – (83 servers infected by eight different viruses)[33]. The attack is said to have taken place in August 2011. The rival companies IHI and Kawasaki Heavy Industries reported being the target of attempted attacks. Supposed origin: China	September 18, 2011
Cyber-attacks on the National Personnel Authority. Supposed origin: China	September 17–18, 2011
Cyber-attacks against the Cabinet Office. Supposed origin: China	September 2011

Table 6.1. *Timeline of official publications, incidents and political eras in Japan (information relating to the rest of the world is shown in bold italics in the table; governmental changes are shaded; the essential aspects are shown in bold)*

---

32 http://www.mod.go.jp/trdi/en/misc/publication/mlterm/body.pdf.
33 http://techland.time.com/2011/09/20/hackers-target-japanese-weapons-maker-nuclear-power-plants/.

Cyber-attacks against a government video broadcasting service. Supposed origin: China	September 2011
Cyber-attacks against the Ministry of Foreign Affairs and various diplomatic outposts the world over[34]	October 2011
Cyber-attacks against Fujitsu Ltd. and the regional governments of Honshu and Kyushu. Supposed origin: Japan itself	November 2011
Cyber-attacks against Parliament. Supposed origin: China	November 2011
Launch of an observation satellite by the Japanese space agency JAXA	December 12, 2011
Fujitsu is said to have created a virus enabling cyber-attacks to be mounted (according to an article by Yomiuri Shimbun)[35]	January 3, 2012
Cyber-attacks against JAXA	January 2012

Table 6.1. *(continued) Timeline of official publications, incidents and political eras in Japan (information relating to the rest of the world is shown in bold italics in the table; governmental changes are shaded; the essential aspects are shown in bold)*

	ISSPN 2010[36]	JVFS 2010[37]	DoJ 2010[38]	DoJ 2011	NDPG 2011[39]	MTDF 2011[40]
Cyberspace	X	X	X	X	X	X
Cyber-attack	X	X	X	X	X	X
Cyber-security	X	-	X	X	-	-
Cyber-defense	X	X	X	X	-	-
Cyber-warfare	-	-	X	X	-	-
Cyber-crime	X	-	-	-	-	-
Cyber-strategy	-	-	-	X	-	-
Cyber-protection	-	-	-	X	-	-
Cyber-operation	-	-	-	X	-	-
Information warfare	-	-	-	X	-	-

Table 6.2. *Use of the concepts in the documents on defense policy, strategy and military doctrine published since 2010*

6.2.2.1. *Cyberspace*

The *Information Security Strategy for Protecting the Nation* defines[41] cyberspace as a "Virtual space on the Internet or other computer systems where information is exchanged using ICT [information and communication technologies]".

---

34 http://www.japantimes.co.jp/text/nn20111027a1.html.
35 http://www.yomiuri.co.jp/dy/national/T120102002799.htm.
36 ISSPN: Information Security Strategy for Protecting the Nation.
37 JVSF: *Japan's Vision for Future Security and Defense Capabilities in the New Era.*
38 DoJ: Defense of Japan.
39 NDPG: *National Defense Programme Guideline.*
40 MTDP: *Mid-Term Defense Program.*

Above all, it is the place of new challenges[42], a global commons[43] (the report uses the expression "international public good"[44], as it does with the sea and outer space) whose use must be assured to be stable (free access).

The *NDPG 2011* also raises concerns over the threat to the accessibility of cyberspace: "Moreover, risks concerning sustained access to the seas, outer space and cyberspace have emerged as a new challenge"[45].

The first part of the 2011 White Paper, entitled *Cyberspace and Security* recalls the dependence of societies on cyberspace. Information and communication networks now form part of our daily lives, and cyber-attacks that affect infrastructures essential to the functioning of society constitute a serious threat, especially given that they appear to grow more complex and sophisticated every day. For the army, networks are the keystone for the functioning of the L2 operational units that cyber-attacks, as part of an asymmetric strategy, are capable of disturbing and endangering.

6.2.2.2. *Cyber-attacks*

Cyber-attacks have four characteristics: they are non-lethal; they can inflict serious damage; they can strike at anytime, anywhere; and it is difficult to identify the aggressors[46].

Japan's new defense strategy was drawn up in response to the attacks suffered by Japan, but perhaps by its allies above all. The publication of the *Information Security Strategy for Protecting the Nation*[47] resulted from the Japanese reaction to the cyber-attacks suffered in 2009 by the US and South Korea, two of its allies. The references here are not to the attacks against Estonia in 2007, nor those carried out during the Russo-Georgian conflict in 2008.

> "After the Second National Strategy on Information Security was resolved, a large-scale cyber attack took place in the United States and South Korea in July 2009. Also, numerous incidents of large-scale private information leaks occurred one after another. The large-scale cyber attack in the United States and South Korea particularly alerted Japan — where many aspects of economic activities and social life are

---

41 Page 20 of the report.
42 *NDPG 2011*, pp. 3.
43 *Expression used in Defense of Japan 2011*, pp. 18.
44 *NDPG 2011*, pp. 5.
45 http://www.mofa.go.jp/policy/security/pdfs/h23_ndpg_en.pdf, pp. 3.
46 *Defense of Japan 2011*.
47 http://www.nisc.go.jp/eng/pdf/New_Strategy_English.pdf.

increasingly dependent upon Information and Communication Technology (ICT) — to the fact that a threat to information security could be a threat to national security and require effective crisis management."[48]

Japan is becoming aware that a major cyber-attack (which is a likely occurrence) could constitute a threat to national security, whatever its target – whether Japan or one of its allies. Such attacks could cause physical damage to infrastructures, provoke financial losses, and have psychological repercussions and effects on the virtual environment.

Japan ranks cyber-attacks with threats that compromise its stability, as well as transnational threats, such as climate change, pollution, natural disasters, epidemics, etc. – threats that have come to substitute the risk of inter-State wars, which have become highly unlikely [COU 10].

Two pages are dedicated to the question of cyber-attacks in the 2010 White Paper, highlighting the crucial importance of the security of information systems, both for the civil sector and for defense. A number of examples of cyber-attacks as part of armed conflicts are cited: Israel/Hezbollah (2006), Israel/Hamas (2008) and Russia/Georgia (2008).

The second part of the 2011 White Paper is entitled "Threats in cyberspace". It recalls some examples of cyber-attacks:

– those launched during the conflict between Israel and Hezbollah in 2006;

– those between Hamas and Israel in 2008;

– those employed in the Russian-Georgian conflict of 2008 (in this instance deeming the cyber-attacks to have had no effect on the functioning of the Georgian army, but merely to have disrupted the government's communication system).

Also mentioned is the introduction of viruses into American networks in Iraq and Afghanistan in 2008. The authors also cite the attacks attributed to North Korea in 2009 and 2011. Finally, the report mentions the Stuxnet worm, underlining that it was able to infiltrate control systems.

In order to illustrate their points and characterize the threat, the various reports draw examples from the US, South Korea, Israel, Russia and Georgia, but are silent about the incidents suffered by Japan.

---

48 *Information Security Strategy for Protecting the Nation, 2010*, pp. 1.

6.2.2.3. *Cyber-defense*

The *Information Security Strategy for Protecting the Nation* report offers a plan of response to large-scale cyber-attacks, and suggests reinforcing the defenses against cyber-attacks. In particular, this plan proposes:

– Preparing the country to cope with a crisis situation (due to a large-scale cyber-attack).

– Utilizing the tools of public/private cooperation for more efficient information sharing, in accordance with the principles seen in the *Second Action Plan on Information Security Measures for Critical Infrastructures.*

– Reinforcing international alliances (with the US, Association of Southeast Asian Nations ASEAN and the European Union).

– Fighting cybercrime[49].

– Consolidating the government's network infrastructure (in particular, developing the use of encryption).

– Reinforcing the protection of critical infrastructures.

The *Defense of Japan 2010* report organizes response to and protection against cyber-attacks around six pillars:

– increasing the safety of information and communication systems;

– upgrading of cyber defense systems;

– development of rules;

– human resource development;

– enhancement of information sharing; and

– research of cutting-edge technology.

In the formulation of this imperative of securitization, we can see the traces of the dilemma that faces all States: how to ensure maximum security – with all the constraints this may involve – while conserving the role that cyberspace must have, i.e. as an instrument of economic and social progress.

> "Implementation of policies to strengthen national security and crisis management expertise in cyberspace must maintain integrity with the policy that is enforced under the principles of the

---

49 Cybercrimes are defined as "Crimes that utilize ICT, such as those using advanced information and communication networks (e.g. the Internet) and those targeting electromagnetic records". Page 20 of the report.

Basic Act on the Formation of an Advanced Information and Telecommunications Network Society, which stipulates promoting the usage of ICT as the foundation of socioeconomic activities."[50]

In order to ensure stable use of cyberspace, Japan will need to *reinforce its capabilities for dealing with cyber-attacks* (*NDPG 2011*). The ways of responding to cyber-attacks[51] are specified in these terms:

"The SDF will respond to cyber attacks by operating functions necessary for defending the information system of the SDF in an integrated manner. By accumulating advanced expertise and skills needed to tackle cyber attacks, the SDF will contribute to the government-wide response to cyber attacks."

The third part of the 2011 White Paper, Efforts against Cyber Attacks, discusses initiatives that must be taken in terms of security and defense at the governmental, ministerial level. The report proposes federation, and grouping of services thus far dispersed throughout the various levels of the administration and State services.

'*Centralization*' is one of the keywords of this approach. The State does not seem able to get away from the logic of centralization of resources, which may appear to be out of phase with the principles that constitute the strength of the hackers and aggressors, who essentially rely on decentralization, the lack of a center or coordination. Japan envisages a vertical model for the governance of its security and defense, where non-State attackers expect horizontal models. It must be underlined, however, that this is not peculiar to the State of Japan. All States follow vertical schemes, where the national authority – the seat of political power – exerts a centrifugal force which, it seems, should provide a response to all problems.

Strengthening this security is also a question of the *extension of the powers* of the intelligence agencies that fight cyber-attacks. The difficulty of this extension lies in the limits imposed upon the actors to whom these powers will be available (the dangers being those incurred by the citizens themselves).

'*Cooperation*' is another of the keywords in this battle plan: cooperation between the public and private sectors, civilians and the military, on a national but also on an international scale[52]. This *leitmotiv* is reminiscent of the adage 'strength in unity'. More than being a choice, cooperation is an absolute necessity because the battle

---

50 *Information Security Strategy for Protecting the Nation, 2010*, pp. 5.
51 http://www.mofa.go.jp/policy/security/pdfs/h23_ndpg_en.pdf, pp. 11.
52 http://www.mod.go.jp/e/publ/w_paper/pdf/2011/07_Part2_Chapter2.pdf   Part II, The Basics of Japan's Defense Policy and Build-up of Defense Capability, section 2, Chapter 1, the New Security Environment.

must be fought on an international scale and because in pooling of capacities and resources there is a not-insignificant economic dimension. Cooperation often entails economy of scale and seems to justify the reduction of means. The flip-side of cooperation may be a relative loss of autonomy, with an encroachment on national sovereignty.

According to the *NDPG 2011*, the reinforcement of security in cyberspace will be achieved through cooperation on a regional and global scale. The problem is ranked on the same level as policies with regards to securitizing space, the oceans, or climate change. As with many international, global questions, which cannot be dealt with and resolved in an isolated manner:

> "Japan will strengthen various regular cooperation, such as joint training and joint/shared usage of facilities, and promote regional and global cooperation through international peace cooperation activities, maintenance and enhancement of international public goods such as outer space, cyberspace and sea lanes, as well as in the field of climate change."

Thus, cyber-security and cyber-defense are domains that enable a State to better its integration into the international community. Through this necessary collaboration, States make choices: Japan has opted explicitly to reinforce its relations with the European Union, the countries in Europe, and the NATO Member States[53].

Standardization could be one of the main axes of this policy. The 2011 White Paper underlines the absence of an international legal norm allowing cyber-attacks to be classed as acts of war and regulating military responses to be made to such acts.

In its reflections on the offensive and defensive use of cyberspace, Japan looks abroad for its examples, with a very particular emphasis on American thinking: the Cyberspace Policy Review in May 2009 (which suggests the creation of a cyber-security coordinator at the White House) and the International Strategy for Cyberspace published in May 2011 (which aims at establishing norms of behavior in cyberspace, based particularly on international cooperation, but particularly underlines the US' desire to respond in ways including military to cyber-attacks that constitute acts of war on the nation), are the two American policy documents that particularly catch Japan's attention. For questions relating to defense, the White Paper refers to America's Quadrennial Defense Review, published in 2010. It also cites a document published by William J. Lynn in August 2010 that offers a

---

53 http://www.mofa.go.jp/policy/security/pdfs/h23_ndpg_en.pdf, pp. 9.

framework for a cyber-defensive strategy by laying the foundations of the rules of engagement.

The *Defense of Japan 2010* report has already enumerated various national initiatives in terms of cyber-defense: the creation of the US CyberCommand, the CCDCOE (in Estonia) and the Cyber Security Operations Centre in Australia. The 2011 edition is far more precise in its analysis of the situation abroad. For the UK, it cites:

– the publication of reports: the Cyber Security Strategy in June 2009 and the National Security Strategy;

– the creation of the Office of Cyber Security, pursuant to the publication of the *Cyber Security Strategy* in 2009 (by the Cabinet Office). The Office of Cyber Security was in charge of coordinating the government's cyber-security strategy. This organization was later transformed into the Office of Cyber Security and Information Assurance;

– the creation of the Cyber Security Operations Centre, a subsidiary of GCHQ (Government Communications Headquarters);

– the Strategic Defence and Security Reviews published in October 2010, which opened the way to the creation of the Defence Cyber Operations Group to unify activities relating to cyberspace in the Ministry of Defence.

For Australia, it is interested in:

– the publication of the Cyber Security Strategy (November 2009) and the Defence White Paper (May 2009), which prioritizes the development of military cyber-warfare capabilities;

– the attribution of the coordination of the whole of the government's cyber-security to the Cyber Security Policy and Coordination body;

– the creation of the Cyber Security Operations Centre in January 2010, in the Defence Department.

For South Korea, it points to:

– the publication of the National Information Protection White Paper, which insists on the necessary centralization of cyber-security questions in a national management structure; and of the 2010 Defense White Paper in December;

– the role of the National Intelligence Service, which coordinates cyber-security policies;

– the role of the Defense Information Warfare Response Center, which protects military networks;

– the creation of Cyberspace Command, in January 2010, a subsidiary of the Defense Intelligence Agency, which implements cyber-warfare capacities.

China[54] is developing offensive capabilities in space (destruction of satellites, for example), and capabilities for cyber-warfare.

With regard to NATO, the report highlights the publication of *the New Strategic Concept* in November 2010; the creation of the Emerging Security Challenges Division in August 2010; the Cyber Defense Management Authority and of the CCDCOE in 2008.

This official literature and these strategic decisions constitute the reference corpus for Japanese strategic and political thinking in terms of defense. This strategy, therefore, is largely inspired by English-speaking foreign countries.

Responses to cyber-attacks are now clearly written into the missions of the armed forces[55]. The responses to cyber-attacks are dealt with more particularly in Chapter I, "Operations of Japan's Self Defense Forces"[56] of Part III: these responses are organized around the Ministry of Defense and the SDF. Those responses which have to be integrated necessitate the deployment of adapted means. In March 2011, the post of Deputy Head, C4 Systems Planning Division (cyber) was created within the Ministry of Defense, with the mission of reflecting on strategies for response. A dedicated cyber-defense unit was also created. Training and research programs in the domain also have to be developed in the National Defense Academy of Japan.

The Mid-Term Defense Program 2011 integrates the reinforcement of the security of the SDF's networks into the defense budget, increasing research efforts and security exercises[57] (particularly with the American ally); training will play an important part in developing the capacities of the army. This effort is part of the structural reform under way within the Japanese army, and proposes, among other things, to recruit some younger personnel[58].

---

54 "Military use of space and cyberwarfare capabilities", pp. 32 of the document:
http://www.mod.go.jp/e/publ/w_paper/pdf/2011/05_Part1_Chapter2.pdf.
55 Chapter 3 "Towards a new system of defense", of Part II:
http://www.mod.go.jp/e/publ/w_paper/pdf/2011/08_Part2_Chapter3.pdf.
56 http://www.mod.go.jp/e/publ/w_paper/pdf/2011/09_Part3_Chapter1.pdf.
57 Cyber-Defense Exercises – CDX.
58 *Mid-Term Defense Program 2011*, pp. 2, and [COU 10], pp. 43. This evolution in capacities must be accompanied by an overhaul in human resources (it is a question of recruiting younger personnel). The management of cyber-attack situations is associated with that of armed attacks and crises (such as natural disasters). In this respect, the role of those in power must also be taken into account. The 2010 report highlights the inaptness of the organization at State level to deal with such situations efficiently: the Prime Minister and

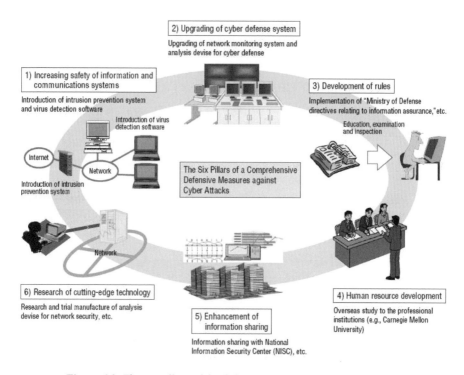

Figure 6.2. *The six pillars of the defense strategy against cyber-attacks.*
Chart published in Defense of Japan 2010 (fig. II-2-6-1, pp. 185)

6.2.2.4. *Cyber-warfare*

One of the chapters of the 2010 White Paper is entitled "Trends Concerning Cyber Warfare Capabilities"[59]: cyber-warfare covers military operations carried out in cyberspace. Thus, cyber-warfare stems from the policies and strategies of defense. Without going into what measures Japan has taken in the past or will take in the future, the report lists the initiatives taken in the matter (strategies, creation of dedicated units in the armed forces) by a number of countries (the US, NATO countries, Australia[60] and South Korea[61]). In view of the army's dependency on

---

his/her government should take part in exercises to prepare for the transition from a state of peace to a state of emergency. The fact that this is said implies that they do not. In addition, Japan has no equivalent to the American National Security Council. Hence, it is more vulnerable than other countries, not having capacities for defining national security strategies – which, naturally, would include cyber-security.

59 http://www.mod.go.jp/e/publ/w_paper/pdf/2010/07Part1_Chapter1_Sec3.pdf, pp. 15.

60 In its 2009 *Defence White Paper*, Australia makes a priority of the development of military cyberwarfare capabilities. This point is mentioned in the *Defense of Japan 2011* report, pp. 26.

61 *Defense of Japan*, pp. 27.

information and communication systems, cyber-attacks are qualified as an 'asymmetrical strategy'[62] that allows the enemy's weak points to be exploited and their strong points to be weakened. In fact, the armed forces may be subject to attack both in wartime and in peacetime.

The 2011 White Paper discusses cyber-warfare, but without dedicating an entire chapter to it, as was done the previous year. It is interested in the priority given to cyber-warfare in the defense policies of the US, Korea, Australia and even China. It highlights the advantage of this for the issue, owing to the importance of information and information space[63]. Japan's international environment makes cyber-warfare one of the priorities of its defense strategies.

6.2.2.5. Mobility, reactivity, rapidity, technology, intelligence, surveillance and reconnaissance capabilities

The National Defense Program Guideline for FY 2011 and Beyond[64] is the expression of the new defense policy of Naoto Kan's government. Its approach lies in prolonging the policies pursued by its predecessors [NIS 11] in the Liberal Democratic Party governments. However, on some points, the strategy is a new departure: particularly in:

– designating China as a source of major concern;

– reallocating resources to the naval forces to the detriment of land forces (in view of the pressure exerted by China in the maritime domain); and

– finally proposing the new concept of 'dynamic defense', which consists of deploying forces to priority areas of Japan and readying them for asymmetrical missions.

The reason for this is the absence of a precise definition of the threats, so the forces have to be ready to deal with any situation. The report introduces the notions of 'dynamic defense capabilities' and 'dynamic defense force', which replace the concept of 'basic defense force'. The security challenges have evolved – more dynamic, flexible forces are needed because reaction times are shorter, particularly because of progress in military technologies.

One of the major concerns relates to improving the capacity to see, to know and to react, ever faster. Speed (of detection, reaction or action) is one of the key factors in the strategy of defense of the territory. It is of the essence, in view of the

---

62 Page 15 of the 2010 White Paper.
63 Chapter 2: Policies for State Defense, Section 3 "Military use of space and cyberwarfare capabilities", p. 32 http://www.mod.go.jp/e/publ/w_paper/pdf/2011/05_Part1_Chapter2.pdf.
64 http://www.mofa.go.jp/policy/security/pdfs/h23_ndpg_en.pdf.

geographic proximity of the threats: China and North Korea are not far at all from Japanese territory. This rapidity in detection and reaction relies essentially on technology: intelligence, surveillance and reconnaissance capabilities (observation satellites, systems for detection, transmission and interception of communications), information processing systems and the decision-making process have to be optimized. Communication capabilities must be kept optimal at every level of the L2s.

Significant alterations in Japanese cyberspace would endanger this entire edifice of security/defense. The securitization of cyberspace thus lies in the process of reinforcing capabilities of intelligence, satellite observation and threat detection[65], which are the foundations of the new policy for defense of the territory. Maintaining control over the flow of information is vital for the country's security. Hence, the redefinition of priorities naturally led to the introduction of cyberspace into the implementation of a techno-centric security and defense policy.

Priority	Provisional budget 2012
Strengthen cyber planning functions of the Joint Staff Office to respond to increasing threat of cyber attacks	-
Strengthen training support functions of the SDFC4 (Command, Control, Communication and Computers) Systems Command in order to improve capability concerning the cyber protection of each SDF group	-
Strengthen the function of the Defense Intelligence Headquarters, which exclusively collects and analyzes information concerning overseas cases of cyber attacks over the long term	-
Human resource development initiatives to defend against cyber attacks Dispatch personnel to study at Japanese and overseas graduate schools, such as Carnegie[66]	-

Table 6.3. *Ministry of Defense provisional budget for 2012. Funds allocated to cyber-defense with the objective of enhancing the capability for effective response to cyber attacks by strengthening the cyber-defense system*

---

65 "Japan will promote its efforts to develop and use outer space, from the perspective of, strengthening information gathering and communications functions":http://www.mofa.go.jp /policy/security/pdfs/h23_ndpg_en.pdf, page 3
66 A photo of Carnegie Mellon University – Software Engineering Institute illustrates this line of the program. http://www.mod.go.jp/e/d_budget/pdf/231220.pdf, Page 7

Enhancement of partnership with the US Participate in Japan-US IT Forum	-
Strengthening of security and analysis devices (device equipped with information collection, analysis and response exercise functions concerning cyber-attacks) for cyber-defense[67]	0.2 billion (Yen)
Research aimed at cyber-attack response. Research and study on the latest technological developments concerning information assurance	20 million (Yen)
Improvement of information sharing capability of vessels and improvement of satellite communication capability	0.9 billion (Yen)
Space programs, enhancement of C4ISR capability, satellite communication, imagery	260.9 billion (Yen)

Table 6.3. *(Continued) Ministry of Defense provisional budget for 2012. Funds allocated to cyber-defense with the objective of enhancing the capability for effective response to cyber attacks by strengthening the cyber-defense system*[68]

6.3. Conclusion

Japan is defining a defense strategy that integrates cyberspace and is aimed at defending the national territory. However, this policy cannot be a strictly national one: in the sense that cyberspace extends massively beyond Japan's borders, being the point of entry for unconventional kinds of attacks, international cooperation becomes an absolute necessity, especially with its American ally. In this effort to define a defense policy that takes account of the cybernetic dimension, the government is looking abroad to a great extent: it is drawing inspiration from the practices of its allies (US, Australia, Europe and NATO), and grounding its action in the context of international cooperation. The defense model that Japan is in the process of drawing up is based on the thinking and approach of the American system.

It must be underlined that in the various official reports, there is silence from Japan about the incidents relating to the security of its own networks. However, there are plenty of examples that are certainly no less serious than the attacks suffered by the US and South Korea in 2009. Could it be that this attitude reflects a certain reticence on the part of the Japanese government to recognize its own weaknesses?

---

67 Funds seemingly have to be shared between four departments: Information Collection Department, Dynamic Analysis Department, Static Analysis Department, and Response Exercise Department.
68 Source: Defense Programs and Budget of Japan. Overview of FY 2012 Budget Request. http://www.mod.go.jp/e/d_budget/pdf/231220.pdf.

The reports prove relatively vague as regards the nature of the aggressors likely to strike Japan. The discourse appears to take place at the level of conflict between States, State actors, and conventional armies who are arming themselves with cyber-warfare capacities in order to skirmish in cyberspace just as they do in the real world. However, this approach seems to ignore the multiplicity of forms of the threat:

– from ordinary crime, but whose accomplishments are capable of upsetting the economy and the normal function of networks and access to cyberspace;

– to hacktivists, non-State actors whose aggressive capabilities are significant (is the anonymous strikeforce negligible in terms of defense?); and

– through organized crime.

This variety of non-state threats is not taken into account in the defense policy. Is Japan's response in terms of cyber-security and the use of cyberspace in defense really apt for the reality of the world? Defense is still thought of in a conventional manner in terms of conflicts with other States. The threat comes also from non-State actors – it is horizontal (attacks carried out over networks and organized spontaneously). Japan's policy sets a centralized defense against it, although it is supposed to be dynamic, evolving, adaptive and flexible; a vertical model, made up of institutions, national and international norms, and a State machine that is cumbersome and therefore slow to mobilize. (It is a question of training, raising awareness, educating... and thus a process that will take time.)

Japan has realized that a great many States are developing offensive capacities in cyberspace[69], and that ideas, examples and models can be drawn from this. However, this also means that Japan is surrounded by nations ready to pounce on it in cyberspace. Thus, there is also a new sort of armament race that has begun. If Japan is involved too, it means that its defense policy is guided by international considerations, that it too must arm itself to ensure the defense of its sovereignty on the global scene. The defense policy including cyberspace thus lends itself to a realistic analysis.

While in the real world the cards are dealt according to the superpowers (US and China), politics in cyberspace puts these cards back on the table. The American hegemony is not as strong; the US cannot guarantee the accessibility of cyberspace, security and peace in the way it does in the real world; the US is no longer able to hold the keys to the "global commons" on its own, and to ensure its free usage in the rest of the world. Cyberspace is part of these global commons. The decline of the hegemonic power results in a more unstable environment, or at any rate a more

69 Defense of Japan 2011, p. 22

threatening one, where actors are demanding new powers and can stand up against the will of the superpower, e.g. by obstructing the development of military forces in the oceans, destroying satellites or launching cyber-attacks. For Japan, the deterioration of access to the "global commons" is a danger [COU 10][70]. Japan is watching the military development of China, one of the actors capable of threatening that accessibility, with concern.

Faced with these threats, Japan is edifying itself with defensive measures. However, the strengthening of its capabilities, which are officially only ever to be used for defensive means, is aggravating the security dilemma. It is because other countries are improving their capabilities that Japan feels the need to do likewise. No longer can the government ignore the resolutely militaristic stance of numerous countries in terms of cyber-attacks; therefore it not only has to equip itself with means of protection, but also of counter-attack [COU 10][71]. This is particularly important in terms of preventing cyber-attacks that could be launched in combination with conventional military assaults (e.g. attacks carried out by special operative forces, directed at critical infrastructures and accompanied or preceded by cyber-attacks).

Japan must learn to anticipate and manage cyber-attacks intended to cause it profound damage, but also attacks that could be provocations, such as the operations carried out by China or North Korea on other territories. The Chinese military, for example, came dangerously close to the Japanese coasts in 2004 when a Chinese submarine entered Japanese waters. In August 1998, North Korea carried out missile launch tests over the island of Honshu. The recent cyber-attacks, attributed – rightly or wrongly – to China and North Korea pose a new challenge for Japan. Could rigorously respecting the Constitution prevent the mounting of a cyber-defense that would inflict blows on foreign territory remotely, without the deployment of defensive forces?

Japan has to maintain its pacifistic stance, and not show the slightest militaristic intention [YIN 08, SZE 06]. In its process of militarizing cyberspace it cannot give too many signals that could be interpreted badly, but must, nonetheless, arm itself in order to defend itself. Japan has to be able to defend itself on its own if attacked, but it cannot do so by way of any sort of armament.

According to an article published in the newspaper *Yomiuri Shimbun* in 2012, the Defense Ministry's Technical Research and Development Institute, responsible for

---

70 Ibid pp. 6.
71 The Council on Security and Defense Capabilities in the New Era, Japan's vision for future security and defense capabilities in the new era: towards a peace creating nation, CSDCNE, Tokyo, Japan, available at http://www.kantei.go.jp/jp/singi/shin-ampobouei2010/houkokusyo_e.pdf

the development of weaponry, awarded a subcontract to Fujitsu Ltd to create a technological solution (a weapon) capable of neutralizing cyber-attacks, tracing their paths and identifying their sources. Results are being tested, following a project carried out over three years and having cost more than $2 million. The main problem that the existence of this tool throws up is legalistic in nature: does Japan have the right to use such a solution? If so, when, how and under what circumstances? Indeed, the process is likely to damage machines and networks situated outside its territory. For the moment, cyber-attacks merely form part of the threats that authorize Japan to exercise its right to self-defense. If such 'weapons' could not be used to pursue the trail of the attacks beyond the national territory, they would no longer hold any interest. Thus, it is the very definition of a 'weapon' that has to be reconsidered.

The same questions are being raised as in 2000 when Japan was (already) exploring the idea of developing viruses and hacking technologies to test its own defenses [YOM 00]: it had already been concluded that to possess such weapons would contravene the principles of the Constitution, which forbids Japan from having strategic weapons [YIN 08]. While Japan had to renounce war as a sovereign right, the Constitution of 1947 (particularly Article IX thereof) raises no objection to Japan's right to defend itself against any foreign invasion. This right to legitimate defense vindicates the implementation of sufficient capacities. Cyberspace poses singular challenges to Japan.

The neo-realists believe that States are encouraged by the pressure of international anarchy to develop offensive weapons in anticipation of the worst-case scenario. Cyber-defense involves adopting a defensive stance: the issue of offensive weapons in this area does not yet exist in Japan. However, the other components are present: international anarchy – or at least anarchy in the international system that is cyberspace – with the entrance onto the scene of actors who do not represent a State, and cannot be controlled, identified or located. Japan's efforts, like those of many other nations, to pin the blame for the attacks on somebody are not only intended to enable reprisals to be carried out or that party to be pursued. They are also intended to reassure, and give the impression that some degree of control is finally being gained over the problem, and that all is not as elusive as it seems in cyberspace. In terms of the worst-case scenario, it is the same as the strategies of all modern and industrialized states who fear major cyber-attacks with devastating effects. It is to defend itself against attacks on critical infrastructures (which would indeed be the worst-case scenario) that Japan is intensifying its efforts in terms of cyber-defense. However, it may also be due to influence or to international pressure: this pressure not only gives rise to attacks but also encourages States to secure their systems, for a cyberspace that is common, in which the weaknesses of one become those of the others – an international system in which numerous States equip themselves with civil and military cyber-units for security and defense. If it is not to be left behind in the comity of nations, Japan cannot remain silent and inactive on the subject.

6.4. Bibliography

[AIZ 98] AIZU I., *Internet in Japan in Asian Context*, ANR, November 1998, available at: http://www.anr.org/web/html/archive/old/html/output/98/PAN98_e.htm.

[AIZ 10] AIZU I., Tokyo Workshop for a Future Internet, report from the conference Keoi University, Tokyo, Japan, May 2010, available at http://www.internetfutures.eu/wp-content/uploads/2010/04/tokyo-workshop-report.pdf

[ATA 10] ATANASSOVA-CORNELIS E., *The US-Japan Alliance and the Rise of China: Implications for the East Asian Security Order and the EU's Regional Role*, K.U. Leuven, Belgium, May 2010.

[BER 98] BERGER T., *Cultures of Antimilitarism*, Baltimore, MD, John Hopkins University Press, 1998.

[CHE 11] CHEN C.S., *Japanese Strategy and Response to the Rise of China*, Fu Hsing Kang College, Taiwan, March 2011.

[COU 10] THE COUNCIL ON SECURITY AND DEFENSE CAPABILITIES IN THE NEW ERA, Japan's Visions for Future Security and Defense capabilities in the new era: toward a peace-creating nation, CSDCNE, Tokyo, Japan, August 2010, available at: http://www.kantei.go.jp/jp/singi/shin-ampobouei2010/houkokusyo_e.pdf.

[DES 98] DESCH M., "Culture clash: Assessing the Importance of Ideas in Security Study", *International Security*, vol. 23, no. 1, pp. 141-170, MIT Press, 1998.

[GIB 84] GIBSON W., *Neuromancer*, Ace Books, New York, 1984.

[GRE 01] GREEN M.J. *Japan's Reluctant Realism: Foreign Policy Challenges in an Era of Uncertain Power*, Palgrave Macmillan, 2001.

[GRE 11] GREEN H.S., *Strategies vs Norms: An Assessment of Theories to Explain Japan's Security Policy*, TOYO, Japan, March 2011, available at: http://www.toyo.ac.jp/law/pblsh/toyo/pdf54-3/0216.pdf.

[HAY 11] HAYS J., *Internet in Japan: Blogs, Rakuten, Broadband, Viruses, Facebook, Mixi and Gree, Facts and Details*, October 2011, available at: http://factsanddetails.com/japan.php?itemid=724&catid=20&subcatid=133.

[HUG 04] HUGHES C.W., *Japan's Re-emergence as a 'Normal' Military Power*, Oxford University Press, Oxford, 2004.

[HUG 09] HUGHES C.W., "Japan's military modernisation: A quiet Japan-China arms race and global power projection", *Asia-Pacific Review*, vol.16, no. 1, pp. 84-89, 2009.

[ISP 06] INFORMATION SECURITY POLICY COUNCIL, *The First National Strategy on Information Security, Toward the Realization of a Trustworthy Society*, ISPC, Tokyo, Japan, February 2, 2006.

[ISP 09] INFORMATION SECURITY POLICY COUNCIL, *Secure Japan 2009*, ISPC, Tokyo, Japan, June 22, 2009, available at: http://www.nisc.go.jp/eng/pdf/sj2009_eng.pdf.

[KAT 96] KATZENSTEIN P., *Cultural Norms and National Security*, Cornell University Press, Ithaca, NY, USA, 1996.

[KAW 01] KAWASAKI T., "Postclassical realism and Japanese security policy", *The Pacific Review*, vol. 14, no. 2, pp.221-240, 2001.

[LIN 03] LIND J., *Continuity and change in Japanese Security Policy: Testing Theories of International Relations*, Department of Political Science, MIT, USA, November 12, 2003, available at: http://web.mit.edu/ssp/seminars/wed_archives03fall/lind.htm.

[NIS 11] NISHIHARA M., *Japan's Defense Policy and the Asia-Pacific Region*, Japan, March 30, 2011, available at: http://www.ca.emb-japan.go.jp/2011_shared_images/Cultural%20 Events/nishihara_lecture_text.pdf.

[PYL 07] PYLE K.B., *Japan Rising: The Resurgence of Japanese Power and Purpose*, Public Affairs Books, New York, 2007.

[RYA 11] RYALL J., "Japan targeted by cyber attacks 'from China'", *Telegraph*, September 20 2011, available at: http://www.telegraph.co.uk/news/worldnews/asia/japan/ 8775635/Japan-targeted-by-cyber-attacks-from-China.html.

[SZE 06] SZECHENYI N, "A turning point for Japan's Self-Defense Forces", *The Washington Quarterly*, vol. 29, no. 4, pp.139-150, 2006.

[WAN 08] WANG K., "Japan's defense policy, strengthening conventional offensive capability", *Journal of East Asian Affairs*, vol.8, no. 1, pp. 87-89, 2008.

[WIL 11a] WILSON D., "Japanese Parliament is under cyber attack", *The Inquirer*, November 2, 2011, available at: http://www.theinquirer.net/inquirer/news/2121964/japanese-parliament-cyber-attack.

[WIL 11b] WILSON D., "Warplane and nuclear plant data were at risk in Mitsubishi Heavy Attack", *The Inquirer*, October 15, 2011, available at: http://www.theinquirer.net/ inquirer/news/2119850/warplane-nuclear-plant-stolen-mitsubishi-heavy-attack.

[YAM 05] YAMAKURA Y., *Network Centric Warfare: its Implications for Japan's Self-Defense Force*, Japan Air Self Defense Force, Japan, August 18, 2005.

[YIN 08] YIN J., TAYLOR P.M., "Information operations from an Asian perspective: A comparative analysis, *Journal of Information Warfare*, vol. 7, no. 1, pp. 1-23, 2008.

[YOM 00] YOMIURI SHINBUN., Defense Agency Considers Developing Cyber Weapons, article of October 23, 2000.

Chapter 7

Singapore's Encounter with Information Warfare: Filtering Electronic Globalization and Military Enhancements

The Singaporean approach to information warfare is best framed in terms of the language of an encounter. It is a phenomenon introduced from outside its sovereign borders. Moreover, informational threats are wholly unconventional ones that cannot be effectively tackled by a standard authoritarian combination of legal sanction and policing. Given these unplanned and unpremeditated features, as of 2011–2012 the Singaporean official response to informational threats tracks the tentative reactions made by governments elsewhere.

In Singapore's case, the authorities have had to reconcile Singapore's capitalist hub status with some form of a pre-emptive defense. The latter description is probably oxymoronic and shrouded in secrecy given its fledgling status as a national security concern. Above all, it is an encounter because information warfare represents either an externality of the 'good globalization' that has brought prosperity to the Republic, or at worst an inevitable 'negative globalization' that causes damage. This binary conceptualization will be evident throughout this chapter, and indeed, aside from treating this as a feature of the preliminary Singaporean experience, it should be queried whether any national encounter with informational threats poses a quandary about the dual nature of globalization.

Chapter written by Alan CHONG.

Since this chapter is situated in a book that calls attention to cyber-conflict or cyber-warfare, it also needs to be noted that the Singaporean discourse does not draw neat distinctions between cyber-warfare, cyber-defence, and the widest umbrella term, information warfare. In this regard, since this chapter is not intended to be a meta-theoretical inquiry into the terminology of various forms of information-related conflict activities. For convenience we will adhere to Daniel Ventre's synthesized definition of information warfare as

> "...the aggressive/defensive use of information space components (which are information and information systems) to reach/protect the sovereignty of a nation through actions conducted in times of peace, crisis or conflict. The concept is then centered on its political and military dimensions, and a connection of dependence is established between the notions of information space and sovereignty – which comes down to saying that an aggressive/defensive action conducted in the information space is not always an information warfare operation: some acts are simply part of cyber criminality or delinquency."[1]

In other words, this definition of information warfare may, on occasion, be loosely invoked by spokespersons of the Singaporean government to justify treating cyber-warfare as an attack upon the sovereignty of its collective citizenry, economy and institutions of statehood, including the military apparatus. In any case, the position of the Singapore Armed Forces (SAF) ambiguously embraces preparations for *information warfare rather than cyber-warfare alone*. In the civilian realm, it is the reverse – the threat is specifically from *cyber-warfare rather than information warfare*.

This chapter will pan out as follows. First, it needs to be elaborated that Singapore's information technology (IT) development is reflective of the Republic's embrace of an electronic globalization that co-constitutes its central role in the global economy. Subsequently, the chapter will branch into two broad sections examining information warfare via the generic discourse of 'defense'. It will become evident in the exposition why this terminology is officially preferred over the highly alarmist tones of American official and academic discourses on the subject. First, in the domestic realm the government acts upon the threat of 'cyber-warfare', which covers attacks by both State and non-State sources employing the World Wide Web, as well as attacks by insiders with access to intranets. There is little official distinction between cyber-crime and cyber-warfare since the laws on internal security, libel and petty crime have also been applied to crimes committed against corporations operating in the Republic. As a result, the government has

---

1 [VEN 09] p. 288.

created the Singapore Infocomm Technology Security Authority (SITSA). This watchdog and strategic controlling outfit, housed within the Ministry of Home Affairs, is trying to engage private sector firms and individuals to collaborate with the government in establishing a joint Cyber Defender Programme to defend against threats to the island state's highly globalized economic links with the world. Cyber-defence is therefore literal in its meaning: to defend against unwarranted penetration via the Internet or through intranets comprising limited networks of computers. This takes place against the background of a steep increase in the number of hacking and viral attacks against private sector corporations in the past three years. Whether this will be a foolproof territorial defense remains to be seen.

On the second front, the SAF subscribes more to the American-originated understanding of information warfare as a realm of military operations designed to disrupt the enemy's decision-making capabilities while enhancing one's own. However, the implementation of military informational measures is often subsumed within the rhetoric of general high-technology improvements. This sort of logic is typical of the military in developing countries aspiring to modernize their offensive and defensive capabilities by acquiring missiles and aircraft. This chapter, however, will argue that the Singaporean defense planners have creatively treated information warfare in three dimensions of capability expansion:

– force multiplication;

– generating asymmetrical advantages in operational transparency; and

– continually revitalizing existing conventional arms capabilities.

In short, the Singaporean military approach is not revolutionary but evolutionary in nature. In summary, both the civilian cyberwarfare and military information warfare approaches render the Singaporean case unique on the grounds of their division of focus. The question of effectiveness, as for most nation-states, however, remains unanswered in this new realm of national defense.

7.1. Singapore: electronic globalization and its pitfalls

The story of Singapore's positioning as a beneficiary of globalization is well known. An island republic devoid of natural resources and a hinterland for hosting a large population necessarily seeks geopolitical and geo-economics strategies of an outward orientation. The Republic's first foreign minister, Sinnathamby Rajaratnam, explained this orientation in terms of an aspiration towards becoming a global city, one which

"is the child of modern technology. It is the city that electronic communications, supersonic planes, giant tankers and modern economic and industrial organisation have made inevitable. Whether the global city will be a happier place than the megalopolis out of whose crumbling ruins it is emerging will depend on how wisely and boldly we shape its direction and growth"[2].

Telecommunications and their financial interconnection networks would integrate Singapore in an institutionalized interaction with the sister global cities of London, New York, Shanghai, Sydney and Tokyo. The economic 'tempo' of economic activity would be sensitively intertwined with trends in the cities that would in turn be attuned to trends in their national hinterlands. Rajaratnam was keenly aware that interdependence may in practice mean lopsided dependence, with Singapore acting more as a follower than a pioneer. The country's governance, even sovereignty, may have to be selectively conceded so as to match foreign arrangements. Rajaratnam nonetheless believed that the risk had to be taken with the full awareness that "if we have the will and the intelligence, [we] *create the necessary anti-bodies within our social system to give us immunity against the many dangers* that close association with giant foreign corporations would pose"[3].

The analogy – derived from the field of medicine, of antibodies, immunity and their antithesis, the virus – is apt for comprehending the political implications of Singapore's embrace of information flows that are carried through wired and wireless means.[4] An early trial of Singapore's media antibodies came through the press. During the 1970s, a few newspapers such as *The Eastern Sun* and *The Singapore Herald* were shut down by the government for receiving undeclared foreign funds in order to undermine the local political system. In the first three decades since Independence in 1965, there had been numerous instances of editors either resigning or being forced to recant editorial positions on the grounds that their actions were inconsistent with Singapore's nation-building directions[5]. According to the official perspectives, then and now, the Republic of Singapore's multi-racial and multi-religious population makeup has to be kept in a condition of mutual tolerance devoid of serious provocation. The People's Action Party (PAP), that has ruled the island state since Independence, regards harmony among the citizens of Chinese, Malay and Indian origin as a sacrosanct part of the internal dimension of national security that must be actively policed.

This authoritarian imperative is based on the fact that Singapore's neighbors in Southeast Asia have been embroiled in inter-racial and inter-religious violence from time-to-time, to the detriment of economic growth and the inflow of foreign

---

2 [RAJ 87] pp. 225-226.
3 [RAJ 87] pp. 230. Italics are mine.
4 See also the Singapore chapter in [VEN 09].
5 [TAN 90] pp. 5-7.

investment.[6] Additionally, the PAP has found many occasions to employ the law to curb the circulation of foreign English-language publications – both offline and online – such as *Time*, *Newsweek*, the *Asian Wall Street Journal*, *Asiaweek*, the *Far Eastern Economic Review*, *Bloomberg News* and *Al Jazeera* for 'inaccuracies' in reporting local political events. Singapore's press is managed by the Newspaper and Printing Presses Acts of 1974 and 1986. Subsequently, the Singapore Broadcasting Act, which was passed in 1994, polices terrestrial broadcasting, digital television through cable, and Internet-based media based in Singapore. Direct broadcast satellite services are still limited to a handful of foreign firms based in Singapore, and selectively to the universities, ostensibly for teleconferencing purposes. When the Media Development Authority was set up in 2003 to consolidate all media regulatory agencies under one roof, its officials promised the 'light touch' regulation of digital media on the premise that total censorship could not be foolproof in the digital age.[7] Moreover, the PAP intended to promote Singapore as a hub for global media corporations. This was not perceived by the PAP as a contradiction. It was in fact a relatively convenient two-way street for both foreign companies and the PAP. The former could avail themselves of Singapore's high-technology communications infrastructure to report world news and process other media products for film and Internet circulation, so long as they avoided 'skewed' reporting of local politics. It is no surprise that most global news agencies, such as the BBC, CNN, Deutsche Press Agentur, Reuters and CNBC Asia, station their Southeast Asian and Asian correspondents on the island to cover the East Asian region stretching from Indonesia to China. Disney and Spielberg Productions also have production facilities in Singapore.

The PAP is nonetheless concerned with the untrammeled flows of information offered by the Internet. An interesting piece of reflection was jointly written by the Chief Executive of Singapore's National Computer Board and the Deputy Director of the government-linked Institute of Policy Studies in 1998 – a significant milestone in the evolution of the World Wide Web and a few years after the first recorded international cyber-attacks. The authors argued that the government of Singapore had run into potentially intractable dilemmas in censoring Internet content[8]. On one hand, it would be possible to censor in the short term when Internet access depended heavily on landline connections and a handful of Internet service providers (ISPs) servicing the island's population. On the other hand, however, rapidly advancing IT geography would mean that Web-savvy citizens could surmount local controls by routing their links via multiple external ISPs; and furthermore, the globalization of overlapping and potentially supranational jurisdictions over Internet content and operational protocols will probably

---

6 [BIR 93].
7 [MDA 12].
8 [YEO 98].

undermine national controls. The trans-sovereign activities of the Internet Corporation for Assigned Names and Numbers (ICANN) – the US-based Web 'authority' – is a foretaste of future Internet governance. Singaporean policing of Internet content could be reduced to mere acts of symbolism amidst the floods of information channels on the Web. It is also likely that a Web-savvy population, ranging from the intelligentsia to students, journalists, chief executive officers and ordinary private sector professionals will object to traditional forms of state control. As the authors of the aforementioned reflection put it, the chief dilemma for the PAP is to reconcile "the [digital] chasm between symbolism and reality in Singapore".[9] How might this pan out when it comes to the matter of information warfare? This is the subject of what I term the 'dual encounter' – civilian and military – in sections 7.2 and 7.3.

7.2. Cyberdefence in the private sector and society at large

In the parlance of the private sector in Singapore, cyber-defense is widely assumed in both private business and governmental publications to be the realm of protecting computers and their software from malicious disruption. It also entails protecting data that is meant by its original creator or designated third-party possessor to remain secret from the general public. In the official Singaporean terminology, cyber-defense is synonymous with cybersecurity. Having clarified the definition of cyber-defense, it is important to situate this discussion within the context of government–corporate sector relations in the dissemination of IT use in Singapore.

Taking after the general pattern in much of Singapore's political economy, the pace of technological embrace in IT can only be explained in terms of a combination of government intervention and *laissez faire* initiative[10]. It was in 1980, incidentally the same year that the Microsoft Corporation forged an alliance with IBM computers, that the government of Singapore made it official policy to spur IT penetration in business. Up until then, computers were treated as the preserve of an estimated 1,000 information systems professionals operating a mere 400 computer installations on the island[11]. After the government initiated bodies such as the Committee for National Computerization and the National Computer Board to implement strategic directions for IT use, the numbers of IT professionals increased

---

9 [YEO 98] pp. 144.
10 [MOT 89].
11 [MOT 89] pp. 881.

1,075% by 1985 to 4,300. The numbers of 'microcomputers' sold quadrupled between 1982 and 1985[12].

IT became even more commonplace in Singaporean homes when the government-linked grassroots organizations led by the People's Association acquired 'personal computers' for home use and conducted demonstration classes in computer appreciation across the island's public housing estates. This helped acclimatize both the young and middle-aged segments of the population, who were also the most economically relevant, to the culture of an information society that had been predicted by Alvin Toffler, Daniel Bell, Peter Drucker and Kenichi Ohmae.

Not surprisingly, by the time the Internet arrived in Singapore, the 'software' of social and professional expectations had prepared the local population to embrace a computer and Internet penetration rate of more than 50% by 2000, placing Singapore ahead of Australia, Hong Kong, Japan, Taiwan and the USA[13]. In 2010, Singapore's Internet penetration rate was determined to be 77.8%.[14] Moreover, the government had fostered an Institute of Systems Science as a partnership between the National University of Singapore and IBM in the US to assist companies with computerization and electronic workflow trouble-shooting. Subsequently, schools of computing, communications and new media sprouted within the local universities and polytechnics ensuring this information economy remained sustainable.

This visible hand of government was obviously not unwelcomed by the private sector, but it did indicate that any threats to the smooth functioning of information society in Singapore would be met by the form of integrated response you might expect of a corporatist relationship between State and society. In 1991, the government announced a top-down initiative called IT2000 in which all homes were to be wired for Internet access by 2000. In July 1998, the government passed the Electronic Transactions Act, which provided the legal foundations for online commerce by placing electronic signatures on a par with written signatures and records and provided legal protection to data sent over networks. Facilities for sending various applications – including tax returns – to government agencies online followed very quickly within a few years.

In August 1998, the Singapore Stock Exchange announced that it would implement an online trading system that would allow stockbrokers to directly interface with its in-house computerized trading system. By late 1998, the government announced the design of an islandwide broadband network named 'Singapore One', which it fully implemented slightly over a year later.

---

12 [MOT 89] pp. 882.
13 [IDA 00, ITU 01].
14 [IWS 12].

Government ministers and IT professionals were continually hosting IT conventions to plug the promise of Singapore as the premier IT hub in Asia. Meanwhile, several incidents involving undersea telecommunications cable disruptions in the Asia-Pacific during the 2000–2010 period highlighted Singapore's role as a vital hub for the physical infrastructure of Asian Internet geography. Although most of these cables were damaged by earthquakes in the Indian Ocean, around Taiwan and in Indonesian waters, Singapore's government-linked company SingTel was relied upon by the private consortium owning the cables to dispatch cable ships to repair the connections. During the disruption, Internet access across virtually the entire Asian side of the Pacific Rim slowed considerably. Despite this hub status, the erstwhile Minister of State for Trade and Industry in 1999, modestly claimed that Singapore's position on the ladder of IT in Asia was "at midstream, where it would bridge the gap between what technology could offer and what the market might require" [KWA 99]. By the early 2000s, the government had established an Infocomm Development Authority to oversee IT regulations and the monitoring of challenges to e-commerce within the island.

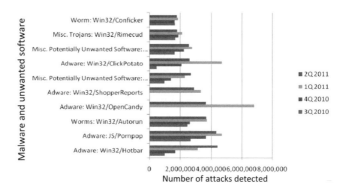

Figure 7.1. *Number of cybercrime cases by category in the 2003–2008 period; X axis – malware and unwanted software families; Y axis – number of attacks detected*

Nonetheless, the wired dimension of Singapore's economy endured several virus attacks, of which the more prominent were the 'iloveyou' viruses beginning in the early 2000s, outright hacking to steal passwords and other data, and 'phishing' attempts. These early threats were sufficiently serious that the government announced in early 2005 that it would spend S$38 million to build capabilities in cyber security. It also established a National Infocomm Security Committee (NISC) to formulate policies and strategic direction for cyber-defense at the national level. The NISC is chaired by the Permanent Secretary of the National Security and Intelligence Coordination and comprises representatives from the Ministry of Home Affairs, Ministry of Defence, Ministry of Information, Communication and the Arts, Ministry of Finance, Defence Science Organization National Labs, and the Defence

Science and Technology Agency (DSTA) [IDA 05]. Another parallel agency, the aforementioned SITSA, was also created in 2009 and housed under the Ministry of Home Affairs to monitor and advise the private sector and individuals on cyber-defense.

Despite the government's proactive leadership, however, cyber-threats in the form of cyber-crime affecting individuals and private firms have grown alarmingly over the period 2004–2011. In a piece of statistical research published in the *Singapore Journal of Library and Information Management* in 2009, researchers found that a whole range of cyber-crime jumped by approximately 50% between 2004 and 2005, and subsequently hacking and fraud have sustained the steady increase in cyber-crime. Figure 7.1, produced by Na Jin-Cheon *et al.* is illustrative of this trend.

In September 2010, Symantec publicly released its Norton Cybercrime Report: The Human Impact with alarming revelations. Seventy per cent of Singaporeans have been victim to cyber-crimes, which was greater than the proportion that Symantec considered to be the global average (65%) [SIM 10]. It is worthwhile quoting the exact words of Effendy Ibrahim, the consumer business head of Symantec in Asia, on this occasion: "Why do we say it is [a silent digital] epidemic? Because 70% of Singaporeans... confessed to having been a victim of cybercrime, and only 12% said they were confident that they would never be a victim," he said. "If you imagine a room full of people, it means that 70% of the people have been robbed by a criminal, and yet it is not taken very seriously" [LUM 10].

Singaporeans had spent an average of 24 days and S$1,660.00 addressing the fallout from cyber-crime, yet this statistic does not factor in the emotional trauma of fixing the computer involved, cleaning up the phishing malware, or negotiating with the transacting institutions to annul fraudulent transactions [SIM 10]. Effendy claimed that the lack of education and awareness were responsible for this state of affairs. Singaporeans tended to be too trusting towards the Internet: "12% said they did not expect to be victims online, against the global average of 3%" [SIM 10]. Effendy felt that simple precautions, such as critically scrutinizing requests for personal information online, purchasing a reliable and constantly updated antivirus program or lowering the credit limit for a credit card frequently used online, could be very useful steps towards limiting exposure to cyber-crime. Although these revelations were all described in the language of crime and its prevention, it could constitute a form of 'soft cyberthreat' to the integrity of Singapore's information society and knowledge-based economy.

Firms have also been hit hard by cyber-attacks. This is evident even though data pertaining to Singapore-based firms have not been made available on a nation-specific basis. Symantec has again been at the forefront of these disclosures. It was reported in their 2010 State of Enterprise Report that 75% of companies in the 'Asia-Pacific and Japan' and 66% in Singapore have experienced cyber-attacks in the past 12 months [REB 10]. These attacks cost enterprise businesses in the region an average of US$763,000 per year and US$2 million globally [REB 10]. A simple 'snapshot-type' comparison between the malware that was reported by Microsoft's Global Security Intelligence Report Volume 11 for the first two quarters of 2011 and Trend Micro's *Threat Encyclopedia for the Asia Pacific* for the period August to September 2011 reveals very different types of malware penetration that further complicate efforts to contain cyber-attacks through software carriers.

Family	Category	3Q10	4Q10	1Q11	2Q11
Win32/Hotbar	Adware	997,111	1,661,747	3,149,677	4,411,501
JS/Pornpop	Adware	2,659,054	3,666,856	4,706,968	4,330,510
Win32/Autorun	Worms	2,454,708	2,624,241	3,718,690	3,677,588
Win32/OpenCandy	Adware	—	—	6,797,012	3,652,658
Win32/ShopperReports	Adware	—	—	3,348,949	2,902,430
Win32/Keygen	Misc. Potentially Unwanted Software	981,051	1,402,417	2,299,870	2,680,354
Win32/ClickPotato	Adware	451,407	2,074,751	4,694,442	2,592,125
Win32/Zwangi	Misc. Potentially Unwanted Software	1,637,316	2,236,990	2,785,111	2,586,630
Win32/Rimecud	Misc. Trojans	1,673,312	1,872,449	2,123,298	1,818,530
Win32/Conficker	Worm	1,648,481	1,636,201	1,859,498	1,790,035

Table 7.1. *Quarterly trends for the top 10 malware and potentially unwanted software families detected by Microsoft antimalware desktop products in 1Q11 and 2Q11, shaded according to relative prevalence*[15]

Malware

Detection Name	Advisory Date	Overall Risk Rating	Pattern Version
RTKT_DUQU.A	24 Oct 2011	Medium	8.509.00
TROJ_DUQU.DEC	21 Oct 2011	Medium	8.509.00
TROJ_DUQU.ENC	21 Oct 2011	Medium	8.509.00
TROJ_SHADOW.AF	19 Oct 2011	Medium	8.429.00
BKDR_R2D2.A	10 Oct 2011	Medium	8.483.00
J2ME_JIFAKE.AA	04 Oct 2011	Medium	8.473.00
ANDROIDOS_JIFAKE.E	04 Oct 2011	Medium	8.461.00
ANDROIDOS_FAKEBROWS.A	03 Oct 2011	Medium	8.465.00
J2ME_FAKEBROWS.A	29 Sep 2011	Medium	8.465.00
ANDROIDOS_ANSERVER.A	27 Sep 2011	Medium	8.461.00

Table 7.2. *Malware listed as part of Trend Micro's Threat Encyclopedia for the Asia-Pacific August 27-September 24, 2011*[16]

---

15 [MIC 11] p. 41, figure 29.

These snapshots reveal a rapid and ever-evolving cyberthreat in just one category – malware, or software that infects your computer with the intent of partially or completely disabling normal functions. In November 2011, the Microsoft report specified that in Singapore's case, the malware infecting computers were mostly what IT experts term the 'social engineering' type. This term refers to the type of cyber-attack where a user is misled into executing commands that open their computers' windows to attack. This is manifested in users clicking on 'pop-up windows' advertising ancillary or unrelated products while surfing the Internet, or installing software patches that promise safety or computer performance enhancement [HO 11]. The viruses with the telltale names beginning with 'ANDROIDOS' and the suffixes 'ShopperReports' and 'ClickPotato' that are listed in Table 7.2 indicate this problem. Microsoft's findings indicate that adware was the most common form of social engineering malware. Adware affected 35.4% of all infected computers in the second quarter of 2011, which was reportedly a decline from 39.3% in the first quarter, but still significantly higher than the global average of 23.5% [HO 11]. Given the ongoing craze for Apple's iPhone, iPad, and other comparable devices in Singapore, as is the case elsewhere in the developed world, Symantec warns of the probable increase in the incidence of malware targeting innocent users using interfacing software across various platforms. In Symantec's words:

> "While the number of immediate threats to mobile devices remains relatively low in comparison to threats targeting PCs, there have been new developments in the field. As more users download and install third-party applications for these devices, the chances of installing malicious applications also increases. In addition, because most malicious code now is designed to generate revenue, there are likely to be more threats created for these devices as people increasingly use them for sensitive transactions such as online shopping and banking.

> "As with desktop computers, the exploitation of a vulnerability can be a way for malicious code to be installed on a mobile device. In 2010, there were a significant number of vulnerabilities reported that affect mobile devices. Symantec documented 163 vulnerabilities in mobile device operating systems in 2010, compared to 115 in 2009. While it may be difficult to exploit many of these vulnerabilities successfully, there were two vulnerabilities that affected Apple's iPhone iOS operating platform that allowed users to 'jailbreak' their devices. The process of jailbreaking a device through exploits is not

---

16 [TRM 11] personal communication with author.

very different from using exploits to install malicious code. In this case, though, users would have been exploiting their own devices."[17]

The Singaporean government's response is to reinforce the 'capacity building and engaging regulators and industry players'. This is SITSA's strategic mission. What this means is that regulators will have to reprise the historical role of government intervention in IT matters. Corporate and consumer IT users will have to follow the government's direction and render their systems compliant with government-dictated rules and informal advice. The NISC provided this concept of a corporatist cyber-defense at its launch, and it is represented in Figure 7.2.

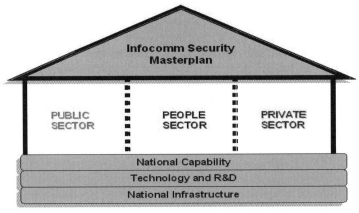

Pictorial Representation of the Masterplan Framework

Figure 7.2. *Infocomm's security masterplan*[18]

Given the government's tendency to set up yet another agency or committee to confront cyberthreats, along with the oft-expressed ancillary interest in fostering international cooperation to govern cyberspace for legitimate traffic, we get the impression that cyberdefence in the private sector and civil society will remain a matter of following the government's lead. This may be helpful in the short term given the ongoing rush by IT professionals to ensure that their systems are security compliant in Singapore. In the long term, however, civil society and private firms have to exercise some initiative and take an active interest in introducing their employees to cyber-security consciousness. This was the point made by Symantec's disclosure of the wanton public ignorance of cyber-crime, and their remedy by commonsensical precautions to take when engaging in online finance transactions and buying protection software. Meanwhile, the government of Singapore seems to

17 [SYM 11] pp. 15.
18 [IDA 05].

be constantly scoping cyber-defense in the widest possible spectrum to focus attention upon curbing *jihadist* proselytization online and the mass mobilization of individuals for extreme causes via social media networking [TEO 11]. This is a disjuncture that may have to be resolved if cyber-defense is not to be treated as a mere elite initiative that carries the imagined prospect of a magically comprehensive solution to all manner of cyber-threats.

7.3. The Singapore Armed Forces and the embrace of third-generation warfare

The SAF was formally inaugurated in August 1965 upon Singapore's separation from the Malaysian Federation. On its official website, the SAF was then described in minimalist terms with no pre-planned aspiration towards a capability that would come to be known as information warfare:

> "Singapore then had only two infantry battalions of 50 officers and some 1,000 men and two ships. There was no air force. Singapore's armed forces had to be created virtually from scratch. With its small population and the need to channel resources to economic development, it was decided that Singapore's defence would be based on citizen armed forces" [LIM 97].

Certainly, there was an element of psychological operation needed to deter potential adversaries across the Straits of Johor (Malaysia) and the Straits of Singapore (Indonesia), as well as to stiffen the population's resolve to supply manpower from their own families to build the armed forces. Yet, as the SAF evolved in tandem with a booming economy over four decades, technological examples of improvement from the corporate sector, as well as the augmented intellectual qualifications of its mostly conscripted manpower, pointed to the possibilities of embracing an information-driven 'revolution in military affairs'.

In 2009, the SAF was officially designated a third-generation armed forces, or in short, the 3G SAF. This transformation entailed exploiting the ever-higher educational qualifications of the vast majority of its citizen soldiers to the full. In 2009, it was reported that 75% of enlistees were GCE 'A' Level graduates or polytechnic diploma holders [CHW 09]. In tandem with this trend, SAF regular officers and non-commissioned soldiers are increasingly being offered in-house opportunities to upgrade their skills and qualifications through professional military courses taught by a pool of academics contracted from both the internationally reputable S. Rajaratnam School of International Studies Nanyang Technological University. These professional courses include leadership, military history, security studies and engineering. For those regulars who are more capable, the SAF offers a follow-on fully-sponsored range of Masters degrees tenable at Nanyang

Technological University and its affiliated schools. This is in addition to the existing array of SAF overseas scholarships and local study awards for basic undergraduate and graduate education, either overseas or at local universities.

An officially-approved news report on the 3G SAF explained the brainpower-reliant dimension in this way: "every 3G SAF soldier has an innate ability to soak up reams of information and act on them" [CHW 09]. It is expected that the 3G SAF soldier will operate in a dense environment of "fluid geopolitical conditions, a glut of high-tech military hardware and different military scenarios [that] require highly adaptable soldiers" [CHW 09].

Some middle-level SAF officers have latched on to US Marine General Charles Krulak's analogy of the 'Strategic Corporal' to digest these implications of becoming 3G. Sample this excerpt from an essay published in *POINTER*, the in-house SAF journal for officers:

> "...the Napoleonic Corporal's role was to listen to orders that were drafted so clearly that no one could misunderstand. With the orders, Napoleon's Corporal will carry out his mission in the exact way required of him. On the other hand, the Strategic Corporal of the information age must be able to function across a range of missions and be able to make decisions that have implications far beyond his responsibilities. With the high-tempo and dynamic battlefield today, the Strategic Corporal needs to be flexible to cope with different demands... This means that soldiers on the battlefield no longer fight alone. He is supported by a larger system for the conduct of his mission. Effectively, the enemy not just faces the soldier in combat, but also the larger system-of-systems that the soldier is connected to".[19]

This is the context for discussing how the SAF encounters the challenge of information warfare. As is the case with most military establishments, it is difficult to obtain an interview with an official spokesperson or to read internal documents clarifying contingent plans for responding to information warfare within a military dimension. Nonetheless, the discussions and selected chronology of events leading up to the implementation of the 3G SAF will offer some useful clues regarding the SAF's information warfare thinking, and whether it stretches into cyber-warfare, as its civilian counterparts would have it.

The SAF's information warfare culture is built around force multiplication, revitalizing conventional arms capabilities and generating asymmetrical advantages

---

19 [TAN 08] pp. 31-32; also see [TAN 09].

with operational transparency. We refer to an information warfare culture because the SAF has not openly announced an information warfare doctrine, while it has been taking steps to ensure that as closely as possible the 3G SAF is capable of functioning as a model information-age military entity.

7.3.1. *Force multiplication*

In the SAF, the notion of force multiplication needs to be understood in terms of the 'folk wisdom' of making a little go a long way. Military hardware does not need to be continually replaced by newer versions of existing equipment. If existing hardware can be extended beyond the manufacturer's specified shelf-life by expedient application of intermediate technology and hybridized processes, it is embraced. Such is the trajectory of the computerization of the SAF and the Ministry of Defence since the early 1980s, coinciding with the civilian push for IT use.

Computer-Assisted Instruction (CAI) was the emphasis in the SAF's officer and technical training schools and administrative departments. CAI ensured that individual learning could be pursued without the disadvantage of placing the student in a position of fatigue due to the inability to keep up with his the pace at which his peers learn. Moreover, the availability of instructors could be economized in terms of not being physically present all of the time; he or she only needs to be beside the student when he encounters a learning block.

Computers understandably would enhance the accuracy of payrolls and meticulous accounting of personnel histories and medical records, logistical readiness, and recording of test performances [TSK 85]. There has been extensive documentation of computerization through the deployment of simulators for artillery, air defense and pilot training. The navy and infantry followed suit very quickly, rendering the SAF a computer-penetrated organization by the 1990s.

Simulator training readies the SAF for war by schooling the human senses in the ability to learn through trial and error without incurring the damage that accompany physical trials; moreover, computerized sensors in the simulators feed back the human operator's weakest spots as scientifically as possible so that they can be corrected. For the trainee, the simulator provides a multisensory substitute for authenticity complete with recorded battlefield sounds and preloaded sights. In this way, the trainee gets to hone his skills while expending virtually unlimited stocks of ammunition, experiencing technical malfunctions, and dealing with damaged equipment until some degree of perfection is achieved in his trials. Only then does he move onto training using the real equipment [LIE 76].

Force multiplication has also been treated through the notion of 'battlefield automation'. According to one in-house journal article written by a signal battalion officer, battlefield automation augments force lethality against the enemy by clarifying where friendly forces have made preemptive arrangements to forestall the enemy, enabling cross-indexing and real-time updates on friendly force positions, recording enemy movements up to the minute, and finally enabling traditional human leadership via 'command and control' decisions [YAP 88]. More recently, at the end of the 2000s, the 3G SAF reformulated battlefield automation into a buzzword: IKC2, or Integrated Knowledge-Based Command and Control.[20] This concept is based upon the SAF becoming a more thoroughly cybernetic organization that is able to transmit assorted details from human and electronic sensors out into the field, process them centrally and enable commanders to deliberate and come to a decision quickly based upon an approximation of the ideal of total information awareness. The sum of an integrated knowledge-based command structure should be more than a sum of its parts. A cybernetic SAF command structure should be able to act and react faster than the enemy in real time, and in so doing defeat the opponent by appearing capricious, menacing and pre-emptive. An in-house SAF journal described IKC2 as information warfare, as shown in Figure 7.3.

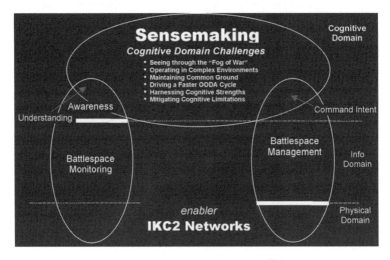

Figure 7.3. *IKC2 in the 3G SAF[21]*

In many ways, this is a direct extrapolation from the thesis presented in John Arquilla and David Ronfeldt's RAND (US think-tank) report titled In Athena's Camp: Preparing for Conflict in the Information Age [ARQ 97]. While it is heavily

---

20 IKC2 is the Singaporean equivalent of network-centric warfare.
21 [CHE 08] pp. 18.

reliant on adapting the latest digital and reconnaissance technologies ranging from satellites and hand-held miniature cameras to breaking news on the Web, it also strives to interpret the better parts of Carl von Clausewitz's warning about seeing through the 'fog of war' to the SAF's advantage *vis-à-vis* the adversary. In an unusual piece of criticism, in the pages of the same journal where the IKC2 concept received its most detailed elaboration, a junior weapons systems officer noted that IKC2 would suffer from information overload, coloration by technological biases, and the imperfections of assuming that adversaries would act rationally according to prior experience with electronically-facilitated war gaming [NG 08]. Von Clausewitz apparently returns to haunt cybernetic decision-making through the back doors of the very human factors of genius and chance. Nonetheless, IKC2 as the culmination of IT-assisted force multiplication in the SAF ought to be acknowledged as a forward development from the angle of virtually upgrading the Singaporean military from a mere brick-and-mortar institution with limited quantities of hardware to one aspiring to creatively transcend its material constraints.

7.3.2. *Continually revitalizing existing conventional arms capabilities*

The 3G SAF extends its preparation for information warfare as part of its longstanding policy of incremental technological upgrades. We might argue that it was consistent with the Republic's impoverished military beginnings in 1965 that weaponry upgrading performed in part by your own defense industry, or by the original manufacturer, was a rational way to stretch the defense dollar over time. Journalist David Boey has coined the term 'defense creep' to refer to this upgrading policy, which often kicks in after equipment systems have undergone several years of service following their initial purchase[22]. Moreover, Boey argues that incrementalism is also a form of information management of the upgrading process; incrementalism does not unduly alarm your neighbors and anticipated adversaries.

Tim Huxley, a major scholar on the subject of the SAF, has observed that Singapore's industrial defense complex manifests itself as the SAF's subtle need to deter the Republic's potential adversaries by maintaining a technological edge that is "not accessible through off-the-shelf purchase in the international defence market"[23]. At the same time, Huxley notes that Singaporean defense planners must certainly realize that such superiority tends to be short-lived unless research and development are pursued existentially with a view towards tailoring innovative upgrades for national needs[24]. In short, the technological edge is an informational

---

22 Boey quoted exclusively in [HUX 00] pp. 173-175.
23 [HUX 00] pp. 181.
24 [HUX 00] pp. 172-181.

edge in terms of scientific superiority. We can understand how the concept of IKC2 ties in with this approach towards industrial defense development.

Although this is not the place to provide an account of the entirety of the 3G SAF's weapons procurement, two examples suffice to illustrate the notion of hard weapons capabilities becoming integrated into a scientifically-conceived information warfare paradigm. The first is an excerpt from the official online description of the Pegasus light howitzer, which is jointly produced by the SAF, the statutory board DSTA, and another government-linked company, ST Kinetics.

The *Pegasus* incorporates several sophisticated subsystems in its design. Some significant features listed in Table 7.3.

Auxiliary Power Unit (APU)	**Ease of Deployment**
The APU is an independent engine unit on the *Pegasus*, which provides the gun with a short-range self-propelled capability. With the APU, the system is able to maneuver over terrain at a speed of 12 km/h. The *Pegasus* is the world's first heli-portable 155 mm howitzer with a self-propelled capability.	As a complex system that needs to be readily deployed for mobility, firing and heli-lifting, the *Pegasus* is easy to configure without any lifting support in the field. Through a simple seesaw action that shifts the gun's center of gravity to suit the different missions, the *Pegasus* can be rapidly engaged for deployment in less than 2.5 minutes with a detachment of eight men.
Ammunition Loading System (ALS)	
Powered by the APU, the ALS automatically loads ammunition to reduce crew fatigue. This allows the gun crew to operate the *Pegasus* for a longer period while maintaining a burst rate of three rounds in 24 seconds.	**Lightweight Materials**
	The *Pegasus* employs lightweight materials such as titanium and high-alloy aluminum that provides the strength and stability required to withstand the recoil force of a 155 mm system.
Mechanical Sight	
	Innovative Recoil Management
Each gun is also equipped with an advanced mechanical sight that can withstand firing shocks of up to 90 Gs. This is critical for sustained operations given the system's lightweight structure.	The recoil of the *Pegasus* is a third lower than conventional 155 mm howitzers. This is achieved through innovative recoil management design.

Table 7.3. *Specifications of the Pegasus Light Howitzer [MOD 11]*

In tandem with the anticipated demands of the IKC2 transformation, a piece of the 'brick and mortar' artillery equipment has been redesigned according to the SAF's information warfare requirements. The Pegasus howitzer has therefore reduced the physical exertions required so that humans can sustain more accurate firing for longer periods of time. Rapid deployment and redeployment, according to the speed of IKC2, is enabled because the structure of the howitzer is lighter and therefore is heli-portable. It can also drive itself if distances are short.

The next sample of information warfare consistency is an innovation on the waterborne craft called the frigate.

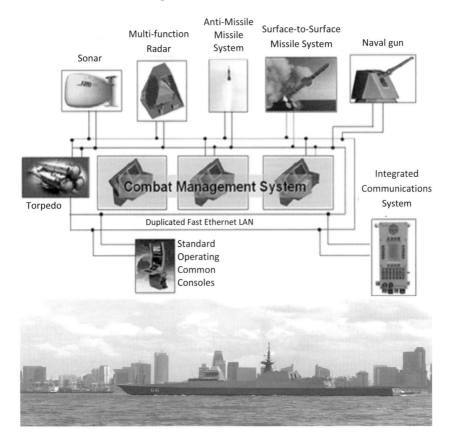

Figure 7.4. *The formidable class frigate's informationally ready combat system architecture*[25]

This diagram of the Stealth Frigate's combat system is a revelation of the scale of the ground-level integration of IKC2 into maritime capabilities. In fact, Figure 7.4 can be superimposed upon Figure 7.3. The electronic sensory capabilities in the

25 [RSN 11].

lower half of the diagram approximate the battlespace monitoring and battlespace management components of IKC2. The 'combat management system' represented by the electronic consoles reproduce the sense-making core of the IKC2, while the panoply of weapons represents the choices for engagement. The electronically-flushed stealth design of the vessel's outer shell is also faithful to the spirit of information warfare: *our side* should be able to see the enemy and its plans in their totality, while remaining inscrutable to them.

7.3.3. *Generating asymmetrical advantages in operational transparency*

Tucked away in the SAF's standing equivalent of a defense White Paper, in the document titled Defending Singapore in the Twenty-First Century published in 2000, is a subsection titled 'Superiority through information technology'. In it, the SAF restates its standard mantras about the need to compensate for the shortage of manpower and hardware resources with sharpened battlespace awareness. More importantly, knowing more implies a new truism: "Having superior information will be as potent, or even more potent, than having an advantage in firepower."[26] Some scholars have read this message into the SAF's expanding SIGINT (signals intelligence) capabilities, ranging from airborne radars mounted on reconnaissance aircraft to air traffic monitoring facilities shared with the civil aviation authorities, to access to satellites operated by local universities and government-linked firms, and most recently, to the SAF's openly declared unmanned aerial vehicle capabilities [HUX 04]. These 'eyes' and 'ears' certainly earn the SAF an enviable reputation among the region's military organizations as a surveillance power.[27] In 2001, a Major Seet Pi Shen, a guardsman with a Cambridge degree, published an essay that won the Chief of Defence Force essay prize for that year. It was titled 'The Manoeuvrist Approach and Dislocation Warfare for the SAF in the Information Age'. In it, Major Seet made a very telling observation:

> "In theory, if there is perfect situational awareness, pre-emption –
> to appropriate or seize for oneself before others – becomes very
> likely. Knowledge of enemy dispositions and intentions enables
> commanders to emphasise speed over caution and make unexpected
> rapid moves before its time. However, as Clausewitz's 'fog of war'
> continues to thrive in the Information Age, *temporal dislocation* will
> be more realistic. *This is the art of rendering enemy strength
> irrelevant through the manipulation of time, and is the basis for
> surprise in war. By acting faster than the enemy can, it undermines*

---

26 [MOD 00] pp. 46.
27 [HUX 04] pp. 204.

his decision-making ability, ultimately leading to the enemy's disintegration".[28]

This perspective reinforces the overall approach of this chapter by couching the Singaporean experience and preparation for information warfare in terms of an encounter where we must comprehend the military adaptation to information warfare as an evolving series of principles that guide operational decisions rather than scrutinizing the SAF for a single grand concept that encapsulates all of its approaches to information warfare.

While it is possible that incremental and ancillary institutions such as an Army Information Centre, the Navy Information Fusion Centre, or the Peace Support Operations Development Group, which were all established in the past decade, are functioning as building blocks for a coherent information warfare capability, we must interpret things in an open-ended manner in the spirit of faithful scholarship on the subject. The SAF's IKC2 may already be operational in peacetime policy and response without a public declaration of it being so. We may therefore leave the inquiry into more tangible evidence of the SAF's institutionalized information warfare capabilities here, and await emerging trends following the accumulation of diverse future field experiences. One case in point is how the guards formation in the army has derived an 'Operations Development Centre/Civil Military Relations Centre' under the umbrella of the Peace Support Operations Development Group in the wake of diverse peacekeeping, humanitarian and disaster relief operations ranging from Afghanistan to Indonesia and New Zealand [SAF 11].

This form of asymmetrical information edge is also ironically dependent upon preventing slippages from the civilian dimensions of the SAF. The SAF has tended to argue that its soldiers are always disciplined in their conscript phases, and that these messages are constantly reinforced. The reality is that the upcoming generations that are likely to staff the armed forces are the same as those who have grown up with 'Facebooking' and photo sharing via Smart phones and iPhones. The SAF must certainly be mindful that the Abu Ghraib prisoner abuse scandal arising from the US Occupation of Iraq between 2003 and 2005 was facilitated by digital cameras and Internet photo-sharing. Moreover, between 2009 and 2010, the Israel Defense Force has been gripped by fears that Palestinian militants may be gleaning militarily-usable intelligence from soldiers' Facebook pages. In some cases the militants had been trying to befriend Israeli troops through those very Facebook pages with a view towards conducting psychological operations against Israeli society. Most recently, the examples of the Arab Spring show that Facebook, Twitter and Flickr social media sites have been instrumental in enabling Arab civil society activists to mobilize supporters as well as bystanders to meet in symbolic

---

28 [SEE 01] pp. 15-16. The italics are mine.

public spaces to confront troops sent to pacify political unrest. A *POINTER* journal article analyzed the problem of the information-savvy 'Generation Why/Y' soldier in terms of a generic enlistment-aged youth avatar (sic) named Heng89 'fresh from junior college, awaiting his enlistment' and plugged into the world of 24/7 email, Facebook, blogs and constant bombardment by SMS and MMS:

> "*Tech-Savvy*
>
> Gen Y grew up surrounded by electronics and gadgets that are constantly vying for their attention. They have played a wide variety of computer and console games that train them to intuitively navigate through new menus and interfaces, master new control sequences and process images faster than they can process words. The advantage of having a new generation of tech-savvy soldiers is that much time and cost could be saved in the training and deployment of new technology on the battlefield. However, they also have a certain expectation of the workplace and a desire for access to new and existing technology. This poses both a challenge and an advantage to the SAF. The challenge would be to manage Gen Y's expectations of technology on the battlefield; despite all the technological advances, soldiers are still needed to fight on the ground. The advantage is that this generation can easily adapt to the latest technologies incorporated on the battlefield.
>
> *Staying Connected*
>
> Technology is no longer just a convenience but has become a defining factor in their well-being. It allows people to establish bonds in virtual space, make friends across continents and oceans, and bridge the gap between religions, races and cultures. Through social networking, (micro)blogging, Massively Multiplayer Online Games (MMOGs) and the entire gamut of communication software, Gen Y have overcome geographical constraints to form ties with people from abroad and beyond. "Heng89" might have hundreds of friends, whose true names he knows not, but who share the same ideology and opinions. They might even know him better than the people who surround him physically. As they seek to stay connected with their online friends, this creates a conflict with the need for information security within the SAF." [SHU 09]

Singapore's corporatist approach to securing society will be questioned by future generations accustomed to a more cosmopolitan existence derived from the borderless electronic globalization occurring worldwide. The SAF must therefore find a way to ensure that the logics of defending a still evanescent Singaporean nation-state remain compelling in spite of the cultural allures of a liberal popular culture permeating the portals of global information flows. At the other extreme, the right wing with causes that mesh with Islamic fundamentalism will also prove to be a threat to national solidarity among all enlistment-age youths.

The question of identity may force the SAF to re-examine the stability of the 'home front' in any information warfare planning. It is worth noting that in 2010 to 2011 alone, there have been three embarrassing photo episodes circulated online among Singaporean-frequented chat rooms and blogs involving the SAF:

– the sight of a gently crash-landed Republic of Singapore Air Force Apache helicopter and its decoupled tail strewn across an open field adjacent to residential apartments;

– the scene of a Filipina maid carrying a national serviceman's full pack for him while he fiddles with his mobile phone; and

– another unforgettable snapshot of an elderly father shouldering his national serviceman son's full pack upon his return from camp.

Facetious online captions are not difficult to create out of these incidents whether for amusement or counter-propaganda purposes: the Air Force's broken blades; Maid's army/army softee; and Dad's army!

Leaving these light-hearted episodes aside, the SAF has also confronted the increase in servicemen posting social and comical snapshots taken on camp premises on Facebook. This led to the SAF reminding Singaporeans that posting inappropriate information on the armed forces might be chargeable offenses under either the Sedition or Official Secrets Acts. Through these experiences, the SAF is beginning to evaluate the complex facets that accompany any aspiration towards information asymmetry using the technologies of globalization.

7.4. Conclusion

With the case in Singapore, the encounter with information warfare has proven to be both enriching and frustrating from an official angle. In fact, the contradictions found between a forward movement (IT producing opportunities for augmenting economics and defense) and a countermovement (IT producing opportunities for destruction, disruption and smear campaigns) are reminiscent of the early theoretical debates from the mid-1990s concerning the precise sociological and anthropological impacts of globalization[29].

This chapter has argued that on the civilian front, involving the private sector and society at large, information warfare has been reduced to dealing with cyber-warfare and cyber-defense. On this front, it is the ordinary citizens and working professionals who need to find ways to tame the excesses of electronic globalization while exploiting the benefits of borderless global commerce. On the military front, it has been argued that the SAF does not address information warfare as an autonomous field of warcraft requiring a dedicated command structure controlling its own wing. Instead, the SAF accommodates developments in information warfare through three prongs:

– force multiplication;

– continually revitalizing existing conventional arms capabilities; and

– generating asymmetrical advantages in operational transparency.

The Singaporean military approach comes across as more evolutionary than revolutionary in nature.

In summary, Singapore's encounter with information warfare is riddled with layers of ambiguity. It is certainly not a case of straightforward offence and defense across demarcated boundaries. IT can both empower and disempower agents that employ them. We can return to the erstwhile analogy offered by Singapore's first foreign minister S. Rajaratnam; Singapore needs to build the robust antibodies that enable its population and government to render electronic globalization a servant of progress and prosperity, but the question remains as to what the formulae of these antibodies might be. One final reflection is perhaps in order, assisted with an insight from Eugene Chang, a panelist at the 2007 e-Government conference representing Singapore's Ministry of Defence. Chang opined that "IT systems are organized in a stovepipe manner… Ideally, we should try and harmonize systems before we even build them" [ZDN 07].

As most studies from mass media scholars would argue, information theoretically distributes its benefits best when it flows through untrammeled channels to equalize the knowledge bases of human beings everywhere. Singapore's encounter with information globalization has, however, produced a position whereby its present antibodies – individuals, firms, government, defense planners and their regulations – are trying to harness the information flows by controlling them for the purpose of isolating some pieces information from others, so that temporary inequalities are produced among the recipients of information. In this

---

29 [WAT 95].

regard, the Singaporean approach thus far approximates what Jean-Loup Samaan predicts, that "there are no truly independent or even autonomous cyberwars *per se*"[30].

Cyber-attacks tend to be deployed as an integrated component of a broader strategic campaign possibly integrating both civilian and military measures. The Singaporeans seem to be gradually taking to heart, even if unacknowledged, the thrust of Martin Libicki's assessment that cyber-warfare can be practiced through open conquest, via generating international software dependence through buying Microsoft products, or through hidden conquest by inserting botnets and malware through innocent-looking Internet shop fronts[31].

This is all happening in Internet 'time', which also means that information warfare, if it is waged, would require rapid learning and the improvisation of countermeasures. Defense against information threats must be equally nimble. The logic of a corporatist Singaporean nation-state with some degree of centralized authoritarian direction may still work best *if* the efficiency of single-minded governance can match intellectual perspicacity. This is something that no nation-state has perfected, not even China with its Web patrols. Therefore, the Singaporean experience in dealing with information warfare will remain experimental, in the realm of open-ended encounter.

7.5. Bibliography

[ARQ 97] ARQUILLA J., RONFELDT D., *In Athena's Camp: Preparing for Conflict in the Information Age*, RAND Corporation, Santa Monica, USA, 1997.

[BIR 93] BIRCH D., *Singapore Media: Communication Strategies and Practices*, Longman Cheshire, 1993.

[CHE 08] CHEN E., PIN C.L, LOON F.K., KHOO J., KOH D., KWOK K., THONG L.K., LONG L.S., SIM G., SINGH R., BIN T.C., MONG T.S., "Knowledge-based command and control for the ONE SAF: building the 3rd spiral, 3rd Generation SAF", *POINTER Monograph*, No. 5, Singapore Armed Forces, 2009.

[CHW 09] CHOW J., "Spirited defence at the heart of 3G SAF", *Straits Times* (Singapore), August 13, 2009.

[HO 11] HO V., "Social engineering still scourge of IT security", *Business Times* (Singapore) November 3, 2011.

[HUX 00] HUXLEY T., *Defending the Lion City: The Armed Forces of Singapore*, Allen and Unwin, Crows Nest, Australia, 2000,.

---

30 [SAM 10] pp. 20.
31 [LIB 07].

[HUX 04] Huxley T., "Singapore and the revolution in military affairs", in Goldman E.O. and Mahnken T.G., *The Information Revolution in Military Affairs in Asia*, pp. 185-208, New York, Palgrave Macmillan, 2004.

[IDA 00] Infocomm Development Authority (IDA), *IT Household Survey Shows Highest Ever Household PC Ownership and Internet Penetration Rates in Singapore*, IDA, January 22, 2000, available at: http://www.ida.gov.sg/News%20and%20Events/ 20061124143944.aspx?getPagetype=20, accessed 19 January 2012.

[IDA 05] Infocomm Development Authority (IDA), *Singapore Gears Up for Cybersecurity*, IDA, February 22, 2005, available at: http://www.ida.gov.sg/News%20 and%20Events/20050712110643.aspx?getPagetype=20, accessed 15 November 2011.

[ITU 01] International Telecommunication Union (ITU), *The E-City: Singapore Internet Case Study*, ITU, April 2001, available at http://www.itu.int/ITU-D/ict/cs/singapore/ material/Singapore.pdf, accessed 19 January 2012.

[IWS 12] Internet World Statistics (IWS), Singapore – Internet Statistics and Telecommunications, IWS, 2012, available at: http://www.internetworldstats.com/ asia/sg.htm, accessed 19 January 2012.

[KWA 99] Kwang M., "Midstream role' for Singapore in technology", *Straits Times* (Singapore), October 16, 1999.

[LIB 07] Libicki M., *Conquest in Cyberspace: National Security and Information Warfare*, Cambridge University Press, 2007.

[LIE 76] Liew M.H., Wong L.C., "Simulators in the Republic of Singapore Air Force", *POINTER* (Journal of the Singapore Armed Forces) vol.2, pp. 12-13, 1976. (This whole issue of the officers' journal is dedicated to trainee reflections on simulators.)

[LIM 97] Lim E., *1965 Independence of Singapore*, Posted August 7, 1997, available at: http://www.mindef.gov.sg/imindef/about_us/history/birth_of_saf/v01n08_history.html.

[LUM 2010] Lum M., *Symantec Releases Cybercrime Report, Launches Norton Internet Security 2011*, Symantec, September 9, 2010, available at: http://vr-zone.com/articles/symantec-releases-cybercrime-report-launches-norton-internet-security-2011/9796.html#ixzz1dld gClsF, accessed 15 December 2011.

[MDA 12] Media Development Authority (MDA), *Policies and Content Guidelines – Internet*, MDA, 2012, available at: http://mda.gov.sg/Policies/PoliciesandContent Guidelines/Internet/Pages/default.aspx, accessed 19 January 2012.

[MIC 11] Microsoft Corporation, Microsoft Security Intelligence Report Volume 11. Worldwide Threat Assessment, Microsoft Corp, 2011, available at http://www.microsoft. com/security/sir/default.aspx, accessed 15 December 2011.

[MOD 00] *Defending Singapore in the Twenty First Century*, Ministry of Defence, Singapore, 2000.

[MOD 11] *Singapore Light Weight Howitzer Pegasus*, Ministry of Defence, Singapore, 2011, available at: http://www.mindef.gov.sg/imindef/mindef_websites/ topics/Weapons/slwh/ capabilities.html.

[MOT 89] MOTIWALLA J., GILBERT A.L., "Managing the Information Revolution", in SANDHU K.S. and WHEATLEY P., *Management of Success: The Moulding of Modern Singapore*, pp. 881-891, Institute of Southeast Asian Studies, Singapore, 1989.

[NJC 09] JIN-CHEON N., HAO W., YONG J., HAO T.M., KANDAN R.M., "Analysis of computer crime in Singapore using local English newspapers", *Singapore Journal of Library and Information Management*, vol. 38, pp. 77-102, 2009.

[RAJ 87] RAJARATNAM S., "Singapore: global city (1972)", in CHAN H.C. and OBAID U.H., *The Prophetic and the Political: Selected Speeches and Writings of S. Rajaratnam*, pp. 223-231, Graham Brash, Singapore, St Martin's Press, New York, 1987.

[REB 10] REBEIRO J., *Where is Enterprise Security Heading in 2010*, Security Asia – Business and Information Security Portal for Asia – securityAsia.net, February 24, 2010, available at: http://security.networksasia.net/content/where-enterprise-security-heading-2010.

[RSN 11] REPUBLIC OF SINGAPORE NAVY AND MINISTRY OF DEFENCE, Navy Frigate – Combat Systems, Republic of Singapore Navy and Ministry of Defence, 2011, available at: http://www.mindef.gov.sg/weapons/frigate/combatsystems.asp#cms.

[SAF 11] SINGAPORE ARMED FORCES, *Guards – Army News Special Supplement #6", 'Subsection – Always Ready – Keeping Our Army's Edge*, SAF, February 2011, available at: http://www.mindef.gov.sg/content/imindef/mindef_websites/atozlistings/army/army_ news/Download_Our_Issues/Issue_2011/_jcr_content/imindefPars/download_1/file.res/G uards_Supplement.pdf.

[SAM 10] SAMAAN J-L., "Cyber Command: The Rift in US Military Cyber-Strategy", *The RUSI Journal* (UK), vol. 155, pp. 16-21, 2010.

[SEE 01] SEET P.S., "The manoeuvrist approach and dislocation warfare for the SAF in the information age", *POINTER* (Journal of the Singapore Armed Forces) vol. 26, pp. 11-28, 2001.

[SHU 09] SHUO H., WAN A., TANG D. "Generation Why – so what?", *POINTER* (Journal of the Singapore Armed Forces) vol. 35, 2009, available at: http://www.mindef.gov.sg/ imindef/publications/pointer/journals/2009/v35n2/feature6.html.

[SIM 10] SIM M., "Seven in 10 here are victims of cybercrime", *Straits Times* (Singapore), September 10, 2010.

[SYM 11] SYMANTEC, Symantec Internet Security Threat Report – Trends for 2010, Volume 16,, Symantec, April 2011, available at: http://www.symantec.com/en/sg/about/news/ release/article.jsp?prid=20110411_01

[TAN 90] TAN T.L., *The Singapore Press: Freedom, Responsibility and Credibility*, Institute of Policy Studies, Singapore, 1990.

[TAN 08] TAN Y.S., LOW J.P., CHUA E.K., YEO L.K., "Networking for integrated ground operations", *POINTER* (Journal of the Singapore Armed Forces), vol. 33, pp. 27-35, 2008.

[TAN 09] TAN T.K., Developing leaders for the third generation Singapore army: A training and education roadmap, MMAS Thesis, Fort Leavenworth, U.S. Army Command and General Staff College, 2009.

[TEO 11] Keynote address by Mr Teo Chee Hean, Deputy Prime Minister, Coordinating Minister for National Security and Minister for Home Affairs at the Singapore Global Dialogue on Wednesday 21 September 2011, 7.45pm, at the Shangri-La Hotel, Singapore.

[TRM 11] TREND MICRO, *Threat Encyclopedia for the Asia-Pacific up to October 2011*, Trend Micro, 2011. Made available to author by an anonymous Trend Micro staff member via email communication on 25 October 2011.

[TSK 85] TSK, "Computer awareness week", *Pioneer* (a publication of the Singapore Armed Forces) vol. 95, pp. 22-24, 1985.

[VEN 09] VENTRE D., *Information Warfare*, ISTE Ltd. London, John Wiley and Sons, New York, 2009.

[WAT 95] WATERS M., *Globalization*, Routledge, 1995.

[YAP 88] YAP W., "Battlefield operation in the army operational context", *POINTER* (Journal of the Singapore Armed Forces) vol. 41, pp. 39-42, 1988.

[YEO 98] YEO S.C.S., MAHIZHNAN A., "Developing an intelligent island: dilemmas of censorship", in MAHIZHNAN A. and LEE T.Y., *Singapore: Re-Engineering Success*, Institute of Policy Studies and Oxford University Press, Singapore, 1998.

[ZDN 07] ZDNETASIA.com, "SINGAPORE: Resiliency Is Top IT Concern", November 13, 2007 reproduced in *Asia-Pacific Informatization Bulletin* vol. 20, Winter 2007, available at: http://unpan1.un.org/intradoc/groups/public/documents/apcity/unpan028293. htm#1ap6_3_3.

Chapter 8

A Slovenian Perspective on Cyber Warfare

8.1. Introduction

Twenty years ago, the small Republic of Slovenia, part of the Socialist Federal Republic of Yugoslavia, decided to exercise its right of self-determination and with confirmation by the plebiscite[1] started to walk along the path of its own independence. The day after the Republic of Slovenia[2] declared its independence was the start of first war in Europe after World War II. A cease-fire agreement was reached after only 10 days of war and the Yugoslav army started to withdraw into other parts of Yugoslavia. Slovenian citizens had achieved independence with strong unity and determination to defend their own freedom by all means.

To fight against a strong army, every aspect of strategy is very important. Every part of society must become a battlefield and every adult citizen has to contribute in his or her role in the fight against the enemy. Despite the bloody war in the neighboring country of Croatia which then spread into Bosnia and Herzegovina, the

Chapter written by Gorazd PRAPROTNIK, Iztok PODBREGAR, Igor BERNIK and Bojan TIČAR.
1 The plebiscite held in December 1990, at which the citizens of Slovenia voted overwhelmingly in favor of a sovereign and independent state. Turnout for the plebiscite was 93.2% of those eligible to vote. Of those who did vote, 88.5% said "yes" to an independent and sovereign Slovenia.
2 Slovenia was declared an independent country by the President on June 26, 1991 at the ceremony held in Trg Revolucije Square, Ljubljana.

Slovenian citizens, in their collective national consciousness, quickly replaced a sense of constant military threat with actual themes for a better standard of living and the desire for political integration in the European Union and the North Atlantic Treaty Organization (NATO) military alliance.

When they reached their main goals in less than 15 years, the compact unity that was capable of achieving almost unreachable goals started to fall apart. Slovenian society has been sharply divided into social classes, which put their own partial interests above the common interests of the whole society. After 20 years, most Slovenian citizens have forgotten the roots of their success and have quickly adapted to a carefree life.

In 20 years the world has changed into a global information village, filled with modern technology and producing a completely new way of life. Information and communication technologies (ICTs) have been implemented in all areas of our society and have started to dominate our lives. Modern technology has not only brought prosperity, but also new challenges, especially in the field of privacy and security. Massive use of the Internet has increased this issue, in addition to the security problems that ordinary people are confronted with every day. Is Internet security only a concern for individuals or does it also concern the State government? What kind of protection must be applied to defend ourselves against modern threats? Can modern threats only be applied through the Internet? To answer these questions, every country should first clearly identify all possible threats and than prepare for their defense in the most optimal way.

Since World War II various forms of electronic warfare have been known, where in order to achieve their goals, in addition to conventional weapons, the conflicting parties have also used various electronic devices. Such electronic devices can be used for direct purposes, such as enemy detection (radar, infrared devices, thermal imaging) or provide different type of communications at horizontal or vertical levels of command (through wired and wireless connections). Most of these electronic devices are used for indirect tasks aimed at increasing the efficiency of kinetic weapons. In the past two decades, rapid development of computer and telecommunication technologies, especially the Internet, has also led to intensive use of these modern technologies for military purposes.

No matter how military electronic devices are used, almost all have something in common – information. The vast majority of military electronic equipment is used for the efficient collection, processing, storing, analyzing and transmission of different types of information. How efficient electronic devices can implement such functions depends on the advancement of the technology used.

Many military analysts believe that the information age will launch a revolution in modern warfare, which will strongly rely upon the digitization of battlefields on land, in the sea, air and in space [CLA 10, PUF 95]. The information age will not only affect existing types of battlefields; it will also produce entirely new battlegrounds in the more abstract areas, such as cyberspace or social networks. The use of modern technologies will affect the future of military affairs, just like the use of canons changed warfare in the 15th Century or the development and massive use of mechanical machinery in the industrial revolution completely changed the course of the modern war. Today it can be assumed with great certainty that in modern warfare it will be equally important for the troops to be equipped with modern conventional weapons as well as with modern technology, which will include information technology, information weapon systems and information channels connected to computer networks.

Due to the specificity and lack of definition of so-called cyberspace[3], it is very difficult to define the boundaries of cyber warfare, cyber-espionage, cyber-crime, cyber-terrorism and even ordinary cyber-hooliganism. The boundaries of battlefields had already started to blur in World War II, but in modern war the boundaries among conflicting parties or soldiers and civilians could entirely disappear. Modern war can theoretically be started by an infected cellphone, owned by a completely innocent person in a different part of the world. Cyberspace can also blur the time boundaries of warfare, because cyberspace allows covert operation over a large time interval (logic bomb).

The specifics of cyberspace – where the main weapon, information, can appear in different forms – mean that the success of warfare in cyberspace mainly depends on the quantity and quality of information held by both offensive and defensive sides. History has demonstrated that in conflicts, technologically advanced countries almost always have an advantage over less developed countries. In real cyber war, the technological development of the country could be also a major shortcoming, since such countries have a high degree of dependence on modern technologies, especially in vital areas such as water and energy supplies, transport, communications, etc.

Unlike conventional warfare, which requires huge human, material and energy resources, effective cyber warfare is possible with limited human, material and energy resources, because it just requires quality information, especially knowledge. The information required can be obtained in various ways. The biggest source of huge quantities of relatively good quality information is the World Wide Web. This information is available to anyone and for this reason the threat of cyber warfare does not only come from countries, but dangerous cyber-attacks may be triggered by

---

3 Word cyberspace was first used by William Gibson in his book *Neuromancer* in 1984.

individuals or interest groups such as Anonymous[4]. Therefore, cyberspace can become an ideal medium for conducting asymmetric operations, where the primary objective is to cause the maximum damage to an opponent by using minimum resources.

Though most of the quality of existing malware is on an enviable level, it is mainly characterized by an evolutionary progression of quality. In most cases malware has been developed by people who have had existing knowledge and have obtained source codes from the Internet, who have downloaded malicious source code and slowly supplemented it with new ideas and then posted it back on Internet sites. The Internet also allows easy integration, communication- and information-sharing among hackers worldwide. A lot of malicious code is created by individuals who lack the necessary coding skills and just "process" existing programs (script kiddie) as a hobby. However, the number of such individuals does not increase, but there is a huge increase in the number of hackers, who produce malicious code in order to obtain various economic benefits. Therefore, the number of different variants of malware is growing at a fast rate. In its Security Threat Report 2011 [SOP 11], Sophos states that in one day it reviewed 95,000 different types of malware.

With regards to different strategic concepts and the different approach to the implementation of digital weapons, it is certain that modern information and telecommunication technology will have a major impact on future warfare and wars. Given that the human imagination has no boundaries, we can expect fighting in a war to occur on all fronts and by all means. The Stuxnet worm has already shown that the success of digital weapons requires combined and coordinated action by different groups of people in different areas. Despite the use of sophisticated technologies, there is still a man in the center of each battlefield that has virtues and weaknesses [ALB 10]. The success of the Stuxnet worm does not rest solely on the use of the high-tech skills, but also on the implementation of classic spy activities that have been known for centuries. To obtain information on the technological specifications to control computer systems used to produce enriched uranium, images from spy satellites do not help; the necessary information must be obtained 'on the ground'.

8.2. Preparations for digital warfare

The rapid developments of modern technologies caused an exceptional worldwide integration of the entire human infrastructure and the heavy dependence

---

4 Anonymous is an Internet-oriented group initiating active civil disobedience and representing themselves as an anarchic, digitized global brain.

on modern ICTs. The whole of human society is becoming increasingly vulnerable in all vital areas of its functioning. Thus, given the importance of the potential benefits of information warfare, most countries, especially large ones, have carefully prepared themselves for the challenges of modern warfare.

The first unsuccessful attempts started in the mid-nineties, when the United States (US) military introduced a concept of digitization called "Force XXI". The concept was based on previous research of the digitizing battlefield and tries to establish a tactical network to connect troops, smart weapons and equipment to operate in near real time (horizontal technology integration). Despite the plans to continue digitization at the level of the brigade (Task Force XXI) and later at division level (Division XXI), the implementation of this concept was stopped because the tests showed the incompleteness of the technology that was designed, which was causing inadequate efficiency and excessive system complexity [GSO 05].

Large countries also started to prepare themselves in the field of cyber warfare. Some senior US military officers have even proposed adding an efficient and effective cyber-branch alongside the army, navy and air force, as the existing structure is not sufficiently prepared and organized for new forms of warfare [CHA 09]. Maybe it is really too early for such drastic change to the army structure, but a new wind will start to slowly move military organizations in this new direction.

In 2009 the United Kingdom started to establish its Cyber Security Operations Centre (CSOC) with around 20 employees [INF 10]. It is based at the Government Communication's Headquarters (GCHQ) in Cheltenham.

In 2010, the US military deployed a fully-operational unit called the US Cyber Command (USCYBERCOM), which aims to conduct military operations based on information technologies and the Internet [DOD 10].

In June 2011, in the former West German capital Bonn, Germany opened the *Nationale Cyber-Abwehrzentrum* (National Cyber-defense Center) with 10 full-time employees from different national security agencies. The center will work closely with the police, customs, the military, intelligence bodies and others [KNO 11].

Even the Chinese Defense Ministry in 2011 confirmed the existence of a cyber unit called "Cyber Blue Team", which aims to improve Internet security, particularly in the military field [CTV 11]. It has also stressed that the cyber unit has been established strictly for defense against attacks by hackers.

The Russian concept of modern warfare introduces information as an important component in its doctrine. Interestingly, this concept associates information warfare with psychological aspects of warfare. The 2000 Russian Military Doctrine, showed a clear definition of information warfare, which was divided into psychological and technical information domains [THO 04]. In 2010 the State of the Internet report by Akamai Technologies stated that Russia had overtaken the US in the number of attacks launched by hackers (12% of traffic attacks came from Russia and 7.3% from the US) [LIN 11]. This is strong evidence of Russian progress in cyberspace in the past decade. Of course, many such attacks have come from Russian criminals and other hackers, but there are also reports of the Russian government's involvement in such hacktivism [STP 08]. Even though in the Russian Armed Forces there is no official cyber-command department, there are some hints as to the military preparations for the establishment of some kind of cyber-command called Information Troops [GIL 11], especially because of a huge criticism of Russia's poor performance in information warfare in the armed conflict in Georgia. Even though the relationship between the Information Troops and the existing REB Troops[5] is not completely clear, REB Troops were one of the few elements of the Russian forces whose performance did not suffer intense criticism. Either way, we can expect that Russia will develop a powerful and huge cyber-army in the near future.

Small countries usually face many problems in the area of cyber-security, especially because of their limited financial and human resources. Although the development of cyber-weapons and cyber-defense is relatively inexpensive compared with the development of modern weapons and defense, the total costs are still too high for the small State budgets. Unlike large countries, which must simply start preparations for future wars, cyber-war preparations in small countries depend on many other factors, such as their geostrategic, geopolitical or economic position.

8.3. Specifics of technologically-advanced small countries

Despite the fact that the vast majority of technologically-advanced small countries like Slovenia possess a sufficient number of highly-skilled professionals in the area of ICTs, the situation in the field of information security is relatively under-represented. In a small country, most of the operational information systems used in the government (army, police, public administration, agencies, etc.) and private (companies, banks, entrepreneurs, etc.) sectors are relatively small. The necessary investments in information security, according to the size of an information system, do not follow the linear laws because the proportion of the costs that are necessary for effective protection is much bigger for small information systems than for large ones. Since the general opinion is that ICT security is a large cost that is rarely found to be justified, those making the decisions rarely decide to invest in a

---

5 REB Troops are the *Voyska radioelektronnoy bor'by*, or Voyska REB – the Russian military's electronic warfare branch.

sufficient level of ICT security. Instead they choose the minimum safety standards. Such an approach is sufficient to prevent the majority of potential incidents, but it still leaves a relatively high degree of probability that unforeseen events will cause extensive damage. Choosing only the minimum of ICT security is also critical in light of the increasing growth in the amount of malicious code, especially in view of its increasing technological sophistication. Due to the increasingly complex malware, the minimum protection of information and communication infrastructure is becoming insufficient.

Since a large majority of small and medium-sized businesses cannot afford the teams that would care for their own information infrastructure, it is feasible to expect a large number of companies that are fully specialized in providing services in the field of ICT security in small countries. Such companies are rare, however, and it can reasonably be assumed that small and medium-sized enterprises would not choose such ICT security improvements. They are satisfied with meeting the minimum standards of ICT infrastructure protection or hire companies that offer a full range of ICT services, including security services.

In addition to the high costs, there is a negative effect of evaluating and selecting the level of information security policy in small countries based on the traditional perception of security in general. This stems from the general belief that small countries are irrelevant and, therefore, uninteresting for various forms of threat (e.g. crime or terrorism). There is also a general opinion that all security measures are much more effective due to the size of a country and a specific language. The level of threat to information technology posed by Internet connection depends primarily on the vulnerability of the systems, so in the long term this approach is naive and harmful [HAY 09].

A good example showing that the level of information security policies in individual countries is mostly dependent on the general attitude of society towards safety is the relatively small state of Israel. Despite its small size it has become one of the leading countries in information security [DAL 08]. A constant threat to the population is not the only factor that led to Israel's highly technological competence in this area, but has significantly contributed to the positive attitude towards the implementation of security measures in all areas, as well as in ICT security. Even a mix of civilian and military spheres with close cooperation between public and private sectors has had a positive impact on the overall technological development of Israeli society, and consequently also the technological development of ICT security.

Another example is Estonia, a small Baltic republic near Russia. In 2007, Estonia was hit by a mass of waves of *distributed denial of service* (DDoS) attacks that hit important websites. DDoS attacks were carried out through a group of infected computers all over the world. A mass of requests for service from infected computers completely flooded major Estonian servers and as a result they were not able to respond to the legitimate demands of users. Attacks were carried out for a few months. Besides the moral damage inflicted, these attacks have caused huge economic damage, as the Estonian economy is very dependent on Internet services, primarily from Internet banking transactions. Ninety-five per cent of its banking operations are conducted electronically.

Partially in response to the cyber-attacks on Estonian public and private institutions, the defense ministers of NATO countries held a meeting in October 2007 in which agreed to create a common cyber-defense policy. In May 2008, NATO established a center in Estonia called the CCDCOE (Cooperative Cyber Defence Centre of Excellence) [NAT 08], which is responsible for making defense policy and cyber-warfare doctrine, providing education and training of personnel, improving cyber-security, etc.

Mainly because of these attacks, the cyber-security sector in Estonia has rapidly emerged [MA 11] and in few years Estonia has become one of the leaders in this sector. Estonia's case has shown that even a small country with very limited financial and human resources can obtain a high degree of cyber-security [BOG 11].

8.4. Geostrategic, geopolitics and the economic position of the Republic of Slovenia

Independent since 1991, the Republic of Slovenia is a small and relatively young country. Slovenia is based at the crossroads of transport routes, so it is in an essential geostrategic position in Europe. It is on the East–West axis that starts in Russia and passes through the Central European countries to Western European Countries. It is also on the North–South axis that binds Central Europe with the Mediterranean zone and links Europe with the Middle East.

Due to its favorable geostrategic position, the Slovenian territory has always been a subject of desire to large countries. Until its declaration of independence 20 years ago, Slovenia has been ruled by foreigners, mostly the Austro-Hungarian Habsburg monarchy. After the First World War, Slovenia became a part of the Kingdom of Yugoslavia and finally, after the Second World War Slovenia, became a part of the Socialist Federal Republic of Yugoslavia. The Slovenian male population has always had to serve in foreign armies, which is the main reason for the existence of negative attitudes in the national consciousness towards the military.

In the 1980s, strong anti-military movements emerged in Slovenia, mostly against the Yugoslav National Army (YNA). For this reason, YNA had become the focus of hateful feelings and such military movements had a big impact on the whole of Slovenian society. At the time of the declaration of independence, when Slovenia really needed weapons and military force, a petition to completely disarm the whole of Slovenia was issued. The petition was signed by a lot of people, even though at that time Slovenia was facing a real threat from the YNA.

Apparently, it was signed by many people who thought that problems would just disappear if the Slovenian people completely disarmed themselves. Few years later, the sad events in Srebrenica[6] showed us that they were wrong.

In 2004, the Republic of Slovenia became part of the NATO alliance and the European Union (EU). Despite some negative attitudes to such an alliance, the majority of Slovenian citizens supported the accession[7]. Despite this, anti-military movements became increasingly strong, so a very similar petition was issued in 2010 calling for the abolition of the Slovenian army [MLA 10]. Again, many prominent Slovenian citizens in the fields of entertainment, science and culture signed the petition.

Slovenia is in currently a huge economic crisis, which is an increasingly common criticism of defense costs. For this reason, such a petition was welcomed by many members of the public, particularly in cases where there is strong support in the media. Therefore, it is currently unrealistic to expect that a small country, in time of huge economic crisis, will start to prepare the Slovenian Armed Forces for cyber-defense, especially because for a lot of people cyber-war is just a futuristic idea.

8.5. Information and communication development in Slovenia

To get a general picture of ICT development in a specific country, several different indicators can be measured. ICT infrastructure (and access) is a very good and simple indicator of ICT development. ICT infrastructure can be adequately sized by counting the number of households and companies with access to the

6 During the Bosnian War in July 1995, in the town of Srebrenica (Bosnia and Herzegovina), there was genocide in which the *Army of Republika Srpska* (ARS) killed more than 8,000 Bosniaks (Bosnian Muslims), mainly men and boys.
7 Turnout for the referendum was 60.29% of those eligible to vote. Of these, 89.61% voted for EU integration and 60.2% voted for integration into the NATO alliance.

Internet. Thus according to the results of the Republic of Slovenia Statistical Office [ZUP 11], at the beginning of 2010, 68% of households had access to the Internet, which is only 2% less than the EU-27[8] average of 70%. This indicator puts Slovenia among the average EU-27 developed countries in ICTs, which means that globally they are a relatively well-developed information country. This high level of development in the field of information technology is also confirmed by statistical data from the Republic of Slovenia in 2010, where 97% of enterprises with at least 10 employees had access to the Internet and 85% of enterprises had access to broadband Internet. Up to 85% of Slovenian companies used a local area network to transfer and exchange information in 2010. Of these, 87% are small businesses and the remaining proportion consists of medium or large enterprises.

Statistical data from the Republic of Slovenia Statistical Office has also been confirmed by statistical data on "e-commerce companies in the EU between 2004 and 2008" [ZUP 10a]. By almost all of the survey criteria conducted, Slovenia is close to the EU-27 average. A big exception in the survey was the criteria of employment or the employment needs of ICT professionals, where Slovenia was ranked 20 percentage points above the EU-27 average. This exception can easily be explained by the fact that in the years from 2004 to 2008 Slovenia underwent extraordinary economic growth, which was much higher than the European average. The survey did not only cover employees in ICT but also industry needs in this area.

Another exception in this study is how many companies use e-services in their operations with the government. In Slovenia, the number of companies using e-government services is among the highest in the EU-27. This has also been confirmed by the *UN E-Government Survey 2010* study, where Slovenia is 29th highest[9] in the world [UNI 10]. Assuming that the development of e-government services and their use is one of the major indicators of the development of information society in each country, based on comparisons with other developed countries, we can gain an overall assessment of the ICT development of Slovenia.

The cheap and friendly service offered by the State institutions via the Internet in recent years means that the Republic of Slovenia e-government has been providing citizens, and companies in particular, with an easy way to carry out many tasks over the Internet. Some State institutions, such as Tax Administration, even require companies to only provide information on their business via the Internet. This approach enables cheap, fast and efficient data transmission, but increases the mutual dependence of the State administration and business upon the Internet.

---

8 EU-27 – the 27 countries in the European Union.

9 According to the *UN E-Government Survey 2008*, Slovenia has occupied 26th position in the world.

Since companies must deliver the required data within specific time periods, it is an open question as to how companies can deliver the requested data in the case of a huge failure in the tax ICT administration, ICT infrastructure or Internet connections, as no alternative solutions exist. Such an approach is acceptable in cases of natural disasters, where destruction is usually so extensive that the entire structure is damaged and businesses can no longer operate. In the event of a prolonged period of DDoS attacks, like the attacks experienced by Estonia, such a shortsighted approach can completely paralyze the proper functioning of the tax administration.

8.6. Cyber-threats in Slovenia

Slovenia has not experienced mass hacker attacks yet, with the exception of minor DDoS attacks from Russian hacktivists in 2009, because Russia lost against Slovenia in the 2010 World Cup (soccer/football) qualifier play off. For one day, Russian hackers attacked the Agency of the Republic of Slovenia for Public Legal Records and related services' webpages, so the damage was relatively minor. This attack was also commented on by the Republic of Slovenia's Ministry of Defense: "The Ministry of Defense is elaborating actions to prevent attacks and protect critical infrastructure as part of the planning of national measures and actions at Alliance NATO in accordance with the financial capabilities" [HAF 09]. So far, the only dangerous cyber-threats that have been detected in Slovenia are from cyber-criminals. From the statistics in a police report for 2010, it can be concluded that 2010 the vast majority of computer criminality (75.2%) related to attacks on information systems [POL 11]. This number had declined from 2009 by 22.4%.

During the summer of 2010, the Slovenian police and FBI agents in Maribor (northwestern Slovenia) arrested two persons accused of participating in the production of one of the largest and most advanced known botnet network – "Mariposa"[10]. A 23-year-old graduate student at the Faculty of Computer Science Maribor in Slovenia with the nickname Iserdo[11] was accused of being the main author of the Mariposa malware.

This network led to the infection of 12 million computers worldwide. The most dangerous capability of this network was its ability to select infected computers for infection with a completely new malware [THO 09]. With this ability, the botmaster can arbitrarily change and develop the functionality of computers that are already infected, and thus he has greatly reduced the effectiveness of antivirus protection. The administrator could send arbitrary commands to all infected computers all over

---

10 Mariposa is the Spanish word for a butterfly.
11 Iserdo, read backwards, means "salvation" in Slovenian.

the world, to all infected computers in a selected country or even just to one individual computer.

Mariposa can be spread via P2P[12] networks, through the IE6[13] security holes, USB sticks or through infected websites, such as via MSN[14] Messenger user connections. Therefore, the malicious code that created the Mariposa botnet network cannot be classified as a virus, a worm or a Trojan Horse, because the administrator can set an arbitrary way to spread malicious code. This has significantly increased the likelihood of the spread of infections on computers equipped with antivirus protection.

Mariposa botmasters, who call themselves the DDP[15] group, have used the Mariposa network to install additional malware on the already infected computers, such as advanced input keyboard loggers (keyloggers), banking Trojans (Zeus), etc. All information obtained (stolen credit card numbers, bank and credit card passwords) is sold through Internet hacker channels. The DDP group has also been selling the control of different parts of the Mariposa botnet, thus allowing illegal installation of toolbars on infected computers and statistical manipulation through their search engines.

Botmasters from the DDP group communicate with infected computers by using encrypted commands. It is extremely difficult to detect such botnet commands, and even harder to decipher them. In addition, the botmasters have established network links via anonymous virtual private network (VPN) connections. Luckily the error of a major botmaster player has led the police to find his identity. It turns out that a group of criminals from Spain, who operated a Mariposa botnet network, did not have much computer knowledge but had bought these services on the "Internet market" from Iserdo. Due to his age, we may conclude with a high probability that Iserdo is not a top professional, but probably only a talented programmer who has skillfully utilized existing tools for creating malicious code and successfully created state-of-the-art malware.

Despite the fact that Iserdo was arrested in the spring of 2010 and the authorities shut down the Mariposa botnet control computers, a year later ICT security experts from Unveillance and Panda discovered an even more extensive network called a Metulji botnet[16] [BAR 11]. The Metulji botnet is the largest botnet discovered so far, since unknowingly tens of millions of infected computers that are located in at

---

12 P2P network – a peer-to-peer network is a distributed application architecture that can communicate between peers.
13 IE6 – Internet Explorer version 6.
14 MSN – Microsoft Network.
15 DDP – *Días de Pesadilla* (in Spanish this means nightmare days).
16 *Metulji* is the Slovenian word for butterflies.

least 172 countries participate in it. Unveillance ICT security experts have even estimated that the size of the Metulji botnet is twice that of Mariposa. The Metulji botnet was created with an advanced version of the Butterfly Bot Kit, which was produced and marketed by Iserdo. All Metulji botnet traces have led to Slovenia, and Bosnia and Herzegovina. The FBI and Interpol conducted Operation Hive, which resulted in the arrests of two Metulji botnet operators in Bosnia [AND 11].

DDoS attacks generated by the botnets are very disturbing for websites and their users and they can cause enormous economic damage as we have seen in Estonia. Although NATO documents have identified DDoS attacks as a military threat, it is very difficult to define DDoS attacks as a military weapon. However, botnet in the hands of criminal groups are threatening funds and can be used for a wide range of serious crimes. Therefore, technologically-advanced countries must be thoroughly prepared for the expansion of cyber-crime, and start to cooperate with other developed countries in this area because this type of crime is usually led by international criminal groups.

If one individual or a small group of people can create a malicious code, such as software code for the Mariposa botnet based only on their knowledge of and the existence of malware source code obtained from Internet sites, we can only imagine the potential to seize power and knowledge from a large organization like the US National Security Agency (NSA), which employs over 30,000 people worldwide including large number of top US experts and scientists in the field of information and communication sciences and technologies. Of course, software code designed by professionals is a secret weapon, so until 2010 it was impossible to obtain any information on cutting-edge technology of such digital weapons.

In July 2010, however, security researchers from the Belarusian antivirus vendor VirusBlokAda discovered a new harmful program code that was later named the Stuxnet worm. The Stuxnet worm had infected less then 100,000 computers and it was not a serious danger to ordinary Windows users but it surprised a large number of security professionals and experts, due to the high complexity and embedded knowledge it contained. The worm was described as the most complex malicious code known and it is estimated that the cost of developing Stuxnet was about $10 million [LAN 10].

Malware is basically an offensive weapon, since it is made to attack the desired target. Whether it only strikes a selected target or attacks causes high collateral damage depends on many factors that cannot be exactly predicted, even by the attacker. Extension of infection by the Stuxnet worm showed that despite the precise definition of the worm's objectives, it caused accidental infection and damage to a huge number of systems worldwide. This led to various speculations about the true purpose of its production, such as damage to an Indian satellite [CAR 10]. It is highly unlikely that the attackers deliberately infected so many computers in order to disguise their true object of attack.

If malicious code is classified as an offensive weapon, then we can consider antivirus protection to be a defensive weapon. With the increasing use of malicious code as a weapon, possessing successful antivirus protection is an increasingly important strategic asset that is necessary for successful defense against cyber-attacks.

8.7. Slovenia in the field of information and communication security policy

The Republic of Slovenia is a small and relatively little country, with a population of around 2 million people – just a little more than the population of Manhattan (in New York). Due to its size and its obscurity, and especially because it has its own language, Slovenia is a relatively safe country embedded in the EU and NATO. Therefore, the vast majority of people feel safe and they do not perceive any immediate threat that would be recognized as a major risk.

This situation is generally reflected in its relationship to information security policy, despite the fact that Slovenian ICT infrastructure ranks among the most highly developed countries and its increased dependence on the reliability of information and communication systems.

According to the data published in the *e-Commerce Companies in the EU between 2004 and 2008* survey, 94% of firms used antivirus programs for protection (in 2006), which ranked Slovenia in the top of the EU-27. Software antivirus protection is the most basic measure of information security protection and it presents a minimum amount of security measures that companies must invest in to protect their own ICT infrastructure. The share of firms that use a firewall for ICT protection is smaller, but its use is still 71% – placing Slovenia above the EU-27 average. The share of the firms that use more expensive hardware ICT protection, however, is dramatically below the EU-27 average (leaving them near the bottom). Thus the share of companies that use secure servers is only 24% and only 12% of companies that use backup systems for data outside the enterprise (off-site backup). These statistical data clearly show that large numbers of Slovenian companies have invested in the basic ICT protection equipment, but most of them have not invested in additional, costly security measures.

In 2010, according to the Republic of Slovenia Statistical Office results [ZUP 10b], only 73% of enterprises in the financial sector with at least 10 employees had formal strategy for the safe use of ICT. Given the sensitivity of financial management, where high security and reliability is a top priority, this percentage is relatively low.

Since the average gains in the financial sector are much higher than in the other sectors, such a situation is not the result of a lack of investment funds, but rather the relationship of management structures to ICT security.

The situation in other sectors is even worse, since the proportion of non-financial enterprises with a formal strategy for the safe use of ICT in 2010 was only 16%, which is more than 10% below EU-27 average (27%). Since these statistics do not include companies with fewer than 10 employees, this situation is dismal. Given that Slovenia has a multitude of regulations that enterprises have to consider in their everyday business, it is unacceptable that in the field of ICT security there are rules to force companies, according to their size and type of business, to take a necessary security measures to protect their ICT infrastructure.

Although there are no specific statistical data on ICT security in government administration, this area is more regulated because in 2002 the Government Center for Information issued a publication entitled Recommendations for the Preparation of an Information Security Policy containing useful guidelines for the implementation of ICT security in the public sector [HAJ 02]. Also included in this publication are security assessments of the current ICT situation in government administration in 2002 [page 6] where it has been found that the state ICT security in public administration was completely unbalanced. In some areas of government, administration ICT security was at a sufficient level while in the other areas it may have been completely ignored or on the back burner. It was found that no branch of government administration at the time possessed a clear ICT security policy. These conclusions suggest that until 2002, the government administration did not have a uniform policy on ICT security. Given the success of the e-government in Slovenia after five years, we may reasonably assume that the ICT security situation has been improved in all public sectors and that no doubt these recommendations have significantly contributed it. It is likely that the recommendations have led to an effective foundation for the harmony of ICT security policy across the public sector.

The Defense Ministry document published in 2011 [MIN 11] states that due to new technological advances, the Government of Slovenia will set up an interdepartmental coordination group to prepare a new document that will update existing recommendations for the preparation of an information security policy. This document will give the government administration completely new guidelines in the field of ICT security and recommendations will be made for other public authorities that do not fall within the government's remit (municipalities, public enterprises, etc.).

Statistical data on the security situation show that in terms of basic ICT security the Republic of Slovenia is at the top of the EU-27 countries. This claim is backed up by the latest Kaspersky Lab's report analyzing vast numbers of ICT threats during the second quarter of 2011, where Slovenia is one of the countries with the lowest percentages of users attacked while surfing the web (17.8%)[17] and with the lowest levels of infection (17.2%) [NAM 11]. If we take into account statistical data regarding the security situation, this report shows that in normal conditions mass use of basic ICT security is almost completely adequate to achieve good results when protecting against everyday cyber-threats. In the field of superior and advanced cyber protection, however, the Republic of Slovenia is at the bottom of the EU-27. Only the future will show whether this approach is the right one in light of the new and sophisticated cyber-threats that are being developed.

8.8. Slovenia's information and communication security policy strategy

Given that Slovenia is a member of the EU-27 and NATO, its strategy regarding information and communication security policies can be divided into several areas that can overlap. In essence, its strategy is divided into the civil sector and military sphere, where Slovenia in association with the EU-27 mostly implements strategic objectives in the civil sphere and in association with NATO implements strategic objectives in the military field. At the same time, Slovenia is also planning its own strategy for information and communication security in both the civil and military fields.

8.8.1. The EU information and communication security policy

Because Slovenia is a member of the EU-27, it must also act within the field of information and communication security in accordance with the recommendations and EU directives, which are mainly concerned with civil governance. In the area of information and communication security, the currently enforced European Council Framework Decision 2005/222/JHA from 2005 [CFD 05] will guide the EU Member States toward a gradual harmony of their laws. This is especially the case in the area of cyber-crime. The directive requires the cooperation of Member States' competent national authorities to ensure the enforcement of effective ICT security.

In preparation there is a European Parliament directive to replace the Council Framework Decision, which is evident from the draft opinion of the European Economic and Social Committee [ESO 11]. In this document, the Committee also stressed the importance of developing strong public and private partnerships with the aim of increasing and strengthening security and resilience (EP3R)[18], thus

---

17 According to Kaspersky Lab's report, in Q2 2011 the lowest percentages of users attacked while surfing the web are in Japan (13%), Taiwan (13.7%), the Czech Republic (16.1%), Denmark (16.2%), Luxembourg (16.9%), Slovenia (17.8%) and Slovakia (18.3%).
18 EP3R – the European Public–Private Partnership for Resilience.

demonstrating the importance of tight cooperation with NATO. Due to the specifics of the emerging information and communication security, the future lies in cooperation between both civilian and military sectors, as well as in cooperation between public and private sectors. This can also be seen from a long-term plan of the European digital agenda [EUC 10]. This plan also stresses the determination to establish a European system for rapid responses to cyber-attacks, including a network of groups to respond to computer threats (*Computer Emergency Response Team* (CERT) [ENI 06] and the strengthening of the European Networks and Information Security Agency's (ENISA's) role. Slovenia also has a Slovenian CERT (SI-CERT) that operates primarily in the civilian area of information and communication security.

In December 2004, the EU Council adopted the European Programme for Critical Infrastructure Protection (EPCIP). Based on the adopted document, the European Commission prepared the Green Paper on EPCIP, where 11 critical structure sectors have been defined. Unfortunately, in the European Council directive on critical infrastructure no. 114/2008, only two sectors were defined (transport and energy). Based on the EPCIP Green Paper, a special inter-sector group for coordinating critical infrastructure protection was established in Slovenia. The special inter-sector group had the task of developing special programs to enforce the EU Council Directive. The program also included a definition for critical infrastructure of national importance. Among other critical infrastructures, it also defined the ICT structure. The inter-sector group included representatives from the ministries of economy, transport, internal affairs, higher education, research and technology, defense, as well as representatives of the Slovenian Armed Forces (SAF) General Staff and the Republic of Slovenia Administration for Civil Protection and Disaster Relief [ČAL 11]. Unfortunately, the group faced similar problems to the EU and was unsuccessful. Its only achievement was the harmonization of the definition of critical infrastructure. In the end, the Slovenian Government did not even succeed in totally implementing European Council Directive 2008/114/ES and received a warning from the European Commission in a formal notice dated March 17, 2011.

8.8.2. *NATO's information and communications security policy*

At the Prague summit in November 2002, NATO leaders agreed to establish a NATO Cyber Defense Program, which would protect NATO information and communication systems from cyber-attacks by setting up the *NATO Computer Incident Response Capability* (NCIRC).

Until the spring of 2007, when attacks were carried out in Estonia, NATO mainly built cyber-defense to protect its own information and communication systems. In light of the cyber-attacks, the defense ministers of NATO countries agreed that NATO must protect all allied countries against cyber-attacks.

Therefore, NATO has developed a mechanism to assist allies against cyber-attacks if they want this assistance. The first step in this direction was the establishment of the CCDCOE in Estonia in May 2008. The CCDCOE's main mission is to foster cooperation, capabilities and information sharing between NATO countries in areas of cyber-security through research and education in cyber warfare, including education and training from specialists from allied countries.

Despite the resolute intention of NATO to defend all allies against cyber-attacks, the major proportion of the security policy still rests with the Members themselves who must take primary responsibility for the safety and security of their systems against cyber-attacks. For a successful mission NATO requires the Member States to have a reliable and secure infrastructure.

8.8.3. Slovenia's information and communication security policy

The Republic of Slovenia, in order to implement its own ICT security policy in addition to meeting its obligations as a member of the EU-27 and NATO, must accept the measures that have been written in key strategic documents in both the civil and military sectors. Unfortunately, the Republic of Slovenia does not possess a clear strategy that would define the objectives it needs to achieve sufficient information and communication security policies and it has even less clear directions on how it can meet the pledged objectives. From most of the adopted strategic documents we can conclude that the problem of ICT security in Slovenia is underestimated. In all these documents cyber-threats are only mentioned, mostly in the domain of cyber-crime, and are not discussed in detail. Defense against these threats is limited to general responses and intentions to design new strategies and new government bodies.

Since the volume of cyber-crime in Slovenia is a relatively minimal and Slovenia has not experienced mass DDoS cyber-attacks yet – certainly not as extensive as that experienced by Estonia in 2007 – its attitude to ICT security is understandable. Because it is already difficult to justify the costly investment of high security in existing ICTs, it is even more difficult to invest in future cyber warfare, which for most people is completely imaginary and incomprehensible. Therefore, it is more important to find appropriate ways to make relatively small investments in order to achieve a high level of information and communication security. This is only possible with concerted action by the whole society, which means close cooperation between civilian and military governmental bodies and successful collaboration between the public and private sectors. This close cooperation enables synergistic effects while avoiding the duplication of various functions and activities that are an integral part of any security policy. Since ICT protection is almost exactly the same in both civil and military sectors, it makes sense to find common foundations and build common defenses against cyber-attacks on them, while only separating those tasks that are specific to each segment (e.g. cyber-crime actions are addressed by the police).

A good example of the successful organization of ICT in a small state is Israel. Studying this example can be a positive experience and, above all, a good solution can quickly be transferred to the Slovenian strategic plans to set out the main courses of its ICT security policy.

Such an approach will also lead to additional boosts in the development of information and communication sectors in the industry, as such activity does not require a huge investment. It requires few material and energy resources; mostly it requires more professional staff. Due to its relatively high technological development in the field of ICT, Slovenia has enough experts who can quickly specialize in the field of information and communication security. Creating the complex botnet Mariposa is proof that Slovenia also has talented hackers whose expertise could be used for worthwhile purposes.

8.8.4. Analysis of key strategic documents regulating the field of information and communication security policy in the Republic of Slovenia

In this analysis we will try to focus only on the most important strategic documents that are directly related to areas that are important for the security of ICT infrastructure. In all of these documents there is no clear specification of cyber-threats, but they generally refer to cyberspace and information technology, which entail certain risks in the event of cyber-attacks. From the documents analyzed it can clearly be seen that not much attention is paid to this issue, because the strategy is limited to the security of ICT in general.

The Republic of Slovenia in 2010 adopted the "Resolution on the national security strategy of the Republic of Slovenia" (*Official Gazette of the Republic of Slovenia*, 27/2010). In Chapter 4.2 on Transnational Threats and Risks of National Security, potential sources of threats are mentioned, such as cyber-threats and the abuse of information technologies and systems. Slovenia is strongly dependent on the continuity and reliability of information systems in both the public and private sectors, with particular emphasis on the key functions of the State and society. In the document, it cites criminal organizations as potential sources of cyber threat. Cyberspace as a potential battlefield is only briefly mentioned. In section 5.3.5 on responding to cyber-threats and abuse of information technologies and systems, the

Republic of Slovenia makes a commitment to develop a national strategy to respond to cyber-threats and abuse of information technologies. It will also take the necessary measures for effective cyber-defense, which will include both public and private sectors. In the near future, the document also provides for the establishment of a new national coordinating body for cyber-security. The resolution on the national security strategy clearly shows that ICT security is not at the top of the list of national priorities and the resolution of cyber-threats but has been moved to a vague point in the future.

In 2010, the military sphere adopted the "Resolution on the overall long-term program for development and equipping the Slovenian Armed Forces until 2025" (Official Gazette of the Republic of Slovenia, 99/2010). In this document, cyberspace is also mentioned as a potential battlefield and only in the annex of this document is the concept of cyber warfare briefly explained. It is described as various forms of attack and defense on information systems that take place in cyberspace. Beside this brief description, the document also explains the concept of cyber-defense, and states the NATO definition of cyber-defense as the use of the security measures in order to protect the infrastructure of communication and information systems against cyber-attacks. Unfortunately in this resolution we cannot find more precise definitions of cyber warfare and the attitude of Slovenian Armed Forces on this issue. This resolution does not indicate any conceivable public–private partnerships in the field of ICT, which would allow more efficient use of human and infrastructure resources.

A condescending attitude towards safety in ICT is also found in the Report on the Implementation of Civil Defense Exercise Doctrine of the Republic of Slovenia [MIN 11], prepared by the Ministry of Defense, where it is noted that at the State level, the center for monitoring cyber threats has not been set up to perform tasks in the field of ICT security in the public and private sectors [page 6].

8.8.5. *National bodies that govern the field of information and communication security policy in the Republic of Slovenia*

In the Republic of Slovenia, competency in the field of ICT security is spread across several ministries and state bodies. It became obvious, during the development of ICT, that there was an urgent need to perform certain security functions. Consequently, many of these tasks in the field of ICT – implemented by the various state bodies – are duplicated or even worse are performed in a large number of departments. As a result of this situation, there are inefficiencies and ICT security has an unnecessarily high total cost.

However, a rapid and complete centralization of these activities would not achieve an optimal effect, since every government department in the field of ICT has its own specifics, which should be carefully taken into account. Therefore, Slovenia should first establish a body whose main concern at the beginning will be to coordinate and guide State bodies on ICT security. Then, in order to achieve the optimizations needed, it should gradually transfer State tasks and processes on ICT security to the relevant branches of the State. Moreover, such an authority will take over the strategic planning of ICT security and also carry out tasks, especially in the field of complex security measures.

8.8.6. *Directorate for information society (Ministry of Higher Education, Science and Technology)*

The main task of the Directorate for Information Society is acceleration, coordination and effective development of the information society. The Directorate also works with various organizations in the field of security and privacy in the cyber world, such as the Center for a Safer Internet (SAVE.SI). It tries to provide information and advice on the safe use of the Internet and other modern technologies to different groups of Internet users (children, teenagers, parents or teachers). Within the Directorate for Information Society, the SI-CERT team operates under the auspices of the academic and research network.

8.8.7. *Slovenian Computer Emergency Response Team*

The SI-CERT organization is the main point of contact for reporting network security incidents involving systems and networks located in Slovenia. By agreement with the Slovenian government, SI-CERT also provides the main role for the government CERT. SI-CERT is the main organization responsible for dealing with all security incidents in computer networks located in the public or private sectors.

For historical reasons, SI-CERT operates under the academic and research network ARNES[19]. In Slovenia ARNES has played an important role since the introduction of the Internet. During the development and adoption of the Internet, help from the academic institutions was understandably welcome, but the massive use of the Internet in all areas of society has exceeded the academic framework. Thus, this form of organization for solving ICT security problems has become completely inadequate. An interesting solution to this issue is provided by the

---

19 The Academic and Research Network of Slovenia (ARNES) is a public institute that provides network services to research, educational and cultural organizations.

ENISA in the [WP2006/5.1 (CERT-D1/D2)] document. The document supports the creation of new groups computer security incident response team (CSIRT) in order to establish an effective network of groups for interventions. Since the CERT Coordination Center has registered the term *CERT* in the US, Europe has introduced the new acronym *CSIRT*. CSIRT groups may be formed as a public–private partnership and in its establishment the government plays a key role. To build a project with a successful partnership, the government should also extend an invitation to academic institutions, private, economic and other interested entities. The CSIRT group can also provide services in the field of ICT security to different customers (academic institutions, government branches, military bodies, small and medium-sized enterprises, traders, etc.). Inadequacy in the SI-CERT organization could be elegantly resolved by transforming the SI-CERT team into a public–private entity CSIRT, where the government contributes SI-CERT shares a capital investment among other interested entities (companies), which could invest their own capital according to their expectations.

8.8.8. *Directorate of e-Government and Administrative Processes (Ministry of Public Administration)*

Under the Directorate of e-Government and Administrative Processes several divisions operate that carry out important tasks in the field of ICT security for the whole country. Thus, the central division for the information infrastructure operates a task forces in the field of public key infrastructure to meet the needs of State agencies, public institutions, enterprises and citizens and the issue of qualified digital certificates for Biometric passports. In this sector they also analyze and prepare domestic and international technology security and regulatory recommendations and standards.

The Department of Local IT Infrastructure gives advice on data security and the protection of local computer networks. It takes care of antivirus protection on information systems belonging to the State authorities.

8.8.9. *Office of the Government of the Republic of Slovenia for the Protection of Classified Information*

The Office of the Government of the Republic of Slovenia for the Protection of Classified Information (*Urad Vlade RS za varovanje Tajnih Podatkov – UVTP*) primarily performs tasks in the field of the security of classified information, and is therefore a key element in information security. UVTP is also responsible for the development and implementation of physical, organizational and technical standards for the protection of classified information in government bodies, local communities, holders of public companies and other organizations that deal with classified information. In this field it cooperates with the relevant agencies from foreign countries and international organizations, unless otherwise stipulated by an international treaty. It is also responsible for ensuring the security of Slovenian national classified information abroad and the security of foreign classified information within Slovenia.

Under the auspices of the UVTP, the Information Security Commission has been established comprising representatives of the Ministry of Public Administration, the Ministry of the Interior, the Ministry of Defense, the Ministry of Foreign Affairs, the Slovenian Intelligence and Security Agency and the Government Office for the Protection of Classified Information[20].

Functions of the Information Security Commission are:

– the production of technical and regulatory solutions to protect classified information in communication and information systems;

– it provides appropriate methods and procedures for the identification and authentication of user access to communication information systems;

– it confirms encryption systems, which can be used in information systems;

– it creates the requirements for the integration of communication and information systems; and

– it prepares the implementation of safety requirements to protect against unwanted electromagnetic radiation.

Although this office works in the area where cyber-threats should be seriously considered, in the official documents there are no specific descriptions of this issue.

8.8.10. *Slovenian Intelligence and Security Agency*

Slovenian intelligence and security operations are regulated by law for the Slovenian Intelligence and Security Agency (*Official Gazette of the Republic of Slovenia*, 81/06-UPB2, *Slovenska Obveščevalno-Varnostna Agencija* – SOVA[21]). It does not directly mention cyber-security tasks, but the agency may perform functions under the Act in accordance with the priorities established by the

---

20 The Information Security Commission has been established pursuant to Part 15 of the Article of regulation on the protection of classified information in communication and information systems (*Official Gazette of the Republic of Slovenia*, 480/2007) and the government decree of the Republic of Slovenia num. 01203-19/2007/7, December 20, 2008
21 Sova is the Slovenian word for owl.

government based on the national-security program adopted by the National Assembly. Given that the SOVA is an important factor in overall security, it would be necessary to update and harmonize legislation on security and intelligence agencies with modern technological trends.

8.8.11. *National Center for Crisis Management*

The National Center for Crisis Management (*Nacionalni center za krizno upravljanje* – NCKU) was established in 2004 under the US initiative to set up centers in Central and Eastern European countries for crisis management at the strategic level. This was to ensure the unified management of the crisis situation at the national level, while also ensuring the regional integration of these countries. At the beginning, the tasks of the NCKU were not fully defined; therefore, in 2006 the government issued a decree to more precisely define the NCKU tasks as they relate to the organization and operation of NCKU (*Official Gazette of the Republic of Slovenia*, 9/2006).

NCKU is organized under the Ministry of Defense, which provides personnel, material, accommodation, financial and other assistance. NCKU operates continuously. Its main task is to provide accommodation, technical, information and communication conditions under the auspices of the government of the Republic of Slovenia in accordance with the law in the event of a state of emergency, war or other threats that may significantly compromise the national security. Although it has been a priority for NCKU to act in a crisis situation, it provides permanent information and communication links between strategic State bodies.

Moreover, NCKU presides over a group that provides analytical and technical support for the ruling government in an emergency or a state of war, and also responds to crises. The analysis group has the task of monitoring potential sources of risk, which include cyber-attacks. In the current legislation, there is no direct guidance for cyber-security; the question arises as to whether the analytical group has sufficient human resources and knowledge to perform such complex tasks. Therefore, it would be prudent to align this area in order to better define the tasks of the group.

8.9. Conclusion

Although the Republic of Slovenia in its strategic documents has mentioned cyberspace as an existing dimension, it should also take into account that the realization and implementation of cyber-security is unfolding very slowly. Slovenia is not adequately prepared for cyber-attacks, especially for advanced attacks on its critical information and communication infrastructure. A very good example of Slovenian cyber-vulnerability is the YouTube affair that occurred in December 2011, when several clips from recordings of closed government of Slovenia sessions were publicized on the video-sharing website [WIK 11]. The Slovenian Armed Forces have neither the personnel nor resources to achieve satisfactory levels of cyber-security [ČAL 11]. Even in 10 years, Slovenia will not be sufficiently prepared to effectively conduct an active cyber-defense [BRA 11]. Besides the high cost, which is really difficult to justify, the main factor preventing investment in ICT security is the relatively high sense of security, which can be seen throughout Slovenian society.

Due to the nature of cyber-attacks, which may be intertwined with cyber-crime, cyber-hooliganism, cyber-espionage, cyber-terrorism or even cyber warfare, all societies, especially in small States, must join forces with civilian and military ICT security, and particularly with the cooperation of public and private sectors, to achieve maximum synergy. This cooperation is cost-effective and would provide ICT protection for everyone.

It is therefore necessary to re-review all strategic documents regulating the field of information and communication security policy in the Republic of Slovenia and coordinate them with the latest trends in ICT security, especially to define cyberspace and cyber-attacks in more detail and trace the optimal defense against them. The focus of the new strategic documents should address the coordination of various government bodies and institutions to affect optimal cooperation between the public and private sectors. Therefore, for effective cooperation between civil and military national authorities, as well as between public and private sectors, it is necessary to set up a group to coordinate the ICT security, which would essentially seek to define common ground among all State bodies and then coordinate all State authorities, municipalities and public or private companies in the ICT security field.

In addition, Slovenia should establish a unit that has the power for rapid reaction in the area of cyberspace, like SI-CERT but with special authorizations. In peacetime this could be a function of the police, and in a state of war this can be transferred to a military unit. Such a unit, in addition to performing preventive measures in the field of cyber-security, could also carry out effective measures to combat cyber-crime and 'cyber-rascality'. At the same time it could take action in the field of cyber-terrorism and cyber-espionage and start to prepare to fight against cyber-warfare.

The key element for an optimal and efficient defense in cyberspace is tight cooperation among all social entities in the country, which could be achieved by careful planning in all strategic documents. Although this applies to all countries, in order to optimize their actions in cyber defense small countries must implement such cooperation even more strictly than larger ones. A good example of such cooperation is Estonia, where an all volunteer-force of programmers and computer scientists has been created that can be mobilized to defend their country during a cyber-war.

8.10. Bibliography

[ALB 10] ALBRIGHT D., BRANNAN P. and WALROND C., *Did Stuxnet Take Out 1,000 Centrifuges at the Natanz Enrichment Plant?*, Institute for Science and International Security, 2010, available at: http://www.isis-online.org/isis-reports/detail/did-stuxnet-take-out-1000-centrifuges-at-the-natanz-enrichment-plant/.

[AND 11] ANDLOVIČ A., *Slovenski Metulji Ropajo po Svetu*, Slovenske Novice, 2011, available at: http://www.slovenskenovice.si/crni-scenarij/doma/slovenski-metulji-ropajo-po-svetu.html.

[BAR 11] BARDIN J. *Metulji Botnet Largest to Date – Unveillance and Panda Team*, CSO online, 2011, available at: http://blogs.csoonline.com/1575/metulji_botnet_largest_to_date_unveillance_and_panda_team.

[BOG 11] BOGIS A., *Lessons from Estonia's Cyber Army*, Homeland Security Watch, 2011, available at: http://www.hlswatch.com/2011/01/20/lessons-from-estonias-cyber-army/.

[BRA 11] BRATUŠA T., Asimetrično bojevanje in strategija posrednjega nastopanja v kibernetski vojni, Master's thesis, Faculty of Criminal Justice and Security, University of Maribor, 2011, available at: http://dkum.uni-mb.si/IzpisGradiva.php?id=19003

[CAR 10] CARR J., "Did The Stuxnet Worm Kill India's INSAT-4B Satellite?", *Forbes*, 2010, available at: 2010, http://blogs.forbes.com/firewall/2010/09/29/did-the-stuxnet-worm-kill-indias-insat-4b-satellite/.

[CFD 05] CFD, Council Framework Decision 2005/222/JHA of 24 February 2005 on Attacks against information systems, Official Journal of the European Union, L 069, pp. 0067–0071, 2005, available at: http://europa.eu/legislation_summaries/information_society/internet/133193_en.htm.

[CHA 09] CHABROW E., *New Cyber Warfare Branch Proposed*, Information Security Group, Corp (ISMG), 2009, available at: http://blogs.govinfosecurity.com/posts.php?postID=160.

[CLA 10] CLARKE R.A. and KNAKE R.K., *Cyber War. The Next Threat to National Security and What to Do About It*, HarperCollins, New York, 2010.

[CNT 11] CNTV, *Defense Ministry clarifies Cyber Blue Team*, CNTV, 2011, available at: http://english.cntv.cn/program/china24/20110526/111784.shtml.

[ČAL 11] ČALETA D. and ROLIH G., "Cyber security in the operation of critical infrastructure – an analysis of the situation in the field of Slovenian defence", in: *Contemporary Military Challenges*, General Staff of Slovenian Armed Forces, available at: http://www.slovenskavojska.si/fileadmin/slovenska_vojska/pdf/vojaski_izzivi/svi_13_3.pdf.

[DOD 10] DEPARTMENT OF DEFENSE, *Cyber Command Achieves Full Operational Capability*, Department of Defense, 2010, available at: http://www.defense.gov/releases/release.aspx? releaseid=14030.

[ENI 06] EVROPSKA AGENCIJA ZA VARNOST OMREŽIJ IN INFORMACIJ (ENISA), Postopen pristop k vzpostavitvi csirt, Dokument WP2006/5.1(CERT-D1/D2), ENISA, 2006, available at: http://www.enisa.europa.eu/act/cert/support/guide/files/csirt-setting-up-guide-in-slovenian/at_download/fullReport.

[ESO 11] EVROPSKI EKONOMSKO-SOCIALNI ODBOR, "Mnenje Evropskega ekonomsko-socialnega odbora o predlogu direktive Evropskega parlamenta" in *Sveta o napadih na informacijske sisteme in razveljavitvi Okvirnega sklepa Sveta 2005/222/PNZ*, 471. plenarno zasedanje, 2011, available at: http://www.toad.eesc.europa.eu/ViewDoc.aspx %3Fdoc%3Dces%255Cten%255Cten437%255CSL%255CCES453-2011_FIN_NI _SL.doc.

[EUC 10] EUROPEAN COMMISSION, A Digital Agenda for Europe, Communication from the Commission to the European Parliament, the Council, the European Economic and Social Committee and the Committee of the Regions, 2010, available at: http://eur-lex.europa.eu/LexUriServ/LexUriServ.do?uri=CELEX:52010DC0245R(01):EN:NOT.

[GIL 11] GILES K. *Information Troops, a Russian Cyber Command?*, Conflict Studies Research Centre, Oxford, 2011, available at: http://www.conflictstudies.org.uk/files/ Russian_Cyber_Command.pdf.

[GSO 05] GLOBAL SECURITY.ORGANISATION, *Force XXI*, Global Security Organisation, 2005, available at: http://www.globalsecurity.org/military/agency/army/force-xxi.htm.

[HAF 09] HAFNAR D., *Nova Zmaga, nov Napad*, Žurnal 24, 2009, available at: http://www.zurnal24.si/print/61307.

[HAJ 02] HAJTNIK T., *Priporočila za Pripravo Informacijske Varnostne Politike*, Center Vlade RS za Informatiko, 2002, available at: www.mju.gov.si/fileadmin/mju.gov.si/ pageuploads/mju_dokumenti/pdf/Priporocila_za_pripravo_inf.varnostne_politike_2.0_1.d el.pdf and www.mju.gov.si/fileadmin/mju.gov.si/pageuploads/mju_dokumenti/pdf/ Priporocila_za_pripravo_inf.varnostne_politike_2.0_2.del.pdf.

[INF 10] INFOSECURITY NEWS, "UK government Cyber Security Operations Centre going live soon", *Infosecurity Magazine*, 2010, available at: http://www.infosecurity-magazine.com/view/8020/uk-government-cyber-security-operations-centre-going-live-soon/.

[KNO 11] KNOKE F, *De Maizière preist neue Cyber-Zentrale*, Spiegel Online, 2011, available at: http://www.spiegel.de/netzwelt/netzpolitik/0,1518,747350,00.html.

[LAN 10] LANGNER R., *The Short Path from Cyber Missiles to Dirty Digital Bombs*, Langner, 2010, available at: http://www.langner.com/en/2010/12/26/the-short-path-from-cyber-missiles-to-dirty-digital-bombs/.

[LIN 11] LATEST IT NEWS, *The Most Hacker Attacks come from Russia*, Latest IT News, 2011, available at: http://www.whioam.com/the-most-hacker-attacks-come-from-russia.html.

[NAM 11] NAMESTNIKOV Y, *IT Threat Evolution: Q2 2011*, Kaspersky Lab, 2011, available at: http://www.securelist.com/en/analysis/204792186/IT_Threat_Evolution_Q2_2011.

[NAT 08] NATO news, *NATO Opens New Centre of Excellence on Cyber Defence*, NATO, 2008, available at: http://www.nato.int/docu/update/2008/05-may/e0514a.html.

[PUF 95] PUFENG W., *The Challenge of Information Warfare*, China Military Science, 1995, available at: http://www.fas.org/irp/world/china/docs/iw_mg_wang.htm

[MIN 11] MINISTRSTVO ZA OBRAMBO, Kabinet Ministra, Poročilo o uresničevanju programa uveljavljanja Doktrine civilne obrambe Republike Slovenije, Dokument 80100-1/2011/10, VlADA, 2011, available at: www.vlada.si/fileadmin/dokumenti/si/sklepi/seja_vlade_2011/133_seja/133sv14.doc.

[MLA 10] MLADINA EDITORIAL, "Peticija Ukinimo vojsko! (Petition for abolishing the army!)", *Mladina*, 2010 available at: http://www.mladina.si/mladina_plus/peticije/ukiniti_vojsko/.

[POL 11] POLICIJA, *Poročilo o delu policije za leto 2010*, Ministrstvo za notranje zadeve 2011, available at: http://www.policija.si/images/stories/Statistika/LetnaPorocila/PDF/LetnoPorocilo2010.pdf.

[SOP 11] SOPHOS, Security Threat Report 2011, Sophos, 2011, available at: http://www.sophos.com/security/topic/security-threat-report-2011.html.

[STP 08] STRATEGY PAGE, *Russia the Evil Hacker Haven*, StrategyPage.com, 2008, available at http://www.strategypage.com/htmw/htiw/20080204.aspx.

[UNI 10] UNITED NATIONS, United Nations e-Government Survey 2010. Leveraging e-Government at a Time of Financial and Economic Crisis, Department of Economic and Social Affairs, New York, United Nations, 2010, available at: http://www2.unpan.org/egovkb/global_reports/10report.htm.

[THO 04] THOMAS T.L., *Russian and Chinese Information Warfare: Theory and Practice*, Foreign Military Studies Office, 2004, available at: http://www.dtic.mil.

[THO 09] THOMPSON M., *Mariposa Botnet Analysis*, Defence Intelligence, 2009, available at: www.defintel.com/docs/Mariposa_Analysis.pdf.

[ZUP 10a] ZUPAN G. *E-poslovanje v podjetjih v Sloveniji in EU, 2004–2008*, Statistični urad RS, 2010, available at: http://www.stat.si/novica_prikazi.aspx?id=2921.

[ZUP 10b] ZUPAN G. *Uporaba informacijsko - komunikacijske tehnologije v podjetjih, podrobni podatki, Slovenija, 2010 – končni podatki*, Statistični urad RS, 2010, available at: http://www.stat.si/novica_prikazi.aspx?ID=3596

[ZUP 11] ZUPAN G., *Svetovni dan telekomunikacij in informacijske družbe 2011*, Statistični urad RS, 2011, available at: http://www.stat.si/novica_prikazi.aspx?id=3908.

[WIK 11] WIKIPEDIA, *2011 Slovenian YouTube affair*, 2011, Wikipedia, available at: http://en.wikipedia.org/wiki/2011_Slovenian_YouTube_affair.

Chapter 9

A South African Perspective on Information Warfare and Cyber Warfare

South Africa is the leading economy in Southern Africa, and is a strategic maritime nation that serves a major shipping lane between the western and eastern hemispheres. Its ports are also vital to the country's economy, as 98% of all exports are conveyed by sea [GCI 10]. The national communications infrastructure in South Africa is 99% digital, and is the most developed telecommunications network in Africa [GCI 10]. The main telecommunications supplier, Telkom, is the largest in Africa; the cell phone industry has also shown significant growth, and by the end of 2008 there were estimated to be over 34 million cell phone users in the country [GCI 10]. The developed nature of the infrastructure necessitates the development of information warfare and cyber-warfare in order to protect the national communications infrastructure from threats; particularly those that are cyber-based.

South Africa is making an effort to develop skills in these arenas; it was first reported in 2004 that an information warfare battlelab had been commissioned by the Council for Scientific and Industrial Research (CSIR) [CSI 04]. In March 2009, the CSIR hosted the 4th International Conference on Information Warfare and Security, and there are numerous local conferences in the country that revolve around information warfare and security. The Military Information and Communication Symposium of South Africa is a biennial conference that ran for the fifth time in 2011.

Chapter written by Brett VAN NIEKERK and Manoj MAHARAJ.

There is a history of the use of information warfare tactics in South Africa. During the apartheid era, the media was heavily censored [MER 01]; and anti-government radio stations were jammed. A ban was placed on sounds or images of racial protests to deny anti-apartheid protestors a stage, aiming to reduce international sympathy for their cause [SAL 11]. Military operations in Angola saw the deployment of electronic warfare. The African National Congress used computers and modems as part of Operation Vula, an underground communications network [SAL 11]. As the prevalence of computers and computer networks was not high during this period, there were no instances of cyber-war.

9.1. The South African structure of information warfare

The South African National Defense Force (SANDF) defines information warfare as:

> "all actions taken to defend the military's information-based processes, information systems and communications networks and to destroy, neutralize or exploit the enemy's similar capabilities within the physical, information and cognitive domains" [BRA 07].

From this definition, there are three 'domains' in which to conduct information warfare. The concept of the 'information sphere' comprises the physical domain, the electromagnetic spectrum, the network spectrum or 'cyberspace', and the human or cognitive domain [COE 11]. Cyberspace is therefore a subset of the information sphere, and is considered to be comprised of the technologies that enable the distribution and storage of data packages in the form of bits and bytes [COE 11]. The human or cognitive domain is also significant as it contains the relevant wisdom and knowledge of the soldiers fighting wars and populations; this is where decisions are made based on experience, information and perceptions [COE 11].

The management and governance of the South African information warfare capabilities fall under the Directorate of Information Warfare, whereas the various branches of the SANDF are responsible for its implementation [BRA 07]. The SANDF organizes information warfare into six functional areas [BRA 07, THE 08]:

– *command and control warfare*: protecting the efficiency and integrity of decision making and the link between the command structure and the soldiers of its own forces, and aims to damage the similar capabilities of the opposing forces.

– *intelligence-based warfare*: protecting the intelligence cycle and dissemination to soldiers of its own forces in real-time (i.e. 'sensor-to-shooter capabilities' [BRA 07]), and aims to damage the similar capabilities of opposing forces.

– *information infrastructure warfare*: the information infrastructure is considered to include the networks and communications as well as the energy infrastructure upon which they depend. Information infrastructure warfare aims to protect South Africa's forces information infrastructure, and to attack or exploit that of opposing forces;

– *network warfare*: this is equivalent to cyber-warfare, computer network operations and network-centric warfare. It aims to protect the information networks of South African forces and to attack or exploit those of opposing forces;

– *electronic warfare*: this protects the availability of the electromagnetic spectrum for utilization by South African forces and aims to prevent, damage or exploit the use of the electromagnetic spectrum by opposing forces;

– *psychological operations* (or PSYOPs): operations aimed to support military objectives by influencing the behavior and attitudes of a target audience, which may be hostile, neutral, or friendly.

The six functional areas are organized into two domains [BRA 07, THE 08]:

– the application domain, which comprises of command and control warfare, intelligence-based warfare and information infrastructure warfare; and

– the enabling domain, which consists of network warfare, electronic warfare and PSYOPs.

The application domain can be seen as the 'target', while the enabling domain is applied to create effects in the application domain. As the military in South Africa is primarily a defense force, information warfare also takes a defensive posture [HEF 09]. This is also evident in the fact that the aims of the six functional areas are described as primarily to protect its own force's information activities and secondly to neutralize, modify, degrade, deny or destroy those of the opposing forces [THE 08].

Table 9.1 compares the six functional areas of the South African model to the seven that are proposed by Libicki [LIB 95] and the Indian model described by Chatterji [CHA 08]. It can be seen that the South African model does not consider economic information warfare but that there is the introduction of information infrastructure warfare in the South African model. The South African network warfare construct is also a combination of cyber-warfare, hacker warfare and network-centric operations. The South African model also segments the six functional areas into the two domains, which is not done elsewhere.

The information warfare functional areas are related to the operational battlespace as follows [THE 08]:

– network and electronic warfare can be used to disrupt the flow of data from sensors to processing units and from processing units to the command structure, or to inject false data into data flows;

– to intercept the information flow between an adversary's command structure to those fighting the war (intelligence agencies), or to disrupt the flow of information or inject false information using network warfare and electronic warfare;

– to disrupt the information flow between the command structure and support units through the use of electronic and network warfare, or to modify and inject false information, with the aim of introducing errors into the logistics supply.

South Africa [BRA 07]	Libicki [LIB 95]	India [CHA 08]
Command and control warfare	Command and control warfare	Command and control warfare
Intelligence-based warfare	Intelligence-based warfare	Intelligence-based warfare
Electronic warfare	Electronic warfare	Electronic warfare
Psychological operations	Psychological operations	Psychological warfare
Network warfare	Hacker warfare	Network-centric warfare
	Cyber-warfare	Cyber-warfare
Information infrastructure warfare	Information economic warfare	Economic information warfare

Table 9.1. *Comparison of the information warfare models*

In addition to its functional areas and domains, the SANDF identifies four layers of information warfare: doctrine, command and control, physical network, and the communications grid [THE 08]. The doctrine layer refers to the operational tactics (both long-term and day-to-day operations) during peace and wartime; it may be possible to utilize information warfare to force an adversary to alter its doctrine, providing an advantage to South Africa's forces. The physical network refers primarily to computer-based networks, and the communications grid refers to the military communications systems, with a focus on the electromagnetic forms of communication (radio frequency and satellite communication systems). Command and control refers to the structure used to manage forces and may include both the communications grid and physical network [THE 08].

In the *SANDF 2020 Vision*, Brazzoli emphasizes the importance of PSYOPs in the African context [BRA 07]. This focus on PSYOPs and influence operations is echoed by Wardini while discussing Senegal's information operations structure [WAR 08]. Wardini attributes the focus on PSYOPs in the African context due to the technological components required for other functional areas being not readily available [WAR 08]. Brazzoli argues, however, that technology may be bought and introduced very quickly, and therefore should not be ignored [BRA 07]. South Africa also has a strong electronic warfare industry; particularly related to the SAAB group [DAR 08].

The 1998 Defense Review indicates that the role of information technology in the SANDF is to provide combat and operational advantages. It recognizes that the convergence of information and communication technologies is resulting in the "erosion of the distinctions between strategic, operational and tactical systems" [DOD 98]. Information technology was considered essential for the transformation of the South African Department of Defense and the SANDF. The term 'information warfare' first appeared in the South African Department of Defense annual report in 2003 [DOD 03]; this indicates that the SANDF has acknowledged the importance of information warfare. In the 2005 annual report it was indicated that the Information Warfare Directorate and Capability Boards had been established, and the draft information warfare strategy had been completed and distributed for comment. It also indicated that the draft information warfare policy and information warfare doctrine were nearing completion [DOD 05]. By 2006, the information warfare committees of the services had been established [DOD 06].

In the 2010 report, it was indicated that the annual implementation targets are being met for information warfare; however a concern is raised that there is a lack of capacity [DOD 10]. This report and the 2009 strategic business plan indicate that the information warfare and security field need development, and that this is an essential area of research [DOD 09, DOD 10].

From these reports it is clear that the development of information warfare in the SANDF is of strategic importance, and there is a clear path for the further development and implementation of information warfare in South Africa. In addition to this, the Faculty of Military Science at the University of Stellenbosch, which forms the Military Academy of the SANDF, has courses that include information warfare, electronic warfare, and cyber-warfare [FMS 11].

9.2. A South African perspective on cyber-warfare

As with many other nations, South Africa is looking to improve its cyber-defense capability following the attacks on Estonia and Georgia. South Africa would regard a cyber-based incident that causes major disruption to national information systems as an act of war [ENG 08]. Much of the country's information warfare and cyber-warfare capabilities are still classified, therefore publications containing doctrine-related material are scarce. What is clear is that there is increasing concern over the growing prevalence and availability of broadband services, coupled with the lack of user awareness. Adequate legislative, incident response and monitoring mechanisms at a strategic level are also lacking to a certain degree, therefore there is no holistic view of cyber-security incidents in South Africa.

9.3. The Southern African cyber-environment

South Africa has a relatively low penetration of Internet services compared to 'developed' countries. The International Telecommunications Union estimates that only 8.82 out of every 100 people in South Africa are Internet users. There are an estimated 0.96 fixed-line broadband subscribers in South Africa for every 100 residents, compared to 10.52 mobile broadband subscriptions per 100 residents; this is a ratio of 11 mobile broadband subscriptions for every fixed-line broadband subscription [ITU 11]. This indicates that in general the South African population is reliant on mobile options for data communications.

There is concern over the vulnerability of the country to cyber-based incidents due to the increasing prevalence and affordability of broadband connectivity; and the lack of security awareness. There is expected to be a drop in the price of broadband in Africa due to the new undersea cables that are being installed. Currently South Africa is connected to three cables, totaling 5,460 gigabits of capacity. This is expected to increase to five cables totaling 15,700 gigabits capacity by the end of 2012. Sub-Saharan Africa currently has six active undersea cables, totaling 9,960 gigabits of capacity, which is expected to increase by the end of this year to 10 undersea cables totaling 23,980 gigabits. While this increase in capacity is good for development in the region, it also brings the concern that the resultant drop in connectivity prices will result in the growth of users who are unaware of online security issues. The primary concern, raised by a number of local and international researchers, is that there will be an explosion of cyber-crime activity and malicious software infections, which will lead to increased susceptibility of the nation's infrastructure to an attack, or an increased risk of the Internet being utilized as part of a cyber-based attack [JJV 10, FRY 10, VAN 10].

There is already a high rate of malicious software infections in Southern Africa. The *Microsoft Security Intelligence Report* [MSC 10a] lists the number of computers (per 1,000) cleaned (CCM) by Microsoft Malicious Software Removal Tool. Table 9.2 shows this malware infection rate of South Africa and the neighboring nations compared to the worldwide figure. The figures in brackets indicate the rank of the nation out of the 212 listed.

There is a general trend where these African nations are moving up the rankings, i.e. having higher infection rates. It should be noted that these figures are only for legitimate Windows platforms; therefore there may be many more infected computers using pirated copies. The rate of pirated software in Africa was estimated at 59% in 2009 [BSA 10]. The pirated software may remain unpatched, leaving the systems vulnerable to infection [FRY 10].

	Jan–Mar 2009	Apr–Jun 2009	Jul–Sep 2009	Oct–Dec 2009	Jan–Mar 2010	Apr–Jun 2010
Worldwide	*12.7*	*10.9*	*10.5*	*9.5*	*10.8*	*9.6*
Botswana	5.5 (136)	4.8 (132)	5.6 (108)	6.7 (78)	7.9 (90)	6.1 (96)
Lesotho	11.9 (52)	8.3 (72)	9.3 (53)	9.8 (49)	22.7 (14)	19.2 (12)
Mozambique	9.9 (70)	7.4 (88)	4.8 (124)	5.7 (102)	10.5 (59)	8 (68)
Namibia	14.6 (38)	11.1 (43)	10.1 (46)	10.6 (40)	10.3 (61)	7.4 (79)
South Africa	9.1 (84)	7.5 (86)	7.6 (76)	9.9 (47)	12.8 (50)	11.9 (44)
Swaziland	13.2 (44)	11.2 (41)	8.6 (63)	8.7 (61)	14.9 (35)	12.1 (43)
Zimbabwe	19.2 (22)	17.2 (20)	16.8 (19)	16.9 (13)	18.8 (22)	18.5 (16)

Table 9.2. *Infection statistics of South Africa and neighboring nations in CCM (rank of 212 nations) [MSC 10a]*

	Jul–Sep 2009	Oct–Dec 2009	Jan–Mar 2010	Apr–Jun 2010
Worldwide	*2.5*	*2.5*	*4*	*3.2*
Algeria	0.2 (78)	0.2 (78)	0.3 (80)	0.3 (79)
Egypt	1.6 (49)	2.8 (30)	3.6 (42)	2.7 (41)
Kenya	0.1 (82)	0.2 (80)	0.2 (83)	0.3 (80)
Morocco	0.1 (83)	0.1 (83)	0.3 (81)	0.2 (82)
Nigeria	0 (84)	0.1 (84)	0.2 (84)	0.2 (83)
South Africa	2.6 (30)	5.8 (6)	9.3 (11)	8.4 (6)
Tunisia	0.2 (79)	0.2 (81)	0.4 (78)	0.2 (84)

Table 9.3. *Botnet infection statistics of African nations in CCM (rank of 86 nations) [MSC 10b]*

Table 9.3 shows the bot infection rate of African nations compared to the worldwide figure; this infection rate is again the number of computers per 1,000 cleaned by the Microsoft Malicious Software Removal Tool. The figures in brackets indicate the rank of the nation out of the 86 listed. As can be seen from the bot infections, South Africa has a very high infection rate compared to other African Nations, and this is higher than the worldwide average.

The figures shown in these tables are ominous signs that a prediction cited by [CAR 10] that 80% of the computers in Africa will become infected by bots may come to fruition; some researchers already claim that 80% have some form of infection [JVV 10]. If this happens, it will establish Africa as a launching point for major cyber-attacks. While the targeted nation will bear the brunt of the attack, it is also highly probable that the networks in Africa will experience severe degradation in performance.

Another concern regarding the increase in broadband activity is that this will facilitate greater piracy, which may result in an increase in unpatched systems, leaving them vulnerable to exploitation [FRY 10]. This will contribute to an increase in the infection rates in Africa. The 2008 survey indicates that 59% of software was pirated in Africa, with Zimbabwe (92%), Algeria (84%), Nigeria (83%), Zambia (82%), Botswana (79%) and Kenya (79%) being listed among the top 30 nations for software piracy rates [BSA 10]. South Africa was relatively low, with a rate of 35%, but it is listed in the top 30 economies with the highest commercial value of pirated software, totaling $324 million [BSA 10]. This indicates that there are many vulnerable systems in South Africa from which an attack can be launched.

According to the Internet Crime Complaint Center [IC3 10], South Africa is already ranked 7th in the world for cyber-crime in terms of the number of perpetrators; consisting of 0.7% of the total. South Africa is also ranked 9th in terms of the number of complainants, totaling 0.15%. Three other African nations appear in the top 10 perpetrators: Nigeria, ranked 3rd with 8%; Ghana is ranked 6th with 0.7%; and Cameroon is ranked 9th with 0.6%. Therefore Africa has four nations in the top 10, totaling 10% of the perpetrators. This indicates that Africa may already be a launching point for cyber-crime activity. As of December 20, 2010, 19,340 South African websites had been hacked since the beginning of the year; of those 74 were government websites [HAC 10]. This indicates that there is a potential susceptibility to hacktivism.

South Africa's neighbors have experienced cyber-warfare tactics due to political conflict. Zimbabwe has reportedly undergone an internal politically-motivated information war. An article cites numerous instances of government attempts to monitor the Internet and cell phones, jam radio stations, instigate denial-of-service attacks on Internet-based newspapers and anti-government hacktivism [MAV 08]. It was also reported that the Zimbabwean government received aid from China to assist with the jamming and monitoring the of country's gateway to Intelsat [MAV 08].

Mozambique recently joined the nations that have experienced electronically-initiated protests. In September 2010, protesters took to the streets over rising food prices, the protest reportedly being orchestrated via short messaging service [JAC 10]. Even though the cell phone penetration is only approximately 29% [BMI 10], it appears that cell phones proved to be a powerful tool to distribute the message. Such use of mobile devices is significant for South Africa, as there is a very high penetration rate of cell phones compared to Internet access; therefore a cyber-based attack on the telecommunications infrastructure may have greater impact than an attack on the Internet-specific infrastructure.

In January 2011, mass anti-government protests in Tunisia and Egypt utilized online social media to spread word of the protests [KES 11]; it is reported that Tunisian authorities attempted to hack into user accounts [MAD 11] and Egyptian authorities shut down the Internet and some cell phone services [KES 11, KRA 11] in an attempt to hamper the co-ordination of the protests. This again signifies the presence of cyber-based conflict in Africa.

Limited denial-of-service attacks are experienced in South Africa and the telecommunications networks do report attempted penetrations of their infrastructure. There is, however, a view that South Africa is unlikely to be the subject of a large cyber-attack unless another nation takes offence to an event or political decision [SCH 09]. Despite this, the growing Chinese influence in Africa may increase the likelihood of cyber-attacks in the region due to its apparently aggressive cyber-tactics; infections of the GhostNet series of malware was reported to be found in some African nations [IWM 09]. The GhostNet cyber-espionage malware has been attributed to the Chinese reportedly targeting those sympathetic to the Dalai Lama [IWM 09]. There have been reports that it was pressure from China that resulted in South Africa refusing entry to the Dalai Lama [SAP 09]. It is possible that South Africa may also have been subjected to cyber-espionage had the Dalai Lama been allowed entry. It is also believed that the ties South Africa has with China also increase the risk of a cyber-attack [JON 09]. The throughput of the undersea cables to South Africa has been calculated at between 500 and 1,000 Kb/s [COT 10]; a distributed denial-of-service attack such as the one that targeted Myanmar in October/November 2010, which peaked at over 14 Gb/s [LAB 10], would severely degrade the country's international connectivity.

Currently there are only three African nations with operational Computer Security Incident Response Teams (CSIRTs): Tunisia, Mauritius and Kenya. Three others are in the process of developing CSIRTs: South Africa, Egypt and Morocco.

As the CSIRT in South Africa is still under development, the country is beginning to lag behind other nations with regards a coherent information security response capability. Robertson, Lessing and Nare advocate the introduction of a military-specific CSIRT with the aim of aiding the military to protect the nation by handling responses to all cyber-security incidents [ROB 08], including cyber-warfare. However, CSIRTs are expensive and complex, and require highly trained personnel [ELL 10]. In South Africa it is also unclear which organization has the political mandate to control the CSIRT, which has hindered the development of the CSIRT in the past [GRO 11]. It has been proposed that community-orientated security, advisory and warning (C-SAW) teams be implemented as a method of protecting cyber-assets within communities; these will not replace the CSIRTs, but provide initial protection while the CSIRT is under development and then operate alongside the CSIRT once it is operational. The benefit of the C-SAW teams is that they are independent of any controlling organization, and therefore will not be hindered by organizational or political mandates [ELL 10].

9.4. Legislation

Legislation relating to cyber-security is currently being introduced. The Electronic Communications and Transmissions Act of 2002 outlines basic laws regarding hacking, intercepting and interfering with electronic communications, including those online [ECT 02]. The second major piece of legislation is the Regulation for the Interception of Communications Act. As the name suggests, this makes provision for security-related monitoring of communications [RIC 02]. The Protection of Personal Information Bill was due to be enacted in 2011, however, this did not occur. The Bill intended to provide basic rights regarding personal information; and places the onus for protecting information on the organization that controls it [POP 09]. In 2002 an Act was passed to allow the establishment of a company to provide services and products that will enable state organizations to maintain communications security [ECS 02].

While these acts are in place, there has yet to be a major, high-profile test of them in court. There also does not to appear to have been a major test in an international incident either. This may create some doubt and uncertainty regarding the implementation and applicability of the acts; organizations therefore may not be fully compliant and have vulnerabilities.

In February 2010, the country's Draft Cyber-Security Policy was released for comment. This document allows for the creation of a national CSIRT, and various CSIRTs for each sector. This policy is a step in the right direction, as the creation of the CSIRT is seen as crucial to the cyber-defense of South Africa. However, most of the legislation focuses on cyber-crime issues, and not specifically on protection from a major cyber-attack.

It is clear that South Africa recognizes the importance of a strong legal framework that can protect organizations and users from cyber-threats. With the advantage of hindsight of a 'late-adopter' it is likely that the legal framework, once in place, will provide adequate protection to users. It is imperative, though, that a strong technical framework is also put into place to support the legal framework. These frameworks will aid in mitigating the impact of a potential cyber-attack against the nation's infrastructure.

9.5. Cyber-security and information warfare organizations in South Africa

There are a number of public and private organizations in South Africa that focus on cyber-security. The following government and related organizations have responsibilities that are related to cyber-security and information warfare in South Africa [BRI 11]:

– the Department of Communications;

– the Department of Defense and the SANDF;

– the CSIR;

– the National Intelligence Agency;

– the Secret Service;

– the South African Police Service;

– the Special Investigation Unit;

– the State Information Technology Agency; and

– Communications Security Pty (Ltd).

The Department of Communications is effectively the government department charged with developing policies regarding information and communications technologies in South Africa; its mandate indicates a focus on socioeconomic development through ICT. The Department of Defense and the SANDF are charged with protecting South Africa through military force. They are therefore responsible for the military aspects of cyber-defense and information warfare. The CSIR is the national research body. As such it is responsible for conducting research into cyber-defense and information warfare for the military and government. The National Intelligence Agency and Secret Service provide intelligence and counter-intelligence services, as well as being involved in anti-corruption, counterterrorism, and countering organized crime. The area of responsibility for the South African Police Service and Special Investigations Unit will revolve around cyber-crime and corruption and fraud [BRI 11]. The State Information Technology Agency is tasked with supplying the South African government and related organizations with information technologies. Communications Security Pty (Ltd) was established to provide the South African government with communications security capabilities [ECS 02].

The disadvantage of having this number of organizations is that it is unclear whose political mandate it should be to lead the national cyber-security efforts, and this often results in hindrances in the existing projects.

There are private organizations that are also involved in the cyber-defense field. The Information Security Group of Africa is a not-for-profit organization that provides a forum for the information security community [ISG 10]. ITWeb is an online news website that has an information security section; it hosts an annual 'Security Summit' [ITW 11]. Ekwinox is an organization that organizes conferences and training in the areas of information security and information warfare [EKW 11]. There are also a number of private organizations in South Africa that provide cyber-security consulting services.

9.6. Estimated cyber-warfare capability in Africa

As much of the doctrine and documentation is not publicly available, estimates need to be made on the capabilities. A study carried out in 2003 ranked South Africa as 37 out of 57 nations with possible cyber-warfare capabilities; Nigeria was ranked 48th, Zimbabwe 55th, and Kenya and Ghana were joint 56th [GIA 03]. Using a different set of data from 2000, the same study ranked South Africa as 22 out of 27 nations [GIA 03]. Given that the first ranking listed China as 43rd, which is now considered to be one of the more capable nations in cyber-warfare, and the fact the term 'information warfare' first appeared in the 2003 South African Department of Defense annual report, it is possible that South Africa has increased in its rankings.

A number of security research projects in South Africa will also improve the defensive capabilities. An example is the quantum cryptography research group based at the University of KwaZulu-Natal, where quantum encrypted networks have been implemented in the eThekwini Municipality (Durban and the surrounding suburbs) [MIR 11]. The internal 'cyber-conflict' in Zimbabwe and the development of CSIRTs in some African nations indicates that there is a growing cyber-warfare capability in Africa.

9.7. Conclusion

The information warfare model adopted by the SANDF is comparable with those of other nations, in that it has similar functional areas to the models of other countries. From the annual reports since 2003, it is apparent that information warfare capabilities will continue to develop and be implemented by the SANDF; however, a lack of human capacity in the area has been noted. The focus of information warfare is on a defensive posture, and this extends to the network warfare functional area, which is analogous to cyber-warfare.

South Africa does not have a particularly high penetration rate of Internet services, and there appears to be a reliance on mobile broadband services. While South Africa has not yet been a victim to a major cyber-attack, there is a particular concern over its vulnerability to cyber-based attacks due to the increasing broadband connectivity and lack of user awareness. High rates of infection, software piracy, and cyber-crime are already evident; this situation is expected to worsen. High rates of botnet infections may see the African information infrastructure employed as a cyber-weapon to launch attacks. There have been cyber-related incidents in Africa. This indicates that despite the low penetration rates, the potential for cyber-power has been recognized. South Africa is not expected to fall victim to a major cyber-attack, however, unless there is an event that attracts the attention of a group with aggressive cyber-tendencies.

Currently Africa, particularly South Africa, is lagging in the introduction of legislation and policies to aid in countering the cyber-threats. South Africa lacks an operational CSIRT, and the general lack of CSIRTs on the continent results in a huge vulnerability to cyber-based incidents. There are a number of public organizations whose mandate is relevant to addressing cyber-security and information warfare; however it is unclear which organization should take the lead responsibility for national cyber-defense.

African countries have been ranked in an information warfare study; this illustrates that some capability exists. The internal 'cyber-conflict' in Zimbabwe, the mass demonstrations throughout Africa, the response by the respective governments and current research indicates that there is a growing capacity in this continent for cyber-warfare. The relevant technology required to conduct cyber-warfare can be purchased and operated with a minimum of human capability; this provides these nations with the ability to 'develop' some cyber-warfare capability almost overnight. Other sympathetic nations may provide both the technology and training to allow African nations to acquire cyber-warfare capabilities. Botnets to conduct cyber-attacks can be 'hired'; providing any state or non-state actors with the capacity to launch an anonymous attack.

Africa, and South Africa in particular, are developing cyber-warfare capabilities. Internal cyber-conflicts and cyber-supported mass demonstrations illustrate that the philosophy and some capability exists. Some African nations have a CSIRT, providing them with a defensive advantage over those that do not; however, the increasing prevalence of broadband in the continent may result in increasing levels of cyber-insecurity due to large levels of piracy and lack of awareness of information security issues.

9.10. Bibliography

[BMI 10] BUSINESS MONITOR INTERNATIONAL, *Mozambique: How Rising Wheat Prices Crippled SMS Services*, Business Monitor International Risk Watchdog, 2010, available at: http://www.riskwatchdog.com/2010/09/13/mozambique-how-rising-wheat-prices-crippled-sms-services/ (accessed 5 November 2010).

[BRA 07] BRAZZOLI M.S., "Future prospects of information warfare and particularly psychological operations," in LE ROUX L., *South African Army Vision 2020*, Institute for Security Studies, pp. 217-232, 2007.

[BRI 11] BRITZ D., "The supporting role of the private sector in the IW sphere," *5th Military Information and Communications Symposium of South Africa 2011 (MICSSA '11)*, Pretoria, July 18-21, 2011.

[BSA 10] BUSINESS SOFTWARE ALLIANCE, *7th Annual BSA-IDC Global Software Piracy Study 2009*, Business Software Alliance, Washington, DC, May 2010.

[CAR 10] CARR J., *Inside Cyber Warfare*, O'Reilly Media, 2010.

[CHA 08] CHATTERJI S.K., "An overview of information operations in the Indian army," *IOSphere*, Special Edition, pp. 10-14, 2008.

[COE 11] COETZEE A.J., "Information warfare: The 5th dimension to project strategic power," *5th Military Information and Communications Symposium of South Africa 2011 (MICSSA '11)*, Pretoria, July 18-21, 2011.

[COT 10] COTTRELL R.L., KALIM U., "New E. Coast of Africa fibre", *SLAC Confluence*, September 2010, available at: https://confluence.slac.stanford.edu/display/IEPM/New+E.+Coast+of+Africa+Fibre (accessed November 30, 2010).

[CSI 04] COUNCIL FOR SCIENTIFIC AND INDUSTRIAL RESEARCH (CSIR), *Science Scope*, CSIR, April/May 2004, available at: http://www.csir.co.za/publications/pdfs/sciencescope/May2004_technobrief.pdf (accessed November 26, 2010).

[DAR 08] DARDINE A., KNOWLES J., "The EW top 20," *The Journal of Electronic Defense*, vol. 31, no. 8, pp. 30-33, 2008.

[DOD 03] SOUTH AFRICAN DEPARTMENT OF DEFENSE, South African Defense Review 1998, Government of the Republic of South Africa, 1998.

[DOD 03] SOUTH AFRICAN DEPARTMENT OF DEFENSE, Annual Report FY 2002–2003, Government of the Republic of South Africa, 2003.

[DOD 05] SOUTH AFRICAN DEPARTMENT OF DEFENSE, Annual Report FY 2004–2005, Government of the Republic of South Africa, 2005.

[DOD 06] SOUTH AFRICAN DEPARTMENT OF DEFENSE, Annual Report FY 2005–2006, Government of the Republic of South Africa, 2006.

[DOD 09] SOUTH AFRICAN DEPARTMENT OF DEFENSE, Strategic Business Plan 2009, Government of the Republic of South Africa, 2009.

[DOD 10] SOUTH AFRICAN DEPARTMENT OF DEFENSE, Annual Report FY 2009–2010, Government of the Republic of South Africa, 2010.

[ECS 02] Electronic Communications Security Pty (Ltd) Act, Act 68, Government of the Republic of South Africa, 2002.

[ECT 02] Electronic Communications and Transmissions Act, Act 25, Government of the Republic of South Africa, 2002.

[EKW 11] EKWINOX, Pasts Events, 2011, available at: http://ekwinox.webs.com/pastevents.htm.

[ELL 10] ELLEFSEN, I., VON SOLMS, S., "C-SAW: critical information infrastructure protection through simplification," *International Federation of Information Processing Advances in Information and Communication Technology*, vol. 328, pp. 315-325, 2010.

[ENG 08] ENGELBRECHT, L., *SANDF Considers Info Warfare Threat*, DefenceWeb, 2008, available at: http://www.defenceweb.co.za/index.php?option=com_content&view=article &id=192&catid=48:Command%20&%20Control&Itemid=109 (accessed November 26, 2010).

[FMS 11] FACULTY OF MILITARY SCIENCE, *Calender 2011, Part 13*, University of Stellenbosch, 2011.

[FRY 10] FRYER, B., MERRITT, K., TRIAS, E., "Security in the emerging African broadband environment," *Proceedings of the 5th International Conference of Information Warfare and Security*, Wright-Patterson Air Force Base, Ohio, USA, pp. 98-105, April 2010.

[GCI 10] GOVERNMENT COMMUNICATION AND INFORMATION SYSTEM (GCIS), *Pocket Guide to South Africa 2009/2010*, South African Government Communications, Pretoria, 2010, available at: http://www.gcis.gov.za/resource_centre/sa_info/pocketguide/2009-10.htm (accessed February 15, 2011).

[GIA 03] GIACOMELLO, G., "Measuring digital wars: learning from the experience of peace research and arms control," *The Information Warfare Site Infocon Magazine Issue One*, October 2003, available at: http://www.iwar.co.uk/infocon/measuring-io.pdf (accessed September 26, 2011).

[GRO 10] GROBLER, M., BRYK, H., "Common challenges faced during the establishment of a CSIRT," *2010 Information Security for South Africa (ISSA 2010) Conference*, Sandton, August 2010.

[HAC 10] HACKING STATS.COM, *Hacking Statistics*, December 20, 2010, available at: http://www.hackingstats.com/hacking-statistics.php (accessed December 20, 2010).

[HEF 09] HEFER, J., THERON, J., "IW into Africa," *Military Information and* Communications *Sumposium of South Africa 2009*, Pretoria, July 2009.

[IC3 10] INTERNET CRIME COMPLAINT CENTER (IC3), 2009 Internet crime report, Federal Bureau for Investigations, 2010, available at: http://www.ic3.gov/media/annual reports.aspx (accessed May 3, 2010).

[ISG 10] INFORMATION SECURITY GROUP OF AFRICA, *About Us*, ISGA, 2010, available at: http://www.isgafrica.org/blog/?page_id=37.

[ITU 11] INTERNATIONAL TELECOMMUNICATIONS UNION, *ICT Data and Statistics*, ITU, 2011, available at: http://www.itu.int/ITU-D/ict/statistics/index.html.

[ITW 11] ITWEB, *Security Summit 2011 – Info*, ITWeb, 2011, available at: http://www.itweb.co.za/index.php?option=com_content&view=article&id=381 00&Itemid=2330.

[IWM 09] INFORMATION WARFARE MONITOR (IWM), *Tracking GhostNet: Investigating a Cyber Espionage Network*, IWM, 2009.

[JAC 10] JACOBS S., DUARTE D., *Protest in Mozambique: The Power of SMS*, AfrOnline – The Voice of Africa, 2010, available at: http://www.afronline.org/?p=8680 (accessed November 5, 2010).

[JON 09] JONES C., *SA Could Face Cyber War*, ITWeb, May 29, 2009, available at: http://www.itweb.co.za/index.php?option=com_content&view=article&id=23157:sa-could-face-cyber-war&catid=296:security-summit-2009&tmpl=component&print=1 (accessed November 29, 2010).

[JJV 10] JANSE N., VAN VUUREN J., PHAHLAMOHLAKA J., BRAZZOLI M., "The impact of the increase in broadband access on South African national security and the average citizen," *Proceedings of the 5th International Conference of Information Warfare and Security*, Wright-Patterson Air Force Base, Ohio, USA, pp. 171-181, April 2010.

[KES 11] KESSLER S., *Twitter Blocked in Egypt as Protest Turns Violent*, Yahoo! News, 2011, available at: http://news.yahoo.com/s/mashable/20110125/tc_mashable/twitter_blocked_in_egypt_as_protests_turn_violent (accessed January 26, 2011).

[KRA 11] KRAVETS D., *Internet Down in Egypt, Tens of Thousands Protest in 'Friday of Wrath'*, Wired.com Threatlevel Blog, 2011, available at: http://www.wired.com/threatlevel/2011/01/egypt-internet-down/# (accessed February 1, 2011).

[LAB 10] LABOVITZ C., *Attack Severs Burma Internet*, Arbor Networks, November 2010, available at: http://asert.arbornetworks.com/2010/11/attac-severs-myanmar-internet/ (accessed November 11, 2010).

[LIB 95] LIBICKI M., *What is Information Warfare?* Center for Advanced Concepts and Technology, 1995, available at: http://www.dodccrp.org/files/Libicki_What_Is.pdf (accessed December 20, 2010).

[MAD 11] MADRIGAL A., "The inside story of how Facebook responded to Tunisian hacks," *The Atlantic*, 2011, available at: http://www.theatlantic.com/technology/archive/2011/01/the-inside-story-of-how-facebook-responded-to-tunisian-hacks/70044/# (accessed January 25, 2011).

[MAV 08] MAVHUNGA C., "The glass fortress: Zimbabwe's cyber-guerrilla warfare," *Concerned African Scholars*, no. 80, pp. 21-27, 2008, available at: http://concernedafricascholars.org/docs/acasbulletin80.pdf (accessed November 26, 2010).

[MER 01] MERRIT C., "A tale of two paradoxes: media censorship in South Africa, Pre-Liberation and Post-Apartheid", *Critical Arts*, vol. 15, no. 1, pp. 50-68, 2001.

[MIR 11] MIRZA A., PETRUCCIONE F., "Quantum technology: A next generation solution for secure communication," *5th Military Information and Communications Symposium of South Africa 2011 (MICSSA '11)*, Pretoria, July 18-21, 2011.

[MSC 10a] MICROSOFT CORPORATION, Microsoft Security Intelligence Report – Global Infection Rates, vol. 9, 2010, available at: http://www.microsoft.com/downloads/en/details.aspx?FamilyID=%20b5f9eddc-70dc-4b11-996b-1bc6987c44b9 (accessed November 26, 2010).

[MSC 10b] MICROSOFT CORPORATION, Microsoft Security Intelligence Report – Global Botnet Infection Rates, vol. 9, 2010, available at: http://www.microsoft.com/downloads/en/details.aspx?FamilyID=%20b5f9eddc-70dc-4b11-996b-1bc6987c44b9 (accessed November 26, 2010).

[POP 09] GOVERNMENT OF THE REPUBLIC OF SOUTH AFRICA, Protection of Personal Information Bill, Bill 9, Government of the Republic of South Africa, 2009.

[RIC 02] GOVERNMENT OF THE REPUBLIC OF SOUTH AFRICA, Regulation for Interception of Communications and Provision of Communication-related Information Act, Act 70, Government of the Republic of South Africa, 2002.

[ROB 08] ROBERTSON J., LESSING M., NARE S., "Preparedness and response to cyber threats require a CSIRT," *IFIP Proceedings on ICT Uses in Warfare and the Safeguarding of Peace*, pp. 84-94, July 2008.

[SAL 11] SALEH I., "The impact of ICT on peace, security & governance in Africa", *Alliance of Civilisations Media Literacy Education*, available at: http://www.aocmedialiteracy.org/index.php?option=com_contest&task=view&id=100&itemid=31 (accessed February 2011).

[SAP 09] SOUTH AFRICAN PRESS ASSOCIATION (SAPA), *Best not to Invite Dalai Lama*, News 24, 2009, available at: http://www.news24.com/SouthAfrica/Politics/Best-not-to-invite-Dalai-Lama-20090322 (accessed April 19, 2010).

[SCH 09] SCHEEPERS W., "Information (cyber) warfare: fact or fiction?", *Military Information and Communications Symposium of South Africa 2009*, Pretoria, July 2009.

[SON 10] SONG S., *African Undersea Cables*, Many Possibilities, 2010, available at: http://manypossibilities.net/african-undersea-cables/ (accessed November 19, 2010).

[THE 08] THERON J., "Operational battle space: an information warfare perspective," *IFIP TC9 Proceedings on ICT uses in Warfare and the Safeguarding of Peace*, Council for Scientific and Industrial Research, Pretoria, 2008.

[VAN 10] VAN NIEKERK B., *Safety and Security on the NET*, TEDx UKZN, May 14, 2010.

[WAR 08] WARDINI A., "Information operations in Senegal", *IOSphere*, Special Edition, pp. 53-56, 2008.

Chapter 10

Conclusion

Throughout the various chapters presented in this book, common issues have manifested themselves – particularly relating to the process of policy-making in terms of cyber-security and cyber-defense.

Although cyberspace emerged during the 1980s, and then really developed in the 1990s with the dawn of the publicly available Internet in a number of industrialized countries, it was not until the latter half of the last decade that concerns relating to cyberspace really seem to have been felt in terms of security and defense policies. The introduction of cyberspace into defense is the fruit of a heightened awareness of threats that States have been able to witness by way of major events:

– the attacks on Estonia in 2007;

– the waves of cyber-attacks that have blighted several governments since 2007;

– the Stuxnet worm which, in 2010, demonstrated the vulnerability of industrial systems; and

– the growing extent of intrusions for espionage purposes affecting the systems of governments and large businesses in all sectors of activity.

This realization has occurred at different paces depending on the country in question. The "slowness" of it, and its "recent" nature, are underlined many times in this book – for while the phenomenon has gained in strength in recent years, it is by no means new. Cyber-attacks have been affecting the entire world for over 20 years. Many nations, led by the US, China and Russia, have written about the offensive

Chapter written by Daniel VENTRE.

and defensive use of cyberspace in their military doctrines and strategies since the early 1990s. This "slowness" means that cyber-security and cyber-defense have only recently become priorities at a political level, the result of an evolution in the perception of the dangers. Anti-militaristic sentiment may sometimes be behind these delays: when military issues are unpopular or when army budgets are constrained by that sentiment, cyber-defense may seem auxiliary, and the subject considered very futuristic and therefore not immediately pressing.

Those States affected by economic crisis may be reticent towards new investments in defense. In these terms, cyber-defense may be viewed in two ways: either as a new source of significant and unacceptable costs, in spite of the necessity; or as an opportunity to reduce costs (a techno-centered approach to problem-solving). The difference is striking between Greece and Slovenia, for instance. In the case of the former, the military enjoy a positive image in the eyes of civil society and political leaders, which enables them to steer choices in terms of defense policy. The military have managed to integrate issues relating to cyber-warfare into the context of Greece's international and strategic policies. In Slovenia, on the other hand, even today the strong anti-militaristic sentiment plays against questions relating to cyber-defense coming to the forefront.

Delays between the emergence of cyberspace, the appearance of threats and the introduction of cyberspace into defense policies highlights the contrast between aggressor and victim models (this is merely a hypothesis). The victim's reaction time is incompatible with the attacker's pace, because their models are opposing: the State machine responds to a vertical logic (it requires hierarchy, planning and organization); the aggressor (who may not be part of a State administrative structure), follows a horizontal logic (with no hierarchy), allowing rapidity, reactivity and capacity for surprise action – capabilities that can be quickly brought together. In addition, this model ignores constraints relating to borders and sovereignty. However, it also falls down on a lack of strategy, and is confined to on the spot actions that may be difficult to concretize (hacker attacks, even *en masse*, usually run out of steam, and very rarely achieve their political goals).

Yet States do not have total autonomy in establishing their priorities in terms of defense. Those who conceive policies and strategies may first draw inspiration from what has been done abroad. A certain form of mimesis may underlie the task of elaborating concepts and policies. There is also the need to place yourself at the same level as others, both friend and foe. Thus, we must behave like the others and be like the others, which will invariably lead to an armament race. The signal this gives may be perceived badly (an aggressive state). However, it is simply the attitude of a State wishing to maintain its position on the international stage, ensure its security and contribute to international peace (adopting a defensive stance aimed at dissuading potential aggressors).

The international context greatly constrains States' actions. Members of NATO and the EU, for instance, must adapt their policies to the common market. The weakness of a Member State in terms of cyber-security/cyber-defense may be damaging, both for that State and for its partners (in a team, the "weak link" weakens the others). Geopolitically important States have a major role to play in managing regional and world peace. Weaknesses in cyber-defense raise provisional questions over a State's stability, and therefore ultimately its capacity to maintain its role as a major piece on the international chessboard. Large-scale cyber-attacks against countries whose geopolitical might is significant are likely to have a greater effect on international stability than those directed at small States.

A State's regional environment and its geopolitical strength largely determine its priorities:

– Japan's considerations relate to defense against China and North Korea, its alliance with the US and its role in Pacific Asia;

– Greece's relate to defense in terms of its relations with Turkey;

– Cuba's choices are defined according to its relation to the US and its political partners in South America;

– Canada's defense strategies relate to the US;

– etc.

Cyber-defense is no exception to this phenomenon. Cyber-defensive policies are not initially conceived in view of the worldwide increase in threats: North Korea is undoubtedly an immediate threat for Japan, but far less so for Greece or Italy, in spite of the progressive removal of boundaries in cyberspace, the globalization of networks, exchanges and communications. A server located in country A can be used by a hacker in country B to attack a server located in country C; however, this does not mean that the question of defense extends to country A. The relation between B and C is central.

Also often raised are the questions of the *efficiency* of the policies put in place, the appropriateness of policies/strategies, means deployed and problems to be dealt with. Strategies for reinforcing cyber-security and cyber-defense rely on a set of developments, an integrated approach, which is common to a large group of nations dependent on cyberspace (including states not dealt with in this book, e.g. the US or China):

– development of the legal apparatus;

– an integrated approach to emergency management;

– involvement of national defense in national security;

– militarization of cyberspace;

– collaboration:

   - between actors at national level,

   - public–private,

   - civil–military, and

   - international;

– formation/training:

   - of experts, engineers, and

   - of directors;

– exercises (CDX)[1];

– participation in international forums;

– creation of organizations, dedicated State, civil and/or military structures (cyber-units, cyber-defense agencies, etc.);

– digitization of armies;

– struggle against cybercrime;

– protection of critical infrastructures: questions about responsibility for defense of civil infrastructures (most of these infrastructures belong to private companies, so who should take care of their defense?); and

– modulation of the budgets allocated to cyber-defense

However, we cannot simply decree that actors (individuals, sectors, organizations, and States) must collaborate for the principle to take effect. The difficulty lies in coordinating, implementing and measuring the effectiveness of that collaboration. The involvement of more actors does not necessarily guarantee the expected efficacy. In addition to the vulnerability of cyberspace due to technical and human factors, there is thus vulnerability due to structural factors (proliferation of actors).

---

1 CDX: Cyber Defense Exercise.

To conclude this book, we wish to make our own contribution to the task of defining the concepts. This phase is essential in implementing common referents, whose usefulness is recalled many times in the various national approaches. Common definitions will, in particular, allow an international legal framework to be drawn up for defensive/offensive operations in cyberspace. The two concepts we are interested in here are "cyberspace" and "cyber-attacks".

10.1. Cyberspace

Defining cyberspace entails defining that fifth dimension which is not solely that of combat but more generally of human activity in today's world.

We define cyberspace as a dimension consisting of three layers, and transversal to the four conventional dimensions.[2]

To begin with, we will look at the conventional dimensions of sea, air and space. The first characteristic of cyberspace is its transversality: it intersects and crosses all of the conventional dimensions.

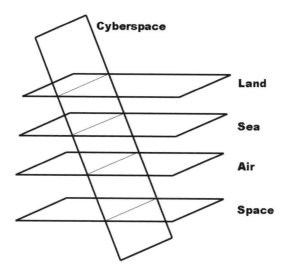

Figure 10.1. *Cyberspace, a dimension that traverses the four conventional dimensions*

2 All the considerations put forward in the section that follows have been expounded in [VEN 11a, VEN 11b].

When we group the conventional dimensions into one, we obtain the real dimension (R), which is crossed by the virtual dimension (V) of cyberspace. Indeed, cyberspace innervates each of the real-world dimensions.

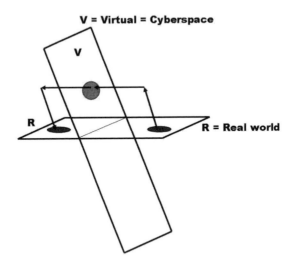

Figure 10.2. *Cyberspace (V) is transversal to the real world (R)*

However, this cyberspace itself should not be understood as a homogeneous whole, or as a block.

We can consider it to be an object made up of three superimposed, interdependent layers:

– a first material, physical layer of infrastructures and hardware;

– a second layer of software and applications; and

– a third, so-called "cognitive" layer.

This formulation is inspired by that advanced in 1998 in *Information Warfare: Principles and Operations* by Edward Waltz [WAL 98] who conceived the "cyberspace dimension" as the middle layer (the informational infrastructure) in the three domains of space in information warfare. These three domains are the physical layer, the informational infrastructure and the cognitive layer.

Our approach, for its part, encapsulates the three layers – the three domains in the definition of cyberspace – rather than being limited to the middle layer.

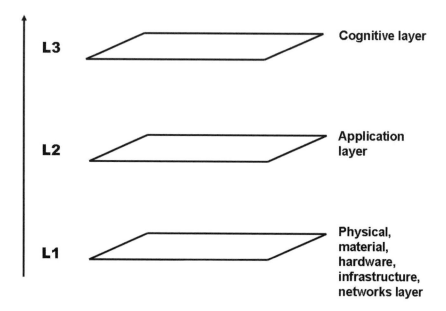

L3   Cognitive layer

L2   Application
                         layer

L1   Physical,
                         material,
                         hardware,
                         infrastructure,
                         networks layer

Figure 10.3. *Representation of the three layers making up cyberspace*

This representation of cyberspace as a matrix composed of three layers and four spaces enables us to reposition incidents, actions, stakes, threats, actors, etc.

From the point of view of the three-layer model, actions carried out on one layer may be targeting the other layers.

This three-layer model can be used:

– To reconsider our perception and representation of the threat: are there particular types of operations, types of aggressors and specific skills that correspond to each layer?

– To organize cyber-defense. This entails taking account of technical aspects, but also of cognitive, political, legal and economic aspects. It must involve multiple skills, different sectors (Internet service providers and telecom operators, technology providers, think tanks and social networks, capable of acting at the level of "manipulation of information"). These considerations validate the holistic approach to cyber-defense.

		Characteristics	**Form of possible attacks against this layer**	**Facts**	**Theoretical perspective**
L3	*Top layer*	Cognitive layer	Modification of displays on computer monitors; introduction of worrying messages; destabilization of the L2; propaganda; psychological operations; website defacement; increasing the sense of threat; divulgation of secrets…	Website defacements; hacktivism; WikiLeaks; use of social networks to mobilize social groups; cognitive hacking. An attack on the cognitive layer consists of manipulating content to manipulate actors	Netwar (Arquilla, Ronfeldt); information warfare (Libicki); psychological operations; manipulation of information…
L2	*Middle layer*	Application layer: software, applications, layer of bits, code, norms, protocols, data	Attacks by code: hacking, virus diffusion…	Website defacement; hacktivism; pirating of Ministry servers; intrusions; distributed denial of service attacks; Internet cutoff by Internet service providers; data theft…	Cyberwar. The L2 layer is at the center of the notion of cyber-warfare. Ultimately, cyber-warfare is only one aspect of information warfare. From a theoretical point of view, cyber-warfare is thus represented by J. Arquilla and D. Ronfeldt (Cyberwar is coming!) [ARQ 93]
L1	*Bottom layer*	Physical, material, hardware layer, cables, networks, satellites, computers, communicative materials…	Cutting of undersea cables; destruction of satellites; steering of satellites away from their trajectories; bombardment of communication infrastructures; launches of electromagnetic pulse bombs…	Cutting of undersea cables paralyzing the Internet in Egypt	Actions at this level are often relegated to the domain of electronic warfare.

Table 10.1. *Association of each layer with its actors, actions and theoretical considerations*

Based on this model, *cyber-attacks* can simply be defined as aggressive operations by R against S, through the medium of V. In terms of transversality, aggressions (cyber-attacks, offensive operations) and defensive actions, initiated in R, are intended to cause an impact in S. Ultimately V is only a vector, a space in which actions are carried out.

An attack on the lower layers always has an impact on the layers above it, but the reverse is not necessarily true:

– an attack on infrastructures prevents the code from functioning and has a cognitive impact;

– an attack on the code by way of the code has an impact on the cognitive layer, but not necessarily on the previous layer; and

– an attack on the code may disrupt computers' function, or even destroy them.

There are combinations of actions on the various layers, in accordance with the equation (act on → to produce an effect on). These are:

– L1 → L2;

– L1 → L3;

– L2 → L3;

– L1 → L2 + L3;

– L1 + L2 → L3;

– L3 → L2;

– L3 → L1;

– L3 → L2 + L1;

– L3 + L2 → L1;

– L2 → L1 + L3; and

– L2 → L1

The layers overlap. In order to affect one, we may or must affect another. For instance:

– cutting in L1 (cutting undersea Internet cables, destroying communication/observation satellites, etc.) to produce an effect in L2 (inability to use networks or communicate) and L3 (disorganization);

– acting in L2 (pirating, intrusion, website defacement, etc.) to produce an effect in L3 (destabilization) or L1 (a viral attack can destroy systems, computers, etc.); and

– acting in L3 to active L2 (broadcasting lists of websites to be attacked, and passing the baton to hackers acting in L2 to pirate the designated sites; providing tools for computer attacks; mobilizing communities of hackers, and so on).

This layer model may be complexified by crossing it with the representation of the transversal dimension, thus defining cyberspace as a three-layered domain over a matrix of four. It is this 3 × 4 architecture that describes or defines the nature of that fifth dimension, which is cyberspace. Table 10.2 expresses the transversality of cyberspace with the real dimension.

	Land	Air	Sea	Space
L3				
L2				
L1				

Table 10.2. *Cyberspace: three layers and four dimensions*

The reading of these models (cyberspace; cyber-attacks) must be complexified by taking account of the following variables:

– civilian/military actors;

– public/private actors; and

– State/non-State actors[3].

Cyber-warfare, for its part, is the cybernetic dimension of conventional warfare.

10.2. Bibliography

[ARQ 93] ARQUILLA J., RONFELDT D., *Cyberwar is coming!*, Rand Corporation, USA, 1993. Accessed at http://www.rand.org/content/dam/rand/pubs/reprints/2007/RAND_RP223.pdf

[VEN 11a] VENTRE D., "Cyberwar and Cyberspace", *Conference CIOR – OTAN*, Warsaw, Poland, August 2011.

[VEN 11b] VENTRE D., *Ciberguerra, XIX Curso Internacional de Defensa*, Jaca, Spain, 26 September 2011, acts to be published in 2012.

[VEN 11c] VENTRE D. (Ed.), *Cyberwar and Information Warfare*, ISTE Ltd., London and John Wiley and Sons, New York, 2011.

[WAL 98] WALTZ E., *Information Warfare: Principles and Operations*, Artech, Boston, 1998.

---

3 For an analysis of these distinctions and their various combinations, see [VEN 11c].

List of Authors

Igor BERNIK
Faculty of Criminal Justice and Security
University of Maribor
Ljubljana
Slovenia

Alan CHONG
S. Rajaratnam School of International Studies (RSIS)
Singapore

Stefania DUCCI
RIEAS
University of 'Roma Tre'
Rome
Italy
and
International University of Social Sciences
Popular University UNINTESS
Mantua
Italy

Joseph FITSANAKIS
Security and Intelligence Studies Program
Department of History and Political Science
King College
Bristol, Tennessee
USA

Lina LEMAY
University of Sherbrooke
Canada

Hugo J. LOISEAU
University of Sherbrooke
Canada

Manoj MAHARAJ
University of KwaZulu-Natal
Westville
South Africa

Iztok PODBREGAR
Faculty of Criminal Justice and Security
University of Maribor
Ljubljana
Slovenia

Gorazd PRAPROTNIK
Faculty of Criminal Justice and Security
University of Maribor
Ljubljana
Slovenia

Bojan TIČAR
Faculty of Criminal Justice and Security
University of Maribor
Ljubljana
Slovenia

Brett VAN NIEKERK
University of KwaZulu-Natal
Westville
South Africa

Daniel VENTRE
CNRS
CESDIP Laboratory (CNRS/UVSQ/Ministry of Justice)
Guyancourt
France

Index

117-121, 124, 143, 154, 156, 159,
167, 170, 175-179, 184-187, 201-
209, 213-217, 219, 224, 233, 261,
263, 270, 281, 284-291, 299, 304,
305
attacker, 90-92, 107, 112, 118, 167,
263, 298
attribution, 118, 167, 184, 186, 187,
212
Australia, 6, 106, 196, 212, 214, 215,
217, 229
authentication, 273, 188
aviation, 119, 120, 242

B

Bacon, 131
Barjavel, 96, 131
battalion, 116, 235, 238
battle, 3, 9, 56, 60, 95, 120, 210
battlefield, 114, 117, 120, 236-238,
244, 251, 253- 255, 269, 270
battleground, 253
battlelab, 279
battlespace, 108, 110, 111, 242,
281
Beijing, 81, 106, 196
Belarus, 168
Belarusian, 263
Belgium, 93, 170
Bellamy, 82, 131
belligerent, 122, 124
biological, 175, 95
biometric, 93, 180, 272
blog, 60, 64, 66, 70
Bosnia, 251, 259, 263
Bosnian, 259

C

Canada, 1-22, 24-39, 299
Canadian, 1-21, 24, 26, 29-31, 34-
38
capitalism, 57

capitalist, 58, 59, 60, 67, 69, 223
Caribbean, 48, 49
Castro, 54, 57, 59, 60, 68, 69, 70
Caucasus, 158
censor, 46, 227
censorship, 81, 227
Chaos, 95
China, 46, 47, 51, 63, 66, 67, 69, 71,
72, 78, 90-92, 95, 106, 137, 167-
169, 171, 185, 194-202, 204-206,
213, 215, 216, 218, 219, 227, 247,
287, 290, 297, 299
Chinese, 55, 66, 67, 92, 95, 97,
105, 120, 193, 196, 198, 201,
204, 219, 226, 255, 287
civilization, 96, 152
Clausewitz, 118, 152, 239, 242
coercion, 108
cognitive, 87, 280, 302, 303-305
colonial, 67, 124
command, 6, 104-106, 116-118, 121,
143, 155, 165, 179, 183, 185, 188,
213, 216, 238, 246, 252, 255, 256,
280-282
complexity, 99, 11, 171, 184, 255,
263
Conficker, 89
confidential, 29, 151, 165, 200, 201
confidentiality, 18, 107, 178
conflict, 9, 45, 64, 69, 73, 77, 79, 86,
91, 94, 100, 104, 109, 118, 120,
128, 129, 139, 140, 152, 166-168,
197, 207, 208, 218, 224, 238, 244,
256, 286, 287, 290, 291
confrontation, 45, 86, 87, 104, 111,
121, 126
control, 46, 54, 56, 60-62, 65-68, 70-
72, 78, 82, 87, 90, 93, 94, 98, 100,
101, 103, 104, 107, 109, 111, 114,
116, 118, 127-130, 139, 141, 148,
152, 165, 170, 173, 176, 179, 183,
187, 188, 208, 216, 220, 228, 238,
244, 254, 262, 280, 281, 282, 288

T

tactic, 9

Taiwan, 106, 198, 199, 229, 230, 266

Tallinn, 106, 156, 182

target, 11, 16, 18, 50, 52, 53, 56, 77, 97, 109, 125, 145, 167, 199, 201, 202, 205, 208, 263, 281

technical, 16, 19, 30, 35, 62, 87, 89, 97, 107, 120, 135, 143-145, 147-149, 153, 154, 174-176, 178, 183-185, 220, 237, 256, 272-274, 289, 300, 303

   technician, 115

technocrat, 157

technological, 5, 7-9, 18, 19, 45, 48, 53-57, 60, 62, 67, 69, 71-73, 114, 115, 119, 120, 130, 140, 148, 152, 158, 169, 187, 199, 217, 220, 228, 235, 239, 244, 253, 254, 257, 265, 269, 274, 283

technology, 8, 16, 17, 25, 33, 34, 45, 61, 62, 69, 71, 72, 82-84, 94, 100, 107, 115, 117, 119, 127, 130, 149, 156, 158, 167, 175, 176, 178, 185, 198, 201, 204, 205, 208, 209, 215, 216, 224, 225, 227, 230, 231, 237, 242, 244, 252-255, 257, 260, 263, 267, 269, 271, 272, 283, 289, 290, 291, 303

telecom, 303

telecommunication, 15, 68, 78, 85, 117, 125, 170, 179, 204, 252, 254

telegram, 124

telegraph, 80, 121, 123, 198

telegraphy, 80, 93, 121, 123, 125

territory, 3, 8, 9, 30, 62, 86, 93, 122, 124, 131, 138, 140, 197, 202, 204, 215-217, 219, 220, 258

terror, 195

   terrorism, 4, 11, 13-18, 20, 21, 24, 30, 37, 58, 88, 92, 95, 99, 150,

166, 167, 172, 179, 196, 203, 204, 253, 257, 275, 289

   terrorist, 8, 13-15, 17, 18, 20, 56, 72, 90-92, 95, 127, 141, 166, 174

threat, 1, 3, 8, 10-13, 22, 24, 29, 32-34, 59, 66, 67-70, 89, 91-95, 97, 99, 100, 140, 168, 177, 178, 179, 181, 184, 187, 193, 195, 196, 199, 207, 208, 216, 218, 224, 232, 245, 252-254, 257, 259, 263, 264, 269, 299, 303, 304

   threaten, 19, 89, 194

   threatening, 93, 219, 263

Tokyo, 197, 198, 200, 219, 226

Toshiba, 202

traditional, 29, 131, 135, 148, 157, 170, 228, 238, 257

trajectory, 140, 237

transborder, 2

transformation, 9, 11, 37, 110, 119, 136, 185, 235, 240, 283

transnational, 87, 168, 172, 178, 208, 269

transversal, 301, 302, 306

triangulation, 167

Trojan, 10, 68, 147, 202, 262

Tunisia, 47, 63, 285, 287

   Tunisian, 64, 287

Turkey, 47, 137-141, 143-145, 152, 156, 158, 299

Turkish, 138-145, 152, 156, 158, 170

Turkmenistan, 63

Twitter, 47, 57, 63, 69, 243

typology, 91

tyranny, 58, 59

U, V

Ukraine, 68, 137

ultranationalist, 140, 141

uncertain, 68, 157

   uncertainties, 117, 118